Curriculum Windows Redux

A volume in
Curriculum Windows
Thomas S. Poetter, *Series Editor*

Curriculum Windows

Thomas S. Poetter, *Series Editor*

Curriculum Windows: What Curriculum Theorists of the 2000s Can Teach Us About Schools and Society Today (2021)
    Thomas S. Poetter, Kelly Waldrop, Kimberly Pietsch Miller,
    Cynthia Sanders, and Andy Hatton

Curriculum Windows: What Curriculum Theorists of the 1950s Can Teach Us About Schools and Society Today (2019)
    Thomas S. Poetter, Don C. Murray, Peggy Larrick, M.A. Moyer,
    Esther Claros Berlioz, and Kelly Waldrop

Curriculum Windows: What Curriculum Theorists of the 1990s Can Teach Us About Schools And Society Today (2017)
    Thomas S. Poetter, Kelly Waldrop, Tasneem Amatullah,
    Cleighton Weiland, Jody Googins, and Vanessa Winn

Curriculum Windows: What Curriculum Theorists of the 1980s Can Teach Us About Schools And Society Today (2016)
    Thomas S. Poetter, Kelly Waldrop, Chloé Bolyard,
    and Vicka Bell-Robinson

Curriculum Windows: What Curriculum Theorists of the 1970s Can Teach Us about Schools and Society Today (2015)
    Thomas S. Poetter and Kelly Waldrop

Curriculum Windows: What Curriculum Theorists of the 1960s Can Teach Us about Schools and Society Today (2013)
    Thomas S. Poetter

Curriculum Windows Redux

What Curriculum Theorists Can Teach Us About Schools and Society Today

edited by

Thomas S. Poetter
Miami University

Kelly Waldrop
The Publish House

Syed Hassan Raza
Miami University

INFORMATION AGE PUBLISHING, INC.
Charlotte, NC • www.infoagepub.com

Library of Congress Cataloging-in-Publication Data

A CIP record for this book is available from the Library of Congress
http://www.loc.gov

ISBN: 978-1-64802-969-1 (Paperback)
978-1-64802-970-7 (Hardcover)
978-1-64802-971-4 (E-Book)

The cover art was provided by Dr. **Katherine K. Smith**. Dr. Smith has provided several beautiful, inspiring covers for the series, including the volumes on curriculum theorists and their books from the 1980s, 1990s, and 2000s. The cover for the Redux volume by Dr. Smith is oil on canvas, titled, "Junction School, Lyndon B. Johnson National Park."

CONTENTS

FOREWORD

I had a happy sense of completion when I finished the Forewords to the Curriculum Windows series of books, stretching from the 1950s through the first decade of the 2000s (a book about several important curriculum books per decade) with Information Age Publishing. I also experienced the nostalgia that accompanies the conclusion of doing something meaningful. Recently, I was surprised that Tom Poetter, Kelly Waldrop, and their colleagues offer readers an additional book list for windows of more reflection: Redux 1, and not only that, Redux 2, both combined in this volume! I have been pondering the lists, each being organized in alphabetical order by author. I have considered discussing them in chronological order of publication date, or the order in which I met the authors or encountered the books, or even grouping them by categories of content emphasis; however, I have finally decided to comment on them in the order received, allowing readers to move, as John Dewey advocated, from the *psychological* (their interests and concerns) to the *logical*, an organization of the literature that makes sense in the world of scholarship.

I want to reiterate my appreciation to Tom Poetter and all connected with this Curriculum Windows project for building upon my (our) curriculum books publications (Schubert & Lopez Schubert, 1980; Schubert et al., 2002) as they developed their contribution to curriculum literature. This contribution, like the earlier ones, is both substantive and pedagogical. It is pedagogical in the sense that the authors, as doctoral students, were introduced to the world of publishing their work. It is substantive in the sense that, as leaders of curricular practice in schools, many of them readily show

Curriculum Windows Redux, pages ix–xliv
Copyright © 2022 by Information Age Publishing
www.infoagepub.com

the continuing relevance of insights to be found in works that are in danger of being lost to those who continue to enter the fields of curriculum theory and practice.

As I reflect on the idea of *redux*, I think not only of Tom Poetter, Kelly Waldrop, and other editors and authors of the Curriculum Windows volumes expanding their own repertoire of curriculum books, I think of the curriculum field itself expanding. Many of the books included here expand what curriculum studies is about, that is, a phenomenon I have been intrigued by and have advocated for a long time (e.g., He et al., 2015; Schubert, 1982; Schubert 2010a). As I have done in previous Forewords in the Curriculum Windows book series, I briefly reminisce about my encounters with each book, author, or a central idea therein. The editors and authors of this volume, like those from the other volumes of Curriculum Windows, offer me novel postures from which to reflect on the books presented. For this I am grateful.

JAMES BANKS

I begin by thanking Nathan Warner for bringing James Banks' (1997) *Educating Citizens in a Multicultural Society* to my attention. It provides context for my reflection on the corpus of Banks' monumental work, along with many other scholars on multicultural education and their influences on curriculum. The focus on educating citizens bespeaks a mode of expansion of curriculum studies that was also being advocated by my first PhD advisee, William H. Watkins. Early in Bill Watkins' career, he wrote a piece that altered my outlook on multicultural education, by arguing that multicultural education must be studied as a basis for critique of the political economy that enables activist contributions by those whose lived experience, ideas, and ideals challenge the dominant cultural views and practices (Watkins, 1994). My brief encounters with Jim Banks and larger encounters with his work over the years should push us all to ask how citizens from diverse cultures can grow by learning from and with each other. By the chance of alphabetical order, we appropriately begin by considering one of the most important curriculum issues today: What does it mean to educate citizens by taking into consideration not only the dominant roots of a nation or culture (e.g., White, male, Western, in the United States) but also the multicultural roots (e.g., Native American, African American, Puerto Rican, Mexican American, and Asian American). The latter were first brought to my attention by Joel Spring (1994) and more recently in a study of curriculum books of previous years by Wayne Au, Anthony Brown, and Dolores Calderón (2016). Nathan Warner's selection of Banks has also made me mindful of another book by Banks (1981), one on an earlier

Redux list: *Multiethnic Education.* This, in turn, reminds me of my admiration for the *Handbook of Research on Multicultural Education* (Banks & Banks, 1995) and the second edition, also edited with his wife, Cherry McGee Banks (Banks & Banks, 2004). These were long deemed paragons of handbooks in education, which I considered models for reference books I have edited or have contributed to substantially (e.g., Husen & Postelthwaite, 1994/1985; Connelly et al., 2008; Kridel, 2010; He et al., 2015, Schubert & He, 2021). Curriculum scholars tapped the ideas of Banks and others; so, his work is clearly relevant to curriculum literature, theory, and practice. Multicultural work of Carl Grant, Christine Sleeter, Gloria Ladson-Billings, Geneva Gay, William Watkins, Cameron McCarthy, Ming Fang He, JoAnn Phillion, among others, also reaches deeply into curriculum discourse. Most recently, I have been impressed with a book by Wayne Au, Anthony Brown, and Dolores Calderón (2016) called *The Multicultural Roots of Curriculum Studies*, which reaches deeply into African American, Native American, Latinx American, and Asian American scholars to show that each of these has parallel histories of thought that should be considered a substantial feature of curriculum theory, scholarship, and practice along with that which has dominated intellectual realm known as *the curriculum field*, that is, the mostly White, too male, and too Western curriculum field. Roots of such work trace back to James Banks and other pioneers, several of whom are represented in this Redux volume.

CHRISTINE BENNETT

I think I need to say ditto here, since much that I relate in relation to Banks is also an expression of appreciation to Jason A. Fine for re-presenting Bennett's (1995) *Comprehensive Multicultural Education,* most recently in its 9th edition. The fact that several editions of Bennett's book have been published indicates that faculty and students in colleges of education value the contribution of this text. It makes me want to add a note to encourage readers to connect this work to Angela Valenzuela's (1999) idea of *subtrative schooling,* a key warning against the distressing tendency of schools to take away the strengths of students from communities of color, when they should as Luis Moll and colleagues have advocated for building upon those strengths as valuable *funds of knowledge* (Gonzalez et al., 2005). The same can be said of Native American education (Grande, 2005/2015) and Asian American education (He, 2003, 2010). Thus, reflecting on Bennett also makes me ponder where the curriculum field has been and where it is headed. Generations of scholars influenced by Bennett, Banks, Christine Sleeter, Carl Grant, Gloria Ladson-Billings, and Michael Apple have formally and informally mentored more recent scholars who add much to multicultural roots of curriculum studies, such as Wayne Au, Anthony Brown, Keffrelyn Brown, and Delores Calderón.

ERNEST BOYER

The selection of Ernest Boyer's (1990) *Scholarship Reconsidered* by Craig Myers connects the need for diversity of educational inquiry itself. While it is a sad truism that many U.S. commissioners of education and secretaries of education have not been known for being intellectuals with scholarly records in education, Ernest Boyer is a noteworthy exception. His *Scholarship Reconsidered* had a major impact on expanding research practices to value the insight and understanding of several categories of persons involved in educational endeavors through intersecting spheres of scholarly endeavor: discovery, application, integration, and teaching/learning. A service-oriented and internationally recognized scholar of physical education curriculum and instruction and colleague of mine at the University of Illinois at Chicago (UIC), Don Hellison, who passed away in 2018, was honored in a physical education journal by characterizing his work along the lines of Boyer's *Scholarship Reconsidered*. Expansion of scholarship has been evident in the curriculum field and portrayed in summary form (Schubert, 1986; Short, 1991; Pinar et al., 1995; Barone & Eisner, 2012). Doubtless connected with Boyer's acknowledgment of credibility for diverse realms of scholarship, was his willingness to support those who advanced mentorship as a significant realm of scholarship, which is clearly evidenced in his accepting Craig Kridel's invitation to write the foreword to what I consider the best book on mentorship in the curriculum field, *Teachers and Mentors* (Kridel et al., 1996). I recall, too, that Boyer directly related his educational concerns to multicultural understanding, as conveyed by a story I heard him tell after traveling to the Amazon to visit the indigenous woman his son was marrying. His daughter-in-law's father said to Boyer, this is what I do, pointing to vast fields of crops, and he asked what Boyer did. He received a strange look when he replied that he flew around the United States and world delivering papers!

DEBORAH BRITZMAN

Whenever I saw Debbie Britzman present at Bergamo or other curriculum conferences, I recalled how much I value the psychoanalytic tradition, that is, a kind of scholarship that illuminates a great diversity of modes of inquiry, including the work that provides her psychoanalytic perspective on teacher education and its creative insightful title, *Practice Makes Practice* (Britzman,

2003/originally 1991). So, Ashley Warren has made me think back to the basis of my practice as an elementary school teacher to conclude that much of that basis, indeed, resided practice itself. When I thought of doing a PhD and a dissertation, I wanted to pursue study by focusing more deeply on what I considered my most important resource as an elementary school teacher, and I concluded it was the connections between my emergent philosophy and my imagination. When I later taught at the university level, I connected this with talks I often had with a friend, former teacher, filmmaker, and novelist and short story writer, JP. On numerous occasions, I tried to tell JP about the curriculum theories I was developing and I interspersed that conversation with stories of my university teaching. Long acquainted with psychotherapy, he suggested that I should look deeply inside my teaching to find my curriculum theory. I did. I am sure I should try more of this, even now—a good retirement project. Britzman's work over the years has helped me reenter my considerable appreciation I developed in a 1967 graduate course in the history of what is often referred to as personality theories, that is, the legacy of Sigmund Freud, Carl Jung, Erich Fromm, Alfred Adler, Carl Rogers, and others. I have been glad to have learned more about radical psychoanalysis from Britzman's presentations and writings, even though I had limited interaction with her. The connections between Freud, Marx, and those who continued to merge their work are rich with provocative insight. Each encounter with Britzman and those she cited made me wish for more emphasis on critical psychoanalytic and related phenomenological perspectives existing in curriculum literature. I remember appreciating it as a basis for *currere* as an alternative to curriculum (Pinar & Grumet, 1976), and later the work of James Hillman (e.g., 1975, 1983).

LINDA DARLING-HAMMOND

While Linda Darling-Hammond is not primarily a curriculum scholar, her research has influenced curriculum and many other areas of education. I thank Kimberly Halley for realizing the germinal importance to curriculum studies of *The Flat World and Education: How America's Commitment to Equity Will Determine Our Future* (Darling-Hammond, 2010). I remember talking with Linda at a symposium called The John Dewey Lecture at the Association for Supervision and Curriculum Development which I developed and chaired each year for 5years for the John Dewey Society in the late 1990s, to help keep alive the relevance of Dewey's ideas. I also recollect less than a decade ago when my UIC colleague, Roger Weisberg, was celebrated for receiving an endowed chair in psychology at UIC for his work on social and emotional learning by the NoVo Foundation headed by Jennifer Buffett, Warren Buffett's daughter, and Linda came to UIC for the ceremony. In these two of several times we have talked, her commitment to equity was apparent, always expanding to think about how curriculum and education could make the future of the world more enriched by collaboration and equity. Linda Darling-Hammond's clarion call needs to be heeded now as ever that pervasive needs around the globe in the context of world economy cannot be met without overcoming much of the prejudice and poverty that threaten the world. This call is based on research and theory that can open windows to reform if educators, policy makers, and power wielders will only open them.

LISA DELPIT

As Marilee Tanner realizes, the concept of *other people* in Lisa Delpit's writings, especially in *Other People's Children: Cultural Conflict in the Classroom* (Delpit, 1995) captures a highly neglected insight for a dominantly White curriculum field. Somewhat earlier, from a quasi-psychoanalytic stance, Madeleine Grumet (in her 1998 book, *Bitter Milk*) published an essay called "Other People's Children," wherein she discussed the tensions within women teachers between relating to their own children and children of others, in her book called *Bitter Milk: Women and Teaching* (Grumet, 1988). Both Delpit and Grumet helped us see children for the loss they have received from a largely White and male field of curriculum theory and research. Lisa Delpit's conceptualization of "other people's children" pertains particularly to ways in which Black and Brown children are often *othered*, because of their racial, economic, and cultural backgrounds. Their histories and contributions for too long have been degraded and ignored. I have not known Lisa Delpit personally, but have often used her work with students and teachers to help them better understand dilemmas and persecutions of race. I still recall teaching a large master's level curriculum course at UIC, in which I was trying to convey, as usual, my critique of testing and advocacy of progressive practices through getting to know students as persons. An African American woman seemed unimpressed and appeared angry. Finally, toward the end of the course she spoke up and explained emphatically that she did not want White teachers to try to get to know her. Experience had taught her that they would not understand her and would use her background in poverty against her, thinking that she could not succeed if her parents were out of work, and possibly debilitated by alcohol or drugs. Unresponsive to my progressive advocacy, she informed me that she would rather be anonymous and judged by objective tests that were not subject to teacher prejudice. I was taken aback, although I did listen and learn from her. Thinking of othering, reminds me of a time I asked Madeleine Grumet, regarding her title, if she ever heard the song lyrics about "other people's sirens"—meaning that we hear the symbol of their stress but cannot open up to feeling it; it would be too overwhelming. I cannot locate those lyrics; however, they might have been in a spin-off from Steve Goodman's "Other People's Troubles."

LISA DELPIT

Appropriate to the image of *othering* in Delpit's (1995) *Other People's Children*, and relevant to the call of Darling-Hammond (2010) to equity in *The Flat World and Education*, Lisa Delpit's (2012) admonition to raise expectations for those neglected in curriculum studies so powerfully in *Multiplication is for White People*. Thanks to Kristine Michael for helping readers realize that Delpit speaks to curriculum workers and educational leaders in schools just as powerfully as she does to students. Moreover, low expectations is an international crisis as well. It makes me refocus attention on Frantz Fanon's (1963) telling title, *The Wretched of the Earth*. There is no larger problem than the all-encompassing dilemma of lives made wretched by greed and the desire for imperialism and colonization, as Edward Said (1993) has brilliantly shown. The pervasiveness of this problem ravages through what we now label The Global South, and clearly exists in the *global south-ness* embedded within first-world and second-world countries, including the United States. Hence, the raising of expectations is necessary, and it must be facilitated by a world economy that realizes that planetary survival for all depends on enactment of living conditions that enable higher expectations to be actualized. If humans and other life on earth are to survive threats of extinction of species, indigenous and minority cultures, and languages that invigorate life on Earth, we in curriculum must be ever aware of past and present Empires that obliterate knowledges—what Bonaventura Sousa Santos (2014) and Joao Paraskeva (2016) perceptively call *epistemicide*.

JOHN DEWEY

The volume by John Dewey (1956) selected by Shanna Bumiller, was one of several combined reprintings of John Dewey's (1899/1915) *The School and Society* and *The Child and the Curriculum* (Dewey, 1902), both written during Dewey's learning from experience at the Laboratory School he founded in 1896 at the University of Chicago. The Lab School, as it was called (Mayhew & Edwards, 1936; Tanner, 1997) was founded to be akin to laboratories in science, that is, places to learn about phenomena by observing and interacting with them. It was not a demonstration school or a prep school in those early years 1896–1904. Instead, Dewey and his wife, Alice Chipman Dewey (the school's director), observed and interacted with the children, and most of all they learned from and with students' experimentation with learning and growing, what Mary Catherine Bateson (1989) called composing their lives. The Deweys and the students learned that the school was a miniature society, and more expansively to fulfill its educative function in society, the society had to be the school. Similarly, the *Child and the Curriculum* can be better understood by also changing the conjunction "and" to the verb "is," understanding that the child is the curriculum and the curriculum is the child. I have found that making that is-to-and conversion, taught to me by one of my doctoral students who learned it from a philosopher with whom he studied earlier, is one of the best strategies for understanding Dewey's many books, the titles of which often consist of two words joined by "and," and then interpreting "and" as "is." Although there is debate over the beginning of the curriculum field, I prefer to locate it in these two books, joined together in the 1956 reprints, selected by Shanna Bumiller. Admittedly, some scholars see the beginning of the curriculum field in the Committee of Ten (NEA, 1893) and Committee of Fifteen (NEA, 1895) Reports of the National Education Association, and others see the field as emerging in 1918 with social efficiency efforts of Franklin Bobbitt (1918), expanded purposes in The Cardinal Principles of Education (NEA, 1918), and the progressive *The Project Method* of William H. Kilpatrick (1918), as a practical instantiation of Dewey, along with the emergent emphasis on vocational education that stemmed from the 1917 Smith-Hughes Act, and raised questions of how to provide curriculum that supports vocational education.

ELEANOR DUCKWORTH

As Eleanor Duckworth (1987) says, we know of teachers and teaching that make education the experiencing of wonderful ideas, in her book entitled similarly: *The Having of Wonderful Ideas* (Duckworth, 1987). Teachers, too, must have high expectations for what they can do in this time when teachers are guided more by mundane accountability standards, test scores, and even scripts, rather than being allowed to flourish by releasing their imagination (Greene, 1995; Lake, 2013). Many teachers became teachers because they wanted to have wonderful ideas with students, and sadly policy demands have sapped this desire from their being. So, I am grateful to Debra Amling for selecting Duckworth's book and commenting on it. Duckworth has been an exemplary teacher at Harvard for many years, now 85 years of age, and still influencing teaching and teacher education around the world, as related to me by my colleague and friend, Bill Ayers, who was recently presenting with her in Asian contexts and was astounded by her continued vibrance. I remember once putting my name in the hat for a position at Harvard, and when I visited there, I asked a few questions about who left to provide the opening. I was told that no one left; however, it was Eleanor Duckworth's position that was opened, and I wondered why. I was told that it is customary at Harvard when someone is considered for tenured professor, they open a search to see if anyone in the world would be better. I was amazed if that was, indeed, their strategy. In any case, I am glad Eleanor Duckworth has had such an amazing career, and I hope that we reach a point when no students or teachers are prevented from experiencing wonderful ideas.

MICHAEL FABRICANT AND MICHELLE FINE

I have known Michelle Fine over the years, and certainly respect her work. Michael Fabricant is a British policy maker who I do not know and find an intriguingly exemplary collaborator with Michelle Fine. I remember when AERA met in San Francisco in 2011 that she had an off-site session at a religious structure in Oakland with New Zealand aboriginal scholar, Linda Tuhiwai Smith (2001/2011). Focusing on aboriginal ways of knowing and being in the United States, New Zealand, and other parts of the world, it was one of the best presentations I have witnessed at AERA Annual Meetings and it was not in one of the usual corporate hotels. This speaks to a message in the book (selected by Mindy Jennings) by Fabricant and Fine (2012): *Charter Schools and the Corporate Makeover of Public Education.* Like many of Fine's books, she is an artist of compelling titles. "A corporate makeover" precisely gets to the point that even though charter schools were ostensibly designed to overcome the educational ravages of poverty, the stark fact remains that many U.S. public schools have not adequately met needs and concerns of the public, especially publics of poverty. Similarly, a central caveat offered by Fabricant and Fine (2012) is that the reform attributed to many charter schools is an illusion, superficial not deep. Thus, Fabricant and Fine offer a caveat about dangers of the corporate makeover of education. Moreover, their poignant question (What is at stake?) resides in the corporatization of education in schools that look better with the cosmetic charter-ness. Fabricant and Fine present a case that charter schools have not provided on their promise. It is not necessarily the fault of educators in those schools; rather, the lack of overall funding prevents the ideals of charter schools from being realized by all who need them. Thus, only a select few benefit. What is at stake, then, is an education that provides worthwhile experiences, and does not merely appear to do so. The authors warn that lack of funds and lack of serious dedication for cultivating students' lives should not be sacrificed on the altar of profit for the few who are already wealthy. The crux of the matter is to enable public schools to be true to the term *public*, that is, responsive to the funds of knowledge, insight, understanding, emotion, compassion, and more that corporate profiteering too often prevents in lives of persons of color and economic insecurity.

MICHAEL FULLAN

Melissa Wipperman selected *The New Meaning of Educational Change* (Fullan, 1991); this is the expanded second edition of Michael Fullan's (1982) *The Meaning of Educational Change*. With these and other books, Fullan became the key educational author on change who influenced the curriculum field since 1980. My own views of educational change applied to curriculum were influenced considerably by an older group of scholars in the generation of my doctoral mentor, J. Harlan Shores, in the book he co-authored with B. Othanel Smith and William O. Stanley, *Fundamentals of Curriculum Development* (Smith et al., 1950). They drew upon key work by philosopher and social theorist Kenneth Benne and Kurt Lewin the psychological field theorist, among others. The second edition by Smith et al. (1957) devoted over 100 pages to four chapters under the heading of "Human Relations in Curriculum Development" (pp. 425–528). Michael Fullan took up the mantle of expert on educational change in the 1970s. I do not know Fullan personally; however, he was a member of Ming Fang He's PhD dissertation committee, in the late 1990s, before I knew her and way before we were married in 2013. I had been convinced, by Fullan's writing on educational change and related topics, that his work was curricular and it is included several times among the entries in our *Curriculum Books* (Schubert et al., 2002). I have been impressed that Fullan (1991) addresses educational change in collaboration with Suzanne Stiegelbauer by adapting a curriculum question as central to his work, as expressed in the Preface to *The New Meaning to Educational Change*: "How do we know when change is worthwhile?" (p. xi). I have argued that in curriculum context one way to know if change is successful is to alter the parlance from change or reform to *improvement*; thus, implicitly defending the *worth* of new ideas and practices as essential to curriculum (Schubert, 1986, pp. 373–379). Nonetheless, I surmise that Fullan continues to study the term *change* to illuminate both its positive and negative character. I am intrigued by his more recent elaborations of the necessity of addressing moral purposes of learning, focus on deep learning, and adapting to change through motion leadership, all of which I encourage readers to explore as germane to focusing on curriculum matters of *worth* (Schubert, 2009a).

ROBERT GAGNE AND M. DRISCOLL

Sometimes we neglect to remember how steadfastly oriented to psychological foundations curriculum development was in the first half of the 20th century. Jeremy Froelich has aptly reminded us to attend to this, by looking to the oft-cited work of Robert Gagne, tracing back at least to his *The Conditions of Learning* (Gagne, 1967). In *Essentials of Learning for Instruction* (Gagne & Driscoll Perkins, 1988), upon which Jeremy Froelich focuses makes me ask readers to investigate the contemporary place of psychology in curriculum studies. Since I was a doctoral student and considerably before, the work of Robert Gagne in psychology has been considered essential for its translation into learning and instructional theories, principles, and applications for those who theorized, researched, made policy, implemented and evaluated it in curriculum development. A substantial dimension of early curriculum development literature has a strong basis in learning and instructional theory and research. Thus, it is valuable to know this realm of curriculum history and practice, which continues in many spheres of educational policy and practice today. There has long been a connection and a rift, as well, between curriculum development and instructional design. An interesting father and son article in *Educational Leadership* decades ago highlights similarities and differences. Wells Foshay and his son, Rob Foshay, engage in dialogue/debate concerning the relative value of their two realms of life work (Foshay & Foshay, 1980). Wells was in curriculum development, research, and theory at Teachers College, Columbia, and Rob was in instructional design in corporate training in the Chicago area. They concluded that Wells' emphasis on the fundamental purposes of curriculum was most important in curriculum studies and Rob's emphasis on instructional design was primarily concerned with the details of scope, sequence, instruction, and evaluation of knowledge and skills taught. Both were influenced by the work of Gagne and his followers; however, Rob more fully than Wells. Still, both respected Gagne's legacy. At the end of the day, Rob and Wells concluded that it is important to combine the quest for meaning of curriculum work with the details of delivery and acquisition in instructional design. To leave either tendency behind is to prevent successful teaching and learning from transpiring.

JOHN GOODLAD

John Goodlad is well known for many curriculum books. However, I am glad that Jaime Ranly reminded us of his *Educational Renewal* (Goodlad, 1994), because the subtitle reminds (*Better Teachers, Better Schools*) me of something I bet Goodlad learned as a dean. His noteworthy and extensive deanship of the Graduate School of Education at UCLA, being able to sustain many scholarly contributions there while succeeding prominently as a dean, and later having a highly productive career at the University of Washington as co-director of the Center of Educational Renewal, puts him in an exemplary position of knowing about the relationship between faculty development and curriculum development. His massive *Study of Schooling* in the 1970s and 1980s was published in many outlets; however, most famously in *A Place Called School* (Goodlad, 1984), which landed him on prime talk shows and in popular media outlets as well as scholarly journals, making him a public intellectual who reflected the stature of his PhD adviser, Ralph Tyler, from his days at the University of Chicago. When I entered the field of curriculum in the mid-1970s, I recall that many held that for someone to be acknowledged in the curriculum field, one had to be recognized by either Arno Bellack at Teachers College, Columbia or John Goodlad at UCLA. So, in the early 1980s I was pleasantly surprised, or lucky, to discover that Goodlad had cited my work. Since Goodlad wrote so much about curriculum, some readers might wonder why *Educational Renewal* (Goodlad, 1994) is selected here as a key addition to the Curriculum Windows collection. My response harkens back to the comment made to me by Richard Johnson, an insightful vice-chancellor at the University of Illinois at Chicago (UIC), who told me that curriculum development and faculty development go hand-in-hand. As I talked with school leaders, I concluded that they considered the act of hiring faculty to be an act of curriculum improvement, because they considered the teacher as embodying a curriculum, not merely a force to disseminate it. As a frequent member of search committees at UIC, and a chair of Curriculum and Instruction, I grew to understand more fully that hiring was a curriculum decision—and at any level better teachers result in better schools.

MADELINE HUNTER

Madeline Hunter was an intriguing phenomenon in the history of curriculum-related matters. So, Tanya Britton Moore is complimented for bringing Hunter into the windows of consideration. *Mastery Teaching* (Hunter, 1982) is one of many books that Madeline Hunter dispensed over 20-some years, books that popularized and combined existing theory and common sense. Between the time I taught in public elementary schools, mid-1960s to mid-1970s, Hunter's persona began to rise. She was likely the first of a plethora of large-scale consultants who have persisted until today and will probably continue into the foreseeable future. Her consulting ventures became so popular and so much in demand that she had to hire a team of helper-consultants to respond to the demand. Hunter had been the director of the Laboratory School at UCLA, which gave her high visibility. She knew how to talk to practitioners and leaders alike. She had a folksy, humorous, though no-nonsense style that made sense to educators, and some of my smartest former colleagues in the schools said that her message seemed useful and practical. She likely convinced audiences that if the widely cited research on *mastery learning* developed by James Block, Benjamin Bloom, and others, that *mastery teaching* surely should be its counterpart for teachers. A university colleague of mine who did a lot of consulting and speaking once told me that Hunter grossed $11 million in 1979. Many others patterned themselves after Madeline Hunter and incorporated, often publishing their own books and packaged materials. Scholars in universities often criticized her lack of peer-reviewed materials and publications in scholarly sources. However, as the popularity of her work accelerated, school administrators from the more prestigious public and private K–12 schools could be heard asking leaders of socially climbing schools, "Have you been *Hunterized* yet?" As sales of her packages, books, and consultancies soared, more prestigious publishers, conferences, and magazines sought to publish her work or to be otherwise affiliated with her success. Madeline Hunter provided a turning point after which organizations such as the Association for Supervision and Curriculum Development (ASCD) began to pave the way for other high-flying consultants. Their exhibits displayed more consulting packages than books for school leaders.The momentum issued in an era in which schools consulted with corporate or privatized consultants, in contrast to their earlier history of inviting well-published scholars to speak to their needs and to provide professional development. Clearly, there were consultants between the beginning of the curriculum field at the beginning of the 20th century and the 1960s: William T. Harris, Francis Parker, George Strayer, William H. Kilpatrick, Hollis Caswell, L. Thomas Hopkins, Florence Stratemeyer, Ralph Tyler, Alice Miel, Harold Shane, Louis J. Rubin, and more. But they were not curricular corporate profiteers. Granted, some of those who had private consulting companies, and might be called profiteers, may have been helpful to schools; nevertheless, Madeline Hunter and those who followed her, changed the kind and quality of consulting. This is illustrated by an incident I recall in the 1980s going to a party where there were a number of school superintendents; thinking that I knew the field, and listening to them talk about the "good deals" they got on consultants I did not recognize for much larger prices than anyone from universities received, made me wonder if I knew the "new field" of these leaders. I remember asking a small group if they ever considered getting Elliot Eisner to speak, and the response was a look of puzzlement, followed by, "Who?"

HERBERT KLIEBARD

Over the years, I spoke with Herb Kliebard many times at AERA and other meetings. I was always impressed with his understated demeanor. He seemed almost shy. At one of those informal meetings, I remember talking with Herb, and my late wife, Ann, casually said that when his children were in school he would always try to come home from his work at the University of Wisconsin to have lunch and talk with them and his wife, Bernice, about how their day was going. We thought that was so thoughtful. Years later I was invited to a party in Chicago by Patrick Roberts, a former doctoral advisee and faculty member at Northern Illinois University. He said he wanted to introduce me to a lawyer friend of his; she was Herb Kliebard's daughter, Diane. My first edition of Kliebard's (1986) *The Struggle for the American Curriculum, 1893–1958* is filled with my underlines and marginal comments. It appeared in the same year as my *Curriculum: Perspective, Paradigm, and Possibility* (Schubert, 1986) was published, and I wish I could have had access to it when I wrote Chapter 3, on historical perspectives. Kliebard's book is packed with insight based on sound historical research on where the curriculum field has been. I gave it a "slow read," a technique his graduate students said he used in defiance of the popular speed-reading fads of the day! He would sometimes devote an entire class session to study and reflection on a valuable paragraph. I am glad Jonathan Cooper encouraged readers to review the curricular window Kliebard has provided. I wonder if Herb struggled with the same dilemma that Ann and I wrestled with in writing *Curriculum Books*, namely, whether to portray the curriculum field as its dominantly White, male participants had created it or to include Native Americans, African Americans, Latinex Americans, Asian Americans, Muslim Americans and others who also had many insights about what curriculum was and should be. I regret not asking Herb about that. I think that both he and we decided to portray the field the way it had been and not so much the way it should have been. Today, when I reflect on the curriculum history of my generation and those before it, I am grateful for scholars (men and women) of color who have helped the field move beyond its White, male, Western history to acknowledge the existence of persons of color and their cultures, and more recently to needing and including their curricular insights (Au et al., 2016; Brown & Au, 2014; Gaztembide-Fernandez, 2015; Watkins, 2015).

ALFIE KOHN

Another kind of popular educational writer is a high-profile writer, speaker, and consultant who became an independent scholar and public intellectual,

Alfie Kohn. Rebecca Wilson selected Kohn's (1996) book, *Beyond Discipline* to illustrate the popular and often controversial perspectives that have accompanied many of his books. His ideas derive from the study of John Dewey, Jean Piaget, and others who are often identified as constructivists. After Kohn became less in need of institutionalized schooling to advance his career, that is, not a member of nor compelled into obedience by institutions for a livelihood, he seemed free to express controversial analyses, interpretations, and prescriptions about the state of education, including focus on such topics as competition, rewards, grades, testing, parenting, homework, and of course his book about moving to self-discipline through community building rather than by enforcing compliance, which fits well with his advocacy of unconditional parenting. I recall how he ruffled the feathers of wealthy readers when he reported in a *Kappan* article that parents from well-to-do families did not want higher scores or better schools for all, because they wanted their own children to have an academic edge in societal success (Kohn, 1998). His call for community involvement and collaboration in many educational and curricular policies is an admonition that all involved should make decisions together. His advocacy is for a kind of participatory democracy that is often at odds with key aspects of rampantly competitive capitalism (Kohn, 1992)—a position that my late UIC colleague John Nicholls (1989) argued so adeptly in *The Competitive Ethos and Democratic Education.*

JONATHAN KOZOL

Jonathan Kozol was another kind of public intellectual, like Herb Kohn, George Dennison, Terry Doran, Myles Horton, John Holt, and others, who were liberally educated, often in literature, philosophy, history, the arts, or social/political theory, and who became teachers to help children and youths become inspired self-educators. They often chose to work with the urban or rural underserved and economically impoverished populations, and hoped to make a difference, often by engaging in countercultural activities. Kozol and these others were more self-educated than lifelong members of the professorial elite, despite the fact that their early credentials were from elite universities. Sometimes they received alternative teaching certifications, as many do today, and they wrote about their adventures in teaching. Some of them, such as Kozol, went on to make a career of writing, speaking, guest teaching at universities, and consulting with alternative educational projects. Kozol's wide range of books and articles illuminated many issues in education and society (e.g., illiteracy, poverty, greed), that is, injustices he showed to be extant in many urban areas in the vividly powerful portrayals in his *Savage Inequalities* (Kozol, 1991) about which I thank Tracy Davis for encouraging contemporary reflection. My experience of working as a professor of curriculum studies in Chicago for 36 years has brought me in close contact with those who suffer from the savage inequalities that Jonathan Kozol depicts so poignantly. These inequalities are still with us in schools, and sometimes full-blown in multiple forms of *miseducation* (Goodman, 1964; Woodson, 1933) that occur among the outside curricula (Schubert, 2010a, 2010b) of everyday life. Of course, mention of Kozol reminds me of counterculture and free school movements Kozol (1972), which I encourage readers to revisit (Fantini, 1976). I met Jonathan on several occasions when my UIC colleague, Bill Ayers, hosted and introduced his presentations in Chicago over the years on several of his outstanding books.

CRYSTAL LAURA

Thank you to Elaysha Wright for encouraging the unsettling view provided by Crystal Laura (2014) in *Being Bad: My Baby Brother and the School-to-Prison Pipeline* whose stories illuminate the dimly lit tunnel that invisibly winds from schools to prisons. Speaking of Bill Ayers relative to Jonathan Kozol above, Crystal Laura was Bill's PhD advisee at UIC and I got to know her through Bill. When I think of her powerful story about her younger brother and his suffering, I think of watching Jesse Jackson speak at The Million Man March when corporations were flaunting social commitment as they acquiesced to pressures to withdraw investments in mining South Africa so as not to appear to support apartheid. I was impressed with Jesse Jackson's starkly insightful predictive warning that we should keep our eyes open to the same corporations' reinvestments in the prison-industrial complex. Stories of racism, Empire, and White supremacy in the school-to-prison pipeline are so necessary to the reeducation of educators, as is the activism that accrues from them, both of which are exemplary in the work of Crystal Laura. To overcome such matters indicates the need to strive for and *demand the impossible*, as Bill Ayers (2016) calls for and as is implicit and explicit in Crystal Laura's story of her brother.

DEBORAH MEIER AND GEORGE WOOD

Thanks to Rhonda Phillips for bringing *Many Children Left Behind* by Meier and Wood (2004), clearly a critique of accountability testing braggadociously offered by the government to leave no child behind. I have known and respected the contributions and examples of Wood and Meier to education over the years. They are amongst the most exemplary scholar-school leaders in the second half of the 20th century. George Wood began as a faculty member at Ohio University and then devoted his career to be superintendent of Federal Hocking Local Schools and before that was principal of Federal Hocking High School in Stewart, Ohio, a rural school leader since 1992. He is a well-known author of *A Time to Learn* (Wood, 1998) which had multiple editions and *Schools that Work* (Wood, 1992), as well as director of The Forum for Education and Democracy. I remember attending some of the events he coordinated at Ohio University, a rural area in Northern Appalachia. We both had PhDs from UIUC (University of Illinois Urbana–Champaign) at about the same time. As I wrote this paragraph, I googled George and read his moving retirement speech that he gave in the Spring of 2020. He focused so meaningfully on the importance of kindness in teaching that I was compelled to call him after not seeing him for about 40 years. So, thanks, Rhonda for helping to inspire our reunion! Debbie Meier, too, worked at universities (e.g., the University of Chicago and Teachers College, Columbia). However, she devoted herself to educational leadership in urban schools, particularly in New York City and then in Boston. In East Harlem she worked with teachers, students, and community members to create public schools that Seymour Fliegel (1993) called a *Miracle in East Harlem*. Meier (1995) wrote about Central Park East in *The Power of Their Ideas* and later moved on to create similar innovations in Boston's Mission Hill School. Both Debbie Meier and George Wood developed communities of teachers, parents, and students in their schools and helped their surrounding communities become intrigued by and involved in educational experiences in and out of school. They have moved progressive education into rural and urban areas where many have deemed it impossible to build new versions of Deweyan progressivism. Central ideas about impediments to such contributions are expressed in *Many Children Left Behind* (Meier & Wood, 2004), such as the ways in which inordinate amounts of competition, layers of testing, threats, and meaningless draconian mandates have pushed our kindness, care, inspiration, and study engendered by needs, interests, and concerns of students and teachers working together—the very ideas that bring dedicated teachers into the profession. There is much to be gleaned from the experience of leaders such as Meier and Wood, if educators, communities, and policy makers will only peer through the window at their example.

VIVIAN PALEY

Kelly Wilham rekindled my positive regard for Vivian Paley and the many books based upon her experiences as a kindergarten and early childhood teacher at the University of Chicago Laboratory School founded by John Dewey and Alice Chipman Dewey in 1896. Paley taught there almost a century later. Paley's (1992) *You Can't Say You Can't Play* is an excellent example of the impressive insights that she made as a teacher for many years in collaboration with children, revealed in books such as *White Teacher* (Paley, 1979/2009), *The Kindness of Children* (Paley, 1999), and *A Child's Work* (Paley, 2004). Like messages in these and all of Paley's books, she portrays the brilliance of children through the lenses of a perceptive teacher who received the coveted MacArthur Fellowship, known as the Genius Grant of the John D. and Catherine T. MacArthur Foundation in 1989. Three years later when William Ayers and I had a book-signing at the 57th Street Bookstore, a public branch of the Seminary Cooperative Bookstore on the University of Chicago Campus for our book called *Teacher Lore* (Schubert & Ayers, 1992), we were highly pleased that Vivian Paley appeared to hear us present and ask us to sign a book for her. I also interacted with Vivian when I was invited to do a 2-year set of monthly presentations to the faculty and leadership of the University of Chicago Laboratory School by its director, Lucinda Lee Katz. Knowing that I did consultancies via role-playing, Dr. Katz invited me to "be" John Dewey, its founder, and to lead discussions, reflections, and curriculum revisions as they reassessed, striving to continue consistency of the lower, middle, and upper schools policies and practices with Dewey's original ideas. It was a pleasure to have Vivian Paley as a participant in those sessions. We became sufficiently acquainted that I invited her to speak in a symposium I organized at AERA in Chicago on the role of students in curriculum studies.

HAROLD RUGG AND ANN SHUMAKER

Many scholars say that *The Child-Centered School* (Rugg & Shumaker, 1928) was one of the first, if not the first child-centered school. Surely it was exemplary and pioneering. Others might say that while educational ideas of such scholar/practitioners as Jean Jacques Rousseau, Johann Heinrich Pestalozzi, Freidrick Froebel, Johann Herbart, Leo Tolstoy, Francis Parker, John Dewey, Maria Montessori, Lev Vygotsky, A. S. Neill, Tsunesaburo Makiguchi, and others could be considered child-centered forerunners of the school of Rugg and Shumaker, since they clearly extended the practical and theoretical image of child-centered schooling in the 20th century. In any case, I thank Lauren Gentene for choosing to highlight the contribution of Rugg and Shumaker. I suggest that Shumaker's emphasis on Rugg may have given him impetus to reach directly to students themselves with his brilliant social studies materials that enabled and inspired them to carefully question the harmfulness of basic values in America, such as capitalism (Rugg, 1929–1932; Rugg, 1941). To some extent these materials made directly for students was another example of learner-centered-ness, that is, not dependent on many years of development, teacher education, institutional dissemination, and filtering through bureaucratic machinery, even though they were developed in collaboration by teams of teacher educators from Teachers College, Columbia.

WILLIAM H. SCHUBERT AND WILLIAM AYERS

Just as child-centered approaches build on the insights of children and youths, Bill and I thought it was possible and beneficial to build on the insights of teachers, and called it *Teacher Lore* (Schubert & Ayers, 1992). The idea of teacher lore was spun as Bill Ayers and I drove from Chicago to a Bergamo Conference on Curriculum Theory and Classroom Practice in Dayton, Ohio. We wondered together about the irony of leaving teachers out of positions of providing insight in research on teaching. So, we talked with graduate students who were experienced teachers and educational leaders. We thought of researchers who praised research projects about teaching by counting the hours spent in classroom observation. Then we asked teachers with many years of experience, how many hours they spent in classrooms. The researchers' hours paled by comparison to those of the teachers. We asked teachers to tell us about some of the most interesting and valuable things they learned from experience and from reflection upon it. We encouraged them to think of ways to talk with other teachers in efforts to excavate their learnings from experience. We presented results at conferences, produced articles, and published the book: *Teacher Lore: Learning From Our Own Experience* (Schubert & Ayers, 1992). Several of the participants developed their PhD dissertations on teacher lore, and other presentations and publications derived from the dissertations (e.g., Jagla, 1994). Bill and I wrote several chapters, and we thank Janet Miller, who 2 years earlier published a book on her learning with teachers called *Creating Spaces and Finding Voices* (Miller, 1990) for writing a chapter and supporting our efforts, too. Also, I thank Carol Witherell and Nel Noddings (1991) for publishing the first paper I wrote on the theoretical justification for *Teacher Lore* (Schubert, 1991a). I want to note authors of other chapters in the *Teacher Lore* book: Pat Hulsebosch, Mari Koerner, Virginia Jagla, Carol Melnick, and Suzanne Millies.

WILLIAM H. SCHUBERT AND ANN LYNN LOPEZ SCHUBERT

I thank Misty Cook and Louis Hacquard III for selecting the first edition of *Curriculum Books: The First Eighty Years* (Schubert & Lopez Schubert, 1980). Of course, *Curriculum Books: The First Hundred Years* (Schubert et al., 2002) is not listed here or in the 2000 volume of *Curriculum Windows*. This is most likely because that volume (sometimes called the 2nd Edition) is the one that has been used as a basis for selecting books for the Windows collections. In any case, a central purpose that Ann (my late wife) and I had in mind for these volumes of *Curriculum Books* was to provide readers with as comprehensive an overview of the curriculum field as possible. We decided to use books rather than articles, since curriculum scholars seem to value books more than articles. A central dilemma we faced was whether to portray the field as it was (dominated by White male and moderately affluent scholars), or to include scholars from other countries, cultures, minority groups, and linguistic groups in the United States and around the world. The reigning belief seemed to be that the British and U.S. Empires founded curriculum studies. The best we could do at the time was to sadly suggest that these groups be recognized as existing, that cultural contexts be characterized, and that the books selected be limited to those published in English. So, we portrayed the field the way it was and tried to encourage the inclusion of greater diversity. We did that by highlighting and coining the term *synoptic texts* that at different times from the 1930s onward provided summary conceptualizations of the state of the field. The term synoptic text was derived from my brief theological study which revealed the New Testament books of Matthew, Mark, and Luke as synoptic texts, that is, summaries of the life of Jesus. Another theological text, now supposedly lost, was called Q, and some said it included more of the primary sayings of Jesus. Applied to curriculum synoptic texts, that could metaphorically be books of readings, that is, primary source selections and excerpts, such as those we included in *The American Curriculum: A Documentary History* (Willis et al., 1993). Or, relative to the first synoptic curriculum text we identified *Curriculum Development*, by Hollis Caswell and Doak Campbell (1935), the Q text could be their edited follow-up volume, *Readings in Curriculum Development* (Caswell & Campbell, 1937). We also tried to show that curriculum scholars could be classified relative to tendencies to reflect different orientations. In the 1980 volume we discussed the intellectual traditionalist, social behaviorist, and experientialist, and in the 2002 volume we added the critical reconstructionist, the postmodernist, and experimented with a couple of other categories. We also coined the terms *outside curriculum* or *nonschool curricula* and *a theory within persons* (Schubert & Lopez Schubert, 1980, pp. 347–348) meaning the ever-evolving images (Boulding, 1956) derived from reflection on experiences that constitute education (Dewey, 1916, 1938). We were grateful for my former students Tom Thomas and Wayne Carroll who added much to the 2002 edition of *Curriculum Books*, and to Bill Watkins (1993) who developed Black curriculum orientations, and of course to my PhD adviser, J. Harlan Shores who encouraged me to keep note cards on all that I read during doctoral studies. These cards were the basis of the 1980 edition that Ann and I wrote.

JAMES T. SEARS

I am glad that *Curriculum, Religion, and Public Education: Conversations for Enlarging Public Square* by James T. Sears (1998) was selected for its contemporary relevance by Erica L. M. O'Keefe. It is, indeed, still relevant. I remember Jim interviewing me by phone in my UIC office for this book which he was partially deriving from a course at the University of South Carolina that dealt with critique of conservative Southern evangelical or fundamentalist opposition to more progressive or liberal aspects of curriculum in public schooling. Sears's emphasis on the public square of course invoked issues around the separation of church and state. I recall that there were fundamentalist protesters in the halls of his classroom and guards were there to keep them from entering his class as he interviewed me on what John Dewey, other critical or social reconstructionists, and I, had to say about this issue. I first met Jim Sears at the University of South Carolina in the record-setting hot summer of 1986, after he finished his PhD at Indiana University under the guidance of Norman Overly (also mentor of Tom Poetter). We talked often during that summer when Craig Kridel and others had invited me to be in Columbia for a summer visiting appointment. Over the years since then, I witnessed Jim's courage in standing up on tough controversial issues in curriculum theory and practice. I recall when he and Dan Marshall invited me to speak at a conference they organized in Charleston, SC, in 1991 at the site of slave auctions on the topic of critically addressing race prejudice and the need for multicultural education. The invited keynote speaker was Molefi Asante, the first Black studies chair in the United States at Temple University, who related curricular aspects of his commitment to *Afrocentricity* (Asante, 1987, 1991). Asante's autobiographical address was videotaped and for years to follow I used it to stimulate discussion of my graduate students at UIC. It is one of the best speeches on the topic I ever witnessed. I already had seen Sears' take on prejudice against gay and lesbian youths in books, articles, and plays he wrote (e.g., Sears, 1992). Today, there is an annual award in Jim's name at the Curriculum and Pedagogy Conference, and he currently devotes much time to helping the LGBT community find and develop safe and comfortable housing. Surely, this is a contribution to the outside curriculum, writ large. I remember, too, contributing to a book that Sears and Marshall (1990) wrote in which curriculum scholars were invited to write creatively about how they taught curriculum. I was pleased, too, to work with Jim Sears and Dan Marshall on a postmodern style history of curriculum studies from the 1950s into the early 2000s (Marshall et al., 2000) and its revision with former students of Jim's and myself (Marshall et al., 2007).

THOMAS T. SERGIOVANNI

The choice of looking anew at Tom Sergiovanni's (1982) *Supervision of Teaching* by Jennifer Penczarski revives a story of my graduate school days at UIUC. When I was completing my PhD studies in 1974, Tom Sergiovanni was a youthful professor in the educational administration area. I had heard good things about his teaching, and I had an elective to select. If I had the course he taught on leadership, I would have all the requirements for an all-grades supervisory certificate, as a side benefit. I was convinced that I wanted to teach curriculum studies at a university; however, I knew that I might like to be a curriculum director or assistant superintendent for curriculum in a good school system, if the university opportunities did not work well. So, I took his course. Wanting credit and not wanting to worry about the grade, I signed up for the pass–fail option. The professor would not know. I liked the course. Sergiovanni drew upon some intriguing business-oriented literature as well as educational administration literature. I did all the work. The course was large, over 40 students I think, and still Tom had a final conference with each of us. When we met, he said he was glad to tell me that he really liked my work in the course, especially my final project and presentation; therefore, was giving me an A+. I don't even think they had A+ grades. Nonetheless, I still cannot forget the look on his face when I said that I took the course on a pass–fail basis. It still makes me chuckle. Thanks to Jennifer Penczarski for bringing back that memory. Seriously, central ideas of curriculum and supervision were once much more entwined in the early days of the field, especially in ASCD, which after all stands for Association for Supervision and Curriculum Development. In those early days it was taken for granted that the curriculum was enhanced by engaging teachers in meaningful supervisory experiences.

CHRISTINE SLEETER AND CARL GRANT

Clearly, pioneering work on multicultural education by Carl Grant and Christine Sleeter has become a valuable feature of the curriculum studies over the years. Andrea Townsend's selection of *Making Choices for Multicultural Education* (Sleeter & Grant, 1988) clearly shows the intersectionality of race, class, and gender in multicultural education. I remember talking with Christine at AERA when I chaired the committee and presented her with the 2016 Charles DeGarmo Award and she delivered the accompanying lecture to members of the Society of Professors of Education. I was intrigued that Christine was continuing to influence multicultural understanding by writing novels. I also know Carl Grant from several sources. Our College of Education at UIC invited him to have a visiting position to attend some of our faculty meetings and advise us on multicultural matters, particularly issues of race. Carl Grant also followed my colleague Bill Ayers and preceded Ming Fang He as AERA vice president (Curriculum Studies), a post that I held in 2000–2001. While earlier work on multicultural education deals with important matters of inclusion and building on strengths of different cultures, Grant and two of his former students Anthony Brown and Keffrelyn Brown, a husband and wife team at the University of Texas wrote a book on the relevance of Black intellectual thought in education (Grant et al., 2015). Such work continues the valuable emphasis on including ideas of eminent Black scholars in curriculum literature (in this case, Anna Julia Cooper, Carter G. Woodson, and Alain LeRoy Locke). It is a big step, indeed, to propose that African American scholars should have been included, were bypassed by White intellectual fields, such as curriculum studies, and need for such inclusion precisely because it enables their neglected insights and understandings to make the curriculum field better, more aware and insightful.

RALPH W. TYLER

By opening the curriculum window of *Basic Principles of Curriculum and Instruction* by Ralph W. Tyler (1949), Brittany Buhrlage helped revive some memories about my association with Tyler, perhaps the most influential curriculum scholar of the 20th century. On Columbus Day (October 12) 1980, I hurried through the corridor of a concourse of the O'Hare Airport in Chicago looking for the gate where Ralph Tyler's plane was arriving. As a young assistant professor, I was excited that he was coming to our house for dinner. In those days you could walk to the gate to pick up a guest. Amazing, by today's rules and regulations. I momentarily forgot the gate number and then heard a shrill whistle. I looked to the side and there was Ralph Tyler, born in 1902, whistling like a teenager to let me know I was passing the gate at which he arrived. He recognized me from our interactions at AERA in Boston, April 1980, when I had organized and introduced a symposium called Curriculum Knowledge and Student Perspectives where I chaired interactions among Tyler, Madeleine Grumet, Philip Jackson, and Max van Manen, and during the same week, as program chair of The Society for the Study of Curriculum History, I introduced him to present on his experience in The Eight Year Study. Since World War II understandably dominated the headlines, the extraordinary findings of the Eight Year Study (Aikin, 1942;

Kridel & Bullough, 2007; Smith & Tyler, 1942) were less apparent; plus, the message of experimentation and participatory democracy were in opposition to the forces that perpetuated the new world empire emanating from the emergent corporate world. Tyler (Tyler & Chall, 1987) had advised six U.S. presidents, many corporate and educational leaders, and depressingly the biggest take-away was making his four categories into recipes for teacher education, lesson plan forms, teachers' manuals for textbooks, evaluation forms—and forgetting his more pronounced emphasis on the importance of social context, student interest and need, philosophy, psychology, research, and participatory democracy. I first met Ralph Tyler in Milwaukee in 1976, when he was an invited presenter on how he would revise his *Basic Principles of Curriculum and Instruction* (Tyler, 1949) over 25 years since it was published in 1949. His presentation is included in an edited book by Alex Molnar and John Zahorik (1977) along with some other papers presented at this Milwaukee precursor to Bergamo Conferences on Curriculum Theory and Classroom Practice. I am still impressed that Tyler said he already made the two main points in 1949, although he would reiterate them more forcefully: the need to see students as active social learners and the need to build on the nonschool learning of students (Tyler, 1977). In any case, after his airport whistle, we drove to our one-bedroom apartment where Ann Lopez Schubert prepared a delicious dinner and we engaged in conversation about many aspects of Tyler's life, including The Tyler Rationale, the tag given by others to his 1949 book, which was an elaborate syllabus for Education 360 at the University of Chicago in the late 1940s. Among many other things, we discussed the emphasis on getting to know students as active social learners and to learn about what they have learned from educational experiences (which I call *outside curriculum*; Schubert, 1981; Schubert, 2010b, 2010c). He stressed that he is not a behaviorist in the Skinnerian sense and that his use of the term *behavior* is merely a simplified way of referring to the consequences of learning experiences in what learners think, feel, and do, that is, a term that prevents having to repeat "think, feel, and do" over again. He was emphatic that his four questions were not a recipe; rather, they were analytic categories and a change in anyone would require educators to attend to reverberations and to make adjustments in the others. In fact, he said just that in a short last Chapter 5 on page 128. Moreover, he reiterated that throughout the considerations about purposes, learning experiences, organization, and evaluation, philosophy is central. Too, throughout the educative process, it is important to keep studying learners and their contexts, because continuing the quest is more important than thinking that one has arrived at a final answer to the central curriculum question about what is worthwhile. Tyler mentioned Herbert Thelen, a colleague at the University of Chicago whose book *Education and the Human Quest* (Thelen, 1960/1972) makes that point. Our interview was published

(Tyler et al., 1986) along with other pieces put together for a special issue of *The Journal of Thought* by Kate Strickland—an early The Society for the Study of Curriculum History (SSCH) president—as a tribute to Tyler's work by SSCH, of which I was a founding member and former president.

DECKER WALKER AND JONAS SOLTIS

The fact that *Curriculum and Aims* by Decker Walker and Jonas Soltis (1997) has been published in several editions speaks to the perception of importance given to translating a generalized sense of philosophical aims into concrete and consistent instantiations for educational practice. Thus, Tammy Yockey has made a good selection for a window from the past for contemporary relevance. When I arrived at UIUC as a doctoral student, I soon heard that Decker Walker had had a visiting position there the prior year, before returning to Stanford. Some faculty and students suggested that in view of mutual interests we would have enjoyed discussion and collaboration. So, I read some of his published and unpublished writings. Having just come from doing practical curriculum work in schools, I liked the way Decker drew upon Joseph Schwab's (1970) curricular writings about the need to move to more practical and eclectic forms of inquiry. I especially liked Walker's naturalistic model of curriculum that he derived from following the work of curriculum leaders in schools and observing that they begin interaction in committee meetings with a position or agenda which he called a platform, then they advocate that platform in deliberation with others, and the result of the process becomes design. Walker (1971) called this the *naturalistic model* of curriculum development. Many theorists saw this movement from platform, to deliberation and design as contradicting Ralph Tyler's more rational model of proposing purposes, selecting learning experiences, organizing them, evaluating their implementation, and then revising. I thought that both can be done simultaneously. Deliberation could deal with how to actualize and revise aims while monitoring the interaction of both Tyler's categories and the curricular commonplaces of Schwab: teachers, learners, subject matter, and milieu. Over the years Decker Walker and I talked from time to time about these and related matters. I met Jonas Soltis at Teachers College, Columbia University, where he was a philosopher of education and on a search committee in 1988 when I was being recruited to be a professor in the faculty of the Department of Curriculum and Teaching. Although I decided to remain at UIC, I continued to interact with professors at Teachers College. I also continued to communicate with Decker Walker, who also wrote a synoptic curriculum text (Walker, 1990).

LOIS WEINER

I commend Kasey Perkins for choosing a book on teacher unions and their contributions to social justice as a valid curriculum window. Lois Weiner's (2012) *The Future of Our Schools: Teacher Unions and Social Justice* portrays valuable examples of how teacher unions contribute to teacher consciousness about curriculum. As a lifelong teacher union activist, Weiner knows her topic well. Unions are not merely about raising salary and benefits for teachers. Instead, when they are at their best, unions also focus on matters that make learning experiences for students more worthwhile, by for instance reducing class size and availability of resources and resource specialists. That work of teacher unions is also the essence of a book written by three of my former doctoral students about teachers strikes carried out by the Chicago Teachers Union, and is well captured in the title of their book on that episode in recent educational history: *Worth Striking For: Why Education Policy Is Every Teacher's Concern (Lessons From Chicago)* (Nunez et al., 2015).

CORNEL WEST

As one of the foremost public intellectuals in the world today, Cornel West has written books and articles on a host of topics, from philosophy and theology to race, class, gender, and a range of social issues. He is adept at drawing upon literary, artistic, philosophical, and religious discourses, as well as popular culture, and can impressively express himself in genres from the most scholarly, to preacher, to debate and dialogue, rap and hip-hop, and more. West appears on talk shows, news casts, and has taught at Harvard and Princeton and has spoken at a huge range of universities and public forums around the globe. Thus, I am grateful for Thomie Timmons for including West's (1993) *Race Matters* as a window on curriculum matters. While not formally a participant in the curriculum field, Cornel West should be welcomed as a window of insight and intelligence by curriculum scholars and practitioners of all sorts. I remember seeing him present as part of a group of (then emergent) young scholars, a few years younger than I was, when the Institute for the Humanities at UIC was inaugurated in Chicago in the early 1980s. While I do not remember the other speakers from that long ago event, I do remember him, and thinking that "Cornel West" was a name that the future scholarly world would hold in high regard for his challenging, radical, and insightful sense of social justice. At least one of my predictions has been realized! When I think of the powerful phrase *Race Matters* (West, 1993), I am reminded of a session at AERA a decade earlier, in 1983. I, as co-program chair with Ann Lopez Schubert, of the Curriculum Studies Division, chaired a session in which Elliot Eisner, the outgoing vice-president and Philip Jackson, the in-coming vice-president, had a short though pungent conversation while exchanging the gavel. One phrase they both invented on the spot is indelibly etched in my mind: "Nothing matters like curriculum matters." This makes me think of Cornel West having to say, yet again, what I interpret as: "Nothing matters like race matters." It is of central import that W. E. B Du Bois asserted in his 1900 message to The Nations of the World in an address to the Pan-African Conference: "The problem of the twentieth century is the problem of the color line." Still, 93 years later, Cornel West had to reiterate and elaborate, and in 2020, revolts in the streets of America and throughout the world cause matters of race, racism, and equity to matter enormously as curricula faced by all, in and out of schools. Race infuses curriculum and curriculum conveys racial messages both implicitly and explicitly. A key message I gather from Cornel West is that educators need to proactively consider what is worth teaching and learning about race, or else prejudices and destructions will emerge by intent and by default.

ALFRED NORTH WHITEHEAD

Alfred North Whitehead, a great philosopher and mathematician, stands in my mind as one of the most insightful and beautiful essayists on the topic of education. His essays on education, in a collection titled by one of them called *The Aims of Education* (Whitehead, 1929), are replete with quotable aesthetic insights. Early in our careers, Ann Lopez Schubert, George Posner, and I did a survey of the professors of curriculum and some other prominent curriculum scholars, asking what articles they found most influential (Schubert et al., 1982). Eight of the top ten were deemed speculative essays (Schubert, 1991b), rather than other kinds of research. Whitehead's (1929) *The Aims of Education* was among the eight. I appreciate the fact that Michelle Banks perceives the contemporary relevance of this book over 90 years later, as did curriculum scholars of the 1970s and early 1980s when they completed the aforementioned survey. Passages that exhibit elegance and meaning in *The Aims of Education* are sampled here: "Every intellectual revolution which has ever stirred humanity into greatness has been a passionate protest against inert ideas" (p. 2). "The present contains all that there is. It is holy ground; for it is the past, and it is the future" (p. 3). And one of my favorite definitions: "Education is the acquisition of the art of the utilization of knowledge" (p. 4). "The solution which I am urging, is to eradicate the fatal disconnection of subjects which kills the vitality of our modern curriculum. There is only one subject-matter, and that is Life in all its manifestations" (pp. 6–7). "The pupils have got to be made to feel that they are studying something and are not merely executing intellectual minuets" (pp. 9–10). "You may not divide the seamless coat of learning" (p. 12). All of these are from the first chapter, for which the book itself is named: *The Aims of Education*. In another chapter called *On Universities and Their Function*, Whitehead says, "The justification for a university is that it preserves the connection between knowledge and the zest of life...in the imaginative consideration of learning" (p. 93). When I was fortunate enough to receive a sabbatical leave from the Downers Grove Public Schools to pursue a PhD at UIUC during the 1973–1974 academic year and the summers before, I felt fortunate to be able to support my family with the sabbatical pay and benefits, house rental, and a teaching assistantship, and a fellowship. However, I knew I should do my best to complete as much of the work as possible during that short period, so I decided to take massive overloads and focus all energy on course work that prepared me for the dissertation. So, I pondered deeply on identifying a topic I could direct my studies toward. I asked myself what I had learned as a teacher that I could share and advance through study about curriculum as a contribution to knowledge. It came to me that my greatest resource was my imagination with children honed by study of philosophy, other humanities, and the arts. I turned every assignment, and a host of audited courses as well, into research ventures on what I later named *Imaginative Projection: A Method of Curriculum Invention* (Schubert, 1975). I did my best to live Whitehead's admonitions during that year, and in 1974–1975, I returned to repay Illinois District 58 for the sabbatical leave by teaching another year and by writing the dissertation while taking some additional course work at Northwestern which could be done through the Traveling Scholar Program of The Big Ten Academic Alliance. It was a busy year of imagining and pursuing my aims of education!

STEVEN ZEMELMAN, HARVEY DANIELS, AND ART HYDE

One of Heinemann's best-selling books, *Best Practice* (Zemelman et al., 1993) reached more educators on progressive education than most recent books; thus, Erin Owens made a good decision to open their curricular window. I knew Zemelman, Daniels, and Hyde, as they were professors at National College of Education (now known as National-Louis University) in Evanston, Illinois when I was a professor at UIC. In fact, I taught a couple of courses at National College of Education before getting fully involved at UIC for the next 36 years. I do not know this for sure; however, I suspect and admire the strategy I surmise they used. Since the authors were progressives and wanted to convey progressive ideas and practices to as many educators as possible, I think they brilliantly thought of calling what they said, "best practices." Moreover, in an era when everyone seemed to be making statements of standards, their subtitle indicates that they were of-fering new standards for teaching and learning. Perhaps they thought that more conservative or traditional educators or communities would eschew or at least question something called *progressive*. Also, since a lot of research and theory backed the ideas they wanted to perpetuate, they selected the term "best practices." Who would oppose the *best*? Who, ridiculously, would advocate for worst practices?! So, I see their choice of labeling as a rea-son Zemelman, Daniels, and Hyde were able to convince a wide swath of educators to adopt progressive approaches without beating them over the head with the "progressive" label. Moreover, they backed their advocacy with theory and research, since there is much theory and research that does, in fact, support progressive practices. And they supported the ideas with "exemplary programs" in the major subject areas and provided advice on making transitions to adopt, adapt, and assess best practices with diverse school populations. Kudos to them! I wish I would have thought to do that. The book, and other writings and consultations that flow from it, has been a "best seller" in the educational world.

BELL HOOKS

It is fitting that the list I was given for composing this Foreword was alpha-betical, except for bell hooks, since her most popular book among educa-tors seems to be *Teaching to Transgress* (hooks, 1994). However, I am glad the hooks book selected by Tiffany Williams is *All About Love: New Visions* (hooks, 2000). Love has been too long left behind in curriculum. As a public intellectual, who has written about many topics particularly relevant to Af-rican Americans, hooks has written books and articles and speaks critically on issues meaningful for all persons concerned with the racist, sexist, clas-sist, patriarchal society and world. Her writing topics include an immense range: freedom, transgression, hope, community, feminism, justice, sister-hood, yearning, race, gender, cultural politics, sex, movies, class, salvation, communion, change, belonging, critical thinking, practical wisdom, self-es-teem, rage, memories, mass incarceration, many others, and of course, love. I urge readers not to forget that love has been a dynamic idea infusing all of hooks' work. Throughout my career I have been concerned with the neglect of love in education and especially in mainstream curriculum studies. Since I retired, I have yearned to write more about love's place in education, and I use the word *yearned* intentionally here, since it is the topic of another of bell hooks' books, namely, *Yearning* (hooks, 1990), which incidentally, a much respected colleague, Denise Taliaferrro-Baszile, has identified as her favor-ite book by hooks. A few years ago, shortly before I retired, I was consider-ing neglected topics in curriculum studies and what I felt was worthwhile to write about, and I settled on love. A former doctoral student, Mike Klonsky, brought John Dewey's short article on Utopians (Dewey, 1933) from *The New York Times* to my attention. In it, Dewey pretended that he had met (or maybe he did meet!) Utopians who taught him a lesson about his own advocacy of democratic education, often known as progressivism. The Utopians taught him that the greatest obstacle to practicing the kind of education that Dewey advocates is the acquisitive society which translates every aspect of education into something to be commodified and acquired. I developed a book as a riff on each sentence in Dewey's essay, extrapolating his points into a meditation on justice in education. I titled the book *Love, Justice, and Education* (Schubert, 2009b) and argued that a Deweyan ideal of education within participatory democracy can only accrue as human beings grow in *agape*, that is, a deep spirit of love, similar to the kind that which Martin Luther King Jr., calls for in *The Strength to Love* (King, 1963). Thus, my argument, drawing on many diverse literatures, moves from a critique of acquisitive society that cannot be overcome without human beings becoming more empathic and just. They must cultivate loving relationships with one another. So, I see a natural progression from recognizing the limitations of the acquisitive society to loving one another as a path to increased justice enabling democratic education. Thus, I return to bell hooks' (2000) *All about Love,* through lenses of a dialogic book she co-authored with Cornel West: *Breaking Bread* (hooks & West, 1991). The symbolism of breaking bread is about a spiritual ascension of love as the seed of social justice and emancipatory education. Again, I am deeply pleased that Tiffany William selected *All About Love* (hooks, 2000) as her window of choice.

CONCLUDING COMMENT

I commend Tom Poetter for this brilliant Curriculum Windows project. I thank Kelly Waldrop for initially inviting me to write the Forewords, and I extend kudos to all of the other editors and authors. I encourage the readers to enjoy looking through the windows opened here and in the other volumes in the Curriculum Windows series, urging you to realize that each of these windows, in turn, opens other windows of authors who provide landscapes of new views onto the continuing flow of curriculum concerns. It is time to move forward from the Foreword.

—**William H. Schubert**
University of Illinois at Chicago

REFERENCES

Aikin W. M. (1942). *The story of the Eight Year Study*. Harper & Brothers.

Asante, M. K. (1987). *The Afrocentric idea*. Temple University Press.

Asante, M. K. (1991). *Afrocentricity*. Africa World Press, Inc.

Au, W., Brown, A. L., & Calderón, D. (2016). *Reclaiming the multicultural roots of U.S. curriculum: Communities of color and official knowledge in education*. Teachers College Press.

Ayers, B. (2016). *Demand the impossible*. Haymarket Books.

Banks, J. (1981). *Multiethnic education: Theory and practice*. Allyn and Bacon.

Banks, J. (1997). *Educating citizens in a multicultural society*. Teachers College Press.

Banks, J. A., & McGee Banks, C. A. (1995). *Handbook of research on multicultural education*. Macmillan.

Banks, J. A., & McGee Banks, C. A. (2004). *Handbook of research on multicultural education*. (2nd ed.). Jossey-Bass.

Barone, T. E., & Eisner, E. W. (2012). *Arts-based research*. SAGE Publications.

Bateson, M. C. (1989). *Composing a life*. Penguin (Plume).

Bennett, C. (1995). *Comprehensive multicultural education: Theory and practice* (3rd ed.). Allyn & Bacon.

Bobbitt, F. (1918). *The curriculum*. Houghton Mifflin.

Boulding, K. (1956). *The image: Knowledge in life and society*. University of Michigan Press.

Boyer, E. (1990). *Scholarship reconsidered: Priorities of the professoriate*. The Carnegie Foundation for the Advancement of Teaching.

Britzman, D. (2003). *Practice makes practice: A critical study of learning to teach* (Rev. ed.). SUNY Press.

Brown, A. L., & Au, W. (2014). Race, memory, and master narratives: A critical essay on U. S. curriculum history. *Curriculum Inquiry 44*(3), 358–389.

Caswell, H. L., & Campbell, D. S. (1935). *Curriculum development*. American Book Company.

Caswell, H. L., & Campbell, D. S. (Eds.). (1937). *Readings in curriculum development*. American Book Company.

Connelly, F. M., He, M. F., & Phillion, J. A. (Eds.). (2008). *Handbook of curriculum and instruction*. SAGE Publications.

Darling-Hammond, L. (2010). *The flat world and education: How America's commitment to equity will determine our future*. Teachers College Press.

Delpit, L. (1995). *Other people's children: Cultural conflict in the classroom*. The New Press.

Delpit, L. (2012). *"Multiplication is for white people": Raising expectations for other people's children*. The New Press.

Dewey, J. (1915) 1899, revised 191. *The school and society*. University of Chicago Press. (Originally published in 1899)

Dewey, J. (1902). *The child and the curriculum*. University of Chicago Press.

Dewey, J. (1916). *Democracy and education*. Macmillan.

Dewey, J. (1933, April 23). Dewey outlines utopian schools. *The New York Times*, p 7.

Dewey, J. (1938). *Experience and education*. Macmillan.

Dewey, J. (1956). *The child and the curriculum* and *The school and society: Two influential works by the father of progressive education.* University of Chicago Press.

Duckworth, E. (1987). *"The having of wonderful ideas" and other essays on teaching and learning.* Teachers College Press.

Fabricant, M., & Fine, M. (2012). *Charter schools and the corporate makeover of public education: What's at stake?* Teachers College Press.

Fanon, F. (1963). *The wretched of the earth.* Grove Press.

Fantini, M. (1976). *Alternative schools.* Doubleday.

Foshay, W. R., & Foshay, A. W. (1980). Curriculum development and instructional development. *Educational Leadership, 38*(8), 621–626.

Fliegel, S. (1993). *Miracle in East Harlem: The fight for choice in public education.* Times Books.

Fullan, M. (1982). *The meaning of educational change.* Ontario Institute for Studies in Education Press.

Fullan, M. (1991). *The new meaning of educational change* (2nd ed.; with S. Stiegelbuer). Teachers College Press.

Gagne, R. (1967). *The conditions of learning.* Holt, Rinehart, and Winston.

Gagne, R., & Perkins Driscoll, M. (1988). *Essentials of learning for instruction* (2nd edition). Prentice Hall.

Gaztambide-Fernandez, R. (2015). Browning the curriculum: A project of unsettlement. In M. F. He, B. D. Schultz, & W. H. Schubert (Eds.), *Guide to curriculum in education* (pp. 416–423). SAGE Publications.

Gonzalez, N., Moll, L. C., & Amanti, C. (2005). *Funds of knowledge: Theorizing practice in households, communities, and classrooms.* Lawrence Erlbaum.

Goodlad, J. I. (1984). *A place called school.* McGraw-Hill.

Goodlad, J. (1994). *Educational renewal: Better teachers, better schools.* Jossey-Bass.

Goodman, P. (1964). *Compulsory miseducation.* Horizon Press.

Grande, S. (2015). *Red pedagogy: Native American social and political thought.* Rowman & Littlefield. (Originally published 2005)

Grant, C. A., Brown, K. D., & Brown, A. L. (2015). *Black intellectual thought in education: The missing traditions of Anna Julia Cooper, Carter G. Woodson, & Alain Locke.* Routledge.

Greene, M. (1995). *Releasing the imagination: Essays on education, the arts, and social change.* Jossey-Bass.

Grumet, M. (1988). *Bitter milk: Women and teaching.* University of Massachusetts Press.

He, M. F. (2003). *A river forever flowing: Cross-cultural lives and identities in the multicultural landscape.* Information Age Publishers.

He, M. F. (2010). Exile pedagogy: Teaching in-between. In J. A. Sandlin, B. D. Schultz, & J. Burdick (Eds.), *Handbook of public pedagogy: Education and learning beyond schooling* (pp. 469–482). Routledge.

He, M. F., Schultz, B. D., & Schubert, W. H. (Eds.). (2015). *Guide to curriculum in education.* SAGE Publications.

Hillman, J. (1975). *Re-visioning psychology.* Harper & Row.

Hillman, J. (1983). *Inter views: Conversations with Laura Posso on psychotherapy, biography, love, soul, dreams, work, imagination, and the state of the culture.* Harper & Row.

hooks, b. (1990). *Yearning: Race, gender, and cultural politics.* South End Press.

hooks, b. (1994). *Teaching to transgress: Education as the practice of freedom.* Routledge.

hooks, b. (2000). *All about love: New visions.* HarperCollins Publishers.

hooks, b., & West, C. (1991). *Breaking bread: Insurgent Black intellectual life.* South End Press.

Hunter, M. (1982). *Mastery teaching: Increasing effectiveness in elementary, secondary schools, colleges, and universities.* TIP Publications.

Husen, T., & Postelthwaite, N. (1994). *The international encyclopedia of education.* Pergamon Press. (Originally published 1985)

Jagla, V. (1994). *Teachers' everyday use of intuition and imagination.* State University of New York Press.

Kilpatrick, W. H. (1918). The project method. *Teachers College Record, 19,* 319–335.

King, M. L., Jr. (1963). *The strength to love.* Beacon Press.

Kliebard, H. (1995). *The struggle for the American curriculum 1893–1958* (2nd ed.). Routledge. (Originally published 1986)

Kohn, A. (1992). *No contest: The case against competition* (Revised ed.). Houghton Mifflin.

Kohn, A. (1996). *Beyond discipline: From compliance to community.* ASCD.

Kohn, A (1998). Only for my kid: How privileged parents undermine school reform. *Phi Delta Kappan, 79*(8), 568–577.

Kozol, J. (1972). *Free schools.* Houghton-Mifflin.

Kozol, J. (1991). *Savage inequalities: Children in America's schools.* Harper.

Kridel, C. (Ed.). (2010). *Encyclopedia of curriculum studies.* SAGE Publications.

Kridel, C., & Bullough, R. V., Jr. (2007). *Stories of the Eight Year Study: Reexamining secondary schooling in America.* State University of New York Press.

Kridel, C., Bullough, R. V., Jr., & Shaker, P. (Eds.). (1996). *Teachers and mentors: Profiles of distinguished twentieth-century professors of education.* Garland.

Lake, R. (2013). *A curriculum of imagination in an era of standardization.* Information Age Publishing.

Laura, C. (2014). *Being bad: My baby brother and the school-to-prison pipeline.* Teachers College Press.

Marshall, J. D., Sears, J. T., & Schubert, W. H. (2000). *Turning points in curriculum: A contemporary curriculum memoir.* Prentice Hall.

Marshall, J. D., Sears, J. T., Allen, L., Roberts, P., & Schubert, W. H. (2007). *Turning points in curriculum: A contemporary curriculum memoir* (2nd ed.). Prentice Hall.

Mayhew, K. C., & Edwards, A. C. (1936). *The Dewey school.* D. Appleton-Century.

Meier, D. (1995). *The power of their ideas: Lessons for America from a small school in Harlem.* Beacon Press.

Meier, D., & Wood, G. (Eds.). (2004). *Many children left behind: How the No Child Left Behind Act is damaging our children and our schools.* Beacon Press.

Miller, J. L. (1990). *Creating spaces and finding voices.* State University of New York Press.

National Education Association Committee of Ten on Secondary School Studies. (1893). *The report.* NEA.

National Education Association Committee of Fifteen of Elementary School Studies. (1895). *The report.* NEA.

National Education Association Commission on the Reorganization of Secondary Education. (1918). *Cardinal principles of secondary education: A report.* NEA.

Nicholls, J. G. (1989). *The competitive ethos and democratic education.* Harvard University Press.

Nunez, I., Michie, G., & Konkol, P. (2015). *Worth striking for: Why education policy is every teacher's concern (lessons from Chicago)*. Teachers College Press.

Paley, V. (1992). *You can't say you can't play*. Harvard University Press.

Paley, V. (2009). *White teacher*. Cambridge, MA: Harvard University Press. (Originally published 1979)

Paley, V. (1999). *The kindness of children*. Harvard University Press.

Paley, V. (2009). *A child's work: The fantasy of play*. University of Chicago Press.

Paraskeva, J. (2016). *Curriculum epistemicide*. Palgrave Macmillan.

Pinar, W. F., & Grumet, M. R. (1976). *Toward a poor curriculum*. Kendall/Hunt.

Pinar, W. F., Reynolds, W. M., Slattery, P., & Taubman, P. M. (1995). *Understanding curriculum*. Peter Lang.

Rugg, H. O. (1929–32). *Man and his changing society* (Vols. 1–6). Ginn.

Rugg, H. O. (1941). *That men may understand: An American in the long armistice*. Doubleday.

Rugg, H., & Shumaker, A. (1928). *The child-centered school*. World Book Co.

Said, E. (1993). *Culture and imperialism*. Knopf.

Schubert, W. H. (1975). *Imaginative projection: A method of curriculum invention* [Unpublished PhD dissertation]. University of Illinois.

Schubert, W. H. (1981). Knowledge about out-of-school curriculum. *Educational Forum, 45*(2), 185–198.

Schubert, W. H. (1982). The return of curriculum inquiry from schooling to education. *Curriculum Inquiry, 12*(2), 221–232.

Schubert, W. H. (1986). *Curriculum: Perspective, paradigm, and possibility*. Macmillan.

Schubert, W. H. (1991a). Teacher lore: A basis for understanding praxis. In C. Witherell & N. Noddings (Eds.), *The stories lives tell: Narrative and dialogue in education* (pp. 207–233). Teachers College Press.

Schubert, W. H. (1991b). Philosophical inquiry: The speculative essay. In E. C. Short (Ed.), *Forms of curriculum inquiry* (pp. 61–76). State University of New York Press.

Schubert, W. H. (2009a). What's worthwhile: From knowing and experiencing to being and becoming. *Journal of Curriculum and Pedagogy 6*(2), 21–39.

Schubert, W. H. (2009b). *Love, justice, and education: John Dewey and the utopians*. Information Age Publishing.

Schubert, W. H. (2010a). Journeys of expansion and synopsis: Tensions in books that shaped curriculum inquiry, 1968–present. *Curriculum Inquiry, 40*(1), 17–94.

Schubert, W. H. (2010b). Outside curriculum. In C. Kridel (Ed.), *Encyclopedia of curriculum studies* (Vol. 2; pp. 624–628). SAGE Publications.

Schubert, W. H. (2010c). Outside curricula and public pedagogy. In J. A. Sandlin, B. D. Schultz, & J. Burdick (Eds.), *Handbook of public pedagogy: Education and learning beyond schooling* (pp. 10–19). Routledge.

Schubert, W. H., & Lopez Schubert, A. L. (1980). *Curriculum books: The first eighty years*. University Press of America.

Schubert, W., & Ayers, W. (Eds.). (1992). *Teacher lore: Learning from our own experience*. Longman.

Schubert, W., & Lopez Schubert, A. L. (1980). *Curriculum books: The first eighty years*. University Press of America.

Schubert, W. H., Lopez Schubert, A. L., & Posner, G. J. (1982, March 19). *Professional preferences of curriculum scholars: A genealogical study* [Paper presentation].

Annual Meeting of the American Educational Research Association, New York, NY.

Schubert, W. H., Lopez Schubert, A. L., Thomas, T. P., & Carroll, W. M. (2002). *Curriculum books: The first hundred years.* Peter Lang.

Schwab, J. J. (1970). *The practical: A language for curriculum.* National Education Association.

Sears, J. T. (1992). *Sexuality and the curriculum.* Teacher College Press.

Sears, J. (Ed.). (1998). *Curriculum, religion, and public education: Conversations for an enlarging public square.* Teachers College Press.

Sears, J. T., & Marshall, J. D. (Eds.). (1990). *Teaching and thinking about curriculum: Critical inquiries.* Teachers College Press.

Sergiovanni, T. (Ed.). (1982). *Supervision of teaching.* Association for Supervision and Curriculum Development.

Short, E. C. (Ed.). (1991). *Forms of curriculum inquiry.* State University of New York Press.

Sleeter, C., & Grant, C. (1988). *Making choices for multicultural education: Five approaches to race, class, and gender.* Merrill.

Smith, B. O., Stanley, W. O., & Shores, J. H. (1950). *Fundamentals of curriculum development.* World Book.

Smith, B. O., Stanley, W. O., & Shores, J. H. (1957). *Fundamentals of curriculum development.* Harcourt, Brace, and World.

Smith, E. R., & Tyler, R. W. (1942). *Appraising and recording student progress.* Harper & Brothers.

Sousa Santos, B. (2014). *Epistemologies of the South: Justice against epistemicide.* Paradigm.

Spring, J. (1994). *Deculturalization and the struggle for equality: A brief history of the education of dominated cultures in the United States.* McGraw-Hill.

Tanner, L. N. (1997). *Dewey's laboratory school: Lessons for today.* Teachers College Press.

Thelen, H. T. (1972). *Education and the human quest.* Harper & Row. (Originally published 1960)

Tuhiwai Smith, L. (2011). *Decolonizing methodologies: Research and indigenous peoples.* Zed Books. (Originally published 2001)

Tyler, R. W. (1949). *Basic principles of curriculum and instruction.* University of Chicago Press.

Tyler, R. W. (1977). Desirable content for a curriculum development syllabus today. In A. Molnar & J. Zahorik (Eds.), *Curriculum theory* (pp. 36–44). Association for Supervision and Curriculum Development.

Tyler, R. W., & Chall, M. (1987). *Education: Curriculum development and evaluation: Oral history transcript* (interviewed by Malca Chall). University of California, Regional Oral History Office.

Tyler, R. W., Schubert, W. H., & Schubert, A. L. (1986). A dialogue with Ralph W. Tyler. *Journal of Thought, 21*(1), 91–118.

Valenzuela, A. (1999). *Subtractive schooling: U.S.-Mexican youth and the politics of caring.* State University of New York Press.

Walker, D. F. (1971). A naturalistic model for curriculum development. *School Review, 80*(1), 51–69.

Walker, D. F. (1990). *Fundamentals of curriculum.* Harcourt, Brace, Jovanovich.

Walker, D., & Soltis, J. (1997). *Curriculum and aims* (3rd ed.). Teachers College Press.

Watkins, W. H. (1993). Black curriculum orientations: A preliminary inquiry. *Harvard Educational Review, 63*(3), 321–338.

Watkins, W. H. (1994). Multicultural education: Toward historical and political inquiry. *Educational Theory, 44*(1), 99–117.

Watkins, W. H. (2015). The neglected historical milieu. In M. F. He, B. D. Schultz, & W. H. Schubert (Eds.), *Guide to curriculum in education* (pp. 303–310). SAGE Publications.

Weiner, L. (2012). *The future of our schools: Teacher unions and social justice.* Haymarket Books.

West, C. (1993). *Race matters.* Vintage Books.

Whitehead, A. N. (1929). *The aims of education and other essays.* Free Press.

Willis, G. H., Schubert, W. H., Bullough, R., Jr., Kridel, C., & Holton, J. (Eds.). (1993). *The American curriculum: A documentary history.* Greenwood Press.

Witherell, C., & Noddings, N. (Eds.). (1991). *Stories lives tell: Narrative and dialogue in education.* Teachers College Press.

Wood, G. H. (1992). *Schools that work.* Dutton.

Wood, G. H. (1998). *A time to learn.* Dutton.

Woodson, C. G. (1933). *The mis-education of the negro.* Associated Publishers.

Zemelman, S., Daniels, H., & Hyde, A. (1998). *Best practice: New standards for teaching and learning in America's schools* (2nd ed.). Heinemann.

William H. Schubert is professor emeritus and former university scholar at the University of Illinois at Chicago where he coordinated the PhD program in curriculum studies, chaired Curriculum & Instruction, and served as director of graduate studies. President of the John Dewey Society, the Society of Professors of Education, and The Society for the Study of Curriculum History, he was honored in 2004 with the Lifetime Achievement Award in Curriculum Studies by the American Educational Research Association (AERA).

PREFACE

When I arrived at Miami in August 2019, I was very excited to be a part of a new scholarly, academic community. I had to travel 9,000 miles to get to Oxford to attend one of the oldest schools in the United States. As an international student, I was quite ambitious to engage in activities that would open new vistas of learning for me. Among these activities, my job as a graduate assistant was a new learning avenue because I had never had such a dynamic role before. Back home, I always looked forward to working on some innovative work. So coming in I had many questions on my mind about my assistantship before my meeting with Dr. Poetter, but as soon as Dr. Poetter started briefing me about my work, I started forgetting them!

I was so excited and jubilant when he finished briefing me. Serendipitously, I was going to be part of a project which I could have only just dreamed about beforehand. I was asked to do edits and minor revisions to some chapters which were going to appear in this book. I was super excited to start working on a project which was going to allow me to hear many new scholarly voices on famous curriculum theorists. The most interesting aspect of the manuscripts came through the voice of doctoral scholars, who after going through the books of notable curriculum theorists expressed their scholarly views of the authors and their work and provided insights into their own lives and work as a result.

My learning, after going through the writings of the 33 scholars presented here, is two pronged. First, I got to know about 30 curriculum theorists through the work of these brilliant young scholars. Second, I particularly enjoyed the writing in the drafts. After reading a couple of pieces, I started

Curriculum Windows Redux, pages xlv–xlvi
Copyright © 2022 by Information Age Publishing
www.infoagepub.com

getting a taste of American English which to me is quite informal, direct, and to the point. I found each author's person-self in the writings. The subjectivity or interpretivism appeared conspicuously in most of the pieces. I had a feeling that the authors could successfully relate their personal as well as professional experiences while narrating their reflections on curriculum theorists.

I hope it is not out of place if I share another personal feeling of mine about the writing pieces of these educational leaders. As I experienced a taste of individualism by going through a variety of unique interpretations and reflections on notable curriculum theorists, I realized that it could be much easier for a beginning scholar to write a scholarly critique by compromising her/his individualistic standpoint. I have a thesis that this feature of American intelligentsia makes this land a heaven for those intellectuals who wish to safeguard their intellectual scholarship by securing their ideas and beliefs on paper without a fear of opprobrium or persecution. As an international student, experiencing a higher education in America becomes a top priority for many international students due to the liberty experienced through disseminating our own personal ideas and beliefs. I am so glad to have contributed to this volume, and to have learned so much from its authors.

—**Syed Hassan Raza**
Miami University

INTRODUCTION

Curriculum Windows Redux

Note: This introduction, for the seventh and final volume in the Curriculum Windows series, is adapted—in some cases nearly word-for-word—from the introduction to the first volume in the series, *Curriculum Windows: What Curriculum Theorists of the 1960s Can Teach Us About Schools and Society Today*, (Poetter, 2013, pp. xxx–xxxiii). I do not use quotation marks to cite the sections that are repeated since they are sometimes several pages long. Sections of that original introduction serve as strong conceptual grounding for the notion of curriculum "window" and helped create a window to the project for the class studying curriculum books for this volume.

HOW THIS PROJECT CAME TO BE

In all of the six preceding volumes of this book series entitled Curriculum Windows, I tell the story of how the Curriculum Windows project came into being. I'll give a shortened version here to get you started as you begin this text on curriculum books redux, that is, of books that probably should have been covered in the previous volumes focusing on decades but either weren't chosen by students at the time or were overlooked by me from the start. After publishing volumes on curriculum books of the 1950, 1960s, 1970s, 1980s, 1990s, and 2000s, this is the final volume in the series, unless

Curriculum Windows Redux, pages xlvii–lvi
Copyright © 2022 by Information Age Publishing
www.infoagepub.com
xlvii

Bill Schubert twists my arm enough to cover the just completed decade of the 2010s at some point in the near future.

Several years ago I "inherited" more than 100 curriculum books from my major professor at Indiana University in the 1990s, Norman V. Overly, a few years after his retirement. I received the books in 2005. I put the word "inherited" in quotation marks above because Norm is still living and going strong. In fact, he won the Lifetime Achievement Award from Division B of AERA, Curriculum Studies, in 2014, based on his rich contributions to research in the curriculum field throughout his career, and especially through two very prominent books, *The Unstudied Curriculum* (Overly, 1970) and *Lifelong Learning: A Human Agenda* (Overly, 1979), treatments of which bookended the 1970s volume in this series. What Norm wanted was for all of the books he gave me to be put to good use; I didn't know exactly how I would do that at first, but I decided to store them initially on a prominent bookcase in my office at Miami University and make them available to students. Students could take them and use them as they willed.

As a result of using Schubert et al.'s (2002) *Curriculum Books: The First Hundred Years* in a seminar, I began to see how so many of the books in Norm's collection could be sorted by decade, which I began to do. At that moment, a window to the past opened up to me. I immediately thought of the idea of teaching a doctoral level seminar in curriculum based on curriculum books by decade. Through several wonderful twists of fate in my department, I got the opportunity to teach a core seminar in our curriculum studies in our doctoral program in Leadership, Culture, and Curriculum (LCC), the first one taking place in the Spring of 2012. In the course, besides studying prominent curriculum books of a particular decade as well as current ideas, theories, and practices in the field of curriculum studies, I would challenge students to study one book in particular from the decade at hand and write a book length chapter (about 15–20 pages, double spaced) for the end of course assignment to be included in a book, like this one, on the subject.

That first seminar in 2012 led to the first volume on the 1960s published in 2013. The second volume deals with books of the 1970s; that book comes from the seminar taught in the Spring of 2013. The 1980s book came out of the seminar in 2014. The chapters on books of the 1990s come from the seminar taught in the Spring of 2015. The book on the 1950s comes from the seminar taught in the Spring of 2016. The book on the 2000s was completed by the last PhD cohort to work on this project with me in the Spring of 2017. The last two classes, made up of students taking the course in our EdD program, completed the seminar in the Springs of 2017 and 2018.

From the beginning, I wondered: "How might a review of key books from the curriculum field from a given decade illuminate new possibilities forward for us today? How might the theories, practices, and ideas wrapped up in curriculum texts of that decade still resonate with us, allowing us to see backward in time and forward in time, all at the same time? How could these figurative windows of insight, thought, ideas, fantasy, and fancy make us think differently about curriculum, teaching, learning, students, education, leadership, and schools? How could they challenge us? How could they help us see more clearly, even perhaps put us on a path to correct the mistakes and missteps of intervening decades, as well as those of today? And, how could I engage doctoral students in curriculum at Miami in a journey like this with me, opening windows to tomorrow by looking back today? How could I get students of curriculum, perhaps on their first formal scholarly journey, to express themselves and new ideas in ways that could be consumed by peers and colleagues in the curriculum field?" (Poetter, 2013, p. xxvii; Poetter, 2010; Poetter et al., 2006; Poetter et al., 2004).

HOW THE SEMINAR WORKS

In the first part of the courses taught over a 7-year period (2012–2018), students studied several book-length works on the field of curriculum studies as well as a book from the decade for study that they would write a chapter about for about 9 weeks. In the last part of the course, about 6 weeks in length, I encouraged students to think of the chapter writing as a qualitative/autobiographic inquiry enterprise, which would involve not only their developing sense of what the book they were studying was about, but more intimately, how the book opened them up personally to new possibilities for seeing their lives and the world. I asked them to connect with the book deeply, by finding a hook in their own lives that would pull them and the reader through a window of insight and experience.

> What I wanted in the end, especially, were chapters that were voiced, meaning that the reader of each chapter could sense both the historical importance of the work but also get a sense of the personal stakes at hand through the chapter author's interests, hopes, experiences, and ideas. I wanted students to write themselves into the book, not out of it. I wanted them to see themselves as conduits for ideas and images and possibilities, that is as "openings," like windows, through which we might see more clearly ahead—or at least somehow differently—the educational possibilities of yesterday, today, and tomorrow. (Poetter, 2013, p. xxix)

During the last part of the course, students had individual meetings with me and they met in small groups to share drafts and engage in peer editing. I didn't engage in this process for the first book and regretted it immediately, so peer editing and continuous drafting have become hallmarks of my ongoing pedagogy with this class. These extra group sessions helped students on this project view the experience more like a collective, group process and less like an ominous, individual project hanging over their heads with a finite timeline. What I do try to make clear to each class that takes this challenge from me is that the project won't be finished at the end of the course. In each case, the publication process takes at least a year, often up to 18 months and sometimes longer, so that students have the experience of seeing a published piece through several editing processes. And the learning doesn't stop at the end of the course, which transforms the doctoral seminar into something with a life of its own that keeps on giving.

ENGAGING THE "WINDOW" METAPHOR

> The word "window," early 13th century, comes from the Old Norse "vindauga," or literally "wind eye." It replaced the Old English words "eagþyrl," literally "eye-hole" and "eagduru," literally "eye-door." Originally an unglazed hole in a roof, most Germanic languages adopted the Latin "fenestra" to describe the glass version and later in English used "fenester" as a parallel word until the late 16th century. (Harper, n.d.)

It's important to recognize that the metaphor of "window" is familiar to us and seems almost natural in terms of its serviceability. Meaning, we have experiences in our own lives of gazing out or into windows (or passing through them), whether they be in homes or cars or elsewhere. Sometimes these are typically present and pleasant memories and actions, tied often to the gift of free time or the opportunity to reflect, dream, ponder, and wonder. Krysmanski (2005) reminds us that metaphor—a figure of speech—grows out of our experiences with objects in the world and explains the unknown through the known. So "windows" had to be *there* before they could be used as metaphors. And literal windows are omnipresent, in our dwellings, works of architecture, the cinema, technology, as well as figuratively, by extension, through literature, poetry, philosophy, religion, and the technology interfaces of present-day computers.

For me, for instance, the literal and figurative notions of "windows" resonate in a very positive way and have had a soothing, almost therapeutic impact on me, and represent, in almost every beat of my heart for nearly 60 years, clarity, beauty, and hope. I remember as a child sitting on the radiator benches just under a picture window in our family's living room facing a busy street. The benches were decorative, with lattice on the sides to let out the heat, but the wooden tops never got too hot to sit on, even in the dead of the frigid northern Ohio winters. I spent considerable time sitting on those benches, that window seat, warming myself, and looking out of the window while taking a break from family action, or from study, or when thinking about next steps for the day or trying to get a grip on life, or dealing with loss, or just taking time to think.

Busy and beautiful, the scene outdoors changed with the seasons, with rainstorms and snow, and sunshine, and familiar faces and characters walking up and down the street. I watched from the inside as my father walked home just across the street from our church at which he was the pastor, at about 5 p.m. each night. I waited for him many an afternoon. I can recall walking or riding my bike home from school or a ballgame now and then, and seeing my sister Anne waving and smiling out to me, beckoning from inside, she, too, enjoying the window. So, the window worked both ways, calming and inspiring from the inside, and welcoming from the outside. And, I realized, I wasn't the only one who loved that window seat and its life altering powers of view.

I also recall the windows of our very large 1972 Chevy Impala as I looked out of them on long western vacation road trips with my family. Squeezed between my brother and sister in the back seat for thousands of car miles before video games and movies in the car helped the current generation of children pass the time, I soldiered on by taking in the landscape through the side windows. Perhaps that's why I dragged my own sons and wife out West in the car several years ago, in an attempt to show them the beauty of the great Western outdoors I appreciated so much as a child myself, or perhaps, to bury them as well in my own pain experienced on those rides. They can tell you the truth now after the fact. I remember saying during patches of boredom for them as the miles rolled by in the car, even beyond the reach of the technology in use, "Just look out the window. There's something new to see every mile."

And on and on it goes, with the stained-glass windows of my home church, especially the rose window behind the chancel (my father preached every Sunday of my youth in a large, impressive protestant sanctuary), majestic, beautiful, and luminous, playing an important role as I listened (or not) and meditated as a youth while surrounded by caring and loving adults and other children. Even broken windows of my youth turned out to yield life lessons, and grace, such as the time when I struck a baseball (a terrific line drive as I recall) through the large drive-up bay window of my neighbor friend's family's insurance business and ran for my life. Of course, since we lived merely steps away and all of us were friends, it didn't take long for his dad to find me and ask me how I intended to pay for it (my first early experience with the application of insurance, how apropos). He also said, "Tommy, it would have been much easier for me if you had just come in for your ball." It's the last time I ever ran from a broken window, both literally and figuratively.

But the metaphor of window, grounded perhaps in the crucible of "real" life experiences outside the sheltered, inviting windows of my own childhood and young adulthood in the 1960s and 1970s and 1980s, isn't always perceived or framed by others, necessarily, in such bucolic ways. In fact, while my experiences enrich me as a person, and make it possible for me to see, imagine, create, and interpret my reality and new realities, sometimes simultaneously, in ways that I think are not oppressive, they may simultaneously cloud my ability to see tragedy, suffering, and pain for others, though I've had my share of such and saw it all unfold on TV and in real life as a child—assassinations, wars, the dead, family deaths, disease, dysfunction, grieving, mental illness, violence, prejudice, racism, extreme social unrest. All of those maladies continue for me, day to day, in the presence, as they do for us all.

What couldn't I see or what did I repress as I gazed out of those windows of my youth? How did my privilege cause blindness? What is it that I see now, or wish I had seen, or think I might have seen with different lenses, born of age, of experience, of context? And how do these images of memory reconstruct my "self," my memory, and my current reality? How do I position myself as a child of privilege, who could look out of windows onto a street without fear of being shot at, or who had time to do so without the responsibilities of earning wages for the family or taking care of family members, soaking up the goods of free time and reflection when so many others my age as children and today as children rarely had or have a free moment to wonder? How enriched have I become at the expense of others as I soaked up the cultural capital afforded simply through the opportunity of "looking out of beautiful windows at a beautiful world"?

These are philosophical questions about experience, the kind that might be asked reflectively given time, and the conflation of context, culture, politics, economics, and experience, and the understanding of privilege as they all bear down on our current concepts of reality as we study the curriculum field and practice it, too. Ultimately, as a result of this deeper "seeing," of course, it's possible that the window, psychologically, can act as a metaphor representing, alternately, the reality or feeling of being enclosed, shuttered, sheltered, hidden, in hiding, even imprisoned, whether there are bars across the panes or not (Crenshaw & Green, 2009).

Krysmanski (2005), a contemporary German sociologist, explores the history of the windows metaphor in a short work entitled, "Windows: Exploring the History of Metaphor," in which he sketches the development of the window metaphor through architecture, fine art, theater/cinema, literature, philosophy, religion, culture, science, and technology. Of particular note in his work are several concepts that may help as you read and interpret the chapters that follow. First is his recognition that the window as metaphor allows humans to use their powers of cognition, perception, intuition, and understanding to connect the seemingly mundane of everyday life with the literal and figurative essence of "light"; this interaction takes us out of our seemingly finite world and helps us connect or not with the infinite, the unknown.

Second is the connection between (a) the literal rise of the window in use in dwellings as a passage for light before the nearly universal access to glass and (b) the subsequent development of early "windows" as "screens." In the dark ages, glass was only available to the extremely wealthy, who could install the windows in frames of dwellings and look out over feudal landscapes at their "holdings." Before the mass production and affordability of glass, which came much later into the early 20th century, "screens" over windows were held in place by "frames," and oftentimes painted and decorated, becoming works of art themselves even as they performed the function of blocking the elements that the window, as an opening by definition, could not keep out (Krysmanski, 2005).

Over time, screens became paintings, works of art in and of themselves, and paintings, for instance, served themselves as metaphorical windows, or screens, representing one reality for a reality in another dimension, simultaneously. Related is the architectural wonder of glass as art, in the case of stained-glass windows, for instance, that became part of churches and other institutional structures across continents. Stained glass doesn't so much let light enter or escape as it does reflect or absorb it, making the glass itself more luminous as opposed to lighting another venue. One's eye is drawn to the glass of the window, and its beauty and/or the story it tells, and not to the inside or outside of the dwelling place (Krysmanski, 2005). Stained glass windows don't so much admit or shield light, in so much instead as they absorb and transform it.

All of this connects with a third point, which is that modern day windows—as they take shape and are framed in so many venues, even as complete walls of buildings, as mirrors in interrogation rooms, or as screens where multiple realities meet through digital technology—continue to act as powerful inspiration for metaphor, and representations of human possibility, growth, progress, and even enslavement, while also opening up the potential for postmodern use and interpretation, that is in the sense that positionality, identity, and perhaps even culture and ideology are subject to new frontiers given the transcending energy of emerging interfaces, or screens, or windows, if you will (Krysmanski, 2005). What might our journey to locate ourselves within the complex worlds, interactions, and experiences of curriculum reveal to us as we seek, explore, open our eyes, shine the light, blaze new trails, and recognize windows of opportunity? What might the process of looking back through time at past windows of meaning reveal to us as we deal with today and dream/act for tomorrow? How might the windows we open or develop serve the curriculum field in ways that lie beyond the "screens" that Tyler imagined, for instance, the ones that would serve to filter the value of objectives "objectively" for the classroom

(Tyler, 1970)? And how might we acknowledge them instead as subjective, value-laden, human, and experiential meanings/questions derived from normative interests at hand and our own lives, as opposed to some arbitrary, meaningless and indefinable truth that lies outside of us (Kliebard, 1992)?

HOW FAR THIS PROJECT HAS COME

The idea of this project, originally, was to teach three of the seminars on this topic while using the writing project as a centerpiece pedagogy over three consecutive spring semesters (2012–2014), and then to hand the course over to one of my colleagues for them to do something different with it and with students. Unfortunately, when it was time for my longtime departmental colleague, Dennis Carlson, to teach the course, he became ill, and subsequently, and tragically, passed away in 2015. I agreed to continue teaching the course that Spring semester in 2015 and through the Spring of 2016, a semester in which I had two sections of the course, probably for the first and last time: one course with PhD students, and one with EdD students. In honor of Dennis, the book on the 2000s featured his curriculum book *Leaving safe harbors: Toward a new progressivism in American education and public life* (Carlson, 2002). Subsequently, as mentioned earlier, I taught the last two versions of this course in 2017 and 2018 to students in our EdD program.

But when this all started coming together, I had every intention of ending this project with the 1980s book. I felt this way, very strongly, for several reasons. First, as stated above, this isn't *my* class. I don't *own* it—it's a core class in our doctoral program. In fact, Denise Taliaferro Baszile, my great colleague in curriculum studies at Miami University, took over the course for the PhD cohort in the Spring of 2017 and taught it for several years before other duties called her away and my duties as department chair kept me from taking it on. For the past several years, department colleague, Durell Callier, has taught the course with great reviews. The students are not suffering by not having this class with me or not doing this project. The fact of the matter is that I wouldn't have even been teaching the 1990s class, let alone the classes on the 1950s and 2000s and the Redux volume, if it weren't for the loss of Dennis Carlson since I had already experienced a substantive 3-year run with the course. And in due time it would have been Denise's turn anyway.

Second, to be honest, I had read almost all of the books featured in this volume but started this entire book series project with the 1960s book and then proceeded by decades because it was an effective organizational device and helped center context in our conversations about curriculum as students studied their books for the course. I didn't really think that much of the curriculum books of the 1990s and 1950s, in particular and in error, and never would have found the depth and texture and marvel of the work in those decades without the course and this project. All of the books in this series and all of the books featured are worth reading! I'm convinced that doing so, if possible, would enlighten any curricularist's understanding of the field, past, present, and future.

And last, of course, it's impossible to cover everything that deserves to be covered in a series of books about great books in the curriculum field, or any field for that matter. I had run out of decades to cover legitimately, in my opinion, by the time I taught the course for the last time in Spring of 2018. But I wanted to keep going with the project because students found it engaging and novel, and a way to center their own emerging grasp of the idea of curriculum studies and how it might center scholarship and practice in multiple educational contexts, even beyond schools. Plus, the project offered a way for many students to experience the publication process and to engage in a meaningful, high stakes, and experiential process in the course.

So, I started to take stock of all of the lists of the books that I had shared with students at the opening of past classes, and took note of all of the books that I had on hand and had read that didn't get chosen over the years by students to use in their course projects. In making the final choices, I did my best to make sure that important books by scholars of color and by women were privileged. There are still books that got left out, but I would challenge any scholar or group of students to create their own review project and inform the field about what has been missed or that should be covered better or more completely!

I also couldn't resist the constant input from Bill Schubert, who has taken a great interest in the series of books and our project and has supported it from the beginning in ways that are rare today, meeting with students individually, visiting class, giving a campus wide lecture on the project and its significance to the curriculum field, and so forth. All of his efforts have been above and beyond the call and a great contribution in and of itself to the field and to me and students as a colleague. I am indebted to him for his guidance and cheerleading throughout the project and beyond.

I hope that you will enjoy the diversity of pieces in this volume, and the rich perspectives of the book authors and the authors of the chapters about them. I have enjoyed learning from them all very much. And except for the circumstances of losing Dr. Carlson, I'm glad I got to work with these classes on this project and to produce this book with them. I hope you'll find enjoyment and insight in the chapters to come, as I and the students have.

—**Thomas S. Poetter**

REFERENCES

Carlson, D. (2002). *Leaving safe harbors: Toward a new progressivism in American education and public life.* RoutledgeFalmer.

Crenshaw, D., & Green, E. (2009). The symbolism of windows and doors in play therapy. *Play Therapy.* https://manguterapeudid.ee/wp-content/uploads/2019/02/The-Symbolism-of-Windows-and-Doors.pdf

Harper, D. (n.d.). *Online etymology dictionary.* https://www.etymonline.com/

Kliebard, H. (1992). The Tyler rationale. In H. M. Kliebard (Ed.), *Forging the American curriculum: Essays in curriculum theory and history* (pp. 153–167). Routledge.

Krysmanski, H. J. (2005). *Windows: Exploring the history of metaphor.* https://web.archive.org/web/20161213080551/http://www.uni-muenster.de/PeaCon/psr/pn/05-krys-windows.pdf

Overly, N. V. (1970). *The unstudied curriculum: Its impact on children.* ASCD Elementary Education Council.

Overly, N. V. (Ed.). (1979). *Lifelong learning: A human agenda.* ASSN for Supervision & Curriculum.

Poetter, T. S. (Ed.). (2013). *Curriculum windows: What curriculum theorists of the 1960s can teach us about schools and society today.* Information Age Publishing.

Poetter, T. (2010). Taking the leap, mentoring doctoral students as scholars: A great and fruitful morass. *Teaching & Learning: The Journal of Natural Inquiry & Reflective Practice, 24*(1), 22–29.

Poetter, T., Wegwert, J., & Haerr, C. (Eds.). (2006). *No Child Left Behind and the illusion of reform: Critical essays by educators.* University Press of America.

Poetter, T., Bird, J., & Goodney, T. (Eds.). (2004). *Critical perspectives on the curriculum of teacher education.* University Press of America.

Schubert, W., Lopez, A., Thomas, T., & Carroll, W. (2002). *Curriculum books: The first hundred years* (2nd ed.). Routledge.

Tyler, R. W. (1970). *Basic principles of curriculum and instruction.* University of Chicago Press.

CHAPTER 1

IS THE ZOMBIE APOCALYPSE UPON US?

Shanna Bumiller

Author/Book studied:

Dewey, J. (1956). *The child and the curriculum* and *The school and society: Two influential works by the father of progressive education*. University of Chicago Press.

THE WALKING DEAD

A desert of silence. Trapped in a cage. Isolation from other human beings. Zombies walking in droves to their next brain-deadening experience. As much as I would like to reveal that this is the description of an episode of the *Walking Dead*, it is in fact what it was like to step into the shoes of a ninth-grade student for one day through the "Shadow a Student Challenge." I only had to endure it for one day, they have to endure this experience 188 days a year. The Shadow a Student Challenge is a national initiative

Curriculum Windows Redux, pages 1–14
Copyright © 2022 by Information Age Publishing
www.infoagepub.com
All rights of reproduction in any form reserved.

in education developed by School Retool. The purpose of this initiative is for educators to experience school through the lens of the student experience. Participants shadow a student by immersing themselves completely in the student experience, which means no walkie-talkies for administrators, dressing the part, carrying the book bag, eating lunch in the lunchroom, and doing all that the student is asked to do in classes. This experience is for educators who are driven by reimagining the school experience, which begins by experiencing school from the student perspective.

My Shadow a Student day began with a quiz in Spanish. This, obviously, was an isolated experience exacerbated by the fact that I took French in high school and had no idea what was being said or what I was reading. Second bell was English where we worked independently on an opinion writing piece for most of the 50 minutes. We did get 10 minutes to talk within a small group about our ideas and it was clear to me why students, when given time to talk to each other, need a few minutes to converse informally—we hadn't been able to talk to each other yet that day and we are social animals! Third bell we were given a reading about Hitler and had to annotate the reading and answer questions—more isolation. Fourth and fifth bell were electives and the best bells of the day because we were allowed to interact with one another and it was a brain break in the middle of the day. After lunch, the real effects of the zombification were felt—we had math and physical science. I was a science teacher for 14 years before I became an administrator, so I felt like I had a pretty good handle on my Algebra I skills but my brain felt like a construction zone—synapses and neural networks were shut down with no detour signs—I had no idea what we were supposed to be doing or how to do it and neither did the student I was shadowing! As I looked around the physical science classroom during the last 50 minutes of the day, students sat in their seats, slack-jawed, not moving, and with a glazed over stare—myself included! The teacher's voice sounded like the adults in a Charlie Brown episode, "Wah! Wah! Wah! Wah!" We were zombies and the end of the day could not come fast enough!

As I relayed my experience to my colleagues, so many agreed that my description of the experience was unpleasant but replied, "Yes, but we all did it and survived." Fighting off the urge to scream and stomp my feet, I instead tried to remember my high school experience. I went to seven bells a day, took similar courses, and "survived." But try as I might, I had a very, very hard time remembering actively participating in my classes or enjoying them. Instead I have more vivid memories of what I would doodle in the margins of my notebooks—flowers, my name in script, perfecting the art of writing my name with my left hand, to-do lists, positive words of focus for my field hockey game after school, and so forth. Is this how we want our students to reminisce about their education, by discussing what coping strategies they used to "survive" education being done to them?

The zombification was not due to the teachers in the classrooms. I can't blame the educators. They were doing what they needed to, in the time they had available, in the way that they had been taught, and then coached to deliver instruction at higher education institutions. It is the way that we play school where I place the blame, with 25–30 students in a classroom, content spewed at students for 7.5 hours a day, 188 days a year, in desks that might be pushed together to resemble tables to give the appearance of a collaborative space but still support isolated exercises in an outdated model of education, teachers whose work identity is rooted in being able to espouse their knowledge much like a silver-back gorilla thumps its chest as a show of dominance, students that are struggling to grab onto some thread of relevance within the curriculum to their lives but continually land in the quagmire of throwing up the facts necessary to get a grade so that they might be able to escape high school and begin a new postsecondary journey. It is insanity!

WE AREN'T IN KANSAS ANYMORE

Just when I thought I might succumb to the gentle calls of "It's always been this way," "We all did it," or "It is too hard to change," John Dewey entered my life and awoke me from my stupor. Prior to taking my first course in my EdD program, I only knew Dewey as a figure in education that was briefly mentioned in some undergraduate education course. It was in that first course that I discovered his philosophy and practice in education. I fell in love with Dewey. During that short 7-week course, the windows in my educational house were shattered and blown out as if an F5 tornado had just ripped through the neighborhood.

John Dewey was a philosopher, an educator, an author, a practitioner, the father of the progressive education movement, and above all else an innovator. Dewey believed that he could influence education by causing action and persuading changes in the traditional model of education. This change would require the focus in education to shift from a focus on the subject matter as sacred and the child gaining an "adult" perspective as the measure of success, to one that focuses on providing the students with learning experiences that allow them to construct meaning through real life experiences. Dewey thought that educators and students should use their knowledge, not just acquire it, and share it with others as the influencing factor to cause action in education.

When it was time for my oldest daughter to learn how to ride a bike without training wheels, my husband and I began to teach her just as we had been taught—get on the bike with a parent holding onto the seat, fall off, skin some knees, and repeat until you figure it out. The first time she fell off, she was so mad and upset she refused to get back on and try again. Instead, she stomped into the house and we found her sitting on the couch with our iPad and watching YouTube videos of other children learning how to ride a bike. The next day she went outside, got on the bike, wobbled a bit, and within 10 minutes had riding a bike figured out, all without the skinned knees.

This experience was the first of many that forced me to grapple with my own pedagogical approaches and philosophy about education. The methods I used in my classroom may not be what my students needed to help them learn. My examples and stories may not be relevant to them and to their learning. And the hardest realization was that I had never asked them about their ideas nor truly listened to them. Just as my husband and I thought that we could teach our daughter how to ride a bike because we had learned how to do it in a particular manner, she learned how to ride a bike in a completely different and "just right" manner for her. We had been successful with that mode of learning how to ride a bike, but there are new methods for acquiring knowledge available to students today. Although Dewey lived in a very different time period, the students he saw and worked with also came to school with a different context for learning than their parents, similar to the students that come to school today. His belief in the importance of student and teacher working together to co-construct the educational experience so that it is relevant and rooted in student experiences was made real to me through the bike riding experience with my daughter.

As I read the two books by Dewey for the project, *The Child and the Curriculum* and *The School and Society,* both published at the turn of the 20th century, I was struck by how relevant the ideas in those books were to our current state of education in the 21st century. More than 100 years later, we are still grappling with the same issues that plagued education a century ago. While I hung on every word in both texts, I was left with a feeling of sadness and hopelessness. How is it that, after a century has gone by, with all the advancements, innovation, knowledge of neuroscience, and supposed reforms in education, are we still, what seems to me like, in the same exact place and discussing the same elements that are missing in the education of our children?

As a young teacher, I can remember sitting in the faculty lounge on my planning period and talking with veteran teachers. I would excitedly talk about a new initiative that was being discussed in the school and look up to see the eyes of those teachers looking at me with a trace of pity, sadness, and sometimes anger. With a slight shake of their heads, they would simply say "been there, done that" or "wait a minute and it will come back around again." Are Dewey's words and thoughts just that—evidence of the cyclic nature of education? Are his ideas and words so relevant to my work and beliefs today because it is that time in the cycle or is it that his true vision for education was never fully realized and there is truth in what he believes? Am I just a victim in the cycle of education and I, too, may one day come to fully believe that my real work is in just learning how to keep my head above the next cyclic wave in education that is coming in to pull the evidence of the last cycle back out into the vast educational ocean? It is these two battling perspectives that shaped my reading of Dewey's books and colored my analysis of his influence on education and his lingering messages left for educators today to ponder.

Line 'Em Up and Spit 'Em Out

In the early 1900s, society was experiencing rapid industrialization and progress characterized by

> the application of science resulting in the great inventions that have utilized the forces of nature on a vast and inexpensive scale: the growth of a worldwide market as the object of production, of vast manufacturing centers to supply this market, of cheap and rapid means of communication and distribution between all its parts. (Dewey, 1956, p. 9)

This growth resulted in the movement of people to cities from rural areas, which created new dynamics for educators to consider when developing and designing the educational experience. The function of the educational experience was viewed by some as a means to prepare students for this new world, that is, the "New Education" (Dewey, 1956, p. 8). There were two competing views of what the educational experience should be for students during this time period. One was the child-centered view that Dewey endorsed and the other was based in the scientific management theory spearheaded by Frederick Winslow Taylor. At the core of Taylor's theory was the notion of efficiency and uniformity in factory production. The manager accumulated the knowledge and then disseminated it to the factory workers en masse. This was termed "task analysis" and it permeated into the curricular realm in schools in complete opposition to Dewey's child-centered vision of education and curriculum. Pinar et al.'s (2004) observation about scientific management's impact on the shaping of the curriculum during this time period provides an important insight into this competing view of what the student experience should be:

> Rather than viewing curriculum as an opportunity to develop mental discipline, as "windows of the soul," or as organized around the needs, interests, and abilities of the child, curriculum became the assembly line by which economically and socially useful citizens would be produced. (p. 95)

Sound hauntingly familiar? It should. Take a look into any school, in any part of the country, and you will see evidence of the scientific management theory in practice. While you are in any of these same schools, listen to what is being discussed in staff meetings, the staff rooms, in the administrative offices, and you will surely hear some iteration of "personalized learning" and "innovation." Zmuda et al. (2015) define personalized learning as "a progressively student-driven model in which students deeply engage in meaningful, authentic, and rigorous challenges to demonstrate desired outcomes" (p. 7). Couros (2015) discusses the need for incorporating an innovator's mindset as the vehicle to redesigning the educational experience for teachers and students. His vision is predicated on similar notions and ideals that Dewey championed; student learning experiences need to be "connected to their lives and make an impact on how they engage with others to make the classroom a learning community" (p. 39).

Is it a coincidence that we have just embarked into the 21st century and our visions for the function of school in the context of the larger society are at a similar intersection? I think not and perhaps this is the explanation for the cyclic nature of education—the state of education is just a reflection of the society at large because we are not unified, as a country, about what the role of education should be in a society. Should it be about preparing our younger generations to be contributing members to the economy, to strengthen and affirm our place in the global economy, or should it be to develop critical thinkers that are able to participate in a democratic society? Is this even an either–or question? Is there no room for both objectives to be achieved? Is there a new iteration or innovative design and development of the educational experience for our children that is child-centered and prepares them for the global world taking shape all around us?

School districts across the country are beginning to develop and craft their own personalized educational experience for the students that they serve. Across the nation, educators are coming to the full realization that the factory model of education is no longer relevant and unable to meet the needs of the vast majority of students who walk through their doors day in and day out. I am fortunate to be a part of this conversation in the district where I am currently a building administrator. We are working towards a vision of personalizing learning for students based upon the belief that students should be able to understand what they are supposed to be learning and have the voice and choice to determine how they demonstrate their learning through experiences that are relevant to their interests and lives. Instead of basing our measure of success on standardized assessment scores, we are developing learner attributes to help guide and redefine what student success looks like in the classroom, while at the same time allowing students to acquire and practice the skills that will help them be successful in their postsecondary journeys. The learner attributes include concepts such as creative and critical thinking, problem-solving, communication, collaboration, and metacognition. Not only does this vision and discussion hopefully give students more ownership in their own educational narrative, but it is also what employers are consistently voicing as the components that they need in their employees to be successful and profitable in our global economy. From my biased perspective, a true melding of the two opposing views of what the purpose of education should be—a little bit Deweyian and a little bit utilitarian, a little bit social efficiency focused.

A PROGRESSIVE VISION

Dewey recognized that life is complex and that the education of students should be as well, meaning that educators cannot simply focus on one component of the educational experience and expect the students that are being educated to become engaged and contributing members of a democratic society. Dewey identified the two fundamental factors that are often in opposition to one another as "the immature, undeveloped being; and certain social aims, meanings, values incarnate in the matured experience of the adult" (Dewey, 1956, p. 4). These two factors should work together to help shape the educational experience for a child. That is not to say that they should or will always work in harmony nor that it is an easy interaction. The complex nature of the curriculum is rooted in the consideration of these two factors. If schools are willing and able to discuss what experiences a child will have in relation to these two factors, then they will most likely develop the curriculum that results in a meaningful learning experience for the child. But, all too often, the easier pathway to follow is when one of these factors, "something in the nature of the child or upon something in the developed consciousness of the adult" (Dewey, 1956, p. 4), is viewed as the pathway to success.

The learning experiences and decision-making factors that determine what experiences children are immersed in should be complex, but not in the sense of being too difficult for children to access, but more so in the notion that their learning experiences and the development of those learning experiences should be complex and not isolated in single subject areas or viewed through myopic lenses. School subjects should not be taught in isolation as parcels of knowledge to just know. Students should be provided the tools to analyze, discuss, and apply their learning to life experiences. Centering the learning experiences in relevant and interesting contexts allows for children to delve into multiple content areas simultaneously and construct meaning which leads to true learning.

Dewey's vision defined what components of the child's life experience are important and how those components could enhance their educational experience. What the child experiences at home and in the local community holds valuable character education and personal responsibility lessons. Children learned their place in their local communities and how their contributions helped the larger community, not just themselves. This was actualized through work on the farm, in their homes, and within their communities. With more people moving to cities due to industrialization, Dewey struggled with the loss of these important life lessons and the effects this would have on the larger society. Schools attempted to recreate these types of life experiences within the curriculum because they were engaging for students, but their implementation was often designed without real purpose. They became an exercise in just doing for the sake of doing. The learning experiences were not embedded in an authentic context. Instead they were embedded in a context that did not value the acquisition of life skills nor promote character development. Dewey saw this as a futile effort because students learning how to actively participate in a larger society were lost.

While these experiences were not available for all students due to societal changes, Dewey also saw the construct of school to be in contrast to these types of learning experiences. School culture was and is set up to be a very individualistic endeavor. Student performance is measured individually and the true impact of working in a larger community, where results are measured as a community, is not present in schools. When a school allows students to engage in activities that are real-life, with the goal being a product that benefits the group then there is a culture created that includes free communication, exchange of ideas, results, failures, successes, and an assurance that they will have experience with the components that make a society successful. Dewey articulates his vision for schools by stating:

> To do this means to make each one of our schools an embryonic community life, active with types of occupations that reflect the life of the larger society and permeated throughout with the spirit of art, history, and science. When the school introduces and trains each child of society into membership within such a little community, saturating him with the spirit of service, and providing him with the instruments of effective self-direction, we shall have the deepest and best guaranty of a larger society which is worthy, lovely, and harmonious. (Dewey, 1956, p. 29)

Learning and Growth

Another buzzword in education that is presented as a new and revolutionary idea, is growth mindset. Much of the credit for bringing this to the forefront for educators as a necessary component to incorporate into education is Carolyn Dweck, a professor at Stanford and the author of the book *Mindset* (Dweck, 2006/2016). Her work is very focused on the concept of growth mindset and what language and practices educators and parents can utilize with children to help them build resiliency and perseverance when they are faced with challenges and failures. While she is credited with the modern growth mindset movement, Dewey regarded this type of a mindset as an essential component of the educational experience for teachers and students—a growth mindset was a part of his vision for education.

Dewey was in strong opposition to the notion that was prevalent within turn of the century schools of "it's always been done that way" and that knowledge was a fixed body of knowledge that was to be passed from one generation to another (Dewey, 1956, p. viii). Dewey's name became synonymous with the phrase "child-centered." This phrase was the foundation for Dewey's vision of what the education of children should look like and the experiences they should have while in school. A major component of this concept was rooted in the developmental stages of children. Just as children grow in their development as humans, the educational experiences of children should grow as well to support their developmental growth. Dewey posited that growth meant "the increase of a child's ability to frame and pursue his or her own purposes" and that in order for that to occur they "needed a stake in the learning activity" (Eisner, 2002, p. 13). The culture within a classroom needed to support students being in a state of disequilibrium, which is defined as "a feeling of having a problem or being upset" (Eisner, 2002, p. 13), to provide students with the motivation and acquisition of inquiry and problem-solving skills that replicate the processes that adults go through in their daily lives.

This is not to say that wherever the child's interests are at any moment in time is where the learning should go, without any direction. The role of the teacher is to take into account the interests and curiosities that a child brings to the learning environment and use those impulses as a mode to connect learning to the larger learning goals. This allows the student to explore and construct meaning through material that is relevant and interesting, while also incorporating several subject areas together, thus emulating how people learn in their everyday lives.

A common critique of Dewey's vision was: "Does this type of experience truly help children be ready to enter the "adult" world?" Dewey identified four key life skills that children needed to practice within the school environment that emulate the experiences and skills adults use in their daily lives:

1. the language and social instinct which included skills such as communication and conversation;
2. the making instinct which were the making and creating experiences;

3. the art instinct which was the ability of the child to express themselves artistically; and
4. the inquiry instinct which included experimentation, inquiry, and problem-solving skills. (Dewey, 1956, pp. 43–47)

These impulses and instincts are the vehicles for growth in a child. They also provide a roadmap on how to make the curriculum and learning relevant to the child, while at the same time, allowing them to take an active role in their own educational experiences, work within real-world conditions, contribute to a larger community, and develop into a contributing member of a democratic society.

Here is a quote from Dewey (1956) that poetically argues against the notion that we are not preparing our students to be adults:

> Life is the great thing after all; the life of the child at its time and its measure no less than the life of the adult. "Let us live with our children" certainly means, first of all, that our children shall live—not that they shall be hampered and stunted by being forced into all kinds of conditions, the most remote consideration of which is relevancy to the present life of the child. If we seek the kingdom of heaven, educationally, all other things shall be added unto us—which, being interpreted, is that if we identify ourselves with the real instincts and needs of childhood, and ask only after its fullest assertion and growth, the discipline and information and culture of adult life shall all come in their due season. (p. 60)

If These Walls Could Speak

An important component of Dewey's professional work was that he vehemently believed in putting his ideas and beliefs into practice, not just in communicating them to the public. He practiced what he preached! Most of his practical work was done at the University Elementary School, which was a laboratory school at the University of Chicago that opened in October of 1897. Dewey relays a story about setting up the school and trying to find a desk that would allow students to move, create, and work—something other than the traditional school desk found in most schools. A dealer at one of the stores quickly realized and made the comment to Dewey, "You want something at which the children may work; these are all for listening" (Dewey, 1956, p. 31). How profound an observation and a moment of realization for Dewey, I am sure!

The physical environment is an unspoken factor in education. It communicates to students and teachers what the intended activity is to be in the classroom, desks in rows, no place or room for construction, no ability to move chairs into smaller groups, no flexibility. The only activity these physical elements can support is passive listening and thus passive learning. This physical setup also allowed for a large number of children to be instructed en masse, efficiently we can educate all of the students with the same material, in the same sequence and say it is done and they have been "educated." It communicates that education is a passive process and if we, the teachers, say it, then the children have learned it or have had the opportunity to learn it. Is it any wonder that so many students dislike going to school when so many classrooms are conveying this message?

Along with the movement in education to define and implement personalized learning experiences for students, there is also a strong movement to redesign the learning spaces that students interact with in their schools. I got to witness the impact transforming the aesthetics of a learning space can have on students and teachers. Prior to becoming a building administrator, I was a science lead learning coach—the person who helps teachers with curriculum and instruction. In this role I got to work with a wonderful woman who was my third grade department chair. She taught all third grade and some second grade science content in a specially designed science lab, which was considered a "special" for these children. This teacher loved the content, working with the students, and she was extremely supportive of her colleagues. Her classroom was a very traditional classroom except for the cages of critters that lined her shelves, and the tables for them to work at, a large carpet in the center for them to listen at, and a Smartboard in the center of the board to display what it was students were learning about that day. The learning experience in this classroom was good. Anytime I visited the classroom the teacher was delivering important content and the students had an opportunity to do an activity related to the content. It was good.

We were very fortunate to have a district office administrator who was very forward thinking who proposed the idea that we turn the science lab into a STEM lab where students could create, design, test, fail, redesign, and solve problems that were interesting to them. I worked with this teacher for the better part of 4 months to help create the curriculum, with most of the coaching consisting of helping her believe in herself and her ability to handle a little disequilibrium in her classroom the following year.

One component of the transformation was to redesign the learning space. We picked furniture that was easier to move, provided moveable cushions that students could pick up and use anywhere they wanted to in the room depending on what they were working on that day in STEM lab, provided whiteboards for collaborative designing, and painted the walls bright oranges and greens to convey that this space was different—it was a student design space.

During the final stages of the physical transformation, I took another position in the district and saw the teacher a couple of months later. When I asked her how everything was going, the look on her face said it all—she could not believe how much the students responded and what she thought was going to be chaos because not all the students were going to be doing the same thing at the same time was not the case at all! She was dumbfounded by how self-directed the students were, the solutions to problems they came up with, and how much more she loved her job. She attributed part of the easy transition for the students to the space itself—students loved coming to the STEM lab and taking on challenging problems. Dewey would have been proud and affirmed with this transformation that not only the physical space but also the learning experiences for students as well were now great!

The Time Is Now

I think it is fair to say that my review of Dewey's works was biased and that I went into reading the texts with a similar mindset and vision for what I want the educational experience to be, not only for my own children, but for all the children that I have worked with and will work with in the future. In my eleventh year as a teacher, just as the true impacts of accountability testing were really making an impact on what we taught and how we taught, I seriously considered leaving education altogether—this is not the job I signed up for! It was that same year that I was asked to implement a new method of teaching into my classroom. The method was very similar to project-based learning, which I was familiar with, but this new endeavor came with ample training and coaching. It was transformational, not only for my students, but for me as an educator. I watched students develop amazing project protocols to demonstrate their understanding of learning objectives, take complete ownership of their own success, come to class excited because they wanted to work, and take great pride in their products as they discussed them with experts in the area of their project. I fell in love with teaching all over again—I asked, listened, and supported their learning and it was awesome! Putting the child at the center of the learning experience is so powerful and it works so much better than throwing content up or all over students on a daily basis.

I also know there is truth in Dewey's vision based upon my own learning story. As I already said, I don't have a great recollection of actually enjoying learning in high school. My experience was more of an exercise in being really good at memorizing information and spitting it back on assessments. The evidence of this was when I got to college and had a very rough first semester as I realized I had no idea how to actually learn and had to figure out what worked for me—quickly! As part of that learning process, I realized that if the course was not relevant to me, I resorted to doodling in the margins again coupled with some belligerent outbursts when I had to do meaningless tasks to earn a grade (such as determine the best route for a garbage truck to take in a course called math in contemporary societies—really?!). I think most educators can also agree that when professional development is not relevant to them, they tune out and that is why they rush out of the room to charge their phones because they just drained them! Dewey's thoughts and ideas are rooted in learning theory. If we cannot see the connection to our own lives and if we are not able to have some choice in how we learn the content, we tune out and become zombies. This is true for adults as much as it is for students—we have got to break the cycle of education and get comfortable living in phases of disequilibrium.

The final piece of evidence I have that Dewey's vision has merit is through the eyes of a parent. As a teacher, I often asked about and discussed with my colleagues when the disengagement begins in school. When I walked into an elementary classroom, the students were so excited about EVERYTHING! They loved to learn, explore, question—they loved school. From my perspective as a high school teacher, the joy and excitement was rarely there and most students were zombies. When did this disengagement happen? Why? Watching my own daughter in fifth grade this year, I now have the answer. I have watched and listened throughout the year to her conversations about school and have come to the sad realization that the current way her school plays school, which is true of most schools, is deadening the learning desire in her. She often comments on how much she sits at a desk during the day. She, in fact, put a suggestion in the suggestion box in her classroom around winter break that asked if they could get out of their seats more because she was bored. She takes a test in social studies every week and has no idea what was on the test the week before and doesn't care. Science consists of vocabulary and activities that she has no idea how they relate to the curriculum. We get emails and notes from the teachers, addressed to the entire fifth grade, about how our students are not studying enough and that they will not be prepared for sixth grade. As I am typing this, my fingers are slowing, my posture is hunching, and my heart is heavy with the reality that her unbridled passion for learning and discovering is slipping through our fingers.

Dewey's vision provides us with the tools to fight off the zombification of students and adults. Learning is such a wonderful endeavor when you understand why you are learning it, how it relates to you, have the ability to discuss your learning with people, and have choice in how you want to demonstrate your understanding. This can only be achieved when the child is at the center of the learning experience and we become comfortable with a little disequilibrium in our schools. Are you ready to go to battle to fight off the zombie apocalypse and change the way we think about educating our students?!

REFERENCES

Couros, G. (2015). *The innovator's mindset*. Dave Burgess Consulting, Inc.

Dewey, J. (1956). *The child and the curriculum: And the school and society*. The University of Chicago Press.

Dweck, C. S. (2016). *Mindset: The new psychology of success*. Ballantine Books. (Original work published 2006)

Eisner, E. W. (2002). *The educational imagination: On the design and evaluation of school programs*. Pearson Education, Inc.

Pinar, W. F., Reynolds, W. M., Slattery, P., & Taubman, P. M. (2004). *Understanding curriculum*. Peter Lang Publishing.

Zmuda, A., Curtis, G., & Ullman, D. (2015). *Learning personalized: The evolution of the contemporary classroom*. John Wiley & Sons.

CHAPTER 2

APPLYING TYLER TODAY

Brittany A. Buhrlage

Author/Book studied:
Tyler, R. W. (2013). *Basic principles of curriculum and instruction.* The University of Chicago Press. (Original work published 1949)

BACKGROUND

Prior to this assignment my understanding and knowledge of Tyler's impact on curriculum was nonexistent. This may be the product of the educational programs I have experienced or my own neglect of truly analyzing the historical nature of curriculum. This may also be due to my brief career in education thus far. Yes, I have been a teacher, and I am an assistant principal, but the reality is that I have not studied or analyzed curriculum until now. As I reflect on this void in my educational preparation and understanding, my experiences confirm Kliebard's (1970) frustrations, "One of the disturbing characteristics of the curriculum field is its lack of historical perspective" and follows up by summarizing that recent curricular work is seldom far from the curricular proposals of the earlier 1900s (p. 259).

Curriculum Windows Redux, pages 15–27
Copyright © 2022 by Information Age Publishing
www.infoagepub.com
All rights of reproduction in any form reserved.

My study of Ralph Tyler, is parallel to an analysis of Eisner (2002) *The Educational Imagination: On the Design and Evaluation of School Programs* and Pinar et al.'s (2000) *Understanding Curriculum* and all include important elements in the historical understanding of curriculum. In addition to the study of Eisner (2002) and Pinar et al. (2000), I also researched Tyler's background and biography, the historical context of his work, critical critics and supporters of his work, read a transcript of an interview with Tyler in the 1980s, and then finally applied Tyler to the current educational landscape. The purpose of my research was to enhance the significance of Tyler's work and to understand why his work is regarded as one of the most influential curricular approaches. Prior to discussing Tyler's rationale, it is critical to understand his background, professional experiences, and historical context that led to his first edition in 1949. In order to effectively and fairly critique Tyler's work, I found it necessary to understand his own development as an educator and how his experiences shaped his work.

BIOGRAPHY OF TYLER THROUGH THE 1940s

Tyler, according to Finder (2008), was raised in rural Nebraska and was the son of a physician and minister and began his teaching career in South Dakota as a high school science teacher. This experience, in a diverse setting comprised of children of unlettered farm workers and other children of civil servants, began his passion for education. He became consumed and captivated by the challenge of teaching and decided to pursue his master's degree in education which he earned in 1923. Following his graduation, he taught at the university's high school and oversaw many students who were pursuing science education. Then in 1926, he enrolled in a PhD program at the University of Chicago and wrote his dissertation which focused on protocols of schooling methods by using quantitative measurement (Finder, 2008).

The next few years provided opportunities to work with educational reformers to pursue the connections between subject content and individual needs of the student. He accepted a position at North Carolina at Chapel Hill as an associate professor of education. Then in 1929, he joined Charters at Ohio State University and was the assistant director of the Bureau of Educational Research and served as the director for the division of testing (Finder, 2008).

Tyler's time at Ohio State in the 1930s overlapped with the Great Depression and its effect was evident within many school settings and the Progressive Education Association devised a study to determine how educational programming could be modified to meet the needs of the students based upon the many barriers they were facing at home and in the community. During this time many high schools were constrained by strict college requirements for admission, but this national initiative backed by funding involved

30 schools that were given freedom to explore innovative courses of study. In turn, nearly every accredited college agreed to accept the participating schools' evaluative records in lieu of their rigid entrance requirements (Finder, 2008). Many educational scholars believe this effort, the Eight-Year Study, remains a major curriculum study in the history of the field.

In 1934, participants of the study formed an evaluation staff to develop a plan to make curricular changes to their organization and structure, and according to Pinar et al. (2000), this process was unique in that it gave local control over curricular decisions. During Tyler's time at the Ohio State University, he was closely intertwined with the evaluative mode to analyze the school's objectives. As part of the initiative, each school identified 10 major objectives and a process which was endorsed by Tyler. Pinar et al. (2000), quoting Madaus and Kellaghan (1992), stated,

> The idea that educational outcomes needed to be defined in terms of identifiable behavior and in operational terms was a keystone of Tyler's Eight-Year Study...objectives that lead to the development of learning experiences, which in turn lead to evaluation of the extent to which objectives were realized." (p. 136)

This development founded and defined behavioral objectives and in 1949 Tyler outlined this process in his *Basic Principles of Curriculum and Instruction* (Pinar et al., 2000).

Unfortunately, the onset of World War II put this dynamic study in the ignored past and despite the curriculum innovations the results were far from radical. However, Pinar et al. (2000) highlighted the viewpoints of teachers who were a part of the study. Many stated that it was an exciting time for teachers and students, and it provided a sense of adventure and genuine freedom to experiment in the classroom. James Michener reflects on his experience as a participant in the study, and stated, "As to the effect on me: it made me a liberal, a producer, a student in my world, a man with a point of view and the courage to exemplify it" (Pinar et al., 2000, p. 139). In summary, many educators often wonder if the impact of this progressive study would have been more powerful in a different time in history when the nation and world weren't filled with so much despair. Unfortunately, the perspective these teachers' provided is contrary to those who have since criticized Tyler's work. Historically, Tyler has been both criticized and praised depending on the educator's philosophy and the historical context of their research. A summary of Tyler's rationale follows.

TYLER RATIONALE

In an excerpt from an interview with Tyler by Nowakowski (1983), Tyler explained that he wrote out his rationale for the first time on a napkin during a discussion about curriculum with his right-hand person, Hilda Taba. Then that outline was used as part of Tyler's syllabus for Education 350 at the University of Chicago, and Tyler later published his work which today is known as the Tyler rationale (p. 27). On page one of his book, Tyler (1949/2013) lays out four fundamental questions which he states must be answered in developing any curriculum and plan of instruction. The four questions are:

1. What educational purposes should the school seek to attain?
2. What educational experiences can be provided that are likely to attain these purposes?
3. How can these educational experiences be effectively organized?
4. How can we determine whether these purposes are being attained? (p. 1)

Tyler (1949/2013) then suggests methods for studying and applying these questions, "Instead of answering the questions, an explanation is given of procedures by which these questions can be answered. This constitutes a rationale by which to examine problems of curriculum and instruction" (p. 2). Therefore, these questions serve as a four-step process and the later part of the book is a further explanation of this process. Many critics believe that the first question regarding purposes is most important. It is also the question he spends over half of the 128-page book explaining and, therefore, the majority of the summary surrounds that question.

When developing the purpose of the school, Tyler (1949/2013) emphasizes that this process has to be locally determined, from many points of view and that we must study the learners themselves as a source. He describes several ways to study the learner, one of which is identifying student need. Tyler then introduces the concept of behavioral objectives and states that education is the process of changing the behavior of students to reach their current needs. At the time, Tyler saw a need for students to find work following graduation during the Depression and therefore he believed there was a gap in instruction and identified employment as a student need. Tyler cited Prescot who classifies student needs into physical needs (food, water), social needs (affection, belonging, respect), and integrative needs (relate oneself to something larger), and states that it is the school's obligation to study their students' current needs. Tyler then recommends using these identified needs to suggest ways to motivate and provide meaning for their students (pp. 3–7). Further, in order to provide a clearer picture of the needs of the students, Tyler suggests gathering observations from teachers regarding students' interests, conducting student and parent interviews, reviewing student records, as well as conducting assessments to gather current academic skills, as well as attitudes and problem-solving abilities (pp. 10–12).

Next, Tyler (1949/2013) analyzes studies of contemporary life outside of school and states that the cultural heritage of schools changed dramatically after the industrial revolution—since previously the body of material that was considered academically important was very small. Then he acknowledges that for each generation there is a tremendous increase in knowledge. Tyler presents two arguments for analyzing this contemporary life to gather suggestions for educational objectives. Tyler recommends studying the life outside of school as you study the learner, "Unless life is analyzed into functional and significant phases it is too big to be attached and any effort in study will result in many gaps" and in order to collect such information Tyler believes it is best collected by analyzing data to identify problems and use the data to suggest objectives (p. 19).

The subject specialist is the next identified source Tyler (1949/2013) suggests in developing objectives. Again, it is important to reflect on the historical context during Tyler's work. Many students were not attending university, and due to the national financial crisis he analyzed the selection of objectives from a viewpoint contradictory to the Committee of Ten. First, Tyler acknowledges that many people criticize the use of subject area specialists since their objectives are too technical, specific, and do not relate to the large population of students. For a long time, the Committee of Ten thought a subject specialist's job was to outline the elementary courses in order to prepare them for more and more advanced work that they will encounter in college aligned with their major (p. 25).

However, Tyler (1949/2013) suggests that the question subject specialists should be asking are, what can your subject contribute to students not going in your field and what/how can your subject help contribute to the layperson (p. 26)? This perspective will then shape students to be prepared whether they have the opportunity to go to college or to enter the workforce. Analyzing this process from many different subject areas may result in "objectives that are more than knowledge, skills, and habits: They involve modes of thinking, or critical interpretation, emotional reactions, interests and the like" (p. 29).

Tyler (1949/2013) further outlines the selection of objects, by analyzing the philosophy of the school, and acknowledges that the use of three sources provides too much information. Therefore, as a next process he recommends schools should narrow this section by screening them based upon the educational and social philosophy of the school, and whether or not they are in line with democratic values (pp. 33–36). Leaders will then "select the number of objectives that can actually be attained in significant degree in the time available, and that these be really important ones" (p. 33). This process will provide consistency as well as harmony between the selected objectives and philosophy with the school.

A second screen Tyler (1949/2013) uses to analyze the information provided by the sources is to apply the objectives to the psychology of learning. For example, he suggests taking the information and establishing feasible goals within a school setting, then determining the best grade and sequence of the objective, and providing students with the opportunity to use the knowledge in their daily life. Tyler also states the importance of developing theory of learning as a curriculum worker. This theory can then be used to determine whether or not the objective is in line with the psychology of learning (pp. 37–43).

As a final screen, Tyler (1949/2013) turns to the teacher/instructor to analyze the objectives that have been selected for them. Next Tyler suggests using their input to divide the objective among these categories: those they will carry out, what the students are supposed to do, and lists of topics to cover. He also, reiterates that the purpose of the objective is to change behavior, and in order to reinforce this sentiment, he states that "the most useful form for stating objectives is to express them in terms which identify both the kind of behavior to be developed in the student and the content area of life in which this behavior is to operate" (pp. 46–47). This process is critical to the development of sound behavioral objectives.

Finally, Tyler (1949/2013) ends the chapter acknowledging that we [curriculum workers] devote so much time to the development and formulation of objectives because they are the critical criteria for guiding all other activities, such as the selection, organization, and evaluation of learning activities and experiences (p. 62). Through Tyler's emphasis and time devoted to this practice, it is evident that this philosophy is critical to Tyler's development of behavioral objectives.

CRITIQUES AND REVIEWS OF TYLER'S WORK

Pinar et al. (2000) provides an historical approach to the field of curriculum, and he thinks that Tyler's work forcefully entered the field at the end of the 1940s. World War II had erased progressivism's influence on education and there was a reappearance of social efficiency and Tyler's work was highly regarded (p. 15). However, overall, critiques of Tyler view his work as too mechanical, and has an end means rationale. One of the main critiques of Tyler's work is given by Herbert Kliebard who analyzed Tyler's work in 1970. Kliebard (1970) begins by summarizing that it is discouraging that Tyler's work is still seen as a reverent process of developing curriculum and states his frustration that little had changed in the 2 decades since Tyler's work was published (p. 259).

Kliebard (1970) summarizes Tyler's use of three sources when developing educational objectives: studies of the learners, the current contemporary life, and input from subject-matter specialists which he states all have their own ideologies, theoretical assumptions, stakeholders, and language. Kliebard attributes Tyler's popularity to the acknowledgement of these three voices, however, he also disputes the fallacy in Tyler's process. Instead, he compares this process to the work of Dewey and states that Dewey's approach is to "creatively reformulate the problem; Tyler's is to lay them all out side by side" a process that is does not exist in reality (p. 260).

Further, Kliebard (1970) refutes Tyler's interpretation and perception of the Committee of Ten's work and states that the committee did discuss whether or not to treat students who are planning to attend college differently than those that do not and the answer was, "No." "The objective of mental training, apparently, was conceived to be of such importance as to apply to all, regardless of destination" (p. 262). Kliebard argues that this was not just a misconception on Tyler's part but instead a fundamental assumption about the subjects in curriculum, which is in complete contradiction with Tyler's curricular process. He then argues Tyler's categorization of subject matter specialists as a source and instead Kliebard defines them as a means to fulfill the student's individual need, vocational aspiration, or social expectation (p. 262).

Tyler's development of needs was also criticized by Kliebard (1970), not because it is not a valid process but instead that it was not a new concept at the time. Kliebard argues that it closely aligns with the process Bobbitt outlined in his first book in 1918 and argues that Bobbitt referred to the process of identifying shortcomings which Kliebard believes is synonymous with Tyler's term "needs." In addition, by analyzing the practice of identifying needs, Kliebard also recommends that the remediation of other needs should be considered. Until schools openly discuss the role of the school as an establishment for the remediation of that need they should not plan a course of remediation. Finally, Kliebard (1970) quoted Dearden who in summary states the whole practice of need is attractive in education because it can offer an escape from the arguments about value. However, Dearden states it is false to suppose judgments can be escaped, since they are based upon assumptions without any awareness they are being made and these assumptions cannot be escaped (pp. 262–263).

One of Kliebard's largest arguments and critiques of Tyler's work is the use of a philosophical screen. The use of a screen in Kliebard's eyes is a criticism on Tyler's part of his own process. Tyler uses three sources to provide diversity—however this process results in several shortcomings. He then uses philosophy as a means for covering them up. Kliebard uses the reference that three sources are mere window dressing and Kliebard states then that understanding of the philosophical screen is most important when studying Tyler's process of formulating objectives. However, Kliebard (1970) evaluates Tyler's philosophical screen as too vague—that it does not describe how we determine what educators leave in and we filter out. He describes this process as just another way to say we are forced to make choices based on the several thousand recommendations one can draw from the sources. Like Bobbitt, this creates an arbitrary process and Tyler's main hypothesis that objectives derive from a philosophy, while probably true, tells educators very little (pp. 266–267).

In his summary, Kliebard (1970) acknowledges that the Tyler rationale is an eminently reasonable framework for developing curriculum and argues that the development of objectives is not a fruitful way to view curriculum planning and that analyzing learning experiences requires a lot more attention and focus than Tyler provides. Nevertheless, Kliebard states that the field of curriculum must recognize the Tyler rationale for what it is, Tyler's own version of how curriculum should be developed, not a universal mode. Finally, Kliebard ends with a quote from Goodlad, "Tyler put the capstone on one epoch of curriculum inquiry" and Kliebard even in 1970 states a new epoch is long overdue (p. 270).

On the other hand, Peter Hlebowitsh is a huge advocate of Tyler's work. While Kliebard uses his similarity to Bobbitt as a criticism, Hlebowitsh (2005) uses the parallels in Bobbitt's and Tyler's work to identify continuity between their work and that of Schwab, who has historically been separated from Bobbitt's and Tyler's work. Hlebowitsh also argues Pinar's view that educators and curriculum experts are still burdened by their obsession for procedural and prescriptive matters and their inability to generate new understanding. Specifically, "the orientation of curriculum studies has been stuck in a simplistic management-style interplay between forming curriculum objectives and telling teachers how to carry them out" (p. 74). According to Hlebowitsh, Pinar argues that Tyler's rationale was a management device that stifles teacher creativity, and does not allow space for choice in the classroom. However, Hlebowitsh argues you cannot use Schwab's work to discredit Tyler's.

While Kliebard uses Tyler's similarity to Bobbitt as a criticism, Hlebowitsh (2005), outlines Tyler's work as an improvement on Bobbitt's. Both scholars appreciate and advocate for more local control in the curricular process. In addition, according to Hlebowitsh, Bobbitt focuses on how activities affect the present-day, whereas like Dewey, Tyler uses curriculum as a means to move beyond the present. Further, Hlebowitsh states that Tyler saw the curricular process as a continuum which focuses first on the purpose, while Bobbitt believed it started with just the activities. Finally, according to Hlebowitsh, Bobbitt does not mention evaluation, while Tyler is now regarded as the father of evaluation. This is all proof that Tyler is an improvement on Bobbitt's work, not just a regurgitation of what had already been published (pp. 80–82).

All-in-all, many perspectives on Tyler's work have been argued, identified, and presented especially when the development of objectives are discussed. However, as I think about the context of Tyler and the perspective he provides to me as an administrator almost 80 years since the book's first publication, Tyler still provides a window to analyze how we prepare students today—what has changed and what work is yet to be done?

ELEMENTS OF TYLER TODAY

Overall, my perception based upon my research is that there are more critiques of Tyler's work than there are supporters. However, I have to argue that many components of Tyler's rationale are still present in the classroom. Therefore, instead of arguing that there is no merit to his work, one must reflect on how Tyler's work provides a window of what is needed to change based upon the current educational philosophy and historical context of that time.

Hammill and Hunkins (1994) argue that we cannot and should not throw out all of Tyler's work. They suggest that moving beyond Tyler and accepting a new paradigm does not require educators to destroy the historical work of Tyler within the field of curriculum. Despite the criticism, evidence of Tyler's work is still dominant in schools across the nation and regardless of your philosophical viewpoint or educational values, Tyler's four questions are apparent in the process to determine curriculum today. Hammill and Hunkins (1994) state that arguing beyond Tyler is not so much just about criticizing his work and time but "to recognize that we are in different times—times that challenge us to think in novel ways about our realities and how to generate curricula within them" (p. 10). Further, they reiterate that curriculum is dynamic and not passive and it is based upon the experiences in which people engage.

In addition, when analyzing the field of curriculum, Pinar (2000) states it is important to preserve the voice of individual scholars and states,

> Fields are comprised of people, sometimes extraordinary, often ordinary people, whose job it is to write material that complies with the rules and principles other people—their predecessors—have established as reasonable. Fields, just like schools, are comprised of people, people with ideas. Both people and ideas change, often not very fast... but they do change. (p. 4)

An interview with Tyler by Nowakowski (1983) provides insight from Tyler on his viewpoint regarding his influence on the field of curriculum and Pinar's ideas as previously presented are very evident. First, when asked to describe individual work with teachers, what has been labeled as pragmatic in Pinar's work, was instead very organic. According to Tyler, in the interview Tyler explained the work he completed with individual teachers, and recommends, "Don't look at some taxonomy to define your objectives. You're a teacher working with students... [and then asked], 'What have you found students learning that you think is important?'" (Nowakowski, 1983, p. 26). He also reflects on his role as a building administrator. When asked if he enjoyed administration, he states, "I like to help people find ways of using their talents most effectively, and that's usually by giving them the opportunity for a time to do what they think is important." In terms of what it means to be a facilitator, Tyler replied, "A person who helps make possible what other dream and hope they can do. I might name a good many others I tried to help" (Nowakowski, 1983, p. 27). Hearing Tyler's own words describing how this practice plays out gives a very different perception than reading his written work. It reminds me that one simple phrase such as maintaining local control in a book seems more cliché than hearing a specific example of how he exercises this in practice.

Most importantly, Tyler notes that the work which led to the Tyler rationale was based upon the changes that he was seeing within education during the Great Depression (Nowakowski, 1983). He stated that when he was a high school student, 10% of his grade went on to high school, in 1929, 25% went to high school, and following the depression 50% of an age group were in high school so their enrollment had doubled in a very short timeframe. He then expresses that many students did not see value in the curriculum which at the time was based upon the expectations of college entrance exams. Principals saw the need to provide programming for students who were now in high school simply because they could not find work. This realization then led to the Eight-Year Study that provided the permission to change the focus from college entrance exams to what they really felt as a local entity was necessary to equip students with the skill set to be employed and to become more complete citizens (Nowakowski, 1983). Therefore, the work of Tyler was specific to his time period and was not necessarily meant to provide a framework for all generations to come.

In addition, Tyler (1949/2013) expresses his viewpoint on the current federal mandates in education in the 1980s and when asked about his perception of these mandates. He stated, "One problem is that they see clients as being the federal government... instead of the teachers and the parents and children. When you have those clients, you have to have different considerations" (p. 27). Finally, when asked the major problems of American education K–12, he references how we are still struggling with reaching all children in all populations. We need to focus more on the transition of youth to adult life, and we need to reflect on the changes in the home such as more mothers employed, the effect of TV and stating those three are enough to keep us busy for a while (p. 29). Today this statement is still true, except changes in the home could be categorized as maintaining a work-life balance, and the effect of TV would instead be replaced with the effect of social media. Again, Tyler's philosophy is sound and it is about reaching all students from all different backgrounds and providing a framework for success after high school.

Admittedly, when I first read Tyler's book, I became very disinterested during his 18 page description of how to organize objectives, using a chart as an example to guide the process. As I reflect on this chart, I believe my aversion was based on the perception that many educators have when they view a curriculum chart. Most educators cringe and see the chart as a predetermined district mandated process. However, having a predetermined district mandated chart for this practice would go against Tyler's intent. He provided the chart as an example to show how one subject area could work through this process. However, at the heart of the process was the local control that teachers have on this process. The chart should be developed by the teacher(s) based upon their current student's needs, goals, and skill sets.

Further, curriculum planning in some school settings is perceived as district mandated paperwork. Over the course of my career, I have observed that the culture of a school district has a large impact on how curriculum initiatives are interpreted. Therefore, some critics of Tyler today could be influenced by negative experiences they have had in districts where there has not been a local control over decisions in their classrooms. As educational leaders, it is important to remember to preserve the organic process Tyler very much intended.

In addition, when applying Tyler's work to today's political landscape and educational initiatives, college and career readiness skills first come to mind. According to the Ohio Department of Education (ODE), college and career readiness is an initiative to meet the current needs and anticipate the future workforce demands of the economy. It also prepares students to succeed in lifelong learning and careers, and it supports the career development and career pathways for high school students (Ohio Department of Education, 2017). As I reflect on this state mandate, while I do believe this initiative is important, I feel the pressure that this adds to school leaders and classroom teachers. In order to adequately follow this initiative additional support and personnel is needed at the building level and this is simply not a capacity that many districts can support. School officials and leaders are continually asked to do more and more with the same amount of resources to a point that schools are forced to implement the bare minimum and the initiative becomes just a check in the box for many schools. Therefore, I can relate that at the time, Tyler's focus on career development may have been perceived in the same way. While the Eight-Year Study supported these initiatives, the support did not last long and its credibility was lost.

This process is complex and varies school to school, but within my own district we are reanalyzing our current programming we offer within our course selection to pinpoint holes in our curriculum in an effort to increase options for students. In addition to analyzing coursework, we have started to develop better relationships with local businesses to develop work-study placements during junior and senior year. This program is designed for students who have been credit deficient in the past, and therefore, did not have the option to attend our local vocational school. These efforts, like Tyler's, intend to provide meaningful instruction for all students so they have better options after graduation. When looking at this initiative through the window Tyler presents, a need for work study opportunities is identified, and whether we acknowledge it or not, we are using input from Tyler's identified sources, and we are screening them based upon the philosophy and democratic values within the school.

Finally, one of the main lessons I learned when analyzing Tyler is that his work of selecting objectives is part of the curriculum planning process and not teaching. I first became very offended at what I first saw as an oversimplification and pragmatic approach to teaching that I believed Tyler was describing. However, it was not until the second reading that I realized I, like many (especially those not in education), had confused curriculum planning with the art of teaching. I was offended at the rote nature that Tyler described and saw it as a one-size-fits-all. I now see Tyler very differently. I see this process as separate from teaching and instruction and that when we are talking about students as individuals there is not one solution, and I think Tyler would say the same.

Overall, reading and reflecting on the interview with Tyler in 1983 changed my perception of Tyler. I saw him more as an ordinary person, who was humble and did not intend for his work on a napkin to last the best part of a century. Truthfully, I believe that he too would be very frustrated and appalled that the work he outlined in 1949 still rings true in many classrooms and schools. He saw kids as many of us see our students, as individuals, with individual needs and unique challenges and therefore we must change our approach in order to meet their needs. At the time Tyler described the work that was occurring in schools with participants in the Eight-Year Study, and to be criticized for describing their work does not seem fair. Tyler's work provides a window to reflect on the current historical context, the federal and state mandates and the challenges our students are facing. We cannot stay stagnant; we have to move.

REFERENCES

Eisner, E (2002). *The educational imagination: On the design and evaluation of school programs* (3rd ed.). Prentice Hall.

Finder, M. (2008). *Tyler, Ralph W.* American Biography Online. http://www.anb.org/articles/20/20-01894.html

Hammill, P. A., & Hunkins F. P. (1994). Beyond Tyler and Taba: Reconceptualizing the curriculum process. *Peabody Journal of Education, 69*(*3*), 4–18. http://www .jstor.org/stable/1492885

Hlebowitsh, P. S. (2005). Generational ideas in curriculum: A historical triangulation. Curriculum Inquiry, *35*(1), 63–87. http://www.jstor.org/stable/3698528

Kliebard, H. M. (1970). The Tyler rationale. *The School Review, 78*(2), 259–272. http://www.jstor.org/stable/1084240?seq=1&cid=pdf-reference#references_ tab_contents

Nowakowski, J. R. (1983). *On educational evaluation: A conversation with Ralph Tyler.* The Association for Supervision and Curriculum Development. www.ascd.org/ ASCD/pdf/journals/ed_lead/el_198305_nowakowski.pdf

Ohio Department of Education. (2017). *College and career readiness.* http://education .ohio.gov/Topics/Career-Tech/College-Tech-Prep/College-and-Career -Readiness

Pinar W. F., Reynolds W. M., Slattery P., & Taubman P. M. (2000). *Understanding curriculum.* Peter Lang.

Tyler, R. W. (2013) *Basic principles of curriculum and instruction.* The University of Chicago Press. (Original work published 1949)

CHAPTER 3

"THERE IS NO BETTER WAY TO STUDY CURRICULUM THAN TO STUDY OURSELVES"[1]

Misty Cook

Author/Book studied:
Schubert, W. (1980). *Curriculum books: The first 80 years.*
     University Press of America.

In 1982, the report "A Nation at Risk" predicted a national catastrophe in America's educational system. Overnight, the crisis in education hit the top of the charts. The national news magazines seem to discover schools, as do the television networks. The prevailing belief from parents to policy makers is that schools are failing to provide a quality education and America cannot prosper unless its schools are successful. Teachers are believed to be the reason for student failure and standardization is the solution. Success can only

Curriculum Windows Redux, pages 29–38
Copyright © 2022 by Information Age Publishing
www.infoagepub.com
All rights of reproduction in any form reserved.

be measured in one clear cut, rational way. Many university researchers, consultants, and policy makers with little knowledge of what goes on in schools across America weigh in on the best ways to improve teaching. They reject the notion of teaching as an intuitive, subjective, and spontaneous endeavor and silence the voice of teachers (Schubert, 1990, p. 99). This silencing allows for little notice of the social-emotional components of student teacher relationships that take place in real classrooms every day. My experience in high school in the 1980s is one example of the impersonal nature of educational reform in this era, a depersonalization that continues to exist today. By the end of the 20th century, the only thing that matters is test scores.

As I reflect on my experience as a high school student during this time period, I am transported back in time to the year 1985. As I drive by the University of Cincinnati on the Metro bus to see my probation officer. I look out the window and see a row of sorority houses that line the street. The window of the bus becomes a window to the unknown world. The students lounging on the lawn, the stately historical buildings on campus pass by and I wonder, "What must it be like to be a student there?" Very quickly this thought is replaced by the knowledge that it is not the place for me. At 14, I already feel like my life is hopeless and I am helpless to change it. I feel like my destiny is already set, with no real possibilities beyond my neighborhood. The ravages of poverty, fear, violence, substance abuse, and isolation make it impossible to see the forest through the trees. For me school is irrelevant. It is a place that emphasizes test scores above all else. School is a place where my absence goes unnoticed except when I am urged to attend to boost the school's state test scores. Clearly, test scores are important, not me. Some of my teachers might mean well, but they are not like me or any person I know. School and home exist in separate compartments that never mix. If I had felt a connection to at least one teacher who knew my story, would my life have taken a different direction? Instead, I was suspended, expelled, and truant from school. I was actively engaged in alcohol and drug addiction. Not until my physically abusive marriage ended after having two children did I, at the age of 20, experience any hope.

Hope and connection came in the form of a GED program run by the local Urban Appalachian council. It was operated by a woman from my neighborhood. A woman who was not constrained by the mandates of policy makers who are largely removed from the day to day interactions in schools. Charlene was not educated beyond high school but she recognized the power of intuition and of creating a contextually based educative experience. She understood her students' circumstances and offered no judgments. She had the time and space in that little dingy basement room to give students the ability to make their own destinies.

My story is one of success but it is crucial to recognize that I am one of the very few lucky ones. I was born with a natural affinity for learning in the traditional sense while so many students' particular talents are not. The failure to educate many students makes it imperative that educators find ways to connect with students and show themselves as the caring and capable adults that they are. Teachers spend more time with students than almost anyone else, therefore what we do in our classrooms has very real world implications. We not only have a moral obligation to prepare students academically but also to help students build an arsenal of tools for a successful life of their own choosing. It is personal connections which enhance educative experiences. We must go beyond simplistic answers and ask ourselves what is best for children and what each of us can do to further that aim. Policy makers, researchers, and teachers must turn away from an overreliance on standardization and recognize teachers' own personal, practical knowledge as a viable option for improving schools.

TEACHER LORE

Teacher lore is one such option. Curriculum expert William Shubert is one teacher/researcher who recognizes the power of experienced teachers sharing their stories. In the book *Teacher Lore: Learning from our Own Experience*, William Schubert and William C. Ayers (1992) "provide teachers with perspectives on teaching drawn from other teachers" (p. vii). They argue that the greatest potential of teacher lore "resides in the oral tradition among teachers who exchange and reconstruct perspectives together" (p. vii). Schubert and Ayers explore the concept of teacher lore developed by Schubert during his Teacher Lore Project as part of the genre of teacher narratives that place teachers at the core of the curriculum rather than predetermined standards. The text is arranged in three parts: Part I establishes the theoretical and methodological framework for the book. In Part II, five contributing authors discuss their own studies of teachers researching and learning from their personal experience. Part III helps the reader to engage in forms of teacher lore themselves.

Teacher lore is a form of action research stemming from the vast work of John Dewey and the Progressives (Schubert & Ayers, 1992). Teacher lore emphasizes the experiential knowledge of real teachers in real classrooms. Schubert and Ayers (1992) define *teacher lore* as "the stories about and by teachers" (p. 9). Teacher lore is also a form of teacher as researcher movement that pairs a university/theorist with a classroom teacher. Editor William Ayers, who is well known for his work in education reform, curriculum and instruction, and radical activism in the 1960s and the controversy during the 2008 presidential campaign when President Obama was accused of having ties to him states, "At its heart, teacher lore, as its name implies, is a storytelling and story hearing activity" (Schubert & Ayers, 1992, p. 155).

Similarly, Janet Miller (in Schubert & Ayers, 1992) a contributing author and researcher states,

> Teacher lore is the shared but mostly unofficial, informal knowledge, revealed in our teaching sagas and lived and created in spaces of our daily teaching, which forms the core of what the contributors of this text have developed as the concept of teacher lore. (p. 13)

The authors/editors/contributors emphasize reflective teaching and the use of personal accounts as the best source for understanding teaching. Placing teachers at the core of the curriculum allows for a more thorough understanding of teaching. This understanding results in improved outcomes for students' development of their guiding principles.

Critics of story as a central analytical framework claim that it is merely a "device for expressing sentiments about teachers" (Carter, 1993, p. 5), but they are wrong. The teacher as researcher movement represents a paradigm shift from "attention to curriculum management, pedagogical tasks, and activities, and even to understanding others in a relational, dispassionate manner to a contextually based, ambiguous, subjective phenomena" (Hollingsworth, 1993, p. 11).

"Scholars such as Cole and Knowles (1992), Clandinin and Connelly (1992), Elbaz (1991), Grossman (1987), Gudmundsdottir and Hollinsworth (in press), and Richert (1990) made story the central element in their analysis of teacher knowledge" (Carter, 1993, p. 5).

A PARADIGMATIC WAR

For the last several years of my teaching career, I have been frustrated, bored, and burnt out. It feels like I have to choose between teaching as a moral calling and teaching as a profession. The prevailing belief among policy makers that there is one single educational program appropriate for all children leaves me with the feeling of being at the center of a paradigmatic war. I feel like I have to choose one side or the other. For me this is a problem. My decision to become a teacher is rooted in my desire to connect with students who have had similar experiences as my own and to provide them with the academic/social/emotional means to overcome feelings of hopelessness and helplessness that pervades many students of poverty. Instilling in them a love of learning is crucial for building a better life for themselves. I want to work alongside students to establish intrinsic motivation for a lifetime love of learning. Lifelong learners are able to contemplate the bigger questions in life. They analyze their own thinking. They can ask themselves what they should do with their lives and who they are. In other words, knowledge allows students to create for themselves a door of opportunity they can walk through. Students have the knowledge of themselves and the world needed to fully participate in society and effect real change both in themselves and society.

This paradigmatic war is not new. It began in the 1980s when Shubert first developed teacher lore as a viable methodological framework for research and continues today.

> For the past thirty years educational researchers have made large claims for the value of research on teaching. Scientific approaches and process-product designs would herald a new day of understanding and enlightened practice. The fanfare has faded, the results turn out to be small. (Schubert & Ayers, 1992, p. 148)

Twenty five years later, the American school system hasn't changed much, and the results continue to be minor for those students at greatest risk of school failure. Many school systems continue to value teachers who practice the science of teaching rather than the art of teaching (Eisner, 2002). They turn away teachers who are very adept at their craft because they are not considered to be scientifically based. It is a mistake. According to Eisner (2002), "Teaching is an art guided by educational values, personal needs, and by a variety of beliefs or generalizations that the teacher holds to be true" (p. 155). Students need teachers to turn away from teaching as a series of routine responses rather than an opportunity for ingenuity. In a similar sense, "Teaching is a form of human action in which many of the ends achieved are emergent—that is to say in the course of interaction with students rather than preconceived and efficiently attained" (p.155) . If given the right skills students can find their own direction in life without having to journey blindly, wasting valuable time they could be using to be their best selves and to do their best work.

Unfortunately in school, we live in an age of depersonalization while outside of school we are in an era of gross personalization fueled by, among other things, social media. Internally educators are expected to compartmentalize ourselves into distinct roles instead of integrating our whole selves as thinking, feeling human beings. This compartmentalization is exemplified in the relationship of the " in school" curriculum and the "out of school" curriculum that are seen as separate and distinct entities that do not overlap.

HOW DO WE MEASURE STUDENT GROWTH?

To have the most effective teaching we need to get back to a personal, context dependent investment in our students where the boundaries between home and school/community are fluid. Not all students have the internal and external resources to grow to their potential without assistance from teachers who spend so much time with them. One of my first teaching positions was at a middle/high school run by a social services agency. The school was created to serve children in the foster care system as well as students who lived with their parents but had severe adjustment problems in school. The students had a myriad of challenges. Most were abused, neglected, and behind their same-age peers in academic achievement. These students had not been dealt a good hand in life, and they knew it. They were unmotivated. They were plagued by the belief that they were doomed to a life of pain. More than a few seemed to have simply given up. School was a place where they simply "did time." What they needed most in their lives was a safe environment with adults who demonstrated patience, kindness, tolerance, and love to allow them to create a connection to life outside their circumstances.

As I engage in my own reflection, one of my students, Dionne, stands out to me. I was one of Dionne's teachers for several years. Dionne was 14 when I met her. She was an angry and traumatized teenager without the necessary skills to deal with problems in a constructive manner. She was very sweet and open-minded at times and other times she would shut down and blow up at the least provocation. Her reaction to adversity was to scream obscenities at anyone who angered her. Dionne was always ready to fight at the drop of a hat. Dionne lived downtown with her father whom she idolized. He cared for her deeply. Her most frequent phrase, said in the voice of a young child, , "My daddy, my daddy. . . ." Dionne's mother was not around due to her own struggles with alcohol and drugs, and as a result, she was very distrustful of women. Her destructive behavior impeded her ability to master the standard curriculum. It was evident from the beginning that nothing by way of the standard curriculum could be accomplished until we established a relationship of trust. Dionne and I became very close. She needed a motherly figure in her life that she could trust.

Establishing trust was intrinsic, as my guiding belief in teaching is to establish an environment where my students can feel safe to open up to me and share who they are, if they desire. In an effort to promote openness, I shared with the class things about my life before I was a teacher. We discussed my life as a child, my difficulty feeling connected in school, my life as a single mother, and ways I have overcome what often felt like a hopeless situation. These students needed more than an academic curriculum; they needed skills for life.

Dionne along with her classmates were academically unmotivated, so they put forth minimal effort. Instinctively I knew my pedagogical knowledge would not be enough but I doubted my intuition and initially unsuccessfully attempted to "play teacher" becoming what I thought I was "supposed" to be. I wrote behavioral objectives, shared them with the students, and designed cooperative learning groups. It was not enough. I thought that was what I was expected to do. The majority of the time they did not complete assignments and instead created chaos among themselves. They needed tasks that meant something to them. I tried all of the scientifically based techniques I had learned in my teacher education program, but most of them failed miserably. My challenge was getting them excited about learning. I knew that one way out of poverty was education, so it was crucial that they learn the necessary skills to be productive members of society.

Playing teacher did not work, so I drew from my own experiences as a troubled youth and directed my attention to meeting the individual needs of all of my students. This required me to synthesize both my personal and professional knowledge. I needed more than technique. I needed to accept that my students were right where they were and strip myself of any predetermined expectations. Every time I tried to control them because "I knew what was best for them," I had to remind myself that acceptance was the key. From this place, I was able to validate for myself the role of intuition and imagination in teaching. This change in perspective provided the necessary conditions for them to make their own connections that took them on their own personal journeys of growth.

The most memorable activities I prepared for these kids was engaging them in reading the Bluford Series novels based on a group of African-American teenagers in an urban high school. The novels were about real problems that students identified as similar to their own. They could identify with the characters. We spent the better part of a year reading those novels for most of the day. Most claimed they had never read nor desired to read one novel before our reading together, but by the end of the year, they were capable of reading and analyzing the whole 15 book series. It was a real accomplishment that we all took pride in. Every day I left school emotionally exhausted but with a feeling of purpose that is its own reward. The students gave me experiences for growth more than I could ever give them. I experienced joy on many occasions that cannot be quantified. I was provided with a much-needed way to give back as a way to heal my own pain and grow as a professional. This was a real gift. I can still vividly recall the excitement on one student's face as he said, "Ms. Cook, I can picture what the room looks like and even the designs on the rug." I built rapport with my students that motivated them to work with me and also motivated them to learn because they wanted to. During the year, many students demonstrated a greater sense of empathy for characters in novels, then for each other, and finally for people with different experiences than the ones they knew. Seeds were planted that can last a lifetime.

For Dionne, I was her teacher, her friend, and the mother she didn't have in her life. I even gave her a baby shower when she was expecting her first child. She couldn't believe that I cared that much for her that I would spend my own money and take my time to celebrate with her. I'll never forget how she paraded me around her neighborhood to introduce me to all the people who were important to her and how much reverence they had for me "the teacher." It was clear in their eyes how much they valued teachers despite their own often unsatisfying experiences in schools. It was also clear how surprised they were at my desire to be a part of their community. This wasn't in my job description nor was it scientifically driven but it was an immensely fulfilling opportunity. By participating in community with them a bridge could be forged between the school and community. It was the kind of experience that informs an entire career.

Despite all her progress, Dionne did not gain as much academically as I would've liked and barely graduated from high school. Many of the things she learned cannot be measured in an objective way, so some might claim I failed her and allowed her to fail herself but this is not true. What she did acquire were ways to handle her anger in more productive ways, to not give up when she made a mistake, and a belief that it is possible to look beyond your mistakes at the bigger picture. Dionne began to talk about a world of possibilities beyond her neighborhood. She showed courage and tenacity by journeying into unknown territories. This courage was exemplified in an outing my family and I went on with Dionne. We went to a county park and decided to rent a paddle boat. She had never experienced anything like this. At first, she was terrified and refused to ride in the boat. After discussing her fear with me, she decided to face it and do something different. I can't say she enjoyed this experience, but she was willing to try something new. I was so impressed by her willingness to step out of her comfort zone, a challenging thing for anyone.

I wish I could report that Dionne's story is all about triumph over adversity, but it's not. Often we take one step forward and two steps back and that is ok. Dionne went on to have six children who became fatherless when their fathers were killed, and 3 years ago she was caught stealing and went to jail. This charge had a domino effect on her life that cost her job and made it tough for her to gain employment at a restaurant or in the retail industry again. This setback did not crush her and she was able to recognize that she had made a mistake and could pick up right where she was and do the next right thing. Despite her problems, I would say that Dionne is a success. She did not reach the predetermined goals outlined in the standard curriculum, but she did gain a sense of self-worth, self-reliance, and an ability to understand herself better. All tools that make her a better mother than the one she has. Her ability to be a more nurturing and growth-orientated person has a direct impact on her children and in turn how they will contribute to society.

To bring about lasting educational reform we need to get back to a personal investment in our students. We need to address the alienation students feel in school. We need to get to know them and their stories to help students make sense of their lives. To accomplish this, we need to give of ourselves by fearlessly sharing our experience, strength, and hope. Teaching students how to reflect on their experiences leads to the development of meaning and purpose in their lives which should be the highest aim of education. It is the intangible benefits in our educational experiences that are part of the real art of teaching.

Both academic skills and skills for life are necessary especially for our students who have experienced trauma and as a result have extremely difficult life circumstances. Caring teachers make it possible for students to find their own direction without having to journey blindly in life wasting valuable time they could be using to be their best selves and do their best work. I wonder what path I would've taken if I had a teacher who embraced the art of teaching, not just the science. What if I had that one teacher in high school, who looked beyond the tough exterior and saw my pain. I am not suggesting all teachers need to get personally involved with students to meet their needs, but I am suggesting we all need to stretch our own boundaries to follow our own hearts. My point is that we need to be willing and unafraid to go in whatever direction that is in the best interest of each child.

PART III: LEARNING FROM TEACHER LORE

Similar to the 1980s, an overriding concern today remains the quality of American education. The voices of teachers were largely absent from the literature in the 1980s and are barely heard today. Everyone agrees that educational reform is needed. What we do not agree on is the best ways to improve educational outcomes for students. Teacher lore is one avenue that can inspire teachers to be the voice of change both inside and outside of schools.

Teacher lore is a potent agent for professional growth. It is one way to create communities of learning among teachers where teachers are free to make meaning of their professional lives, where teachers are free to develop in unique ways and are permitted to come together to share without fear of being judged.

We often hear the word choice when talking about professional development for teachers, but the options offered are pieces of the same pie. Many districts are turning toward conference type arrangements. They provide a multitude of mini-workshops to choose from such as: "How to Use Technology More Effectively," "Special Education and the Law," and "Data Driven Instruction." These training workshops send the message that the answers to our questions are predictable in advance and one only need to use the right techniques to get to the predetermined results. Professional development must acknowledge teachers as whole human beings, something that rarely happens at the pre- or service level. Teachers need the autonomy to pursue education that suits their individual needs. Teachers who are acknowledged as whole human beings, in turn, learn to recognize students in the same way.

The concept of teacher researcher can transform the traditional view about the relationships between knowledge and practice and the roles of teachers in educational change. It can provide ways to connect teaching and curriculum to wider contextually based social and political issues. Not only does teacher lore provide a way for teachers to share their knowledge, but it can also be a mode of communication that allows those who are not part of the everyday lived experience in schools to understand the complex, ambiguous, challenging nature of teaching. "Not only teachers themselves but students, administrators, parents, communities and policy makers can learn about theories, issues and ideas that propel school reform" (Schwartz, 1998, p. 163). Teacher Lore can bring about change from the bottom up by providing an inside-out view to policy makers and legislators. Teacher lore can be a curriculum window to a more humanistic curriculum that encompasses standardization and allows for the art of teaching and inevitably increased student learning.

NOTE

1. Connelly & Clandinin (1988, p. 31).

REFERENCES

Carter, K. (1993). The place of story in the study of teaching and teacher education. *Educational Researcher, 22*(1), 5–18. https://www.jstor.org/stable/1177300

Connelly, M., & Clandinin, J. (1988). *Teachers as curriculum planners: Narratives of experience.* Teachers College Press.

Eisner, E. W. (2002). *The educational imagination: On the design and evaluation of school programs.* Merrill Prentice Hall.

Schubert, W. H., & Ayers, W. (Eds.). (1992). *Teacher lore: Learning from our own experience.* Educator's International Press.

Schubert, W. H. (1990). School culture: Acknowledging teachers' experiential knowledge: Reports from the teacher lore project. *Kappa Delta Pi Record, 26*(4), 99–100. https://doi.org/10.1080/00228958.1990.10518605

Schwarz, G., & Alberts, J. (1998). *Teacher lore and professional development for school reform.* Bergin & Garvey.

CHAPTER 4

THE STRUGGLE TO THE SUMMIT

Jonathan Cooper

Author/Book studied:

Kliebard, H. (1995). *The struggle for the American curriculum: 1893–1958* (2nd ed.). Routledge. (Original work published 1987)

THE FOURTEENER

When my wife and I were first married, we took a backpacking trip to Colorado with another couple in our family, but who are also our very dear friends. My wife's brother married a wonderful girl from out west, and she knew all of the ins and outs of backpacking. We wanted to climb a fourteener. In mountaineer terms, that meant a mountain that was 14,000–14,999 feet above sea level. We chose Mount Uncompahgre. Uncompahgre Peak is the sixth highest summit of the Rocky Mountains. We were very unskilled and "green" in a sense, but we were up for the challenge.

Curriculum Windows Redux, pages 39–50

To climb a peak that high, we planned for three overnights in the mountains. We wanted plenty of time to explore and reach our summit and not run out of food or supplies. We planned our routes, a general idea of where we'd set up camp, the food we'd pack, how we'd evenly distribute the weight to carry, how we'd filter our water *and* where we'd find our water, where we'd set up camp, what trail we'd take for the first leg, what trail we'd take for the second leg. We packed our first aid, read up on how to recognize acute mountain sickness in case any of us experienced it, and made sure we knew how to reach the nearest ranger if we needed help. There was a lot of planning and preparation and exact measurements to be sure we had all we needed, but nothing more. Everything you need is on your back, so you must think wisely about the necessities. And you had to remember your end goal. To reach the summit. If you made all these plans, but never reached the summit, well, let's just say that'd be pretty disappointing.

Once on our trail, there was much to see in the way of nature. When climbing a fourteener, it's unlike hiking up Pike's Peak or Stone Mountain. You really don't see many other people, but you see much wildlife, nature, and unbelievable views. There are paths and trails and it's very remote. You are, after all, truly in the middle of a steep climb upward in the middle of the Rockies. Once we set up camp our first night, we made our fire, cooked our dinner, and let it all sink in. We were really doing this. All of our hard work and preparations and planning were coming to fruition. That night we built a cairn.

A cairn is a human made pile (or stack) of stones. Cairns have been used since prehistoric times and are still used today. They have many designated uses. Perhaps you buried something special and need to remember where it is. Perhaps you have made a burial site. Perhaps you have climbed a mountain and need to leave markers for trails you have taken. In our case, it was a bit of a memorial we established to remind ourselves of this monumental moment. The cairn was a physical representation of something that would forever be embedded in our memories. We knew once we'd left that campsite, we'd probably never see it again. But anyone who came after us, while not knowing exactly what that cairn represented, would know that someone had built it and erected it for a purpose.

The next few days, we spent exploring upward. We left a few more cairns along the way. Some of them to mark a sweet memory and serve as a memorial, some of them to simply serve as a landmark confirmation we were on the correct route back to our campsite. Either way, the cairn became something that was memorable and useful and served a purpose. Our daily treks were difficult, left us sore, and coming back to a very thin pad on rocky ground to sleep. Our days were filled with vistas that projected out into the vastness of the sky or trails that were tucked in and covered with wildflowers. We often struggled through difficult paths and a few times, life-threatening moments, but not without excellent reward. We knew what we wanted. We wanted to get to the summit because we believed it would be so breathtaking that it would make anything we risked losing, whether our sleep or feet that were blistered or even a limb, completely worth the challenge. We knew that if we made it to the top, it would make all of the preparation worth it. We believed this opportunity was what was best for us in that moment of our lives.

The Struggle, so aptly titled by Herbert Kliebard, reminds me of a four-teener experience. Many paths, many ways of doing it, some definitely better than others. Not an easy path. Not an easy summit. All people want to get to the top, but why? And how? Have you felt the struggle? The struggle is real and it is not new. The struggle matters. The struggle demands our attention. The struggle that Kliebard writes about is for the American curriculum. Before reading Herbert M. Kliebard's (1987/1995), *The Struggle for the American Curriculum*, I viewed the history of curriculum as a nice string of events that originated as a response to what was happening in the world at the time. For example, when the second industrial revolution hit heading into the 20th century, we started preparing our students as if they were all going to join the factory in order to grow our economy. Most educators and our public are somewhat aware of the key events through history that seemed to influence the direction of education and our society. What most people do not often consider are the voices behind the scenes that have battled in word and philosophy to influence and control the direction of the American curriculum. These influential voices had power and often took the American curriculum in a direction that had lasting impact on our students, teachers, and society as a whole.

BASECAMP WITH THE AUTHOR—HERBERT M. KLIEBARD

Herbert M. Kliebard, the author of *The Struggle for the American Curriculum* (Kliebard, 1987/1995), was considered by many a leader in the field of curriculum theory and educational history. Kliebard served as a professor at the University of Wisconsin, Madison from 1963 to 1999. His work included approximately 100 articles and publications that influenced the ongoing conversation about the history of the American curriculum. His most influential piece of work was the book that has influenced this chapter, *The Struggle for the American Curriculum* (Kliebard, 1987/1995). *The Struggle,* as it is often referred to, is now in its third edition. Kliebard passed away at the age of 84 on June 8, 2015. However, his work lives on and is referenced often in writings that address curriculum history, especially during the progressive era.

The reason that Kliebard's book is regarded by many scholars to be an essential fixture in the broader body of literature addressing curriculum history is because he strategically illuminated four key groups or voices that played a significant role in the struggle. Whereas, most curriculum historians and theorists lump several key voices from the past together in the progressive era of curriculum development, Kliebard intentionally differentiates and helps the reader train his or her ear to listen for the slight yet significant differences from one group to the next. The four camps that Kliebard uses to group the different voices are the humanist, child development, social efficiency, and reconstructionists. Each of these groups erected their own cairns, invisible landmarks, or trails heads that are still visible in our educational landscape today.

I would compare Kliebard's work of spotlighting these cairns to that of a master sommelier. Just as a master sommelier understands the slight yet significant differences in wine, Kliebard mindfully pairs similar voices from curriculum history into teams that share common philosophical differences. He then artfully infuses the passionate and often antagonistic arguments of John Dewey. Kliebard uses Dewey's voice throughout the book to help the reader define the boundaries and values of the four camps. Dewey sets up many of his own cairns across the landscape of educational history.

Most books that attempt to address curriculum history typically do a decent job of establishing a timeline of key events. The authors then work to make the connection between these various historical events and the parallel change in direction in our approach to the curriculum and the impact it has had on our schools. The key difference in Kliebard's book is that he works hard to take the reader behind the scenes. He shows the reader behind the curtain. As Kliebard (1987/1995) himself states in his book,

> The struggle I tried to depict, in other words, is primarily a symbolic one over whose most fundamental beliefs shall occupy center stage in a continuing drama. In that drama, protagonists representing competing values and beliefs vie for public validation and approbation on the national stage. (p. xi)

Kliebard considered completing a sequel to *The Struggle for the American Curriculum* to include the next decade of the struggle, then influenced by his reading of Joseph R. Gusfield's epilogue in 1986 (Kliebard, 1987/1995, p. x), he chose to publish a second and then third edition to his work. He added an afterword in the second edition to help readers frame the political context of the book. In his third edition, he went on to add two additional chapters to dig deeper into a specific decade in the book that he felt needed to be unpacked further for people to understand the influencing voices throughout our history.

As mentioned above, Kliebard creatively grouped the most influential voices into four distinct groups. As you read further, you will be able to make connections from each of these groups and their contributions to the struggle and the evidence we still see of each of them today in our schools.

CAIRN ONE

The humanists were by far the most influential voice and had the largest audience over the span of time. There are several implications in today's curriculum that are clear connections rooted deep in the original humanist movement. This movement included recognizable names back in curriculum history such as Charles W. Eliot, William Torrey Harris, and Robert Maynard Hutchins. They believed schools were instruments for imparting the traditional values, sensibilities, and cultural highlights that accumulated within Western civilization. Most leaders of this group were not in the educational community, but they commanded an audience throughout the intellectual world as a whole. And they fought hard to hold onto their sacred traditions and establish their cairn signifying the importance of their beliefs.

The conversation became official when the National Education Association Committee of Ten formed in 1893. This Committee originally began to deal with a problem that high schools were facing as they were looking for a consistent process for students entering college. Eliot, who was then the president of Harvard, was appointed as the first chairman of the National Education Association's (NEA) Committee of Ten. Eliot was a humanist but also a mental disciplinarian meaning he believed in all students' ability to develop mental reasoning. He was known for leading educational reform at both the elementary and secondary levels. Even though Eliot had a different view than the committee on his pro-elective stance (he would have liked to have seen a high school set up that was based on purely electives), he inevitably found compromise with the rest of the committee and settled for a system that established a core set of curriculum offerings that would be given equally to all students as if all students were preparing for college.

One of the strongest viewpoints that was in unanimous agreement among the committee was that the purpose of the curriculum was to prepare all students equally for college whether or not they were planning on going to college. This essentially aligned with the beliefs of the mental disciplinarians. The committee argued that all students were entitled to the best education for life, which is essentially the best preparation for college.

After the Committee of Ten came the Committee of Fifteen (1895), reporting on the condition of elementary education in the United States. William Torrey Harris fully embodied the doctrine of the humanist curriculum. Harris, previously a member of the Committee of Ten, worked hard, though, to disassociate himself from the mental disciplinarian position. He began to argue for a new understanding of the humanistic curriculum. He developed the five windows of the soul: arithmetic, geography, history, grammar, and literature. He espoused that this is how we would carry on tradition and cultural knowledge.

During this time period, a group of educational leaders who were scientific in thought studied schools in Germany and became followers of the beliefs of Johann Friedrich Herbart. Many believed that Herbart's philosophy had the most promise in changing education. And among those in that group was the young John Dewey in 1895.

Signs of the struggle became clear in 1895 in Cleveland at the NEA meeting when the Herbartian voice of Charles DeGarmo (who later became the president of the National Herbartian Society) began to attack Harris and the humanistic doctrine:

> The meeting in Cleveland became, in a sense, the Fort Sumter of a war that was to rage for most of the twentieth century. Whatever may have been the merits of the Herbartian criticism, the clash between Harris and the Herbartians marked the beginning of a realignment of the forces that were to battle for control of the American curriculum. The atmosphere at that 1895 meeting was so tense and the sense of drama so great that, thirty-eight years later, DeGarmo, at the age of eighty-five, was moved to write his friend Nicholas Murray Butler, "No scene recurs to me more vividly than on that immortal day in Cleveland, which marked the death of the old order and the birth of the new." (Kliebard, 1987/1995, p. 17)

While the Herbartian movement was powerful, Kliebard (1987/1995) points out that it existed only for a short amount of time before it virtually disappeared. However, it posed a challenge to those in the camp of mental disciplinarians and classical curriculum and ultimately opened the pathway for the child development theorists to build a cairn of their own.

CAIRN TWO

While there were important transitional players leading the child-centered team, none stands out more than G. Stanley Hall. Hall dominated the pathway for this group initially. He embraced the ideas of individualization. He was preoccupied with the health and wellness of the whole child claiming that Harris and company were harming the child by only focusing on the cognitive aspects of school. He irately opposed the Committee of Ten findings.

The child-centered movement focused on the child as the center of the curriculum. So, what the child was interested in and what the child needs is then the direction the curriculum goes. Unlike the humanists who were sold on the classical curriculum of memorization, recitation, pouring in information, and developing only the intellect, child development focused on the interests of the child in developmentally appropriate stages and somewhat as a whole person. However, "For Hall, the purpose of individualization was not to provide opportunities for maximal development of each individual. Rather, it was to identify the gifted child" (Pinar et al., 2014, p. 89). He advocated for differentiated instruction based on genetic heredity believing that there were limits to human educability determined by nature's endowment (Kleibard, 1987/1995, p. 40). And thus students should be segregated based on these determinations.

Kliebard highlights that Dewey shows up on the scene to make sense of the mix of beliefs set out by the classical curriculum supported by the humanists like Harris and the child-centered curriculum led by Hall. He actually embraced thoughts from both teams, but still held different core values that set him in a camp of his own. However, many people of his time were not ready for his ideas to transition into actual practice.

While there were many who applauded Dewey for his progressive thinking, and truly believed in his ideas, he was unable to create a trail that drew enough attention to gain traction. His cairn was being erected, but not enough people were looking at it as a landmark quite yet. A louder crowd of society was chanting for social efficiency and a stable social order as the second industrial revolution was upon America. The idea of the educational summit was varied for many, and it was at this time that the team of social efficiency educators emerged.

CAIRN THREE

Social efficiency educators (i.e., Leonard Ayres, John Franklin Bobbit, Charles Ellwood, Ross L. Finney, Charles C. Peters, David Snedden) believed there was no use in training or educating students beyond what they needed to know to perform their societal role.

> The fact that their brand of reform differed dramatically from that of Hall's and was the virtual antithesis of Dewey's should not obscure the fact that the basic intention was to overthrow the established order in education as represented by the traditional humanist curriculum. (Kliebard, 1987/1995, p. 78)

No matter what pathway you were on, the cairn built by the humanists group was always visible.

There were rumblings that kids were complaining that school was boring and unengaging. The second industrial revolution was in full swing, and there was an ever-growing demand for more railroads, sewage systems, and so forth. The social efficiency group saw this as a time to think of schools as a way to train kids into the adults they would become. Everyone got an education, and an education that was tailored exactly to what they needed to be productive in society, nothing more and nothing less. It was a way toward social control, which is what Edward A. Ross, a renowned sociologist of education at the time believed was urgently necessary. His work strongly influenced the work of many other educational sociologists of his time. Ross believed the schools were focusing too much on intellectual development and felt that "the schools [should] adopt a much more direct and more pronounced social purpose" (Kliebard, 1987/1995, p. 80).

Besides social control, the other theory that social efficiency educators adopted was efficiency itself. John Franklin Bobbitt stands out as one of the most efficiency-minded educators. He published an article titled "'The Elimination of Waste in Education' and his career in curriculum was launched" (Kliebard, 1987/1995, p. 84). It was promoted that schools needed to be as efficient as factories and kids should be moved from location to location similar to a factory model or platoon and be trained for what society deemed him good for.

CAIRN FOUR

As you can imagine, there were many who fought against this idea of the factory model for schools no matter how practical it might have appeared. Enter the social meliorists or reconstructivists (George S. Counts, Harold O. Rugg, Lester Frank Ward, William Heard Kilpatrick). This group set up their cairn based on the belief that there is an inherent tendency toward progress (also known as progressivism) or improvement in the human condition. And they aimed to bring the curriculum back to the center of the child. However this group had "two related but distinguishable streams. One of those was rooted in a conception of the nature of human experience and intelligence, the other in social reform" (Eisner, 2002, p. 67). Among their beliefs arose the project-based curriculum specifically led by William Heard Kilpatrick, who was a learner under John Dewey. The idea that children could learn through their natural senses and experience and explore their environment was in direct contrast to the traditional schooling that focused on memorization, strict order, and authoritarian type teachers, as well as the factory model. It eventually led to the Montessori movement.

George S. Counts, an influential educator and early follower of John Dewey, was very concerned "with the social and economic inequities of American society and thought schools had a positive obligation to change the social order" (Eisner, 2002, p. 67). "Because schools were run by the capitalist class who wielded social and economic power, Counts argued, school practices tended towards the status quo, including the preservation of an unjust distribution of wealth and power" (Westheimer, n.d., para. 3). He wanted education to be seen for what he believed it was—having enormous potential for creating positive change in society.

SO MANY PATHWAYS, SO MANY CAIRNS

This book was particularly full of many different viewpoints, and even individuals from the same group would often find variations to the exact details of how it was believed curriculum should play out. Who was it about? What was it for? What was the end goal? Is it to satisfy curiosity or simply for performing tasks? Many individuals had views that changed throughout the beginning of the 20th century. While Kliebard's book was fascinating at a lot of levels, it was ultimately so full of information and overlapping, that it was difficult to keep track of the movements and when and what history was taking place at the time. However, one thing is certain, and that is that many, or possibly most, of the ideas that were being fought for from 1893–1958 are still in debate in some form today. And we can point out tendencies in our curriculum as well as the overall function of schools from each of the four groups that are thoroughly discussed in this book. One important lesson Eisner (2002) points out is that you cannot assume that the public visibility of an idea meant that it was actually being practiced at the school level. And that, in and of itself, would be an interesting study (p. 72).

The trek to the summit is still on . . . and ultimately there is still much debate over what is the best pathway or trail for kids today. And for that matter, what is the ultimate summit? John Dewey once said, "We do not learn from experience, we learn from reflecting on experience" and that "Failure is instructive. The person who really thinks learns quite as much from his failures as from his successes" (John Dewey Quotes, n.d., para. 1, 3).

MY PERSONAL PATHWAY

Kliebard's thorough description of the four major cairns that were established along the pathway of curriculum history from 1893–1958 has challenged me to reflect on my own experience as a teacher, a building principal, and now an assistant superintendent. When I first started teaching in 2003, I was in a self-contained third grade classroom. My largest concern as I started off as a teacher was whether or not I had the best lesson plan for maximizing student learning. It did not take me long to learn that my main goal was not to create a beautiful lesson plan. Planning was just part of the journey. I quickly realized that the future success of my students depended on my ability to differentiate and at times personalize my plans to meet the needs of the whole child. This also meant that I needed to begin giving students more ownership in the learning process.

This sharp switchback in the steep pathway up Mount Rookie, only came about because of the experienced mentors that supported and challenged me to grow as a teacher and a learner. This process of efficacy built my confidence to begin taking risks that would open up new learning opportunities for my students. I began designing disruptive experiences that led my students to apply what we referred to as 21st century skills to move forward as a learning community. My goal was very similar to Dewey's even before I had deeply studied Dewey. My approach truly stemmed from a dissatisfaction combined with a vision to use my passion and talent to fight for a world that expects a more personalized approach to learning.

I recall one of the first times I decided to rethink my approach to the classroom learning environment and make a significant shift to the way my students would experience the curriculum. It was my third year of teaching and I had just transitioned from teaching third grade to fourth grade. I had finished reading Thomas Friedman's (2005) book, *The World is Flat* and instantly knew something had to change in my approach to the classroom. The book challenged my core beliefs of how I believed we should be preparing our students for the future. It caused me to ask the question, what is the purpose of public education? This reflection caused me to begin blazing a trail that had no clear destination or trail guide.

I stood up in front of my fourth grade class and with a calm, serious voice and a skosh of urgency in my tone, I told my students that the president of the United States had made an executive decision to establish Ohio as a centralized air base. His order required all Ohio citizens to relocate out of the state so that the government would be able to essentially bulldoze the state and build the ultimate global runway and centralized command centers.

As you can imagine, some of the young fourth graders were not sure whether to laugh or cry. Either way, they were hooked and ready to save our state. This launched my students in a yearlong pursuit to save our state. At that moment, the curriculum became alive and living. Students owned every part of their learning and the development of the learning experience. They transformed our classroom environment into the S.O.S. headquarters. They became researchers, lawyers, scientists, botanists, and many other real life experts in order to prove with evidence that the President should save our state.

At the end of the year, the students invited local and state leaders, field experts, and peers from other buildings to witness a full day of well-developed arguments, visual presentations, and compelling evidence that we need to essentially come together as one voice to save our state.

Since fourth grade standards were aligned with the thorough study of the state of Ohio, it was easy for my students to connect their deep self-driven learning on the myriad of topics to our goal of learning more about Ohio history, geography, culture, and more.

After the final arguments were made and the case was fully shared with the guest jury, the students had convinced the guest jury to save our state and preserve all that is great about the state of Ohio. Our student experts erupted in cheering and celebration. Through self-designed learning, passion, and personalized learning experiences, my students accomplished an authentic learning goal.

When I reflect on this detour from the typical pathway, I realize that there is evidence of each of the four cairns that are described above. I would argue that as we begin to provide more project-based or personalized learning experiences, we need to recognize that we are continuing the struggle and the experiences that we are providing for our students are anchored from the lessons learned by the historic cairns set before us. I would also argue that it is no longer simply the struggle for the American curriculum. It is now the struggle for the global curriculum.

In the past 3 years, I have been on a relentless pursuit to see educational leaders across the United States begin owning the definition and development of personalized learning. I would argue that the next pathway that needs to be defined on our eternal journey to the summit of the curriculum struggle is personalized learning. We, as educational leaders, must take bold ownership and fight for our voice as we clear the path for our students and staff in their experience in personalized learning. The pathway is crowded with an endless list of vendors and political leaders who would like to define personalized learning from the top down as they struggle for control of the pathway. This is why it is critical that educational leaders wake up and courageously shape the conversation as a service to our students and our society as a whole. Many of the innovative thoughts that John Dewey argued with his colleagues ring true today as we begin to give our students a voice and choice that align with mastery of standards with the larger overarching purpose of strengthening our community and democracy.

SEEKING THE SUMMIT

The summit was in our sight. However, we were immediately faced with three life-altering decisions that would determine whether or not we would actually arrive at the peak. First, my brother-in-law was experiencing symptoms of acute mountain sickness (AMS). He had made some comments about feeling light-headed and he was behaving very slap happy. We assessed the situation, and as a team, decided to push forward in the struggle to the summit. We would monitor his symptoms and safety as we pressed on. We were so close.

Second, we quickly observed ominous storm clouds to the west. We understood based on our information gathering that a cause of death while on a mountain top was getting caught in a lightning storm while at the peak. Again, faced with a very difficult decision, the team voted to press on. We were now within an hour of the peak.

We faced our final and most terrifying moment in our journey when we encountered a 15-foot icy ridge that went alongside a crevice. We basically had to sidestep while holding onto any rock we could find to make it past this crevice. There was not enough room for our entire foot to gain traction. One misstep and it was a definite fall. Possible death, definite injury. Again, we discussed as a group. We unanimously decided to cross. We created a human rope to support each other through the most deadly stretch of our journey. Scaling our way past this crevice, we finally had the peak safely in view.

We experienced one of the most breathtaking 360 degree glorious views I have ever witnessed. It brought an emotional response to the beauty and majesty of the mountain and a deep respect for the journey itself.

As educational leaders, we must press on in the struggle for a learner-centric global curriculum. We must support each other in making courageous decisions to press on toward the summit with the goal of providing our students with personalized learning experiences that will lead to a stronger community of learners.

REFERENCES

Eisner, E. W. (2002). *The educational imagination: On the design and evaluation of school programs* (3rd ed.). Merrill Prentice Hall.

Friedman, T. L. (2005). *The world is flat: A brief history of the twenty-first century.* Picador.

John Dewey Quotes. (n.d.). Good Reads. https://www.goodreads.com/author/quotes/42738.John_Dewey?page=1

Kliebard, H. M. (1995). *The struggle for the American curriculum* (2nd ed.). Routledge. (Original work published 1987)

Pinar W. F., Reynolds, W. M., Slattery, P., & Taubman, P. M. (2014). *Understanding curriculum* (Vol. 17). Peter Lang Publishing.

Westheimer, J. (n.d.). *George S. Counts (1889–1974).* State University. http://education.stateuniversity.com/pages/1891/Counts-George-S-1889-1974.html#ixzz4gkCY6fH8

CHAPTER 5

CHALLENGING WORLDVIEWS
Facing Down Educational Injustices

Tracy Davis

Author/Book studied:
Kozol, J. (1991). *Savage inequalities: Children in America's schools.*
Harper Perennial.

NOT JUST A COINCIDENCE

Last fall, I was introduced to a book by Nel Noddings (1995) entitled *Philosophy of Education.* In her book, she referenced Jonathan Kozol's (1991) book *Savage Inequalities.* At the time, I had not read nor even heard of his book. Several months later, I was attending an IEP meeting for my son at his school. As I scanned the bookcase in the principal's office, the first title that caught my eye was *Savage Inequalities* (Kozol, 1991). The next week, I started a class and Kozol's book was an option for me to read for a final project. The fact that Kozol's book kept showing up in my life could not have been a

Curriculum Windows Redux, pages 51–64
Copyright © 2022 by Information Age Publishing
www.infoagepub.com
All rights of reproduction in any form reserved.

coincidence, so I requested and was given the opportunity to read the book for this project. Part of me wished I hadn't.

After reading the first chapter of the book, I had to put it down and decompress. It was so depressing, sad, and hurtful that I couldn't pick it up again for days. Putting it mildly, I was upset. I am not naive to the existence of racism and its influence on all systems of America. Nor is my head in the sand about the continued racist society we still have and that is growing in 2017. One only has to reflect on the last 8 years of the disrespect of the Obama administration to see this truth.

I was furious because systematically the odds have been stacked against people of color even before the annihilation of the Native Americans. Imperialism, expansionism, and manifest destiny historically are the reasons used to justify those in power staying in power and abandoning those who are not. *Savage Inequalities* (Kozol, 1991) crystallizes the inherent inequities not only in school systems, but in society generally. Kozol's book was an admonition of the injustices and inequalities that continue to plague our nation's poor, people of color, and disenfranchised. It illustrates the lack of community care and support necessary for all systems to flourish. His book reminded me of how far we have *not* come.

In this chapter I discuss issues related to school funding, quality of schooling, and the systemic inequalities that perpetuate the problems found in our neighborhoods and from my perspective, why these inequalities continue to exist. Solutions vary but money, school reform, nor privatization of public education are the answers. As you will see, the answers may lie in things money can't buy or that policy can't dictate.

RUDE AWAKENING

I couldn't help but wonder as I read Jonathan Kozal's (1991) book *Savage Inequalities* if he was really one of the good guys? Was he writing it for the notoriety? Or, was he one of the few who genuinely abhorred the injustices heaped upon poor inner city children? His privilege alone allows him to walk in and out of these situations unaffected because "this is not his life." At the end of the day, he could pretend these issues do not exist and no one would care. But Kozol did not walk away and in fact he continued his crusade against inequalities in the inner cities and inner city schools. For his dedication, I applaud his tenacity for fighting against these injustices for the past 40 plus years. In addition to this book, and in others such as *Death at an Early Age* (Kozol, 1995), *The Shame of the Nation* (Kozol, 2005), and *Fire in the Ashes* (Kozol, 2012), he shares first-hand accounts of his experiences and provides insights to the readers about social problems such as segregated and inadequate schools, inadequate school funding, illiteracy, and vagrancy (The Famous People, n.d.).

Born to a middle-class Jewish family, Kozol graduated summa cum laude in English literature from Harvard in 1958. He was awarded a Rhodes Scholarship to Magdalen College in Oxford but did not attend. Instead, he traveled across Europe to study fiction and nonfiction writing. When he returned to the states it was the height of the civil rights movement. He says he returned in the summer of 1964 to learn about the disappearance of three civil rights workers in Mississippi. He immediately tried to find out how he could help.

Kozol (2015) admits that he is neither a teacher by degree nor training, but he began his teaching career as a kindergarten substitute teacher in an inner city school in Boston. The school was so crowded and so poor that it could not provide his fourth grade children with a classroom. He was fired shortly after he started teaching for introducing Langston Hughes poetry to his students. After his short tenure, he took a teaching position at Newton Public Schools, the school district he attended as a child. The shock of going from one of the poorest to one of the wealthiest school districts cannot be overstated (Kozol, 2015, p. 2). It was this rude awakening that fueled and inspired his involvement in social justice work.

Beginning in 1988, Kozol travelled across the nation, visiting schools coast to coast and was startled to find that racial segregation and inequality in public schools was still very common. At that time, it was more than 100 years post *Plessy v. Ferguson* (1896) which supported the segregation of schools for Black students with the stipulation that those schools were equal to those of White schools. It was also 37 years post *Brown v. Board of Education* (1954) in which the U.S. Supreme Court ruled segregated education unconstitutional because it was inherently unequal (Kozol, 1991). He suggests these conditions continue to exist in many inner cities mainly due to unfair funding protocols, governmental neglect, and poor quality of education perpetuated by political greed and institutional racism.

A NATION AT RISK

All, regardless of race or class or economic status, are entitled to a fair chance and to the tools for developing their individual powers of mind and spirit to the utmost. This promise means that all children by virtue of their own efforts, competently guided, can hope to attain the mature and informed judgment needed to secure gainful employment, and to manage their own lives, thereby serving not only their own interests but also the progress of society itself. (U.S. National Commission on Excellence in Education, 1983, p. 7)

Issues surrounding school reform tend to pivot around a document published in 1983 called *A Nation at Risk* (U.S. National Commission on Excellence in Education, 1983). This government report suggests that the American public school system is not effectively educating our youth. It basically says that public schools are churning out illiterate students who are not prepared to enter into and be successful in the job market. This was the case made in 1983. In 1991, Kozol made the same substantial claims, but based on a different set of conditions. *A Nation at Risk* suggests the educational curriculum is to blame; what students are being taught is what hinders the success of America's youth. This document also deems school reform as the answer to this problem. Kozol suggests that inequalities in access to basic tools necessary to facilitate schooling are hindering community after community of poor inner city youth. Kozol's visits to several of the country's poorest school districts yielded reports that decaying and dilapidated conditions create safety issues in school buildings in which children are expected to learn and teachers are expected to teach. Conditions like these reek of economic, social, and political inequalities that go far beyond school reform.

A Nation at Risk (U.S. National Commission on Excellence in Education, 1983) suggests that all students regardless of race, class, or socioeconomic standards deserve a "fair" chance of bettering their lives through education. This fair chance would be based on equitable learning environments, equitable access to information, and equitable distribution of funding for "all" but none of this is the case. I believe one reason for this inequity lies in the *Brown v. Board of Education* (1954) decision that deemed separate schools for Black and White students' unconstitutional and forced public schools to desegregate. What Black schools lost was more than what was gained by desegregation. The bottom line was that White America still believed Black students to be inferior and did not want them in their schools. White students were not sent to Black schools so many of the Black schools closed. Along with those closures came the loss of jobs for many Black teachers and administrators. Ladson-Billings (2004) puts the number of jobs lost at about 38,000 in 17 states in the South between 1945 and 1965. As "White flight" gained momentum and families moved away they left their schools along with White teachers who had no interest in educating Black students. Those Black students left behind had no good Black teachers who could show them the educational brilliance that lay within. There was no one to motivate them to strive toward the excellence of which they too were capable. There was no one to inspire them as students. Instead, you have generations of Black students forced to conform to a school system that did not want them in the first place and manages still to inflict its miseducation on them. Rothstein (2014) notes additional policies such as redlining, zoning laws, and restrictive covenants kept Blacks in overcrowded neighborhoods with few jobs and even fewer homes. Funding for these neighborhoods and schools became nonexistent because property taxes could not support the school districts. What remains is what Kozol witnessed in the 1990s: a nation still at risk complete with poverty stricken neighborhoods, poorly funded schools, underqualified teachers, and students left in educational situations no one wants for their child.

WORLDVIEWS CHALLENGED

I was encouraged by Dr. Poetter to explore and try to explain how and why these inequalities happened and unfortunately still exist. Through Kozol's research, interviews, in-depth observations, and historical accounts from written publications, I am convinced that other forces were at work long before Black people were poor and crowded into the inner city. Long before the extreme poverty, lack of educational funding, sewer filled lunch-rooms, and dilapidated schools, societal and political racism was at work. We need to keep in mind that in the beginning, many of these neighborhoods were middle-class/wealthy White neighborhoods and as immigrants and Blacks from the south came for better jobs, Whites started moving out and property lines were drawn. Not being able to move into better living situations, overcrowding and lack of jobs bred what Kozol witnessed in his travels across the county. All these ills in one area of any city would make it difficult to survive (Rothstein, 2014).

Ladson-Billings (2004) writes that the answer to the inequities we see in the schools lies much deeper in societal issues. "These issues emerge from a much higher level of abstraction. We have the schools we have because we have the culture we have. The real answer lies in cultural transformation, a much more difficult and unpopular solution" (p. 11). I do not believe money is the only answer. Will it help? YES, but that is not the only problem. The problem supersedes something money cannot buy and that is the ethic of community and care. The idea of "community" and what that means has been mutilated in these cities and the denigrated mindset of society has a large part to play in its demise.

In *Understanding an Afrocentric Worldview: Introduction to an Optimal Psychology*, Myers (1988) introduces a concept of suboptimal and optimal worldviews. This book helped me understand how something like these savage inequalities could occur, remain in existence, and be completely acceptable by both Black and White communities. The suboptimal or Eurocentric worldview is characterized by competition, individualism, division, and fragmentation. It operates from the premise that resources are finite and in order to survive you have to compete for those resources. Those who operate from this perspective believe that all things, including one's self-worth, are rooted in who has more and seeks to find these things externally.

In this worldview, issues of human development, relationships, or anything concerning the quality of life are minimized if not completely ignored.

It is understandable how schools in poor or predominantly Black neighborhoods could end up in these conditions. The concern is not to help people in these conditions, but to continue to oppress them as they seek to get more for themselves. Therefore, if an educational system is rooted in this type of thinking, the schools as Kozol has described are a byproduct of the greed and individualism characterized by this worldview. Additionally, the fact that it has persisted for all these years is a testament to the fact that this worldview still dominates. This worldview is entrenched in the fabric of society and the foundation of which this world is anchored and until this mindset can be reversed, these savage inequalities will continue.

Myers (1988) defines an alternative conceptual system termed *optimal Afrocentric worldview*. This way of viewing the world assumes that everything revolves around both the material and the spiritual. "When the spiritual/material ontology is adhered to, one loses the sense of individualized ego/mind and experiences the harmony of the collective identity of being one with the source of all good" (p. 12). "An optimal conceptual system yields a world view that is holistic, assuming the interrelatedness and interdependence of all things." (p. 13). If one has, we all have. When an educational system is rooted in this worldview, then the inequalities witnessed by Kozol would not exist. Based on the idea of interconnectedness, all stakeholders in education are responsible for these schools and the children who attend. There would be more sharing of resources through the optimal view. The "we" and not the "I" are more important than the success of individuals. For instance, pollution in the community would be minimal because the community would understand their connectedness to the environment. It sounds utopian perhaps, and a little odd. This is because society has been operating from the suboptimal for so long, anything different is radical, maybe even cultish.

This also is not to suggest that Black people solely operate from the optimal worldview, nor does it denote solely White people operate from the suboptimal. Both options exist in everyone, the choice to operate in either mindset is a choice. Dr. Myers suggests that the reorientation to an optimal worldview is possible and although the complexity and size of the world makes it a challenge, the real barrier is the ingrained suboptimal worldview. Changing people's views is more daunting of a task than size. From this perspective, all things interconnected and interrelated, that are both Afrocentric and feminist in nature, are disregarded and ignored. For these reasons, we can see how an optimal way of thinking disappears and the suboptimal view is propagated and perpetuated in societies where the White male influence is most dominant. In the sections that follow, I attempt to show how the dominant suboptimal worldview continues to perpetuate these inequalities.

SHOW ME THE MONEY

Inner city schools and their communities' inability to escape generational and systemic poverty does not occur by happenstance. Once communities lose businesses that create revenue and jobs, the scaffolding of the community is weakened and ultimately decimated. In Sauget, East Saint Louis, the chemical plants responsible for toxic waste and pollution of the air did not pay taxes. Being a small, self-governed town, not only was it tax exempt, but also free from supervision by health agencies. This allowed the plants to operate and fill the city's land, air, and water with toxic waste and pollutants. The major industries other than the chemical plants were topless bars and lottery stores. Lottery proceeds were supposed to go into education, but instead they went into state revenues once again leaving education coffers empty (Kozol, 1991). Homes that did exist in these neighborhoods did not have the property values to create revenue for public schools. In another example, Kozol describes driving through the Southside of Chicago and seeing block after block of old, abandoned factories. Once where companies such as Campbell's or Pfizer thrived and created jobs and taxable revenue, now they were closed and created nothing but blight in these struggling neighborhoods.

I have stated before that there are several explanations as to why the inequities continue to exist in education. Let's consider school funding. Funding is typically based on a three prong approach. Federal, state, and local monies are designated to fund public schools. According to a 2016 NPR report, the average breakdown of these funds is as follows: 45% from local funding, 45% from state funding, and 10% from federal funding (Turner et al., 2016).

> Sales, property, and personal income taxes are the most important of these revenue sources, together contributing roughly half of total state and local general revenue. Other tax sources include corporate income taxes, severance taxes, and "sin" taxes. (e.g., taxes on alcohol and tobacco). (National Center for Education Statistics, 2003, p. 34)

In middle-class and wealthier communities this formula yields adequate if not exorbitant amounts of money for their public schools. However, in poorer communities, because of the extreme poverty, lack of jobs, lack of homes, lack of businesses, and the overall "lack" means that there is not a lot of money to be gained from local taxes to fund their schools. What ensues is a vicious cycle of impoverishment wherein property taxes continue to dwindle, schools continue to deteriorate, students continue to fail, while the government continues to withhold or steer funds into other private enterprises (i.e., choice vouchers or publicly funded but privately run charter schools). What we have is a systemic formula that is not only inequitable but insufficient to meet the needs of these communities.

Both Kozol and I agree that property tax is an insufficient way to fund public education. No communities are going to have the same property values. As long as poor neighborhoods have schools, they will never be funded at the same level as neighborhoods that are more affluent. Also, the funding of public schools is in danger because of privatization efforts through vouchers, school choice, and charter schools. Kozol believes the voucher system to be the most vicious possible device to enable affluent people and middle-class people to flee the public system and to take tax money with them into the private sector. This only serves to leave poor public schools poorer (Scherer, 1992/1993).

This controversial topic continues to be a focus of debate for Secretary of Education Betsy DeVos (Higgins & Gray, 2016). DeVos, a former Republican Party chairwoman in Michigan and a former chair of a pro-school choice advocacy group American Federation for Children (AFC) supports the privatization of public education. The AFC creates programs and laws that require the use of public funds to pay for private school tuition in the form of vouchers and similar programs. The fate of public education and access to quality schools is at stake. The biggest issue for poorer students is that these programs typically do not cover the total cost of private school tuition and thereby limit their access to that level of education. If the tuition was somehow affordable, the location of the school might be inaccessible again creating a barrier to access. If for some reason both affordability and access were not an issue, the school may not participate in the voucher program at all. What is left are underfunded and in many cases academically failing schools, and students mostly are left with no viable options despite the "efforts" to provide them.

Affordable, accessible, quality public education must remain an option for everyone. While funding is not the primary answer, it can't hurt. Instead of increasing military spending, the government needs to get back to supporting its nation's children … all of them. Earmark $10 billion federal dollars to education. Have states identify the public schools in most need of repair or renewal and repair or rebuild them. Make them places that students want to learn and teachers want to teach. Salaries for teachers are abysmal. Increase the base salaries of teachers by $10,000–$15,000. Earmark funds to assist teachers with professional development opportunities to help them learn strategies that can help students. Smaller classes might come with making teaching a more attractive professional option for incoming college students. There are other solutions to improving failing schools than mass exodus out of them. Let's try reinvesting in them instead of short changing them.

In addition to inadequate funding policies, governmental leaders need to be held accountable for their roles in allowing such inequalities to continue. Legislators use the words "sink holes" to describe inner city Chicago Schools, more specifically and pejoratively calling them "black holes" to justify withholding of funds (Kozol, 1991, p. 53). In 1991 the Governor of Illinois refused to allow an emergency state loan of $40 million for the city of East St. Louis. He blamed the mayor and his administration, almost all of whom were Black, and refused to grant the loans unless the mayor resigned. He was quoted as saying, "It's unfortunate, but the essence of the problem in East St. Louis is the people who are running things" (Kozol, 1991, p. 9). This is the type of suboptimal political thinking that still exists today.

As recently as February 2017, The Chicago city school system filed suit against the governor and the Illinois board of education alleging the way the state allocates funds is against the civil rights of minority children (Madhani, 2017). The Chicago Public Schools (CPS) have been without a full-year budget since 2015 and to add insult to injury, Gov. Bruce Rauner vetoed a bill that would have sent $215 million to Chicago Public Schools, funds desperately needed by schools, teachers, and students. Without major funding turnabouts, the Chicago Public Schools will continue to have funding issues (McDermott, 2017). In an optimal worldview act, musician and Chicago Public School alumnus Chance the Rapper and the NBA's Chicago Bulls pledged $1 million dollars each to support Chicago Public Schools. But, these two generous donations to the Chicago Public Schools are mere drops in the proverbial bucket and mean little to nothing in a school system racked with poverty. As long as the worldview of hoarding resources for the wealthy continues, these funds will never reach the schools that so desperately need them. We need systemic, major action, large acts of generosity, as well as small ones to shift our cultural view of schools, communities, and children who have been marginalized by the real and devastating suboptimal views and policies at work.

WHAT CURRICULUM EXACTLY?

Generally speaking, curriculum entails the topics taught in school. It's deciding on a set of learning goals and setting up steps to achieve those goals. The overarching goal of school is to educate its youth to participate in the social and political process. However, curriculum as we have learned in Elliot Eisner's (2002) book *The Educational Imagination* varies based on how it is defined by individuals and their goals. Interestingly, curriculum is also defined as all of the experiences kids have while attending school and "the quality of the experiences that the child had" was the real curriculum; the one that made a difference in their lives (Eisner, 2002). The experiences of the children in East Saint Louis, North Lawndale, or New York City are clearly not at the top of the list when it comes to making sure the "experiences" are redeeming. By not allocating funds to improve schools, but choosing to build prisons or buying handcuffs, what message are we sending the youth, the community, and the world about the value of children in these areas?

I believe the quality of education suffers for all students when the explicit curriculum does not inspire students to be better people. For students in deplorable conditions, getting to the intentional lessons and activities used to teach are unrealistic for many of these schools. Students can't learn if there are not enough books for each student. Computer skills suffer if the schools have outdated software or no computers at all. Students cannot compete academically with other well-funded, well-staffed schools when their school employs mostly substitute teachers who rarely show up to teach because the salaries are so low and morale is in the tank.

The implicit curricula, the unspoken or unintentional messages, are loud and clear and only serve to deepen the despair of these students and their communities. As one contributor stated, "They call it America's Soweto, a repository for a non-White population regarded as expendable" (Kozol, 1991, p. 8). They are learning about the injustices and inequalities that exist in schools and in the world. They are learning where they rank in society...the bottom. Implicitly, they are learning that their future is not important nor their contributions wanted because their schools are in turmoil and nobody is doing anything to change the circumstances or conditions. What I find even more disheartening is that these students are being taught that education is not for them and that there is no expectation for them to succeed. I don't believe that these are unintended outcomes. The suboptimal system is working exactly as it should because it is designed to suppress and alienate the voices of marginalized students from the social and political process. It's no wonder in Chicago Public Schools 27% of students who get to their senior year read at an eighth grade level or that they have a noncompletion rate of 97% (Kozol, 1991). Yet, these are the same students society believes should be able to contribute to the democratic process, but lack the tools to do so.

As I read story after heart wrenching story, Kozol manages to find slivers of hope in all this gloom. He finds people in small spaces who care. Mrs. Hawkins, a fifth/sixth grade teacher at Mary McLeod Bethune elementary school on the Southside of Chicago was unique because she was one of only a few teachers who found a way of connecting to students so that they give 100%. Her contagious energy excites the kids to want to learn. Kozol (1991) describes her class as "an island of excitement, energy and hope" (p. 47). She provided materials, books, and supplies from her own pocket for her students. In addition to teaching the basics, she also takes field trips on weekends, tutors parents for their GED, and she directs the gospel choir. More importantly, Mrs. Hawkins teaches them "1) self-motivation, 2) self-esteem, and 3) to help your sister and your brother" (Kozol, 1991, p. 48). I believe that without knowing it, Mrs. Hawkins was operating from an optimal worldview. This kind of empowerment and care is crucial in the educational success of Black children and the way to begin sharing the idea of an optimal worldview.

THE ETHIC OF CARE: AN OPTIMAL CONCEPTUAL SYSTEM

I struggled with how to write this portion of my chapter because of how important this type of empowerment is to me. I did not want my points to come off as trite or contrived. The phrase "No one cares how much you know until they know how much you care" is a very true statement. For many Black students, especially in Kozol's experiences, it does not seem like they are experiencing or hearing things they need to sustain them not only as students, but as people. Mrs. Hawkins showed them something different. Nel Noddings (1984) talks a great deal about the ethic of care in her book *Caring: A Feminist Approach to Ethics and Moral Education*. She states, "The community of care is rooted in relatedness and responsiveness" (Smith, 2016, p. 140). While this is very much a feminist point of view, it also parallels the Afrocentric/optimal worldview. Noddings (1984) writes, "We have to show in our own behavior what it means to care" (p. 230). As I recall my educational journey, I remember those teachers who made me feel good about who I was as a person and valued me as a student. Their encouraging words and reminders of the strong, proud legacy I came from helped to sustain me as a student and encouraged me to excel in my studies so I could carry on that legacy.

I believe this is what is lacking in many inner city schools. Though basic knowledge is important in everyone's schooling, if Black students knew the significance of their ancestors' contributions to science, technology, and math, might there be a change in how they approach these subjects? If these students learned more about the systematic social and political injustices that exist and the impact they have on their education, would they be more willing to fight against them? If exposed to more Black teachers and administrators, would it change how those students viewed themselves and their importance to society? What if they were taught that Black lives really did matter? Could we alter their worldviews from the suboptimal to the optimal?

I believe what we don't teach is equally as important as what we do teach. The idea of the "null curriculum" includes those ideas, subject matters, or historical references that schools do not teach (Eisner, 2002). Whether it is accidental or purposeful, the exposure to the typically null curriculum may make a positive impact on how Black students view themselves and their success. Systematically, Black people have been taught that we are inferior and that is explicitly stated (Delpit, 1988). The counter argument lies in the null, where those golden nuggets of truth are not taught. I am suggesting one way to improve the quality of education of Black children is to bring those ideas and discussions into the explicit curriculum in order to counteract all of the negativity and suboptimal exposure they experience daily. This will be a challenging task and won't happen overnight. Not only are the right people and environments important, but the mindset and world-view from which they approach the students will be crucial.

DEARLY BELOVED . . .

April 21, 2017 marked the 1-year anniversary of the death of Prince. Anyone who knows me can tell you how much of a devoted fan I am. To most people, Prince was associated with cutout booty pants and *Purple Rain*. But, what most people don't know is that he also wrote about serious political and social issues that plagued the world. While I was contemplating the wrap up of this chapter, a song came on the radio that I had not heard in years and it immediately found a place in this chapter. Prince (1988a) penned a song called, "Dance On" from his 1988 CD *Lovesexy*. After running down a list of political evils, Prince goes a step further by suggesting a broad societal solution: "It's time for new education; the former rules don't apply. We need a power structure that breeds production instead of jacks who vandalize." What I believe Prince was trying to convey was that the way we have been doing things in the past has not worked and we need to do something different. This is precisely what I have been attempting to do in this paper is to suggest that an optimal worldview mindset is doing something different.

A solution to many, if not all, of the social and political injustices and inequalities lie in the renewing of the minds of the generations to come. The future of the world hinges on giving up the idea of individualism, fragmentation and power, and opening up to an alternate way of viewing the world. This is the time to begin dismantling the falsehood that only one structure has all the right answers. All races, genders, and socioeconomic statuses bring cultural capital to the table and is better experienced when more people can use it. Educating children is not about the suboptimal premise of money and material gain. Repeatedly, I have suggested the business of repairing our inner city schools is beyond money. Social problems require social solutions, not money. If we go back to an optimal worldview, the idea is to have society adopt a worldview of interconnectedness and spend more time working on how to be part of the solution and not the problem.

I have alluded the injustices of the systems as being a primary player in the inequalities of education. No one system is to blame because the system encompasses everything. The social, political, economic, religious, business, and educational structures are all interwoven. If one string is plucked, all the others respond. I have not specified which system is most responsible for the ills that plague inner city schools because as long as our system operates from the suboptimal construct, they are all problematic. An optimal worldview would seek to bring all of these systems into some type of harmonious discourse. When one system is in operation, the others provide the support. Then at some point another system is going to need to move forward and another step back and provide the support. It can't be just one system in control all the time. This is what has gotten us into the position we find ourselves in today and what fueled the savage inequalities Kozol witnessed those 20 plus years ago.

The optimist in me wants to believe that someday the idea of an optimal worldview might come to pass. I don't believe I will see it occur in my lifetime. If 20+ years from now, another bright-eyed student reads these words, maybe they can continue to move this idea forward. It takes courage to change these savage inequalities. But the current state cannot stand forever. The late Prince "Rogers" Nelson (2004) penned a song called "Dear Mr. Man" on his 2004 CD *Musicology* that provides a great conclusion to this chapter. Paraphrasing this excerpt he states: Voting is a useless political act because although the leaders change, the hegemonistic, suboptimal mindset remains the same. You claim you want to help the poor, marginalized, and disenfranchised, but your assistance is useless and the resources inadequate. The people are fed up with your shenanigans and greed and it's time for a change.

REFERENCES

Brown v. Board of Education of Topeka, 347 U.S. 483. (1954). https://supreme .justia.com/cases/federal/us/347/483/

Eisner, E. (2002). *The educational imagination: On the design and evaluation of school programs* (3rd edition). Pearson.

Higgins, L., & Gray, K. (2016, November 23). Betsy Devos: Fighter for kids or destroyer of public schools? *Detroit Free Press*. http://www.freep.com/story/news/ education/2016/11/23/betsy-devos-trump-secretary/94357370/

Kozol, J. (1985). *Death at an early age: The destruction of the hearts and minds of Negro children in the Boston public schools*. Plume.

Kozol, J. (1991). *Savage inequalities: Children in America's schools*. Harper Perennial.

Kozol, J. (2005). *The same of the nation: The restoration of apartheid schooling in America*. Crown Publishers.

Kozol, J. (2012). *Fire in the ashes: Twenty-five years among the poorest children in America*. Broadway Books.

Kozol, J. (2015). Speaking on education. Lecture given during the Leaders in Education Lecture Series at the University of Northern Iowa. Cedar Falls, IA.

Ladson-Billings, G. (2004). Landing on the wrong note: The price we paid for Brown. Educational Researcher, *33*(7), 3–13.

Madhani, A. (2017, February 14). Chicago sues Illinois, governor over school funding formula. *USA Today*. http://www.usatoday.com/story/news/2017/02/14/ chicago-sues-illinois-governor-over-school-funding-formula/97907074/

McDermott, M. (2017, March 31). Chance the Rapper Chicago Bulls will donate $1M to CPS. *5 Chicago*. http://www.nbcchicago.com/news/local/chance-the -rapper-major-announcement-cps-funding-417786933.html

Myers, L. J. (1988). *Understanding an afrocentric world view: Introduction to an optimal psychology*. Kendall/Hunt Pub. Co.

National Center for Education Statistics. (2003). *Overview and inventory of state education reforms: 1990 to 2000*. U.S. Department of Education.

Noddings, N. (1984). *Caring: A feminine approach to ethics and moral education*. University of California Press.

Noddings, N. (1995). *Philosophy of education*. Westview Press.

Plessy v. Ferguson, 163 U.S. 537. (1896). https://supreme.justia.com/cases/federal/ us/163/537/

Prince. (1988). Dance on [Song recorded by Prince]. On *Lovesexy*. Paisley Park Studios.

Prince. (1988). *Lovesexy* [Album]. Paisley Park Studios. https://genius.com/Prince -dance-on-lyrics

Prince. (2004). Dear Mr. Man [Song recorded by Prince]. On *Musicology*. Metalworks Studios.

Prince. (2004). *Musicology* [Album]. Metalworks Studios. https://genius.com/Prince -dear-mr-man-lyrics

Rothstein, R. (2014). *The making of Ferguson: public policies at the root of its troubles*. Economic Policy Institute.

Scherer, M. (1992/1993). Students at risk: On savage inequalities. *Educational Leadership, 50*(4), 4–9.

Smith, K. C. (2016). The legacy of a woman: A hero of the 1980s. In T. S. Poetter, K. Waldrop C. Bolyard, & V. Bell-Robinson (Eds.), *Curriculum windows: What curriculum theorists of the 1980s can teach us about schools and society today* (pp.131–143). Information Age Publishing, Inc.

The Famous People. (n.d.). *Jonathan Kozol*. http://www.thefamouspeople.com/ profiles/jonathan-kozol-1992.php#7mckwcQc88vf5gh

Turner, C., Khrais, R., Lloyd, T., Olgin, A., Isensee, L., Vevea, B., & Carsen, D. (2016, April 18). Why America's schools have a money problem. *NPR*. http://www.npr .org/2016/04/18/474256366/why-americas-schools-have-a-money-problem

U.S. National Commission on Excellence in Education. (1983). *A nation at risk: The imperative for educational reform: A report to the nation and the Secretary of Education, United States Department of Education*. https://edreform.com/wp -content/uploads/2013/02/A_Nation_At_Risk_1983.pdf

CHAPTER 6

MAKING PERSONALIZED LEARNING STICK

Using *The Child-Centered Schools* to Criticize and Bolster Personalized Learning

Lauren Gentene

Author/Book studied:

Rugg, H., & Shumaker, A. (1928). *The child-centered school: An appraisal of the new education.* World Book Company.

Freedom, not restraint. Pupil initiative, not teacher initiative. The active, not the passive, school. There is a fourth new article of faith—child interest as the orienting center of the school program.

—Rugg & Shumaker, 1928, p. 60

> *Personalized learning is a progressively student-driven model in which*
> *students deeply engage in meaningful, authentic, and rigorous challenges*
> *to demonstrate desired outcomes.*
> —Zmuda et al., 2015, p. 7

DÉJÀ VU: PERSONALIZED LEARNING AND ITS PREDECESSOR

At nearly every turn, I'm told that personalized learning is the next new thing in education, even that it is the next *iteration* of education. Personalized learning is exciting, and in many ways, seemingly intuitive. Of course students' learning should be at the center of education. Of course we should be meeting the needs of our individual students. Of course students shouldn't be hindered by a standardized curriculum in an age where they hold powerful computers in their pockets. Recently there was an entire edition of *Educational Leadership* devoted to personalized learning. My own school district has listed on its goals the implementation of personalized learning over the next 5 to 10 years. Coincidentally, I picked up *The Child-Centered School: An Appraisal of the New Education* by Harold Rugg and Ann Shumaker (1928) for my graduate program around the same time I was reading *Learning Personalized: The Evolution of the Contemporary Classroom* by Alison Zmuda, Greg Curtis, and Diane Ullman (2015) for my school district. The relevance of Rugg and Shumaker's work was simultaneously thrilling and disheartening. How is it that this book published in 1928 with rich discussion and visions for curriculum, student choice, and child-centered education has not only failed to revolutionize our school systems but appears to chronicle the same journey on which I'm embarking with my school district almost 100 years later?

Every new teacher has had "that conversation." It's when the rookie teacher is talking with a veteran—not in the teacher's lounge, of course; all new teachers know to avoid the teachers' lounge by now. No, this is the time that, just prior to the conversation between rookie and veteran, administrators have rolled out a brand new initiative that sounds exciting and falls right into the "What's Best for Kids" bucket. The new teacher leaves the meeting energized and willing to tackle the challenges of the new initiative. She even sends her administrator a quick email to say how excited and grateful she is to work for a school that is on the cutting edge of what students need. This is when that conversation occurs. It's when the veteran teacher rolls her eyes and points out it's the same thing the school tried 5 or 10 years ago but packaged with a different buzz-wordy title. Disheartened and annoyed, the rookie retaliates with an equally exasperated eye roll. It's just what she thought that crotchety veteran would say; the rookie shakes it off, assuming the veteran is cynical, jaded, and maybe even a bit lazy. That conversation will be long forgotten when 5 or 10 years later the once-rookie stands in the hallway bemoaning the school's most recent but vaguely familiar initiative with new hoops through which the teachers must jump. Is this the story of personalized learning? Let's hope not.

In order for today's educators to truly and effectively push forward with personalized learning for students, a careful analysis of its predecessor, the child-centered schools movement, is important. By understanding the vision and work of child-centered schools, personalized learning might just have that sticky-staying power that will prevent it from being the next fad veteran teachers lament in the hallway with rookies.

Defining what is meant by personalized learning is as important as it is challenging. There are many different visions, ideas, and definitions floating around today's schools about what personalized learning really is. It is useful to arrive at a concise definition to understand personalization in light of its predecessor, child-centered schools. As defined by Allison Zmuda et al. (2015), personalized learning "is a progressively student-driven model in which students deeply engage in meaningful, authentic, and rigorous challenges to demonstrate desired outcomes" (p. 7). Among other facets, the authors imagined personalized learning could be accomplished by customizing learning experiences to students' interests, creating collaborative classrooms "where students *own* the learning process," connecting learners to experts and audiences, and fostering resilient learners who overcome obstacles (Zmuda et al., 2015, p. 6). In an executive summary for *Students at the Center*, Yonezawa et al. (2012), astutely recognized that personalized learning begins with a student-centered approach to education. That student-centered approach is fundamentally a "web of positive relationships . . . to promote learning" (p. 1). For Yonezawa et al., "the idea is that educators get to know their students well—not just their abilities and learning styles but also their interests and motivations—and they use this personal knowledge to design more effective individualized instruction and guidance and help students feel competent in and connected to the world" (p. 1). Any student of curriculum can see that the principles of personalized learning, then, are nothing new.

Though there were many educational and social components that led to the progressivist movement and beyond, it's useful to examine the 10 years which preceded the publishing of Rugg and Shumaker's *The Child-Centered School*. Many were disillusioned by the social efficiency movement which anchored so much of America's schools at the turn of the 20th century. Like progressivist educator John Dewey, William Heard Kilpatrick (1918) worried that the social efficiency movement would produce "selfish individualists" (p. 334). Kilpatrick published the "Project Method" in 1918 which claimed "that although it was acceptable for the child to adopt the teacher's suggestion as his or her own, it was preferable for children to have practice in all four steps or aspects of any given project: purpose, planning, executing, and judging" (Pinar, 2002, p. 115). The project method quickly became both a method and a theory of curriculum development (Pinar, 2002, p. 115). In 1919, the Association for the Advancement of Progressive Education formed (Pinar, 2002, p. 110). Important tenets of the association related specifically to child-centered schools and today's personalization movement included "interest should be the motive of all work"; and "the teacher is a guide, not a task-master" (Pinar, 2002, p. 111). Despite the possible benefits of progressivism, private and public schools struggled to sustain effective progressive education models for both political and practical reasons; politically the progressivists struggled to overcome social efficiency theorists, and practically progressive schools were falling prey to harsh criticisms (Pinar, 2002, p. 119).

Published in 1928, *The Child-Centered School: An Appraisal of the New Education* by Harold Rugg and Ann Shumaker turned a critical eye on the increasingly popularized child-centered schools of the day. Rugg writes in the foreword that "tolerant understanding and creative self-expression—the two great aims of the new education" are the "two criteria on which [Rugg and Shumaker will] appraise the child-centered schools" (Rugg & Shumaker, 1928, p. ix). To be clear, Rugg and Shumaker were believers in child-centered schooling. Yet it was their fervent belief in the child-centered school that led them to turn a critical eye on the movement, with hopes that the schooling model would be sharpened, improved, and ultimately would endure as a model of school for students. Rather than expound on the entirety of *The Child-Centered School*—which is a worthy read, indeed—it is most useful to begin with a celebration of its criticism of child-centered schools followed by carefully extrapolating relevant tenets so educators today can ensure that personalized learning is not just another fad.

Rugg and Shumaker, in part, offered their appraisal of child-centered schools because they believed this kind of schooling was the inevitable—and good—future of education. Even though there were previous tweaks to schooling before child-centered schools, Rugg and Shumaker (1928) argued that "practically every innovation was an attack upon the surface, an attempt at administrative rearrangement, not at fundamental reconstruction" (p. 12). They pushed deeper by saying, "not once from the signing of the American constitution to the present time has the school caught up with American life" (p. 12). My point here is this: Rugg and Shumaker were not fervent believers in child-centered schools because it was the next new "thing" that happened to be defensible. Rugg and Shumaker believed in child-centered schools because they equally believed traditional schools were detrimental to educating children.

I don't remember with precision the moment or its circumstances, but I do have a vague memory that has stayed with me for many years. The details of the memory I do have are as follows: I come home from a high school basketball practice my senior year, aggravated with our new coach who seemed to be yelling at and criticizing me more than anyone else on the team, and more than anyone had ever criticized me. I knew I was not a perfect basketball player. I had always loved playing basketball, but unfortunately my talent was not in direct proportion to my affection for the game. On this particular evening, I was standing in the kitchen while my parents prepared dinner when they asked how practice was. Frustrated and dejected, I told them our new coach was being too hard on me. I reminded them that I never got yelled at like this by last year's coach. That's when *they* reminded *me* that I never got off the bench with last year's coach, either. With our new coach, I was a starter. I don't remember which of my parents said it, but one of them said something like, "Lauren, if Coach didn't care about how you played, he wouldn't waste his time getting on you. If Coach gets quiet, you need to get worried. The more he yells at you, the more he cares." *These people are crazy. They get on me all the time, too, and now they're just using this as a way to get away with yelling at me*, I thought. But of course, you and I know they were right.

Criticism seems to be a lost art in today's world, in many respects. Society has plenty of examples of those who criticize for the purpose of tearing down, ostracizing, or stamping out altogether. One is hard-pressed to recall examples of public criticism that are transparent and vulnerable, that come from a place of deep care with a genuine desire to improve. This kind of criticism was the work of Harold Rugg and Ann Shumaker (1928) in *The Child-Centered School.* The final paragraph of the book's introduction is a thoughtful articulation of their work: "We launch upon our task of description and sympathetic criticism. The new education has had an abundance of episodic exposition, especially of the casual retrospective type. More than all else it needs critique. That is the chief task we have set ourselves in this book" (p. 10). With this in mind, Rugg and Shumaker succeeded at this task. With sharp rebuke of "traditional schooling," they carefully and thoughtfully advocated for new education as a necessary endeavor. Because they believed it was a necessary endeavor, they also extrapolated the many ways in which new education had been unintentionally perverted or ineffectual. What makes Rugg and Shumaker "sympathetic" critics of new education? They not only sought to understand how it went off course, they offered pathways to get it back on track. They did not criticize what was currently being done at the time and leave those schools to figure it out for themselves (which is, perhaps, how they ended up where they were anyway).

After a lengthy chapter describing the state of child-centered schools, Rugg and Shumaker (1928) concluded: "We are confronted, however, by one important fact. We are in the midst of a vigorous and widespread re-form movement in education. The second stage in the educational revolu-tion is thoroughly launched. There is no going back now" (p. 53). In my first reading of the book, I was so struck by this statement I highlighted and scribbled in the margin, "Really? But didn't we?" Rugg and Shumaker's optimism toward the future of education only makes the reality of today's personalized learning movement even more upsetting. Rugg and Shumak-er believed there was no going back, but today's educators are drafting the same concerns about schools. Using Rugg and Shumaker's model of sympa-thetic criticism is an important part of ensuring that personalized learning is the next *iteration* of education, not just an *initiative.*

Proponents of personalized learning rest firmly on the premise that stu-dents need more control over their learning. The recognition that students need more control is likely an evolution of the standardization movement. Educators today are deep in the trenches of standardized learning repre-sented by Common Core, an attempt to standardize national curriculum. With the standardization movement came the accountability and testing movement. While the two movements need not be inextricably linked, it is easy to understand the natural evolution from common curriculum to stan-dardized tests or vice versa as a way of comparing student achievement on normed content standards. As a result of standardized test fatigue, it should come as no surprise that many educators are crying out for more autonomy for both themselves and their students.

Yet there are a number of educators concerned that personalized learn-ing means tailoring education to an individual child's needs and interests. Can students really choose what they want to learn? Benjamin Riley (2017), in "Personalization vs. How People Learn" worried about letting students "have it their way" (p. 70). In addition to his scientific appeal that personal-ized learning works contrary to what we know about long- and short-term memory, Riley (2017) expressed concerns about the content students learn:

> Defenders of personalized learning might counter by arguing that if students are allowed to explore what fascinates them through good resources on the Internet, they might be more motivated to commit facts about that subject to long-term memory. There are at least three problems with this notion. First, it's often difficult to discern what makes something a "good" Internet resource versus an untrustworthy source. Second, the process of searching for information is not, in and of itself, an effective strategy for committing that information to long-term memory. Think back to the term papers you wrote in college—how many facts from these exercises can you recall now? Finally, I believe every practicing educator can affirm that what students find fascinat-ing on the Internet tends toward social media and messaging with friends rather than the subject matter of lessons. (p. 69)

In a less damning but equally cautious article on personalized learning called "Let's Celebrate Personalization: But Not Too Fast" by Carol Ann Tomlinson (2017), the concern about curriculum is raised but with a bit more nuance. Tomlinson wrote, "It's unwise to select an instructional direction without clarity about how compatible that direction is with local understandings about the nature of curriculum. Instruction is a means of enacting curriculum. It works in service of a curriculum, and the match between the goals and the means of achieving those goals is critical" (p. 12). But the battle for balance between students' choice in curriculum and predetermined content is not something new to schools at all.

A prevalent criticism of child-centered schools was that students had too much freedom and control of what they were learning, and that relying on spontaneous activities did not actually teach students enough of what they ought to know. Rugg and Shumaker (1928), after surveying hundreds of schools nationwide, admitted "the evidence is convincing that [child-centered schools] have erred in unwillingness to define in advance and to provide systematically for the intellectual outcomes of their activities. The problem is very important and very difficult" (p. 125). Schools must find a balance. If the answer to curriculum is not relying on total student freedom and choice, it probably isn't curriculum that is totally controlled either. "The new schools are laudably uninterested in teaching isolated facts," wrote Rugg and Shumaker (1928, p. 125). Though today's educator may wish to dismiss this portion of the book, believing it irrelevant in a world where students hold powerful computers in their pockets, it may be worth exploring more deeply. Riley (2017) argued that "the principles of personalized learning conflict with some basic principles of cognitive science" (p. 68). To bolster this claim, Riley (2017) elaborated on the cognitive science and argued that students should not have control over what they learn, explaining that "the relationship between working memory and long-term memory should make us deeply skeptical of" giving students control over what they learn (p. 70).

Rugg and Shumaker (1928) conceded that *some* planning and forethought in curriculum development were important. But they resist the full pendulum swing of teaching those isolated facts that are usually not relevant or meaningful to students. Rugg and Shumaker (1928) were confident that the balance could be found by the school determining important and relevant concepts ahead of time: "The curriculum cannot be planned for effective growth unless the relative importance of these in human living is determined" (p. 127). With careful consideration of what students need to know for their contemporary society, schools can carefully develop units of study—overarching understandings which help students situate themselves in society as a whole. Rugg and Shumaker (1928) "do not propose to determine in advance the details of the specific units of work. [They] do propose, however, to have a large array of units, analyzed in advance for their ideational possibilities, their concept-developing power; to determine what relationships of cause and effect may reasonably be expected to appear from participation in them" (p. 126). The concern over balance and curriculum is just as fervent today as it was when Rugg and Shumaker wrote *The Child-Centered School.*

If we can agree that there ought to be a balance between students' ownership of what they learn and a predetermined course of study that illuminates important skills and concepts for students, then the next key player in the child-centered school and personalized learning is the teacher. If we can determine the teacher's role, then we can better understand the form and function of curriculum from there. There is no question that the role of a teacher changes in a child-centered or personalized approach to education. Equally, there is no question that the teacher *has* a role—a vital one, at that—to play in the classroom. Rugg and Shumaker (1928) used a case study to recognize the impact of a teacher's "expert guidance." In understanding the essential role of a teacher in the classroom, members of the child-centered schools movement as well as the personalized learning movement would agree. Rugg and Shumaker posed a series of questions to illuminate the possibilities of teaching using this approach: "Can the stage be set so that pupils will recognize those problems which are suggested by the teacher as of enough importance to stimulate whole-hearted effort and thus to bring about intense and broadly integrated learning?" They concluded, "The need for expert guidance, therefore, is very great" (p. 109). Likewise, Zmuda et al. (2015) argued that "the ultimate intention of moving along the Personalized Learning Evolution is to have students believe that the work they are doing matters" (p. 107). Rugg and Shumaker pointed out, "It was the teacher's questions which directed the pupils' thinking" (p. 109). Here it becomes clear that the role of the teacher as guide is paramount. Students are not to be left to flounder through school learning only what happens to be accessible to them. Rather, teachers are to expertly guide students toward learning outcomes that are both personally relevant and meaningful.

To further examine the role of the teacher in a child-centered classroom, it is particularly helpful to look at the ways in which Rugg and Shumaker (1928) described the work of the teacher. These descriptions include the following phrases: "It was her foresight. It was the teacher's planning in advance... It was her insight... It was the teacher's guidance..." (p. 109). The teacher is carefully considering both the understandings at which students need to arrive, and the students themselves to determine how they will arrive at those understandings. Rugg and Shumaker believed

> that an important force behind the organization and development of these
> units of work is the teacher's judgment of what is real to the pupils. Selective

discrimination must be employed, for, after all, the school must maintain its role as an educational institution. (p. 110)

The teacher is not an autocrat in utter control of the information disseminated to students in the classroom, but they are not mere chaperones of learning either.

In their effort to define the teacher's role in schools, Rugg and Shumaker (1928) turned to several teachers they interviewed in their research for the book. In their case for creative arts in schools—and the kinds of artists schools should employ as art teachers—Rugg and Shumaker wrote:

> Hence a teacher, instead of being an encyclopedia or a force pump, must, in the words of Peppino Mangravite, become "a person who is clairvoyant, who is able to penetrate the mind and soul of a child. A teacher must comprehend what the child wants to do . . . He must never interfere with the child's mental image by telling him how to begin. The idea—the mental picture—must be the child's. Once he is started, a teacher can help him." (p. 229)

However, this description could aptly apply to any teacher in schools, not just the one who teaches artistic expression; this kind of teacher is of particular importance when students have the most exhaustive and dynamic encyclopedias with them in their pockets every day.

Advocates of personalized learning understand that the role of the teacher shifts from the traditional "sage on a stage" to a more dynamic, relationally-based partnership with students. Zmuda et al. (2015), in describing how the teacher's role changes, explained,

> We grow our partnerships with students as they have a greater stake in the development of the tasks. We deliberately expand student voice and choice in task creation, timely feedback and opportunity to take action, sharing and enlarging the target audience, and taking stock of the accomplishments to consider future goals. (p. 95)

In a recent joint report called "The Shifting Paradigm of Teaching: Personalized Learning According to Teachers" (Jenkins et al., 2016) published by Knowledge Works and National Commission on Teaching and America's Future, the authors claimed that teaching should shift from practice-based education—that is, education that "values standardizing inputs for standardized outputs"—to knowledge-based instruction (p. 6). Furthermore, Jenkins et al. (2016) argued that, in a personalized learning environment,

> teachers must facilitate the transition to student ownership through projects and activities that help students understand and assess metacognitive skills,

standards, and learning targets. They also guide students to the appropriate resources and continually monitor and respond to students' data. (p. 6)

Thus, proponents of personalized learning are not sidelining teachers. Like Rugg and Shumaker, today's experts envision the teacher's role changing but with no less importance. Good, effective teachers remain the crux of the classroom.

If the notions of student-centered approaches to learning persist, but without fundamental adoption, how do we maximize the opportunity the personalized learning movement presents to schools today? How do we make sure the fundamental premise of personalized learning, like customizing education to maximize students' engagement and learning, sticks?

Before I discuss ways for schools to make sure personalized learning perseveres beyond a buzzwordy initiative into the next iteration of education, let me take a step back for a moment. It's clear that personalized learning is not a new idea for instructional design. Educators 100 years ago were advocating for the kind of learning personalized learning provides. Why is it so important for personalized learning to stick around? Why do we need an overhaul of traditional schooling? Rather than worry about why it was important 100 years ago, let's just focus on today's students. Why do our students need personalized learning? According to Zmuda et al. (2015) there are two important ways in which personalized learning is needed. First, "personalized learning is a better way to attain current learning outcomes ... [it] allows for deeper, more lasting learning in an engaging and relevant environment" (p. 7). Second, "personalized learning is a better way to grow children ... personalized learning is the best way we know to grow these people into the best versions of themselves, with all of the skills and mindsets needed to succeed and contribute to our shared future" (Zmuda et al., 2015, p. 7). Without delving into pedagogical and curricular details, personalized learning is fundamentally about focusing on the growth and development of each individual child in the classroom, not just as academic performers but as whole children. I could drop statistics of dropout rates; student, teacher, and parent dissatisfaction; the changing economy; low voter turnout; and a multitude of other facts to build a case for why personalized learning is important. Yet I don't think that's necessary. Schools and all of the people in them are working hard. People are doing the best they can. I don't want to spend time highlighting those statistics and painting an abysmal picture of education today, because that simply isn't the case. Exciting things are happening in schools, regardless of whether they include models of personalized learning.

But fundamentally, personalized learning is a child-centered approach to education that does not focus only on academic performance. We want personalized learning to stick around because we want to keep our students at the center of education—not test scores, not government policies, not even the economy. We want to develop people into their best selves. As long as personalized learning stays laser focused on the growth and development of the whole child as an individual, we want personalized learning to stick around. So how do we make sure it happens?

THREE WAYS TO ENSURE PERSONALIZED LEARNING IS EDUCATION'S NEXT ITERATION, NOT INITIATIVE

Personalized Learning Starts With Professional Development

If we expect teachers to radically shift their roles in their classrooms effectively—and to persevere through the inevitable challenges of change processes—we must provide ample and adequate professional development to help them successfully shift their classrooms. That teachers receive professional development for the purpose of cultivating personalized learning in their work with students is not enough. Let's take a moment to consider the implicit condescension of teacher professionalism that occurs when we implore teachers to empower students with more autonomy, more flexibility, and more trust, but then turn around and demand our teachers "sit and get" their professional development from the same place in the same seats nailed to the floor. Before we expect our teachers to maximize student learning by tailoring instruction for individual students, schools and their leaders must tailor professional development to suit the needs of individual teachers.

In Daniel Pink's TEDTalk about motivation, Pink (2009) argued against businesses using rewards and punishments to motivate employees. According to Pink, rewards and incentives might be effective for simple tasks but for complex tasks, the model does not improve employee performance and, in some cases, even harms it. Pink presented an alternative model for employee motivation, which he called "a new operating system" based on three concepts: autonomy, mastery, and purpose. Pink defined autonomy as "the urge to direct our own lives"; "mastery as the desire to get better and better at something that matters"; and "purpose as the yearning to do what we do in service of something larger than ourselves." If we want to motivate teachers to do their best in the classroom, we must engage them with personalized professional development. This means that teachers ought to have choice and voice in their professional development, teachers should be able to learn in flexible environments and at flexible paces, and school leaders ought to be learning guides for teachers rather than top–down task-masters. The school leader's role should reflect at a macro level the teacher's role shift that occurs at the microlevel in the classroom. Administrators should be instructional leaders who partner together with the teacher to provide meaningful coaching and professional development. Personalized professional development should be the number one priority of schools to provide to teachers; even for teachers—perhaps even *especially* for teachers—who are reluctant to embrace personalized learning for their students, the experience of effective personalized professional development will naturally evolve the teachers' work with students.

Technology Is a Tool, Not a Talisman

It is important to note that technology is purposefully absent in my previous discussion of child-centered schools and contemporary personalized learning. In order for us to effectively and efficiently personalize learning, we would be remiss to ignore the power and possibilities technology affords. However, technology in and of itself is not the magic force behind effectively personalizing learning. Like Will Richardson (2013) argued in "Students First, Not Stuff," "Few people seem to understand that the web and the technologies that drive it are more than just vehicles for delivering the traditional curriculum more effectively as measured by those assessments" (p. 10). Too often schools fail to harness the power of technology.

In years past, the primary technology goal was for schools to increase students' access to personal technology devices. Now that most students at least carry one in their pockets, the focus should shift from access to pedagogical use of technology. If we think that we are leveraging technology in a pedagogically rich way because students are typing their essays on a laptop instead of using a pencil on paper, then we have seriously fooled ourselves. Instead, what we have is a $300 pencil at our students' fingertips. Furthermore, access to technology is not the end-all for education. It has been previously well established that the teacher plays an integral role in the child-centered, personalized learning classroom. We cannot relegate teaching to computers; technology cannot supplant the teacher. Furthermore, in the spirit of personalized learning, we should always keep in mind that there is not a one-size-fits-all model for anything—including technology. Technology is not the magic of a personalized learning environment. Rather, it is a tool that teachers and students can leverage. But the magic of the classroom is the network of democratic, egalitarian relationships fostered between and among teachers, students, and even those outside the classroom.

Advocates for personalized learning would be remiss to assume that technology is the talisman for effectively implementing and sustaining personalized learning; and it would be equally foolish to deny the potential that technology offers to teachers and students alike. Schools should carefully consider the role that technology plays in personalized learning. Just like effective personalized learning environments will have models of curriculum to guide learning with opportunities for nuance and tailoring, so too should the role of technology be nuanced and tailored to the needs and interests of learners in the classroom. Getting technology right will be key to ensuring that personalized learning is not a fad that flickers as quickly as the next social media craze.

The Walls Must Fall

If we do not want to lose personalized learning to the next buzzword initiative, the classroom walls must both literally and symbolically fall. We must be willing to concede that it is possible that learning takes place outside of the four-walled cinder block classrooms we have built. Casting vision for purposeful spaces is more important here than prescribing a blueprint for school architects. Schools should carefully consider their purpose and values and craft flexible work spaces that meet the needs of their students. Look to innovative corporate offices, for some ideas. Notice that even the most innovative corporations have still tailored their environments to best fit the values and culture of the company. Innovative schools need not look exactly like. Furthermore, we must be willing to embrace a more dynamic vision for how learning occurs. The "classroom" is no longer a place with a teacher standing at a chalkboard in the front of the room, desks nailed down to the floor in neat rows. The classroom is where learning takes place, wherever that may be.

In addition to literally changing the physical confines of the classroom, for personalized learning to endure we must see classroom walls symbolically fall. The single, most fundamental premise of personalized learning is a network of democratic relationships. For teachers and students alike to be successful, their relational networks must be rich, democratic, dynamic, and global. If we want to see personalized learning truly become the next iteration of education, we must see schools foster partnerships with entities outside of their physical school and outside of the educational industry altogether. If teachers are going to liberate themselves from being content experts who deliver a set of rudimentary facts, they must be willing to point students to practicing content-area experts. (I refuse to use the term "real-word" here and instead am in favor of "practicing." If school is done right, it doesn't just mimic the real world, students and teachers are acutely aware that they are a part of the real world.) When students are studying physics, they need to be able to connect with a practicing physicist. When students are trying to solve an environmental problem, they need to be able to connect with organizations, locations, and people outside of the confines of the school building.

SUMMARY

At the center of today's traditional schooling is teaching, a noble calling which requires a balance of technical skills and artistry. But teaching cannot be the center of our schools; learning must be. Whether we call it child-centered schooling, progressive education, personalized learning, or something else entirely, we must remember that each student's education is the moral imperative of our schools. With this in mind, we cannot allow the personalized learning movement to pervert into prescribed technologies nor can we let it combust under the pressures of political policies. We must stay committed to each individual child in our school, and we must persist in guiding them deep into meaningful learning.

For personalized learning to persist despite (sometimes in spite of) the next government initiative or lucrative scheme, we must carefully plan for the implementation and evolution of personalized learning. But most important, we must stay laser focused on each individual student's learning. Like the progressive educators who built child-centered schools nearly 100 years ago, today's educators recognize that teaching is not the most important thing happening in the classroom. Learning is. Effective schools will make learning both the means *and* the end.

REFERENCES

Jenkins, S., Williams, M., Moyer, J., George, M., & Foster, E. (2016). *The shifting paradigm of teaching: Personalized learning according to teachers.* KnowledgeWorks; National Commission on Teaching & America's Future.

Kilpatrick, W. (1918). The project method. *Teachers College Record, 19*(4), 319–335.

Pinar, W. F. (2002). *Understanding curriculum: An introduction to the study of historical and contemporary curriculum discourses.* Peter Lang.

Pink, D. (2009, July). *The puzzle of motivation* [Video]. TED Conferences. https://www.ted.com/talks/dan_pink_the_puzzle_of_motivation

Richardson, W. (2013). Students first, not stuff. *Educational Leadership, 70*(6), 10–14.

Riley, B. (2017). Personalization vs. how people learn. *Educational Leadership, 74*(6), 68–72.

Rugg, H., & Shumaker, A. (1928). *The child-centered school: An appraisal of the new education.* World Book Company.

Tomlinson, C. (2017). Let's celebrate personalization: But not too fast. *Educational Leadership, 74*(6), 10–15.

Yonezawa, S., McClure, L., & Jones, M. (2012). *Personalization in schools: The students at the center series.* Students at the Center. https://create.ucsd.edu/_files/publications/Personalization%20in%20Schools.pdf

Zmuda, A., Curtis, G., & Ullman, D. (2015). *Learning personalized: The evolution of the contemporary classroom.* John Wiley & Sons, Inc.

CHAPTER 7

SCHOLARSHIP RECONSIDERED

The Art of Teaching

Craig Myers

Author/Book studied:

Boyer, E. (1990). *Scholarship reconsidered: Priorities of the profes-soriate*. The Carnegie Foundation for the Advancement of Teaching.

We've all been there before on the first day of class, sitting through the presentation of a professor who seems knowledgeable and qualified but unable to connect with the students in the room. Your intuition told you before she referenced the first line in the syllabus that she is a researcher at heart, but not necessarily prepared to share the wealth of knowledge accumulated. This individual doesn't lack passion for the subject; she just doesn't know how to share it with the students sitting in an undergraduate

Curriculum Windows Redux, pages 79–91
Copyright © 2022 by Information Age Publishing
www.infoagepub.com
79

class. Ernest Boyer's (1990) *Scholarship Reconsidered: Priorities of the Professoriate* tackles the functions of the professoriate and how professors have become more heavily focused on research resulting in a lack of attention paid to teaching. Boyer provides highlights of the history of the professoriate and describes four roles he feels the professoriate must adopt to remain essential today. Boyer's feelings about the professoriate are qualified by the results he shares from a survey of professors across the nation. *Scholarship Reconsidered* concludes with a call to arms for the professoriate to stay relevant. Staying relevant in an ever-changing dynamic world is a concern for the professoriate and always has been. Throughout the book it is easy to recognize Boyer's personal feelings about service, community, and the importance of connecting with future scholars in order for the professoriate to have a meaningful impact.

Boyer's (1990) book is a significant contribution to the field of education and curriculum because it forces higher education to examine what has been its focus in recent history and how that has impacted the professoriate which has other unintended consequences. The unintended consequence of an undergraduate not receiving the full benefit of a higher education and how that will impact society and the future of our country is a compelling argument for a recalibration of the professoriate. Boyer's approach to this topic is one that can be adopted for all areas of education. We need to ask at all levels, "What historical forces have led to the current state of education and how can we return to a greater emphasis on teaching?" I believe this book calls educators to embrace the other three R's that all levels of education must embody: rigor, relevance, and relationships. All educators must be reflective and examine the quality of what they are providing as well as producing for the greater good. Educational options continue to increase making it even more important for educators to be reflective about what they offer students, society, and the country. In a digital age of increasing connectivity, but potentially superficial connections, all educators must not devalue the importance of genuine relationships with their students. Ernest Boyer did not use the terms rigor, relevance, and relationships as a metaphor for his work in *Scholarship Reconsidered*, but the argument he proposes runs parallel with this focus. This argument of a service-focused professoriate has roots in Boyer's personal history.

Ernest Boyer was born in 1928 in Dayton, Ohio, a year before the stock market crash that would lead to the great depression. One of the most influential people during his early life was his grandfather, William Boyer. Ernest would learn about being people focused through the dedication to service displayed by William. This dedication to service can be seen throughout the different positions he held after completing his doctorate.

Boyer received his doctorate in speech pathology and audiology from the University of Southern California in 1957. Boyer began teaching speech pathology and audiology at Upland College in California and by 1960 took a leadership role as the director of the Commission to Improve the Education of Teachers at the Western College Association. By 1965, Boyer would take a role at the State University of New York (SUNY). While chancellor of SUNY, Boyer created the rank of "Distinguished Teaching Professor" (Bucher & Williams, 1995). Boyer emphasized the importance of teaching and learning and would also stress a sense of community during his leadership at SUNY. He remained at SUNY until he was asked by President Carter to become the U.S. Commissioner of Education in 1977. As a reformer during his time as U.S. Commissioner on Education, Boyer would focus on closing the achievement gap for those in poverty. Boyer would then take a position at the Carnegie Foundation for the Advancement of Teaching in 1979, where his top priority was on the relationship between high schools and higher education. Boyer would recommend the adoption of a core curriculum in 1983 based on the results from his study *High School: A Report on Secondary Education in America.* In 1987 Boyer would publish his concerns about how college professors were focused more on research than on teaching in *College: The Undergraduate Experience in America.* In his publications and his work leading to *Scholarship Reconsidered,* the recurring theme is that good teaching, strong community, and relationships will lead to great results.

SCHOLARSHIP RECONSIDERED: PRIORITIES OF THE PROFESSORIATE

Higher education and the professoriate have continuously changed through time and Boyer (1990) provides a brief 350-year timeline highlighting the ebb and flow that brings us to the 1990s. Boyer provides this historical examination to show how the professoriate adapted to the needs of society throughout history in America. There are three specific phases that Boyer provides historical context to: the colonial college, nation building, and research. The "colonial age" marks the first colleges in America, which in large part mimicked the model found in British colleges. The intent of the college was to produce students of great character who would be able to lead the citizenry especially as clergy and in business. Morality and spiritual development took precedence over scholarly achievement. The professoriate was considered a calling and those that entered it did so given their religious commitment, not necessarily their scholarly aptitude.

Boyer (1990) describes the "nation building" phase of higher education as America moves into the 1800s. America was in need of a more scholarly professoriate as the nation grew. The need for workers with the ability to propel America's emerging industrial economy and agricultural needs became the focus of the professoriate. The idea of educating students with a focus on serving the country through their newly acquired technical skills was the central theme during this nation building time period. The Land Grant College Act of 1862 and the Hatch Act of 1887 incentivized colleges to further produce students who would help further our agricultural industry. Others classified this focus as a weakening of academic standards, and did not accept the "common man" attending college.

The idea that the professoriate would further the knowledge of scientific fields was not always considered higher education's responsibility. The focus on research by the professoriate also emerges in the 1800s. A transition was taking place from "faith in authority to reliance on scientific interaction" (Boyer, 1990, p. 8). This transition would usher in the modern "research" focus of higher education that Boyer feels has become too heavily weighted.

Boyer (1990) writes:

> By the late nineteenth century the advancement of knowledge through research had taken firm root in American higher education, and colonial college values, which emphasized teaching undergraduates, began to lose ground to the new university that was emerging. (p. 9)

Colleges also began to grow their graduate course offerings increasing the number of graduate and doctoral degree opportunities for students. As we enter the 1900s, historical events such as the great depression and world wars would result in the government looking to colleges to provide stability and answers to key problems through the use of science. The most dramatic redefining role of colleges would come from Harry S. Truman's Commission on Higher Education in 1947. The report emphasized that college should be the pursuit of all of the citizenry and that all children and adults should carry their education as far as possible. As the number of colleges and professors grew, the focus on research would increase. The professoriate found an increased emphasis on research and being published if they wanted to secure tenure. While more students entered college, the professoriate began to focus less on their relationship with undergraduates. The context of teaching being thought of as a calling and the focus on producing a moral citizenry of great character were becoming secondary to research.

WHAT DOES SCHOLARSHIP MEAN?

"Scholars are academics who conduct research, publish, and then perhaps convey their knowledge to students or apply what they have learned" (Boyer, 1990, p. 15). Boyer (1990) contends that we must reevaluate the focus of the professoriate. Through the use of a national survey of faculty, Boyer highlights how the professoriate agrees with redefining their job responsibilities. The survey results provide insight into how the pressure to research and publish are the primary concerns. The expectation to research and publish is of primary concern as well when looking at the evaluation systems of higher education. Higher education has deemed that the only way to reach tenure is through research and publication in many colleges and universities. Boyer proceeds to describe four specific functions that scholarship should include in addition to the current focus on research. These four areas should be given consideration in order to provide a healthy balance to the professoriate and higher education. The four specific scholarships include: discovery, integration, application, and teaching.

DISCOVERY

The function most associated with where our professoriate finds its current focus is the scholarship of discovery. The scholarship of discovery is the pursuit of knowledge, the commitment to academic growth, and the lifeblood of an educational institution. Without the research contributions of our colleges and universities many of the advancements in the past 100 years across all of the fields would not exist. The scholarship of discovery not only invigorates scholars and students on a college campus but also advances the growth of our society.

INTEGRATION

Closely linked to discovery is the scholarship of integration, which is the ability to take knowledge gained from research and apply it across disciplines and a larger perspective. This function takes what was learned from research and asks, "What does it mean?" "Interdisciplinary, interpretive, and integrative" (Boyer, 1990, p. 21) are noted as the scholarly trends of integration. Boyer (1990) confronts the age-old question asked by every student, "Why do I need to learn this and how will this help me in the career I want?" Along with answering this question Boyer insists that the professoriate must communicate with colleagues across fields in an effort to find meaning that may not have been apparent in the department where the original research was conducted.

APPLICATION

Taking a theory and making it a practice is the simplest way to understand the scholarship of application. Though this is a simple premise, it is one that Boyer (1990) contends the professoriate has rejected. Academic pursuits now take precedent over service or application. Boyer contends that the scholarship of application is increasingly important given the complexity of problems that the world faces each new day. The professoriate must be concerned with academic content that can be applied to real world problems. Being able to apply what is being taught will also lead to further academic understanding.

TEACHING

The scholarship of teaching is often one that does not receive the credit it deserves given a lack of understanding about what is involved. Boyer contends that teaching cannot be the last priority of the professoriate. Boyer (1990) explains how great teachers "stimulate active, not passive, learning and encourage students to be critical, creative thinkers, with the capacity to go on learning after their college days are over" (p. 25). Great teachers not only transmit information but also push their students and themselves to extend their understanding. Great teachers inspire their students and continue scholarship beyond their classroom.

EXPECTATIONS OF THE PROFESSORIATE

Boyer is clear that research is critical to remaining professionally alive, but a balance of expectations for the professoriate needs to be reexamined. The expectation to publish research findings on a regular basis is of great concern based on Boyer's *National Survey of Faculty*, 1989. Boyer emphasizes that not all staff should be expected to publish and that the increased pressure to publish can dilute the quality of the research or even result in plagiarism. A need for excellence in research and publication is critical and should replace the current priority of quantity of publications. But the system exists due to the reward systems in place at colleges.

Professors pursuing tenure work in a field in which publishing is rewarded, may result in placing a lesser importance on teaching. The importance in publishing can be linked to its inclusion in the process for receiving tenure and evaluations. Faculty evaluations need to be broader in scope of how they measure the professoriate. Boyer proposes that there are other ways we can measure the intellectual contributions of the professoriate to the institution. Faculty should be allowed to include a record of the ways in which they have applied their knowledge. We must also reconsider the evaluation model to emphasize the importance of teaching as equal to research. Boyer proposes the creation of a flexible evaluation model that is not stagnant; he calls this the "creativity contract" (Boyer, 1990, p. 51). This evaluation model can contain different options to choose from for professional growth. The goal is to provide faculty with the opportunity to grow in the profession regardless of their experience in addition to including a minimum expectation for teaching, research, and service.

IN SEARCH OF PRESTIGE

In an effort for colleges and universities to gain more notoriety, they copied the strategies of older more established institutions. Specifically, colleges looked to improve their status in the academic community by focusing heavily on research. With more colleges pursuing this recognition they became more alike than different. The uniqueness and character of these academic institutions began to fade as they all pursued the same recognition. In pursuit of status, they also jeopardized their purpose of being a student-focused institution that enabled undergraduates to grow. Boyer (1990) contends that higher education must maintain a diversity of programs that make each of them unique while still focusing on the lifeblood of education, teaching.

If teaching is not at the heart of higher education, these institutions will be lessening their value. Who will carry on the torch of research and teaching to inspire the next generation? What will be the quality of the next generation of scholars? There is a concern that the next generation of professoriates will not be able to connect with students or with colleagues across disciplines. Furthermore, we see Boyer's (1990) focus on service in his belief that the professoriate must extend its focus beyond the classroom. Faculty members must be civically engaged on campus and attentive to the current issues of our time. "If the nation's colleges and universities cannot help students see beyond themselves and better understand the independent nature of our world, each new generation's capacity to live responsibly will be dangerously diminished" (p. 77). Boyer contends that the professoriate must transform in order to maintain the vitality of scholarship and ultimately to contribute positively to society.

I believe Boyer's (1990) description of the focus of higher education and the professoriate to be insightful and accurate based on when it was published. Boyer is not providing a scathing critique of higher education but is deeply concerned with the direction that the professoriate, students, community, and potentially the nation are heading. The current path that higher education is on due to the expectations of the professoriate needs to be changed. The survey data provided in the book is referenced at various times to reinforce his thesis of how the expectations of the professoriate have become out of kilter and need to be reexamined.

CURRICULUM WINDOW

There are two different windows or insights I find myself drawn to after reading *Scholarship Reconsidered* (Boyer, 1990). I am writing this from the perspective of a professional educator at the high school level and as someone who is concerned about the focus and perception of education in K–16. First, Boyer's (1990) scholarship of application and teaching are of the greatest importance to the future undergraduate. Second, Boyer's focus on reexamining the professoriate should be applied to K–12. There are similar circumstances that have been distracting forces resulting in a change in teaching for K–12. Ultimately, there is a need for both K–12 and higher education to focus on rigor, relevance, and relationships.

THROUGH THE EYES OF A FUTURE UNDERGRADUATE

I contend that a future undergraduate looks through a blurred window when contemplating which path to take after high school. As an administrator in a high school, I am constantly pursuing ways in which we can help students (many of whom would be the first generation to attend college) become college and career ready. All freshmen take a course designed to focus on their interests and the type of career they feel best suits their strengths. We expose our students to a variety of choices in curriculum and pathways to career fields as they move from being an underclassman to an upperclassman. Students research colleges and universities that have degrees that coincide with their career goals and understand the necessary prerequisites to enter these institutions.

However, by the time students reach the beginning of their senior year, we see a minority of students with solid goals and a clear path established. Most students who want to pursue a 2-year or 4-year college feel overwhelmed by their choices. They can find multiple schools with the same focus, but will the time and money invested in their education lead to knowledge that can be used in the real world? Will the professors create an environment where they are welcomed and challenged to grow academically? Future undergraduates don't speak of the scholarship of application or the scholarship of teaching but these two areas are exactly what they are concerned about when choosing a college or university. I've had countless conversations with students and their parents in which they have decided that pursuing higher education is not worth their time and money for a degree that has no application in the real world. Additionally, their experiences or what they have heard from others have shown them that the professoriates at certain schools are not invested in enabling them to grow further academically and prepare them for their desired career.

To make things more complicated, many institutions of higher education now advertise that they can help everyone reach their goal and that they are the correct choice for almost everyone. Boyer (1990) alluded to higher education emulating one another in *Scholarship Reconsidered* and it is certainly visible today through the marketing campaigns targeted at students of all kinds. An increasing number of higher education institutions boast of a larger diversity of programs, but in an effort to duplicate successful institutions they are becoming more ubiquitous and less unique to a student trying to narrow the choices. Students are searching for that factor that makes one school different from another and this task is only getting more complicated.

Today a future undergraduate student has more choices for higher education than any other time in history, but an abundance of choices can be paralyzing. Iyengar conducted a recent study on choice comparing two groups. One group had the choice of 6 jams and the other had the choice of 24 jams. Though people were drawn to the larger group of 24 options, Iyengar (as quoted in Tugend, 2010) found that "people might find more and more choice to actually be debilitating (para. 6). When Boyer published *Scholarship Reconsidered* in 1990 there were 3,559 degree granting institutions of higher education in America as compared to 4,724 by 2014 (Snyder, 2015). A growth of more than 1,100 new institutions in 14 years all in search of students to attend their institution. In my experience, high school students can relate to looking at the choices for higher education and feeling paralyzed. The push to publish research findings across all fields of study by higher education is partially driven by the goal of advertising the diversity of an institution. Institutions of higher education want to attract as many students as possible to their programs and one way to do that is to point to the research taking place in that field. In different areas where there are multiple choices for higher education, the deciding factor becomes cost rather than which institution is the best choice after the consideration of application and teaching. The undergraduate needs to carefully vet their choices for higher education in an era of seemingly similar choices. The undergraduate may find that once they arrive at the school with an outstanding array of choices at their price point there is very little attention given to the scholarship of application and teaching.

THROUGH THE EYES OF A K–12 EDUCATOR

Boyer reexamines scholarship to find the best balance among the responsibilities for the professoriate while better serving the needs of students. The window through which an educator should view Boyer's book is more of a mirror in which we should reflect on our own practice in the same way. How can we look at our roles and better meet the needs of our students?

This is not a simple task but rather a process of continually examining your profession as an educator. The heart of this for educators in K–12 will be to examine who they are as a teacher given the current state of education. The current political pressures making decisions on behalf of educators do not understand the profession and are applying business models for outcomes. Teaching is not as simple as retooling or recalibrating machinery on an assembly line to get the right product.

Eisner (2002) writes:

> Teaching as an art: There are classrooms in which what the teacher does—the way in which activities are orchestrated, questions asked, lectures given—constitutes a form of artistic expression ... Second, teaching is an art in that teachers, like painters, composers, actresses, and dancers make judgments based largely on qualities that unfold during the course of action ... Third, teaching is an art in that the teacher's activity is not dominated by prescriptions or routines but is influenced by qualities and contingencies that are unpredicted. The teacher must function in an innovative way in order to cope with these contingencies ... Fourth, teaching is an art that the ends it achieves are often created in the process. (p. 155)

I believe that educators struggle to see themselves as artists anymore given the high-stakes assessment driven environment that has grown in the past 20 years. When inundated with analytics about how your students perform, you are being placed in a business model of outcomes yet being asked to inspire and create the next generation of critical thinkers. Furthermore, when your evaluation system is changed to take into account your results on standardized tests, you have no choice but to at least partially adopt a concern for outcomes of state assessments. That is a dichotomy that is difficult to navigate and parallels the struggles that the professoriate faced in Boyer's book. K–12 education needs the voice of a modern day Boyer pointing out how we are more interested in results on state assessments and we are doing this at the peril of teaching as an art, as described by Eisner.

As Boyer mentions in his book, education must continually evolve in order to sustain its vitality (Boyer, 1990, p. 81). In addition to being artists in the classroom, educators at all levels need to exercise resolve about their profession and focus on what I call the other three R's: rigor, relevance, and relationships.

THE OTHER THREE Rs

Rigor

In order to understand rigor, we must understand what it means in an educational context. "Rigor is the result of work that challenges students' thinking in new and interesting ways" (Sztabnik, 2015, para. 12). Boyer (1990) was concerned that the professoriate was engaged in research and no longer challenging their undergraduates. They were providing information but not engagement that leads to further growth. Becoming rigorous means challenging our students to a deeper understanding of challenging material. Engaging them with thoughts and ideas that will lead them to pursue a deeper understanding and ignite their interest to pursue what they don't know. This is the lifeblood of education at any level. Connecting with students and their intellect where it is and creating an environment where they are pushed, pulled, or propelled on their own into further understanding.

Relevance

In the year that this book was published, it is estimated that 3 million people in the world had access to the internet out of an estimated 5.2 billion population. Today there are more than 3.5 billion people, out of an estimated 7.5 billion, that have access to the 1.1 billion websites in existence (Jacobs, 2016). The internet information age has changed the accessibility to information on an immeasurable scale. Staying relevant is a primary concern whether you are a kindergarten teacher or a professor of undergraduates. Boyer (1990) was concerned with the lack of teaching in lieu of a focus on research in a time period before you could "google" any question you have. The need for educators to stay relevant and engaged with the needs of a society that moves at social media speed is increasingly more complicated. What is perceived as a dire social issue today may not exist in a few years or even months. Educators must find the appropriate balance of staying relevant while not becoming consumed in the minutiae of topics that don't have their place in a classroom.

Relationships

Successful educators have always understood the importance of having relationships with students. We now live in an increasingly remote information age in which 28% of college students are taking at least one course online according to the Babson Survey Research Group (Smith, 2016). With an increase in distance learning and a decrease in face-to-face interactions, teachers are challenged even further to build relationships with students. Fostering relationships contributes to a healthy learning environment in which students can grow and be challenged. Educators that have built relationships create a healthy socio-emotional environment that enables academic growth. Even with the onset of remote and blended class models, building relationships is still the primary ingredient for academic growth and leads to a positive sense of belonging. Students of all grade levels are connoisseurs of genuine adults and know within seconds how vested a teacher or professor is in them and their academic growth. Educators must be self-reflective and examine whether or not they are building relationships through their interactions with students.

WHERE DO WE GO FROM HERE?

Boyer's (1990) thesis proposing that the professoriate be redefined with more emphasis on teaching, displays how at times education can become fixated on one task leading to potential neglect in other areas. Through reviewing the history of higher education, Boyer clearly outlines why and how research became the driving factor and why teaching became secondary. I believe that Boyer was accurate in his assessment and respected enough to have his voice heard. In examining Boyer's concerns 27 years later, we see that higher education is making efforts to better meet the needs of students. There is a greater focus on receiving feedback from college students today that I did not witness during my undergraduate years in the 90s. Campuses are much more attentive to the socio-emotional needs of students and are providing more supports for academic success.

It is a healthy process to critically examine the factors that are influencing the field of education and the impact that has on the students in the classroom at all levels. Education has a short attention span around the instructional strategies and fads that it adopts only to be replaced by something that was tried 20 years ago. If we were to reflect on the focus of education in 2017, what would we identify as the issues that need to be reconsidered? Boyer may have been compelled to further write about the loss of some individuality in higher education. One thing remains, education must be fluid and adapt to an ever-changing world in order to remain relevant and inspire students.

REFERENCES

Boyer, E. L. (1989). *The condition of the professoriate: Attitudes and trends, 1989: A technical report.* Carnegie Foundation for the Advancement of Teaching. http://files.eric.ed.gov/fulltext/ED312963.pdf

Boyer, E. (1990). *Scholarship reconsidered: Priorities of the professoriate.* The Carnegie Foundation for the Advancement of Teaching.

Bucher, G., & Williams, A. (1995). *Ernest Boyer (1928–1995): D.C. Washington, Carnegie Foundation for the advancement of teaching, reports and publications.* State University. http://education.stateuniversity.com/pages/1798/Boyer-Ernest-1928 -1995.html

Eisner, E. (2002). *The educational imagination: On the design and evaluation of school programs.* Merrill Prentice Hall.

Jacobs, I. (2016). *Internet users.* http://www.internetlivestats.com/internet-users/

Smith, D. F. (2016, February 25). *Report: One in four students enrolled in online courses.* EdTech. http://www.edtechmagazine.com/higher/article/2016/02/report -one-four-students-enrolled-online-courses

Snyder, T. (2015). *Digest of educational statistics 2015.* NCES. https://nces.ed.gov/pubs 2016/2016014.pdf

Sztabnik, J. (2015, May 7). *A new definition of rigor.* Edutopia. https://www.edutopia .org/blog/a-new-definition-of-rigor-brian-sztabnik

Tugend, A. (2010, February 26). Too many choices: A problem that can paralyze. *The New York Times.* http://www.nytimes.com/2010/02/27/your-money/27shortcuts .html

CHAPTER 8

THE ROAD LESS TRAVELED

The Best Practice of Teacher Choice

Erin Owens

Author/Book studied:

Zemelman, S., Daniels, H., & Hyde, A. (1998). *Best practice: New standards for teaching and learning in America's schools* (2nd ed.). Heinemann.

OLD FRIEND, NEW FACE

My office bookshelves, home bookshelves, one shelf of my downstairs bookshelf, and one shelf of my upstairs bookshelf, are all devoted to volumes and volumes of professional books. I rarely read them cover to cover. Instead, I look for parts that are of interest to me, are relevant to a project I'm working on, or are related to my work with teachers as a professional developer and curriculum director. Twenty pages into *Best Practice* (Zemelman et al., 1998), I realized I have read parts of and regularly consult and

Curriculum Windows Redux, pages 93–105
Copyright © 2022 by Information Age Publishing
www.infoagepub.com
All rights of reproduction in any form reserved.

recommend the fourth edition of *Best Practice* (Zemelman et al., 2012), and teachers love it!

Actually, the six academic coaches with whom I work closely first recommended the book to me 3 years ago when they were faced, in their first year of coaching, with supporting all the teachers of every content area on best practices for instruction. No matter their individual teaching backgrounds, *Best Practice* (Zemelman et al., 2012) became the coaches' first "go-to" resource when planning for any teacher meeting. In 2014, when academic coaching first took place in our district, the fourth edition was still "hot off the press," but the first edition was originally written in 1992. How had I missed 22 years of such practical tips? The pages are filled with strategies from years of research by a myriad of councils, institutes, and researchers important to the education field (please see a shortened list of research reviewed for *Best Practice* by Zemelman, Daniels, and Hyde at the end of this chapter[1]). From 1992 to the present, the authors have collaborated to revise this foundational curriculum work FOUR times! As a professional educator, a curriculum director, and (more important) a voracious reader, why do I only recognize the fourth edition as an old friend?

When handed the second edition, the cover was completely different, and the authors' names were unfamiliar. In connecting the two texts, what was evident was the marked visual difference between the books—inside and out. Why the extreme change, not in language or message, but in branding, between the second edition and the fourth?[2] What has changed in education, the teaching community, and with the authors? I quickly found myself more interested in why the editions looked so different than in learning more about the best practice within the texts. It is important to understand one of the major differences between the 1992 publication of the first edition of *Best Practice* and the 2012 publication of the revised fourth edition of *Best Practice* is that education had changed drastically because of national standards, even though the authors' message about what is effective teaching had not.

THE NATIONAL STANDARDS MOVEMENT

Zemelman et al. open *Best Practice* (2012) by clearly articulating that the "what" of teaching began its emergence with the national standards movement. While the movement was only a pipe dream in 1992, it progressed into a reality called the Common Core State Standards by 2010. At the same time, the esteem of public education, under the pressure of accountability to the "what," lowered to almost near universal public dissatisfaction. Despite what has changed in education, the goal of the authors is, and always has been, to help teachers see the "how" of educating America's future in an effort to make the reform promise of the "what" come to life. Indeed the single most powerful variable in student achievement—more than socio-economic status or school funding—is the quality of the teaching learners receive.

When the first edition of *Best Practice* was published in 1992, *A Nation at Risk* (National Commission on Excellence in Education, 1983) was nearly 10 years old and had set forth five recommendations for educational reform. Two of the five recommendations included language that focused on standards in the form of content minimums for graduation, a call for standardized testing and better textbooks, and increased rigor by raising the bar for admission to college and universities. While *A Nation at Risk* was only a report, the 10 years that followed were dedicated to numerous councils and summits that would attempt to articulate actionable steps in moving forward with the document's five recommendations.

In response to those ideas for educational reform, it was the National Education Goals Panel (1999) under President Bill Clinton that finally produced a report that put measures and action steps to the recommendations of *A Nation at Risk* (National Commission on Excellence in Education, 1983). This was the Goals 2000: Educate America Act of 1994. Of the eight goals outlined in the Act, the following goals focused on what students learned in school and effectively spawned the creation of the national standards movement:

1. By the year 2000, all students will leave Grades 4, 8, and 12 having demonstrated competency over challenging subject matter including English, mathematics, science, foreign languages, civics and government, economics, arts, history, and geography, and every school in America will ensure that all students learn to use their minds well, so they may be prepared for responsible citizenship, further learning, and productive employment in our Nation's modern economy.
2. By the year 2000, the United States students will be first in the world in mathematics and science achievement (National Commission on Excellence in Education, 1983, Sec. 102. National Education Goals).

In order to move these goals into implementation, the National Education Summit convened on at least two separate occasions to discuss the Goals 2000: Educate America Act (1994) and to begin setting the standards for what America's students should learn throughout K–12 education. Though standards were not produced by the National Education Summit, there was much discussion and debate about the "what" of teaching, to be sure. The National Council of Teachers of Mathematics (NCTM, 1989) had already agreed on a common set of standards years prior to the summits. During the time that the summits convened, the National Council of the Teachers of English (NCTE) and the International Reading Association (IRA) were in the throes of writing national standards in English language arts.

Enter *Best Practice: New Standards for Teaching and Learning in America's Schools* (Zemelman et al., 1998). While councils and committees were focusing on the "what" of teaching in an effort to improve America's schools, Zemelman, Daniels, and Hyde saw the answer as lying in the hands of *how* America's teachers were teaching. The preface to *Best Practice* contains one of the best quotes I have read in regards to the habit of lawmakers of focusing on student achievement instead of focusing on teachers through meaningful direction in curriculum and instruction: "It costs far less to raise the bar than to help someone jump over it" (Zemelman et al., 1998, p. xi). *Best Practice* (any edition) serves as a way to help teachers impact students by making the content stick for students through powerful and engaging instruction. It really doesn't matter where we want kids to be at the end of their K–12 career if we do not equip our teachers with the tools to get them there.

Move forward 14 years to the publication of the fourth edition, Zemelman et al. (2012) maintained their focus on the "how," while the standards and standardization movement marched forward. The 2010 advent of the Common Core State Standards becomes the focus of the preface in the fourth edition, rather than the legislative efforts for standardization outlined in the preface of the second edition. Through much political and academic turmoil, reaching agreed upon standards in English language arts and math took an unbelievable 20 years! However, a lack of common science and social studies standards remains because a consensus on the "what" simply cannot be reached among academics, and certainly in conjunction with the public.[3] Yet, the authors' conviction that teachers need knowledge of how to get over the bar, rather than only knowledge of the bar termed "more rigorous content," remains steadfast.

Over the course of 14 years, the best practices recommended for teachers to grow student potential remains largely unchanged, while the sociopolitical nature of public school has continued to roil with mandates, controversies, and misaligned attempts to improve the entire system without improving the social support system of the nation. *Best Practice* (Zemelman et al., 2012) is a practical guide for teachers looking to meet student needs in the changing landscape of educational reform.

According to Zemelman (personal communication, March 2, 2017), *Best Practice* has remained a best seller since the first edition. Yet, I cannot help but wonder how teachers come to discover the book and its enlightening recommendations for delivery of meaningful and engaging classroom instruction. After all, it took me quite some time to realize *Best Practice* as a book worth reading and recommending to others.

INTO THE HANDS OF EDUCATORS

When the first edition was published, I had just entered my teacher education program at a liberal studies university. In reflection, I wonder why I would not have seen *Best Practice* (Zemelman et al., 1992) as a text during my teacher education classes. Then, the second edition came along during my second year of teaching. I have always attested that my first teaching experience provided some of the highest quality leadership and mentorship I have experienced or have seen for new teachers. Yet, as those first few years passed, not one colleague referred to *Best Practice* (Zemelman et al., 1998) as a resource. Shortly after the publication of the third edition, I transitioned from a 12-year classroom teacher to a curriculum specialist and teacher leader in the area of mathematics in the curriculum department, where I have continued to focus for the past 9 years. During this time, I have packed up my books and moved offices several times as my roles have changed, yet, *Best Practice* (Zemelman et al., 1992, 1998, 2005) was never a part of any of those moves. It was 2014 when I was finally introduced to the fourth edition of the book by the very teachers I currently lead.

Public education is not just my job, it's my passion. So, I question why it took so long for me to come across one of the best curriculum texts that situates teachers and teaching as the greatest and most important asset to the long-term maintenance of America's renowned educational system. Twenty-two years seems like an unreasonably long time for a book to stay relevant, and for an educational leader to have to wait to discover its wealth of ideas for classroom practice. Again, I wondered, is there something to the improved look of the text that has helped it to become more widely read by teachers and teacher leaders like me? After all, I discovered its wealth of instructional guidance a full 22 years after publication. When I look out across the sea of best practices in education, and even professional publications, what causes a book to gain popularity and then result in widespread change? My curiosity about the authors' and publishers' roles in influencing teaching in the United States prompted me to seek an interview with one of the authors, Steve Zemelman.

AN AUTHOR'S VIEW

> **Me:** Hello, Mr. Zemelman, thank you so much for taking time to speak with me about your book. I'm not sure if you saw my list of questions in the email, but I was recently assigned to read the second edition of *Best Practice* as part of a curriculum class in my doctoral program. After reading for about 20 minutes, I realized that I was very familiar with the fourth

edition, and, in fact, it has become a widely popular professional book in my district. Several buildings have done
teacher-led book studies around the book.

Steve: Oh, that is flattering to hear. What are they getting out of it?
I am sorry. I do not have that book in front of me. I probably
should.

Me: Actually, I doubt you will need it. My curiosity and focus
of the call is to understand the visual changes between the
two editions. I find the fourth edition to be so much more
friendly and appealing to the teaching audience. It's laid
out differently, and it seems as though there was effort to
direct teachers to key points without the need to read every
chapter word-for-word. Can you speak a little bit about the
changes? And has readership grown because of the changes?

Steve: The book was a hit from the beginning, but you never know
if they will be. Heinemann takes a lot of chances when they
contract with authors. They know that only about 10% of the
teachers are going to read the books.

Me: Did Heinemann influence the changes to prompt sales?

Steve: When a book does well, they are willing to spend more
money. That is the gist of it. They will spend more time on
layout and getting photos and graphic designers; but teachers change and I changed as a writer. We all changed as writers. We got better at it, better at understanding what readers
wanted, while our readers were changing, too.

Me: Fourteen years ago, did readers prefer a text?

Steve: Maybe I did. Donald Graves,[4] he is a brilliant author. I try
to be like him. He has directives and asks teachers to try
something specific. That's not me, but I learned some things
from him. I try to get the first chapter to say what the purpose is. I put my thinking there. Chapters after that become
more "how to." (S. Zemelman, personal communication,
March 2, 2017)[5]

It seems what I really learned about books and publishers and teacher
appeal is that we all grow. *Best Practice* (Zemelman et al.) changed over
time, not because of some ploy to sell more books or become more widely
recognized, but because when you know better, you do better. In 14 years
there is a lot of time to reflect and improve. The evolution of *Best Practice*
is akin to the same growth we all experience in the classroom or as administrators. We learn along the way: what our students want and respond to
and what the standards really mean or intend because, frankly, we have
spent more time with students and standards. As Zemelman has spent more

time writing books and working with teachers and publishers, he can simply make a better product than he did in 1998.

The world, education included, has changed the way that information is consumed. Authors and publishers respond to our demands for products that can be skimmed and easily reviewed. Pictures, color, and visual appeal define American culture. It is news feeds in line at Starbucks, not newspapers at the breakfast table that inform the American public. While my phone conversation didn't confirm a wild hypothesis about the backhanded influences of publishers today, I did take away so much more as it relates to my own practice as a teacher leader based on the next 35 minutes of collegial conversation with Mr. Zemelman. Our conversation that grew naturally used no scripted questions as a guide. He opened for me an unexpected window into my beliefs about teachers, and I began to understand how my teacher leadership was steeped in a belief that may be stifling.

As we continued, the rest of the conversation shifted from the actual book to some wonderful, philosophical conversation about what we each believe about teachers. We enjoyed some debate about the teacher leader versus the leader in all of us. On my initial read of *Best Practice* (Zemelman et al., 2012), I worried that there were too many "best practices" outlined in the book. In fact, my original thoughts about the formation of this chapter centered around the way *Best Practice* (Zemelman et al., 2012) might not be at all helpful to teachers. I thought that, because each practice outlined in the book takes many years to perfect, a teacher would certainly feel overwhelmed or scattered if they read the book and began to try it all. Steve's response was that "balance is giving enough information that teachers have freedom." The authors' intention with the book was to give teachers choices on what to do to improve their classrooms and engage students. Throughout the text, I had worried that it was simply too much. Perhaps I am not giving teachers enough credit.

Roughly 40% of my work revolves around professional leadership, development, and teacher practice. My goal is, and has always been, to empower teachers to believe that giving students the freedom to choose, to lead, and to speak results in the greatest learning. The irony is that, in order for teachers to believe this is right for students, they need to see that it works for them. The telephone conversation with Mr. Zemelman gave me a needed perspective on teacher leadership. *Best Practice* (Zemelman et al., 2012) was written to include a myriad of things that teachers can do better in their classrooms. Teachers, not academics, were intended to digest the material and make choices about where to begin and then what to pursue further.

Why have I insisted on being the dreaded "sage on the stage" and telling teachers to focus in on one practice just because it works well for me? As a result of reading *Best Practice* (Zemelman et al., 2012) and of my interview with Mr. Zemelman, I aim to focus on teacher freedom by suggesting teachers study and implement more instructional strategies, not fewer. Teachers deserve multiple choices about effective instruction, rather than having to settle on one and trying to make it into a single exemplary practice. During our conversation, we reflected on instructional strategies.

> **Me:** I spent 4 years with a staff developer from Columbia University in order to fully understand writing workshop, and that time has impacted every fiber of who I am as an educator. I was able to take that deep study and apply it to everything in my classroom—make those connections. Without that time, I don't think I would have the toolbox I do.
>
> **Steve:** Lucy Calkins is a friend of mine, so I'm not saying anything she hasn't heard; but I think the flaw with Writing Workshop is, that at its underlying core, it believes that teachers are not smart enough to figure out the pieces themselves.

Moving forward, the choice I plan to make for teachers is to help them realize that the best practices in *Best Practice* are based on a quasi meta-analysis of common practices outlined in over 20 different studies. Choosing what to study, try, and adapt from those best practices should certainly be their choices, not mine. By digesting and synthesizing the whole of the text, it is possible to weave together a whole new classroom practice that takes fibers from each fabric of *Best Practice*.

As information consumers that is how we have changed over time. We all want many different snips—10 short news articles—rather than one whole newspaper. Only then can we make sense of the news as a whole. As educators, should we not be learning as much as we can in order to create our own best practice? In the study of the text and through my phone conversation with the author, the belief in the teacher as a capable and critical consumer has begun to take hold.

BEST PRACTICES

Zemelman et al. (1998) describe the seven structures that constitute pillars of best practice teaching as a "'new' integrated and holistic educational paradigm [that] can fairly be called a continuation of progressive thinking" (p. 19). They are referring to the ideas espoused and studied by the late John Dewey in the 1930s called "progressive education." Dewey's foundational work served to shape American education if only, at times, to draw opposition that created new conversations about the way that children should learn in our public school system. Dewey's ideas have become a steady part of the ebb and flow of education and, when revisited, are consistently rebirthed in a new light. For Dewey, school was for learning through experience, not learning about experience. He believed that the learning process was at least as important, if not more important than, the content. Curriculum is to be driven by students rather than the subject matter (Yoder, 1992). To be student-centered, school had to be democratic in nature and not an authoritative, teacher-driven experience.

Using Dewey's ideals of progressivism, the authors of *Best Practice* put democratic curriculum development and students at the center of their seven best-practice structures. Zemelman et al. (2012), see their book as "philosophical orientation [that] is better balanced with pedagogical pragmatism" (p. 20). Their book is dedicated to the following seven structures and their examples in practice, in content areas, and in classrooms across the nation. The seven practices are derived from common agreements found in documents published from what one would consider to be a "pretty fractious field" known as education (Zemelman et al., 2012, p. 5).

The first best practice structure is the *gradual release of responsibility* (GRR) and is the only one of the seven structures that does not appear in the 1998 edition of *Best Practice* (Zemelman et al., 1998). Developed in 1983 by Pearson and Gallagher, GRR outlines steps for transferring the learning responsibility from teachers to students. In curriculum today, we refer to the steps of GRR as the process of "I do, we do, you do." First, the teacher teaches a skill, and then the students try it with help from the teacher or other students. Finally, the students are asked to try the task or demonstrate the new learning on their own.

Best practice number two is called *classroom workshop*. Classroom workshop is actually a particular example of GRR. Developed as a model for teaching writing out of Columbia University Teachers College by Lucy Calkins, workshop fundamentally believes that students learn by doing the work of the content. They become readers by reading, writers by writing, and mathematicians by investigating math concepts. The workshop model is defined by student choice, teacher facilitation and expertise, and time spent "doing" the work in the classroom. The beauty of workshop is that teachers and students have clearly defined roles within that structure, and, therefore, know exactly what they should each be doing, rather than having an unstructured experience during the workshop time.

A third practice is a small, but important, strategy for long-term, student success called *strategic thinking*. As humans, we spend all day thinking, yet have rarely been taught efficient and effective ways of how to think through new learning. Strategic thinking is about teaching students to be cognizant of their thinking and to learn from it in order to adjust during the learning process. As a best practice, strategic thinking comes from recent brain research, as well as foundational research in the area of reading, conducted by Pearson and Gallagher. Teachers help students to become strategic thinkers by demonstrating their own thinking and learning through a think-aloud or by modeling questioning in conversations with students. Students then apply the strategy in their writing or in conversations with each other.

The best practice of *collaborative activities* is about students learning from each other when they work in small groups. To do this, students must be taught to work effectively with others. Putting students in groups and expecting quality production requires that teachers explicitly teach students certain social skills. Research on and knowledge of collaborative learning has at least one foundational link to educational psychologist Robert Slavin's (1983) first work on cooperative learning in 1983. When done well, students not only learn from each other, but have a transferrable and marketable skill for the rest of their lives.

Integrative units as a best practice is essentially about student-led learning and teacher planning that facilitates inquiry. The teacher as curriculum developer must "back-map" from student interests and questions to the mandated curriculum (Zemelman et al., 2012, p. 70). James Beane (1997) first developed this approach in his book *Curriculum Integration: Designing the Core of Democratic Education.* Integrative units "make students real, responsible partners in their own education" (Zemelman et al., 2012, p. 70). In such units, students identify the topics, create the questions to pursue, conduct the work of learning, and then share out. Currently, schools are investing in learning about problem-based learning, which follows the same model outlined in *Best Practice* (Zemelman et al., 2012) for integrative units.

The sixth best practice, *representing to learn,* is about students showing what learning and thinking they are doing as they work through problems and units. Students should be talking about what they are learning. They can use writing as a learning tool, not just for finished products. Representing to learn includes dramatic representation and drawings, essentially anything that activates the brain to commit learning to memory. Representing to learn is the process used to transfer what is heard from a teacher or a classmate into the student's memory bank. The practice was developed out of work in the 1970s based on the idea of writing to learn (Zemelman et al., 2012, p. 72).

The final best practice is *formative-reflective assessment.* This structure is an upgrade from the reflective assessment structure mentioned in the second edition of *Best Practice* (Zemelman et al., 1998, p. 206). Formative-reflective assessment is when the teacher gathers and uses qualitative data for instructional decision-making. The authors go so far as to term it as "adapting the tools of ethnographic, qualitative research" (Zemelman et al., 2012, p. 79). Teachers are encouraged to use interviews, observations, and portfolios to assess student learning and to plan next steps.

Within and across these seven structures are 14 key principles that bind the structures and effectively position them as the "best." Figure 1.1 found on page 10 of *Best Practice* (Zemelman et al., 2012) shows how the principles relate to one another in a Venn diagram. After reading about the seven Best Practice structures and putting them in a classroom context, one can see how they complement and overlap with each other. For instance, classroom workshop is an example of GRR; and within classroom workshop, a teacher can use collaborative activities and strategic thinking—all in one day. Perhaps Zemelman's view that teachers need just enough information to get them interested in learning comes more from the fact that the best practice structures relate so closely. In fact, each best practice stands to enhance another.

RESEARCH–PRACTICE–
PROFESSIONAL DEVELOPMENT NEXUS

If I circle back to my original ponderings about *Best Practice* (Zemelman et al., 2012) and wind around the road that has been my personal journey into academics, I sit at the fork that requires me to act. The choice I must make is either to change my professional practice and continue making choices for teachers about what to study for improvement or to walk through this new window forged through conversation and reflection that has me considering professional development as a process for teachers to digest research to impact their practices.

Initially, I was awestruck by the profound visual differences in the different editions of *Best Practice* (Zemelman et al., 1992, 1998, 2005, 2012). Wanting to get an answer for why the authors had made so much change to the layout of the book, while changing little in the message during a time of radical educational change, prompted me to reach out to the author. In that conversation, I learned that like all people, Zemeleman did better because he knew better. The editions looked strikingly different because the way that society consumes knowledge has changed in 22 years.

However, that same conversation challenged my beliefs about focusing on a single best practice in my own district, so I began to reflect on what I have learned over the last year in Miami's doctoral program. Bombarded by new and exciting academic research in all areas of education and leadership, I had just started to question my own professional practice as a curriculum leader. Have I been making the right curricular choices for 100s of teachers and 1,000s of students over the last 9 years? I have made no secret of my distaste for the textbook publishers and my desire for teachers to master their content. When I examine the ways in which I have designed and led professional development for teachers, I can't help but note the lack of choice. While founded on research, I have rarely provided opportunity for teachers to become "research-engaged" (Dimmock, 2016).

But I can get there. I can take the road less traveled, as I have in many leadership roles. Dimmock (2016) lays out a framework for research engagement that focuses on leading teachers and schools to consume, practice, and share research with each other. His framework calls for three specific actions that result in the "nexus" where research, practice, and professional development will meet. He states that all teachers and leaders must engage in research. My call to action is to continually put research before teachers. During each meeting, each coaching session, each interaction, I can offer relevant research to help build the norm that everyone is exposed to research.

Next, Dimmock builds on DuFour's work about professional learning communities by suggesting that schools be created as learning communities to bridge the walls of the school. Dimmock's imperative for a learning community is a network. Of course, the inclusion of researchers in the network of a school's learning community is at the crux of his ideal. In my roles, professional and academic, I spend substantial time in connecting with university professionals. In order to help the teachers in my district create the professional learning network that leads them to a point of nexus, I must use my connections to bring people in, beyond my office door. Teachers need the support of researchers, and researchers need the support of teachers if they are ever to make an impact in education. After all, Dewey created a school so that he could research alongside teachers.

Finally, Dimmock insists that a workable methodology be adopted that allows teachers and leaders to put research into practice. This means that I must examine the culture of my district and adjust accordingly so that teachers and leaders have the support needed to put research into practice and reflect on the effect. It boils down to the freedom to fail. Without a doubt, we want our students to experience failure in order to learn. To do this, we must also set that up for our teachers and administrators.

Fundamentally, *Best Practice* (Zemelman et al., 2012) has changed me as a person and as a leader. It was not the words on the page, nor the single phone call with the author, that shifted my thinking from controlling professional development to encouraging action research by teachers. Instead, it was the timing of the book and the project that have made me reflect on my role as a district leader. To plan to empower teachers to be learners alongside researchers has become my number one goal. I do not intend that teachers simply need to know more about what researchers are saying and doing, but that they need to be researchers of practice. And, with Dimmock, I have found a framework. It is now time for my own action research in teacher leadership.

NOTES

1. Some of the "major stakeholders" whose research informed *Best Practice*: American Association for the Advancement of Science, Carnegie Corpora-

tion, Center for the Improvement of Early Reading Achievement, Center for the Study of Mathematics Curriculum, National Board for Professional Teaching Standards, National Center for History in the Schools, National Institute of Education, Partnership for 21st Century Skills.

2. I was unable to locate a copy of the first edition published in 1992; not online, in stores, or within my district employing over 900 teachers. Zemelman claims the book was a best seller from the start. I was able to locate the third edition online but not in local stores or within my district. Therefore, I choose to focus my comparison on the second and fourth editions of *Best Practice* (Zemelman et al., 1998, 2012).

3. In my opinion, both topics, science and social science, are so rife with controversy that completion of national standards accepted by our tumultuous political system will be nearly impossible.

4. Donald Graves passed away in 2010 but was also an educator/writer with Heinemann that wrote mostly about teaching writing.

5. This is not a transcription of the interview but a reconstruction of the conversation according to this author's memory.

REFERENCES

Beane, A. J. (1997). *Curriculum integration: Designing the core of democratic education.* Teachers College Press.

Dimmock, C. (2016). Conceptualising the research-practice-professional development nexus: Mobilising schools as "research-engaged" professional learning communities. *Professional Development in Education, 42*(1), 36–53.

Goals 2000: Educate America Act of 1994, P.L. No. 103-227 (1994). https://www.govinfo.gov/content/pkg/BILLS-103hr1804enr/pdf/BILLS-103hr1804enr.pdf

National Commission on Excellence in Education. (1983). *A nation at risk: The imperative for education reform.* https://edreform.com/wp-content/uploads/2013/02/A_Nation_At_Risk_1983.pdf

National Council of the Teachers of Mathematics. (1989). *Principles and standards for school mathematics.* http://www.nctm.org/uploadedFiles/Standards_and_Positions/PSSM_ExecutiveSummary.pdf

National Education Goals Panel. (1999). *The national education goals report: Building a nation of learners.* http://govinfo.library.unt.edu/negp/reports/99rpt.pdf

Slavin, R. (1983). *Cooperative learning.* Longman.

Yoder, F. (1992). *The University of Chicago faculty: A centennial view. John Dewey.* https://www.lib.uchicago.edu/collex/exhibits/university-chicago-centennial-catalogues/university-chicago-faculty-centennial-view/john-dewey-1858-1952-philosophy-and-education/

Zemelman, S., Daniels, H., & Hyde, A. (1998). *Best Practice: New Standards for Teaching and Learning in America's Schools* (2nd ed.). Heinemann.

Zemelman, S., Daniels, H., & Hyde, A. A. (2012). *Best practice: New standards for teaching and learning in America's schools* (4th ed.). Heinemann.

CHAPTER 9

TURNING TOWARDS THE LIGHT

Jaime N. Ranly

Author/Book studied:

Goodlad, J. I. (1994). *Educational renewal: Better teachers, better schools.* Jossey-Bass.

Plato's idea of a teacher is one whose soul boldly faces the sun, a self-motivated seeker of truth. In his allegory "The Cave," he describes guiding minds toward what is real and important and allowing them to seize it for themselves. In this cave, prisoners' backs are to the sun and they are only experiencing life through the shadows that the sun casts. However, by removing the shackles and turning towards the light, the prisoners will be able to see and experience the real things that have cast the shadows. Consequently, a student's back can be to the light and only with education will she "see." Plato believes that "there is the person, who for as long as they live, will remain a voluntary prisoner in the darkness of the cave. For such a person, education will merely amount to training" (Gonzalez, 2013). I

Curriculum Windows Redux, pages 107–120
Copyright © 2022 by Information Age Publishing
www.infoagepub.com
107

am left asking myself, if our preservice teachers are prisoners of Plato's cave, studying the shadows instead of the real thing, should we not develop programs that allow teachers to turn to the light so that they can see and experience the tangible things that are casting the shadows? John Goodlad believed so. In his book, *Educational Renewal: Better Teachers, Better Schools* (1994), he explores how real-world teacher education curriculum can improve teacher effectiveness.

JOHN I. GOODLAD

John Goodlad was an educational researcher and theorist who published work on renewing schools and teacher education. He began his education in a one-room schoolhouse in Canada and after graduating from high school, Goodlad attended a normal school in Vancouver. The completion of studies at the normal school qualified Goodlad to teach in an elementary school. He taught in a one-room schoolhouse. He then attended summer school for two consecutive summers to gain a permanent teaching certificate. He eventually went on to earn a bachelor's, master's, and finally a doctoral degree at the University of Chicago.

Goodlad then moved from elementary school teacher to a university professor. He spent his years in higher education in various positions within teacher education. This included teaching at a Laboratory School, as dean of UCLA's Graduate School of Education, and director/co-director of the Center for Educational Renewal at the University of Washington. Goodlad is known for publishing influential models for renewing schools and teacher education. He "authored or co-authored more than 30 books, wrote chapters and papers in more than 100 other books and yearbooks, and published more than 200 articles in professional journals and encyclopedias" (Encyclopedia.com, n.d., para. 5). He went on to become the co-director of the Center for Educational Renewal where he created centers of pedagogy. His work centered on creating a working relationship among universities' schools of arts and sciences, colleges of education, and K–12 institutions. His work included creating a teacher preparation curriculum that equipped teachers for subject matter delivery, inquiry, questioning, curiosity, and fostered a desire to learn new ideas (Goodlad, 1994). In Goodlad's (1994) book, *Educational Renewal,* readers explore how he planned to transform the way universities prepare teachers.

Goodlad believed that the time has come when teacher education must be redefined and reconstructed in a way that raises expectations, eliminates weak educational ideas, and increases professional honor. His experience and work as the director of teacher education in four different universities afforded him the foundation and knowledge to begin researching a better way to educate future teachers. Such research led him to begin setting the foundation for a new and robust teacher preparation program through the development of 19 postulates. These postulates indicate specific responsibilities for teacher preparation institutions and their collaborations with school districts. By directly including top university leaders, the postulates aim to help them understand that it is their societal responsibility to adequately support and advance teacher education programs. It is imperative that these programs be of the same rigor and quality as other professional education programs. In postulate four, Goodlad (1994) goes so far as to say,

> There must exist a clearly identifiable group of academic and clinical faculty members for whom teacher education is the top priority; the group must be responsible and accountable for selecting diverse groups of students and monitoring their progress, planning and maintaining the full scope of sequence of the curriculum, continuously evaluating and improving programs, and facilitating the entry of graduates into teaching careers. (pp. 78–79)

Other postulates focus on curricular aims that encompass an educated person. These relate not only to developing critical thinking and social reasoning skills, but also developing a program that enables a student to interact in laboratory settings for simulation, observation, and hands-on experiences. Goodlad (1994) encourages his readers to use the postulates not as a checklist, but as an inquiry into what currently exists and what should exist.

Goodlad frames the 19 postulates as a basis for what he called *centers of pedagogy*. These centers are the focus of the book and the ideas associated with them were developed to provide an academic setting and identity for the education of educators. The center of pedagogy brings together what Goodlad calls *key players*. The key players include the university's Department of Education, the Department of Arts and Sciences, and K–12 school districts. Although two of these players are housed at a university, a partnership must be created with school districts in order to have all the key players essential for a center of pedagogy.

I related to this book in so many ways as I have spent a significant amount of my career in some facet of the ever-evolving Ohio teacher induction program. I spent 11 years as a teacher mentor in urban school districts and nine of those years were as a full release mentor. Currently, I serve as the program coordinator for our district's induction program. As a full release mentor, I was released from my teaching duties in order to mentor 15–25 teachers each year throughout a large urban district. Over my career, I have mentored nearly 200 new teachers. My time spent with new teachers quickly revealed concerns about their knowledge and preparation, the weaknesses of the induction program, and most important, the harm the two concerns had on student learning and development. My experience taught me that teachers are often unprepared for the realities of teaching and more times than not, especially in an urban setting, struggle severely with classroom management. Pedagogy often takes a back seat because new teachers were unable to instruct because of management concerns. While mentoring, I often found myself being a social-emotional support for the new teachers. It was not uncommon to console a crying teacher who felt overwhelmed, exhausted, ineffective, and/or defeated. The most concerning moment came when a new teacher told me that on her way to school that day she thought about wrecking her car into a tree so that she didn't have to go to work. This teacher had been one of the most effective new teachers that I had ever worked with. She was differentiating for her students, classroom management was in place and working, she incorporated projects, used data to drive her instruction, and had made a personal connection with all her students. She was getting noticed by the administration. However, she was exhausted, overwhelmed, and constantly concerned with being effective and reaching the students she couldn't seem to reach ... the realities of teaching. I think it is fair to say that all teachers, new ones and veterans, experience times of mental and physical exhaustion, of being overwhelmed, and are in a constant state of making sure they are effective at reaching all their students. However, the way in which our current teacher preparation and induction programs are structured, I don't believe we are preparing our future and current new teachers for this reality, and Goodlad didn't think so either.

THE HISTORY OF TEACHER EDUCATION

To improve teacher preparation programs, we must first examine its history. The idea and implementation of teacher education in America did not begin until the middle to late 19th century. During this time, the common school movement was also beginning. With common schools came a need for teachers who were educated in the particulars of the common school method. The leaders of the common school movement supported teacher education. Prior to common schools, anyone who had completed a given grade in primary or secondary school could become a teacher and teach up to the highest level of grade completion. For instance, if you attended school until the eighth grade, you could teach any grade, K–8. These types of schools and teachers existed in America long before teacher education programs. The earliest example of teacher education was during the middle of the 19th century when summer teaching institutes became prominent. According to Labaree (2021), these institutes were a set of lectures and classes aimed at developing the skills of teachers in both pedagogy and subject matter. This was the first formal effort to give teachers on the job training (professional development) opportunities.

With the adoption of the common school, the demand for teachers increased. There was a need for not only more teachers but teachers with higher qualifications. This resulted in the creation of normal schools. Normal schools "resulted from nineteenth-century education reformers' efforts to adapt the German teacher seminary and the French Ecole Normale to train teachers for the growing system of American common schools" (Ogren, 2003, p. 641). Major cities began setting up their own normal schools within their high school so that they could train teachers to work in their local system. In 1839, the first state normal school opened in Lexington, Massachusetts, with a purpose of providing professional schooling for future teachers (Labaree, 2021). According to Labaree (2021),

> In the eyes of reformers like Horace Mann, the primary aim of the state normal school was to prepare a group of well-educated and professionally skilled teachers who could serve as the model for public school teachers throughout the country. (p. 292)

During this time, there was a high demand to fill empty classrooms with teachers. Therefore, the country saw a large increase in the number of state normal schools. After getting their start in 1839, they grew from 103 in 1890 to 180 by 1910 (Labaree, 2021). As these institutions grew, the students' expectations for these institutions grew as well. Students began to demand that the normal schools begin to offer an array of programs that would offer access to other occupations outside of teaching. This push would eventually lead normal schools to begin transitioning into teachers' colleges by the start of the 20th century. It was between 1911 and 1930 that 88 of these normal school conversions took place with the last of the normal schools ending by the 1950s (Labaree, 2021). Now, with the formal teacher preparation programs beginning to look more like liberal arts colleges, many made the switch to a more marketable label of state college and then finally to that of state university.

As teacher education evolved from summer institutes to normal schools to teacher colleges and finally to state universities, teacher preparation programs evolved. As mentioned earlier, the early purpose of normal schools was to fill empty classrooms with much-needed teachers and so the debate between program quality and quantity, relevance versus academic rigor began. The normal schools had to decide whether to provide a high degree of professional training for a few model teachers or provide a large number of teachers a relevant but watered down version of professional training. Due to the high demand for qualified teachers at this crucial time, institutions chose relevance over academic rigor so that they could mass produce teachers (Labaree, 2021). Although not necessarily true today, these foundational decisions and other factors have caused a long and persistent notion that teacher education programs are of low status despite studies that say otherwise.

In the article "Teacher Education: Historical Overview, International Perspective," Ducharme et al. (n.d.) discusses the low status of education preparation programs:

> College and university-based teacher education is often the target of many critics contending that students in teacher education programs are academically weaker than students in other programs, that preparation programs are vacuous, and that the faculty are second-rate. Despite reliable studies responding to these criticisms and demonstrating some of the criticism as ill-founded, the attacks continue. (para. 14)

Unfortunately, According to Ducharme et al. (n.d.), the programs that prepare teachers today remain remarkably consistent with their beginning roots. It is because of this that they struggle to eliminate the unflattering and detrimental perceptions of teacher education programs. Like their early founding, "traditional teacher education programs are typically marked by three components: foundations of schooling and learning, teaching methodology, and practice teaching" (para. 18). Although teacher education has always provided opportunities for classroom experiences for decades, this experience typically came during the last year of the preparation program, in the form of student teaching. It wasn't until the 1960s that teacher education programs started requiring experiences beginning as early as a student's freshman year (Ducharme et al., n.d.). For additional information on the history of teacher education in the university, I would highly recommend David Labaree's article that is cited in this chapter.

CENTERS OF PEDAGOGY

Goodlad (1994) reiterates that teacher education hasn't changed much over time and in fact, he states that for decades there have been basically two routes to becoming a licensed teacher in the United States. The first, and longest standing is the 4-year program that consists of 2 years of general studies, and 2 years of specialized study. The specialized study includes specific courses and teaching experiences. The second includes a postbaccalaureate program that has additional coursework that would earn the student a master's degree, typically in a fifth year. Goodlad proposes a change en masse to the teacher preparation approach using a 5-year model. He describes this type of program as having seven major components. He first begins with recruitment. Goodlad believes that colleges of education should begin recruiting a diverse group of students during their junior and senior years of high school. Once admitted to the university, the 2 years of general studies must have an educational perspective associated with learning. The restructuring of general studies is important to Goodlad. He discusses how little influence colleges of education have on the general studies taken by those students pursuing teacher education. This is quite the opposite of other professions such as doctors, lawyers, and engineers. The schools of medicine, law, and engineering exercise far more influence over the general education of their undergraduates than that of the school of education. Goodlad believes that departments of education do teachers a great disservice by not immersing themselves into the planning of undergraduate curriculum. He believes that

> curriculum should be designed to produce broadly educated citizens and that all students should have intellectual encounters within major concepts, principles, and ideas within six knowledge domains: the nature of the human species, social, political, and economic systems (the global village); the world as a physical system; the world as a biological system; evaluative and belief system; and communicative and expressive systems. (Goodlad, 1994, p. 142)

This includes courses in multiculturalism, ethics, comparative religion, aesthetics, and government.

No longer should colleges of education allow only the schools of medicine, law, and engineering to dictate the general education requirements. These professions are no more important than teaching. In fact, I am reminded of a poignant quote by the educational psychologist, Lee S. Shulman, who has made notable contributions to the study of teaching, assessment of teaching, and the fields of medicine, science, and mathematics. He stated,

> The practice of teaching involves a far more complex task environment than does that of medicine. The teacher is confronted, not with a single patient, but with a classroom filled with 25–35 youngsters. The teacher's goals are multiple; the school's obligations are far from unitary. The only time a physician could possibly encounter a situation of comparable complexity would be in the emergency room of a hospital during or after a natural disaster. (Danielson, 2009, p. 1)

With that being said, teacher educators' voices must be at the table to ensure that future teachers have access to the classes needed to prepare them for their profession.

Another significant portion of Goodlad's work focused on school and university partnerships. These partnerships are significant as the personnel from each organization come together to strengthen the final stages of teacher preparation during the internship stage. A school–university partnership entails one college or university and several school districts. Here, experienced teachers, professors of education, and professors of the arts and sciences come together to create a more natural and clinical environment for teacher education. Goodlad proposes one example of how this partnership could work. Within a partnership, approximately five certified, licensed teachers work with a cohort of university students for the entire 4-year period. Among these five teachers is one head teacher who holds a doctorate in pedagogy with specialization in reading and language arts and four licensed teachers with varying full-time equivalencies. This group would also include four teacher education students. Between these nine teachers, they would educate 80 students with the help of parent volunteers. Although this is just one example of how the school–university partnership could run, Goodlad stresses that there is not just one way to make this partnership work.

Restructuring curriculum, bringing together colleges of education and the arts and sciences, and creating school–university partnerships encompasses Goodlad's vision for a center of pedagogy. Goodlad believed that colleges of education should create centers of pedagogy that stand apart from the university or college and have their own budget and faculty. This center must also work collaboratively with school districts as partner schools. In the late 1990s, universities across the country implemented centers of pedagogy, including our own Miami University. However, only one extremely strong example still exists today, at Montclair State University.

MONTCLAIR STATE UNIVERSITY

Montclair State's Center of Pedagogy, as envisioned by Goodlad, coordinates all aspects of teacher education. To support their center of pedagogy, they have a number of programs and offices. Included is the Montclair State University Network for Educational Renewal (MSUNER), Agenda for Education in a Democracy, Advocacy Center, Office of Admissions and Retention, Fieldwork Department, Urban Teaching Academy, and Urban Teacher Residency Program. Not unlike what Goodlad directed at the University of Washington, Montclair State also has a Network for Educational Renewal. In this program, the focus is on a collaboration among the university and what they call member school districts (K–12 institutions). The program is designed similarly around Goodlad's ideals and is a key feature of Montclair State University's Center of Pedagogy. Montclair's faculty members from both the college of education and the arts and sciences teach courses and provide professional development and coaching to the teachers who work in the member school districts.

According to their website,

> The Montclair State University Network for Educational Renewal sponsors professional development activities for more than 11,000 teachers and administrators in its member districts. Over the past 20 years, the MSUNER has developed an extensive research-based professional development program offering members an array of opportunities for professional and intellectual growth. (Montclair State University, 2019, para. 12)

Teachers in the member school districts have the opportunity to become clinical faculty members for the university. In this role, they can serve as cooperating teachers, on-site mentors, co-facilitators of workshops and seminars, and adjunct faculty (MacKnight, 2022). These relationships create a bridge between the university and school district where one is an extension of the other; each is invested in the other's success.

In 1990, John Goodlad first introduced the idea of centers of pedagogy and in 1995, Montclair State University was the first to open a center. Although many universities across the nation attempted to implement and design programs around Goodlad's ideas, Montclair State is still effectively implementing Goodlad's work today. Although I do not have the reasons why so many failed to fully create and/or maintain a center of pedagogy, I can only assume a myriad of political issues came into play as it so often does at universities and school districts. I have spent years immersed in the professional lives of new teachers and have continuously wondered why there is such a disconnect between the schools and universities. Goodlad's book both excited and saddened me. I have spent so much time daydreaming scenarios in which school districts partner with universities to strengthen teacher preparation and practice. Therefore, it was exciting to see that so much of the work and ideas already existed. However, the failure of this concept to be fully realized by universities and school districts left me feeling a bit defeated. How could this work, this movement, be tossed away when the potential to transform how we prepare teachers was right in front of us? What did we lose by tossing it away? According to a 2014 White House report, almost two-thirds of new teachers report that their teacher preparation program left them unprepared for the realities of the classroom (The White House, 2014). What would these types of reports have said today if the concept of centers of pedagogy were embraced, supported, and implemented in the 1990s by every college of education across the nation?

Unfortunately, education today continues to have the problems which Goodlad so passionately talked about in his book. Although his transformational ideas never took hold at most universities, new teacher issues and retention continued to concern school leaders. It was because of these concerns that teacher induction programs were developed. Teacher induction programs have a short history in America. According to Ashburn (1986), there has been an evolution of teacher induction programs over the past several decades with states beginning to mandate them in the 1980s. Teacher induction programs were developed because studies showed that it takes 3–7 years to become an effective teacher. Also, low retention rates of new teachers are significantly higher than their experienced counterparts, as a high number of teachers leave within the first 5 years of teaching (Moir, 2014). The low performance and turnover rates of teachers not only cause school districts significant financial burdens, but it also has a negative impact on student learning, especially for the schools that serve low income and students of color (Haynes, 2014). The turnover rate in low-income schools is 50% higher than that of their counterparts, therefore, our hardest to reach children are being taught by our least experienced teachers (The New Teacher Center, 2007).

One method of solving this problem has been the implementation of state-mandated teacher mentoring and induction programs. Although there are no clear-cut definitions of teacher induction programs, there is a distinct difference between induction programs and mentoring programs.

> Mentoring is one-on-one support and feedback provided by an experienced veteran teacher to a new or struggling teacher. An induction program is a larger system of support that often includes mentoring, but also includes additional supports, such as help with curriculum planning and professional development. (Potemski & Matlach, 2014, p. 1)

Ohio and many other states implement state-mandated induction programs. These programs support new teachers by coaching them through best practices of teaching in the hopes that they are teaching at a higher, more effective level sooner, rather than later, in their career.

However, research studies show mixed results on the effectiveness of new teacher induction programs. Many states require these programs in public K–12 school districts and are costly to districts. According to the New Teacher Center, one of the leading institutions for teacher induction programs, the average cost of a high-quality induction program can run as high as $7,000 per teacher. These high-quality induction programs have the potential to increase teacher retention and increase new teacher effectiveness, which, in return, should save districts a significant amount of money. Research has shown that it costs an average urban school district an estimated $15,000–$17,000 when a single teacher leaves the district (The New Teacher Center, 2007). Although research from the New Teacher Center shows that quality teacher induction programs produce improved teacher retention rates by over 20% (Moir, 2014), Kane (2013) states "there is limited evidence of the degree to which current policy investment in induction programs adds value in terms of teacher professional learning, teacher quality, and student learning" (para. 1).

In the State of Ohio, the induction program is referred to as the Resident Educator Program (REP). The REP is a 4-year program. The first 2 years are the mentoring years and the last 2 years focus on assessment. The assessment required is the Resident Educator Summative Assessment (RESA). If the new teacher passes all four parts of the assessment in year three, then the fourth year is used to explore teacher leadership. This program is not only required of new teachers but their licensure advancement is dependent upon the successful completion of the program. Ohio's teacher induction program was loosely based on the medical profession's residency structure, hence the 4-year program. However, there are not many similarities beyond that.

Medical students, for example, are practicing on cadavers and working side by side with an attending doctor, in real world situations, as they learn medical skills and how to think like a doctor. In Ohio, the school of education prepares preservice teachers by having them take the core classes and clinical experiences needed to graduate. Upon graduation and employment, new teachers have limited support while they are expected to teach students in a manner that meets the high expectations set by the school district and the Department of Education. One can argue that the reason so many new teachers feel unprepared is because none of the aforementioned metrics and requirements of undergraduate education include real world teaching scenarios. During the clinical/field experience, preservice teachers walk into a fully functioning classroom, where the rules and procedures are set, a community of learners has been established and an experienced teacher is in the same classroom to offer instruction, guidance, and support. This is unlike what new teachers experience when they walk into their own classroom for the first time. Often, they are hired after the school year has begun, given a classroom that has been stripped bare, lacking supplies and materials, and are often given a class roster full of students who have learning and/or behavior concerns. It is at this time that the teachers become part of the induction program and are referred to as *resident educators* (RE).

During this time, the RE is often the sole teacher in a classroom and held accountable for student outcomes. During this time, the RE should be receiving support from both their administrator and mentor teacher. Unfortunately, the reality is that they often have very little support because their mentor teacher is teaching his/her own students while the building administrator is dealing with a myriad of building issues. Nonetheless, it is the job of this teacher mentor and administrator, who are not in the new teacher's classroom, to support, mentor, and develop this new teacher into an effective educator. During the mentoring years, conversations, concerns, and reflections between the RE and mentor rarely happen in real time but are saved for a time when they can both meet without students. This could be daily, weekly, or even biweekly, depending on the school. Additionally, Ohio mentors are only required to attend a 2-day training that introduces them to instructional mentoring. Additional online training is available but is not required. Not only are the mentors often insufficiently trained, but many districts must plead to get veteran teachers to agree to take on the position instead of choosing the best educator for the job. None of the factors stated above create a conducive environment for a high level of on the job training and support as intended by the program.

Today, Ohio's resident educator program is on the chopping block. In 2017, the Ohio senate voted to eliminate the program in its entirety only to be saved by the governor. I believe that as a district we must view these moves as a sign that the program is near its end. If removed, past practice has shown that a new program will replace the current program. As an educator who believes that new teachers need to be supported through a strong teacher induction program, I think it is time for school districts to plan and develop their own programs of support that cater to the needs of their teachers and school culture, one that can survive the whims of government mandates. We must not let the caprices of government cause us to drop the ball on new teacher support. If we, as individual districts, create induction programs based on best practices, one that creates resilient, self-reliant, and instructionally strong teachers, then they should withstand whatever the state department throws at us.

John Goodlad has reawakened my desire to challenge the status quo of teacher induction. I have devoted countless hours to thinking about how I can better support new teachers. As I discussed earlier, I have envisioned a relationship of communication and collaboration between higher education and K–12 school districts but never pursued the possibilities of a partnership. After reading *Educational Renewal* (Goodlad, 1994), I am committed to exploring this possibility. Although Goodlad's book and 19 postulates are geared towards changing teacher education curriculum and programs, his ideas resonated with me, causing me to reflect on how I can use his ideas to change how we support our new teachers. I may not have control on what program the state department will require of us but I can facilitate change within my own school district. I plan to begin this change by reaching out to local universities. I would propose an idea of collaboration and anticipate that one would be willing to work with our district in a way that would support both our new teachers and mentors while also offering levels of support to their teacher preparation program.

Taking from both Goodlad's work and that of Montclair State University, there are a few ways I believe a collaboration with a university could help support our local induction program and their teacher education program. The first would be through professional development. Although Ohio mentors are required to go through a 2-day training, this training does not fully prepare them to be effective instructional coaches and mentors. Additional training could include cognitive coaching, facilitation techniques, and collaborative practices. New teachers could also benefit from professional development by having the mentors and university professors support them as they begin to bridge the gap between theory and practice.

The collaboration can also extend into the undergraduate's teaching experiences and student teaching. I envision our teaching staff working with the university to create classroom experiences that elicit high levels of learning through real world hands-on experiences, critical conversations, and problem-solving strategies. An experience where university professors, veterans, and preservice teachers are all experiencing and interacting with both higher education and K–12 curriculum. The university's department of education and the administrative staff of my school district would also meet to discuss the areas of strength and weakness of the programs for refinement and growth. I believe that through this type of experience, we all gain a greater understanding of each institution, leading us to build and create better systems of learning for new and future teachers.

Although the aforementioned ideas may be minimal, I believe that these conversations could start laying the foundation for something bigger. With the research and knowledge that university professors could bring to the table along with the knowledge and experience of veteran teachers and administrators, we have the opportunity to transform the way we prepare and support new teachers.

In the opening of this chapter, I explored the darkness of Plato's cave, a cave in which the prisoners could only see and experience life through the observation of shadows cast by the sunlight behind them. Plato's allegory expressed concern for those who never break free of the shackles that bind them to the cave, forever unable to educate themselves on what is true and real. The allegory resonates with me and the work I do with new teachers every year. Goodlad gave us a plan for preservice and university/ school district partnerships that could break open windows of light into those caves by directing students' minds toward what is real and important and allowing them to apprehend the knowledge and experiences for themselves. Through these windows, we can view a new beginning. I challenge educators of today to research and learn from the past as to move into a more prolific and purposeful future. The practice of education is multifaceted and imperative to maintaining a democratic society. What can we learn from Montclair State University in order to implement similar programs? The time has come to stop viewing school districts and universities as two separate entities. We are all in the profession of education, a never-ending spiral of light, a circular organism that molds, shapes, and produces all other professions. Together we must rise.

REFERENCES

Ashburn, E. A. (1986). Current developments in teacher induction programs. *Action in Teacher Education, 8*(4), 41–44.

Danielson, C. (2009, June 1). *A framework for learning to teach.* ASCD. http://www.ascd.org/publications/educational-leadership/summer09/vol66/num09/A-Framework-for-Learning-to-Teach.aspx

Ducharme, E. R., Ducharme, M. K., & Dunkin, M. J. (n.d.). *Teacher education: Historical overview, international perspective.* State University. http://education.stateuniversity.com/pages/2479/Teacher-Education.html

Encyclopedia.com. (n.d.). *John Inkster Goodlad.* https://www.encyclopedia.com/people/history/historians-miscellaneous-biographies/john-i-goodlad

Gonzalez, P. (2013). *Plato's idea of the teacher.* http://www.kirkcenter.org/index.php/bookman/article/platos-idea-of-the-teacher/

Goodlad, J. I. (1994). *Educational renewal: Better teachers, better schools.* Jossey-Bass.

Haynes. M. (2014, July). *On the path to equity: Improving the effectiveness of beginning teachers.* All4Ed. https://all4ed.org/publication/path-to-equity/

Kane, R. (2013). *Beginning-teacher induction.* Oxford Bibliographies. https://www.oxfordbibliographies.com/view/document/obo-9780199756810/obo-9780199756810-0077.xml

Labaree, D. F. (2021, August 26). *An uneasy relationship: The history of teacher education in the university.* David Labaree on Schooling, History, and Writing.

MacKnight, D. (2022). *Montclair State University Network for Educational Renewal FAQs.* https://msuner.org/page/2927079:Page:130

Moir, E. (2014, July 17). *Improving the effectiveness of beginning teachers* [PowerPoint]. https://all4ed.org/wp-content/uploads/2014/07/Ellen_ppt_-Alliance-briefing_july_17_2014_DRAFT-V5.pptx

Montclair State University. (2019, August 20). The 2019 MSUNER Summer Conference. *Alumni News.* https://www.montclair.edu/alumni/2019/08/20/the-2019-msuner-summer-conference/

Ogren, C. A. (2003). Rethinking the "nontraditional" student from a historical perspective: State normal schools in the late nineteenth and early twentieth centuries. *The Journal of Higher Education, 74*(6), 640–664.

Potemski, A., & Matlack, L. (2014). *Supporting new teachers: What do we know about effective state induction policies?* Center on Great Teachers and Leaders. http://www.gtlcenter.org/sites/default/files/Induction_Snapshot.pdf

The New Teacher Center. (2007). *New teacher support pays off: A return on investment for educators and kids.* NTC Policy Brief. http://dcntp.org/wp-content/uploads/2012/12/making-the-case-new_teach_support.pdf

The White House. (2014, April 25). *Fact sheet: Taking action to improve teacher preparation.* https://www.whitehouse.gov/the-press-office/2014/04/25/fact-sheet-taking-action-improve-teacher-preparation

CHAPTER 10

THE CULTURAL STRUGGLE IS REAL IN OUR CLASSROOMS

How Our Students' Culture Effects Educating Them

Marilee R. Tanner

Author/Book studied:

Delpit, L. (1995). *Other people's children: Cultural conflict in the classroom.* The New Press.

CULTURAL INJUSTICE

Delpit's (1995) major theme in *Other People's Children: Cultural Conflict in the Classroom,* is to teach the children and they will perform. In schools today, we have children who know the rules of the school because they reflect the rules of their culture. However, what about those outside of the culture of the majority? When are they taught the rules or codes they need to be

Curriculum Windows Redux, pages 121–133
Copyright © 2022 by Information Age Publishing
www.infoagepub.com
All rights of reproduction in any form reserved.

successful in school and who is responsible for teaching them? A theory of Delpit's is to teach children the code of the culture of power and this will create success for these children well into their future. All children would then be on the same playing field as they moved about their school years and no miscommunication would result.

LISA D. DELPIT

Lisa Delpit is an African American researcher whose work emphasizes elementary education and focuses on language and literacy development. Delpit grew up in "Old Baton Rouge." Her parents' example of helping children in need by providing free meals to elementary schools fostered a desire to help at-risk children. Her father owned a restaurant and she worked most of her youth in the restaurant. Her mother was a high school teacher. Delpit spent her school age years regurgitating basic skills back to her teachers, skills such as diagramming sentences and practicing multiplication facts. It was not until her 10th grade where this award winning author broke free from her low level of learning and challenged the "status quo." Delpit went to Antioch College in Ohio. At the time Antioch was known for its radicalism, and after graduating she went to South Philadelphia to teach. It was at the school in South Philadelphia where she realized that all children do not learn the same way or at the same pace. There were individuals in need of different strategies. Delpit went on to study at Harvard's Graduate School of Education where she received her master's and doctorate degrees in curriculum, instruction and research. She received a fellowship grant and traveled to Papua New Guinea where she evaluated school programs and conducted her own research. In reading Delpit's writings, readers may find the following themes: granting students' access to the culture of power; preparing teachers for cultural, linguistic and ethnic diversity; and developing open mindedness and eliminating the bias of the "other."

CRITIQUE

In *Other People's Children: Cultural Conflict in the Classroom,* Delpit (1995) expresses her beliefs on racism, mistreatment, and ignorance in our culture today. Delpit divides the book into three sections: "Skills and Other Dilemmas of a Progressive Black Educator"; "Lessons from Home and Abroad"; and "Looking Into the Future."

In the first section of the book called, "Skills and Other Dilemmas of a Progressive Black Educator," Delpit (1995) delves into topics such as power in the classroom and how it affects the environment within the classroom, as well as the rapport the teacher has with the child. She speaks to the curriculum that is being taught to African American students. Delpit touches on the benefits of teaching skills within a meaningful context rather than in isolation. This is an important part since some educators choose the program the child should work on due to the student's skin color or upbringing rather than assessing the student and using curriculum that meets the need of the child. Delpit makes a point in this section that Black children need to see the subject matter connect with their own life to have success. Further in the section, she continues to discuss differences in family expectations such as the differences between African American families' expectations of schools versus White families' expectations. African American expectations, according to Delpit, are to teach their child how to be successful in the world; White families expect schools to provide a good education. I do not agree with Delpit on this statement. I feel families of all races expect schools to provide a good education. It would be more accurate to say Black families are expecting a school to provide a good education along with helping their child understand the culture of the world around them to ensure success. White families do not say they expect a school to help their child with the culture of the world around them since the majority of the population is White, thus holding the codes and culture for success.

This first section also includes a key chapter of the book titled, "The Silenced Dialogue." Here Delpit (1995) discusses the curriculum, pedagogy, culture, issues with progressive education, and explains what children of color need in an education. In my experiences as an educator, I feel students of color are in need of the same environment and teacher that any other student needs. This would be a teacher who is knowledgeable, can build a rapport with his/her students, and makes the content relevant and engaging. When these best practices are at work, the teacher will reach and be successful with all of the children.

In the second part of the book, "Lessons From Home and Abroad," Delpit (1995) uses her experiences when she was in Papua New Guinea and the time she was working with the Native Americans to specifically show examples of other cultures and communities. Her stories are true testaments to cultural acceptance within their communities. While Delpit was working in Papua New Guinea in combination with Australian researchers, they were trying to find out what people wanted in education. She found that families wanted an education where their children would not lose their culture. As a result, the islanders began 2 years of preschool instruction at age 7, followed by 6 years of English-language primary school which would begin at age 9. The preschool focus would be on basic skills such as reading, writing, and counting in their native language. Congruently, the children would receive cultural education which would include customs, values, and acceptable behavior in the community. The program was successful in both achievement and retention of the children's culture. From this study, Delpit began to think of how Black students should be taught the culture of power—which will help them be successful in their school—and their own culture so they do not lose their identity. According to Delpit (1995), "When it reaffirms rather than negates a people's knowledge of its culture and heritage, then there is no better prospect for its success" (p. 90).

In a diverse district like mine, we embrace the culture of the 49 plus countries that are represented. There are opportunities for families and students to proudly educate others of their countries with a cultural night. Students are encouraged to share their stories of their heritage in social studies classes. High school students perform dances of their culture during lunch time. Many of the schools have a cultural club which includes all students in which students can learn from one another various cultures from around the world. The district supports our diversity with a lunch menu that reflects our diverse population. There is a district cultural diversity committee. This committee is charged with understanding the needs of our diverse students and families, helping them feel welcomed and looking at bringing awareness on teaching a diverse population to our staff.

The final section is about the call to action from Delpit regarding what she would like to see happen to aid the success of educating African American and diverse children in the United States. Some of her suggestions include: relooking at teacher evaluation systems and ensuring there is no bias, curating interactions between teacher and family to help better understand one another, including more diversity in the teaching staff at schools, and offering a more diverse (non-Eurocentric) curriculum. She calls for the staff of schools to be more open-minded when working with a diverse population and as stated previously, a wider perspective when dealing with the students, student issues (i.e., discipline), and families.

Delpit has a strong voice in regards to curriculum, pedagogy culture, progressive education, and what students of color need to have a successful education. In thinking about today's educational system, I reflect on Delpit's thoughts on these topics and try to understand her voice. However, when I think about Delpit's recommendations I question, aren't these best practices that we should be implementing to ensure all students receive an equitable education?

TODAY'S CURRICULUM

With the push of Common Core in today's schools, ideally a student who moves from one school to another will experience the same standards from district to- district and state to state. This helps prevent large gaps in educating our transient students. However, Delpit would argue a big flaw in the Common Core curriculum today would be assuming that all the students began in the same place, with the same skills. For example, I see many students who transfer from district to district (in and out of the state) who have gaps. Even though we are all using the Common Core Standards, there are still more gaps within a student's education when the student has moved frequently, providing for a fractured educational profile.

Delpit would also argue that the curriculum is based on the Eurocentric education which is only one viewpoint and does not account for the history of the Africans. She would argue that a one-sided curriculum does not allow African American children to connect to the history being taught to them or give their culture relevance. Their disproportionate education, Delpit would state, is what causes children of color to fail in the school system today. The push today is for a multicultural curriculum. This will bring diversity back into the curriculum. However, this does not solve the problem since teaching staff is not prepared to deliver the contents in a multiculturalist way (Pinar et al., 2006).

PEDAGOGY

Delpit speaks to specific skills being taught for children of color in order to be successful in schools. She states that there needs to be an understanding of the written and spoken language within the culture of power and an understanding of the power of language for children of color to be successful. In order to help teach the written and spoken language, students are exposed to many different genres and teachers discuss author's voice.

Within our school, fifth and sixth grade students participate in project based learning. Students take a school-based problem (i.e., second chance breakfast) and ask interviewees questions about the problem, gather data, and write persuasive presentations. This allows the students to have a voice, a purpose, and allows them to be part of the learning process. Students make real life connections to the content being presented and it becomes relevant to their life and practice their speaking and writing skills. Delpit would agree project based learning would benefit African American students due to their strong need to see relevance of the content to their lives. This style of learning would also pay attention to specific skills children of color may need specifically in speaking, writing, and presentation skills.

Another form of best practice that was implemented within our school district was formative checks within a lesson. The purpose of the checks was to help see growth and mastery of all students. After the formative checks were completed by each student, teachers looked at the data and were able to group students and differentiate lesson plans for individual needs. Teachers then were able to reteach specific skills to certain students, conference with them, and make the content more relevant. Students are able to show mastery of the content and even partake in graphing their own progress. The differentiation the teachers began as a result of the formative checks that we began helped students begin to grow and master content and not just be compliant. Delpit (1995) would agree these forms of checks would help teachers form relationships with students of color, teach relevance, and help the student feel the teacher believes in him/her.

THE MAIN ISSUES WITH PROGRESSIVE EDUCATION

One of Delpit's major issues was with progressive education. She talked about how progressive education assumed that all children started at the same place. Recently I heard a discussion amongst a team of teachers. The teachers were discussing students' scores on a universal screener. The teachers talked about how some students were growing when others were not. However, one important point was brought to light, "How could these few very low students make several points growth when they did not even know the content being taught in the classroom?" The teachers were assuming the growth was first based on the content taught in the classroom and that each child would have the same knowledge and then grow from that point. This relates to Delpit's point that the issue is more of a miscommunication and alienation between the Black and Whites' cultural perspective. Delpit (1995) gives an example of a miscommunication between cultures, "Progressive white teachers seem to say to their black students, 'Let me help you find your voice. I promise not to criticize one note as you search for your own song,'" she writes in the first of her essays. "But the black teachers say, 'I've heard your song loud and clear. Now, I want you to harmonize with the rest of the world'" (p. 18).

As I continue to read books and journals, I wonder if children of color can succeed in a White middle class world without losing their identity. How can an average White, middle class woman teach a child of color in today's society? Delpit answers these questions with two main ideas: (a) teach the codes of the culture of power and (b) be effective instructors in education.

NEEDS OF CHILDREN OF COLOR AND THE CULTURE
OF POWER—MENTORING

Delpit discusses cultural aspects of education and how they can affect children of color. A great way to accomplish educating children of the cultural aspects of education would be by providing a mentor to children of color. The mentor would help facilitate understanding of the culture of power, the code of the culture of power, the value of the code, and why the people within the culture of power do not recognize they have power. Mentoring would allow the codes of the culture to be taught to the children in a nonthreatening way. The children could be taught what value the code has to them in society and how this will help them with their future success—making the connections to their life in the future. Mentors could lead by example, providing their own life experiences from when they were their age. Most importantly, mentors could teach the children how to succeed in the educational and political world while also keeping their own identity by switching codes when necessary. Additional skills taught by the mentors would also be writing, speaking, and self-presentation skills that would go along with the culture of power.

NEEDS OF CHILDREN OF COLOR—ADVOCACY

Children of color will also need a person to speak for them in the educational process/world, that being an advocate. Their voice and educational needs should be heard. This means the community, parents, and students should be gathered when discussing a child's concerns and how to succeed in schools. One strategy in our school is students prepare student-teacher conferences to help the students' voices be heard. Prior to these student-led conferences, teachers and students establish goals the student wants to accomplish for the year. If a student is misbehaving or has missing assignments, it is pertinent the teachers work with the student and families. This may be the following steps: meet with the child privately, meet with the child as a team of teachers, communicate to the parents the observed behaviors and what plans have been in place or what they are planning to do. All of these steps need to include the student.

School wide, we have a progressive discipline system. Students are always asked what happened prior to stating the punishment. Many times, parents are called to collaborate when problem-solving with the student on the choices he/she made and how they can be corrected. In addition to these steps, Delpit would suggest school administrators putting in place conflict resolution and a "check-in, check-out" program as part of their discipline procedures. These best practices would help children of color feel part of the process, know that the adults believe they can learn, and therefore begin to develop the personal relationship that they so desire. Within the classroom, on a daily basis, Delpit would suggest teachers foster environments where directions are clearer, concise, and direct, have high standards for learning, and a general acceptance for minority groups.

CONNECTION TO THE STRENGTH OF THE CULTURE
OF THE CHILDREN IN OUR CLASSROOMS

While reading Delpit's (1995) book, a window opened for me in regards to ways in which diverse populations process through interactions, their values, and the expectations on education, and what schools should provide children of color. Things began to get clearer when I thought about students and their culture. One particular connection I made to Delpit's book in this area was with an African American family who moved into our district. The students were moving from a predominantly African American community to our school district which had a predominantly White population. The boys had moved through several different school districts, all in African American communities. Not long after the boys entered our school, the boys began to exhibit behaviors. The behaviors were mostly insubordination and disrespect. The boys were unable to see a purpose of being at this new school and even stated they were afraid of losing their identity. The boys' behaviors created barriers between their peer groups and the adults in the school. After a month, the team, which consisted of the teachers, administrators, counselors, and psychologist, convened and began notifying the parent regarding the boys' behaviors and lack of work completion. After 2 months, the team became smaller and only consisted of one teacher, one administrator, and the psychologist. This team met more frequently, communicating and having discussions that were more purposeful about what the boys needed to be successful in their environments and work completion. Collaboration and solutions became the topic of the conversations and a plan was implemented. In reflection on this situation, Delpit would agree the boys needed to have someone speak on their behalf, someone who did not represent the culture of power. In the meeting, the school district brought in a social worker, their mom, and a wrap-around-service provider. All these voices were alternative voices other than the culture of power at the school district.

With this example of the boys, two-way communication between the White educators and the children of color needed to be opened. At the beginning, the interventions with the boys were not successful because there was notification to the parent and the parent was not being heard about what she felt was best for the boys. Delpit makes the point of Blacks not being heard by Whites, and miscommunication results. All of the White educators' perception was that the boys were misbehaving and the mother was not supporting the school. A perception such as this happens when there is only one side of the story—whether the other side has not been voiced, not being taken in account or completely ignored. The mother did not understand why our school was saying her sons were misbehaving all the time and not completing work because the boys did not act this way at home. The boys' behavior was a direct result of not understanding the code of the culture of power they were experiencing in their new school district. The educators were perceiving that this child was acting out because he wanted to be defiant and they were not listening to the mother's solutions. Had the team began with communication and problem-solving sessions which happened at the end, the mother and the team would have not been as frustrated for so long. It is important to make sure all parties are represented and heard.

Delpit (1995) discusses how we want to start with understanding the culture of power within our environment:

> If we are to succeed in this quest, we must recognize and address the power differentials that exist in our society between schools and communities, between teachers and parents, between poor and well-to-do, between whites and people of color. (p. 133)

She explains that within the classrooms today there is a culture of power which is enacted by the teacher over the students. The person of power then enacts codes, or rules, for participating in the culture of power. All of these rules, or codes, are a reflection of the culture which has the power. If a student is not part of the culture of power (i.e., children of color or children of poverty) then obtaining this power is difficult. It must be taught. The persons who are within the culture of power are least likely to know they hold this power since they are not struggling within the culture and obtaining the power is easy (Delpit, 1995, pp. 24–28).

Delpit (1995) speaks to the uneven power, "Those who are less powerful in any situation are most likely to recognize the power variable more accurately" (p. 26). This suggests that the teachers were unaware of the power they held in the classrooms during the meeting. The boys were struggling with acclimating to the school culture since they were not part of the culture of power. All the codes and rules that were expected of the boys were very different from their culture and the cultures of their previous schools. The educators at our school were unfamiliar with the culture the boys were coming from and the majority of the educators did not actively take interest in the boys. Delpit would suggest addressing the miscommunication and culture differences by teaching the boys the code of the culture of power directly and explicitly. This would help them become successful in the environment. The boys also needed teachers who formed strong relationships with them to help mentor them through this transition. If possible, Delpit would suggest having teachers of the boys' same culture so they could identify with each other.

To continue to open this window of ongoing dialogue about cultures of power and giving students of color a voice, we must explore how schools can accomplish this task. In our classrooms and schools, we have children who will be entering from many different cultures. It would be best if we focus on teaching the students how the culture of power works, what its value is to them, how to speak within the culture of power, and how to write and present themselves in the culture of power. This may include the conventions, grammar, and rhythms of the middle-class life. According to Delpit (1995), "They (parents) want to ensure that the school provides their children with discourse patterns, interactional styles, and spoken and written language codes that will allow them success in the larger society" (p. 29).

The way we teach children of color and poverty is as important as the background of the person who teaches them. An article by Horsford et al. (2011) supports this,

> Thus this growing racialized demographic divide between students and teachers, coupled with limited training in culturally relevant and antiracist epistemologies and educational practices, has significant implications for student learning, engagement, and achievement in cultural and racially incongruent contexts. (p. 588)

Delpit (1995) explains that the school systems should be ensuring that educators are as diverse as their population. She supports this due to the difference in the learning styles between African American children and "mainstream" children. Delpit discusses how people of color begin with relationships rather than content. She states, "Research suggests that children of color value the social aspects of an environment to a greater extent than 'mainstream' children" (p. 140). Bittner (2017) discusses students' perception in regard to their teachers: "Students perceive black teachers more than their white peers to hold students to high academic standards and support their efforts, to help them organize their content, and to explain clearly ideas and concepts and provide useful feedback" (p. 16). Delpit also explains how children of color want persons of authority to act authoritatively and not as a student's friend. Students expect the person in authority to earn the authority by effort and by personal characteristics. If these things do not happen, the student will not revere the person who is supposed to be an authority figure as an authoritarian in their environment. Students of color and poverty are consistently having the authority figure prove characteristics to ensure he/she knows that she is the authoritarian. For example, if the teacher cannot control the classroom, she will lose the authority figure for most children of color.

I observe this playing out in the school environment frequently. There was an African American student who I knew who constantly challenged the teacher and bus drivers at our school. An incident early in the year happened which brought him to the office. I asked him what happened and he explained that his chips fell on the floor and the entire class laughed. The teacher did not address the laughter yet when he became upset and disrespectful she sent him to the office. There were incidents on the bus where he would get in trouble and in his eyes, others on the bus were having behaviors, too. However, he felt they were not getting disciplined. The student continued to exhibit behaviors to challenge the teacher and bus drivers to see if they were authority figures. He came to the conclusion the teacher was not controlling the classroom and the driver was not controlling the bus which led him to decide that the teachers and bus drivers are not authority figures. He then had an experience where he went into a room with a sub who happened to be an African American woman. He explained to her that she was a good sub. She asked how he knew that when they were only there for a few minutes. He said, "Because you have control of the classroom."

The curtains have been pulled back and I can now see a bit more clearly. My thoughts veer to understanding Delpit's discussion on culture of power, codes, and rules that go along with the culture of power, and specifics to aid in the success of African American students and students from low socioeconomic subgroups. Ladson-Billings (2009) talks about successful characteristics and practices of teachers of African American children, or implementations of mentoring programs and initiatives on hiring practices to ensure minorities are getting jobs in schools. These have made me wonder about my long-term goals for this topic. I question myself, "How can I make a larger impact in this area and open up the dialogue in my district, community, and state?" I then wonder about the impact I can make in my current building. What difference can I make with referrals in the office, communication I have with families of color and poverty, and how can I work with staff regarding understanding the concept of culture of power. I believe I can start with an awareness of the concept of the culture of power and how White educators, the majority, need to understand the culture of power, others' perceptions, and understand and build relationships with those that are not in the culture of power. I want to open up the conversation on both sides with the purpose of understanding each side's perception in order to help our children grow successfully in society.

OUR IMPACT AS EDUCATORS

Today's children of color are still a minority in the education system. The curriculum, the teaching staff, and the culture of the school do not often reflect the values and interests of marginalized children. In order for all our children to succeed, we need to ensure they are able to see themselves and their culture through what is being taught to them and their surroundings. The children should be able to be viewed by their teachers as unique individuals and given instruction based on their need. This is truly best practice in education. In order for this to happen with children of color, we need to get more families involved in the education system. This means we need representatives for people of color in every facet of the educational arena; from Washington, DC to our teachers in our classrooms. I would like to see school districts making more of an effort to recruit and sustain teachers of color in their school districts. With African Americans and Latinos teaching in the schools, children will be able to identify and trust that their voices are heard. In her review on Delpit's book, Viadero (1996) states,

> If you really want to know how best to teach urban children, Delpit maintains, then you must ask them and their parents. You also must ask the teachers who know them best because they come from the same cultural groups. (para. 21)

When there are issues and academic and behavioral concerns with a child who is African American, administrators and teachers need to contact the parents and request face-to-face meetings to problem solve and ensure that all parties' voices are heard. When curriculum, schedules, and district changes are happening, I ask that we make sure there are African Americans represented on committees. It is important to make sure everyone is involved in the educational process. The most important piece is to involve all stakeholders in the decision-making process. Having all stakeholders represented in decisions for our students is important. As Delpit (1995) states, "We must keep the perspective that people are experts in their own lives," she writes. "There are certainly aspects of the outside world of which they may not be aware, but they can be the only authentic chroniclers of their own experience" (p. 47). When all perspectives are represented, then all experiences are represented and everyone will feel heard and we may just fulfill Delpit's goal of an equitable education for every student.

REFERENCES

Bittner, R. (2017). The diversity divide. *Principal, 96*(3), 14–18.

Delpit, L. (1995). *Other people's children: Cultural conflict in the classroom.* The New Press.

Douglas Horsford, S., Grosland, T., & Morgan Gunn, K. (2011). Pedagogy of the personal and professional: Toward a framework for culturally relevant leadership. *Journal of School Leadership, 21*(4), 582–606.

Ladson- Billings, G. (2009). *The dream keepers: Successful teachers of African American children.* Jossy- Bass.

Pinar, W., Reynolds, W., Slattery, P., & Taubman, P. (2006). *Understanding curriculum: An introduction to the study of historical and contemporary curriculum discourses.* Peter Lang.

Viadero, D. (1996, March 13). Lisa Delpit says teachers must value students' cultural strengths. *Education Week.* https://www.edweek.org/teaching-learning/lisa-delpit-says-teachers-must-value-students-cultural-strengths/1996/03

CHAPTER 11

TEACHING HUMANS TODAY

Andrea D. Townsend

Author/Book studied:

Sleeter, C. E., & Grant, C. A. (1988). *Making choices for multicultural education: Five approaches to race, class, and gender.* Merrill Publishing Company.

Christine Sleeter is an educator whose work regarding respect for diversity and education continues to impact the way practitioners in education implement strategies that foster respect for diversity and differences. Her collaborative work with Carl Grant titled *Making Choices for Multicultural Education: Five Approaches to Race, Class, and Gender* (Sleeter & Grant, 1988) elevated her work to an international level as it outlined five choices for educators addressing diversity in their classrooms. With this book she and Grant empowered the profession as a whole to think critically regarding their response to diverse populations of students. Her work continues as an activist, teacher, and speaker on the topic today. Her experiences as a high school teacher during desegregation helped her to formulate her earliest ideas about multicultural education. Sleeter and Grant build on their

Curriculum Windows Redux, pages 135–147
Copyright © 2022 by Information Age Publishing
www.infoagepub.com
135

experiences to lay the foundation of the work in multicultural education that continues today.

As a reader, the work of Sleeter and Grant resonates with theories developed by Miami's own Richard Quantz, which provide a solid foundation for critically analyzing the impact of social interaction, including education on the identity of the human. In this way, *Multicultural Education* (Sleeter & Grant, 1988) highlights the shift in the accepted purpose of education. Originally education existed as a tool for assimilation or indoctrination. The nature of indoctrination allows little to no room for recognition or respect for cultures other than the dominant culture. Multicultural education calls educators to examine the role of culture in the student identity and, thus, the role of student identity to student success. At the heart of multicultural education is the discussion of the purpose of education as our society broadens its view of the citizen.

Sleeter and Grant (1988) outlined five options for addressing multicultural education that existed in the 1980s. During that decade, the work in multicultural education was barely out of infancy and the focus seems to be on what programs or strategies would work to incorporate the impact of culture on students and learning.

Sleeter and Grant (1988) compared five approaches to multicultural education that were a part of classrooms in the 1980s. Classrooms then could be seen as a microcosm of the larger society with diverse groups of people participating in parallel endeavors and masking their differences with pop culture and fashion. While this allowed many of the educators and leaders to celebrate this as a success in race relations and multicultural education, the need for multicultural education can be seen in the continued stratification of students and then therefore adults by race, gender, ability, and socioeconomic status. The achievement gaps and therefore gaps in potential outcomes continue to be stagnant between minority groups. These gaps were glaring in the 1980s and for the most part exist today. After Sleeter and Grant reviewed the literature, they boiled down the multicultural approaches into five approaches and then recommended one.

APPROACHES

Sleeter and Grant (1988) identified one approach as *teaching the exceptional and the culturally different*. This approach works primarily to train students to fit into the contrived parameters of school so that students can find their proper place in society.

When considering the demographics of school, we find a significant discrepancy in representation of minorities among teachers and staff members and the representation of minorities among students and community members. This allows for an approach that considers the minority characteristics as a weakness that teachers must teach students to overcome. This approach is still widely used when teaching students with diverse intellectual ability. We continue to see these differences as weaknesses and then justify segregation within instructional time and space so that the students can catch up.

Sadly, in districts where this approach is continued, over-representation of students of diverse racial, cultural, socioeconomic status and gender occurs in special education classes. Many great and caring special education teachers work hard to build compensatory skills in students and encourage appropriate social choices by students with the hope that they will correct or "fix" the weakness of the students all with the vision of their successful adult outcomes. On the surface, this approach appears to be most considerate of the student and the students' needs. In reality, it contributes to the stratification of subgroups through segregated instruction that only further develops weaknesses rather than catches students up.

The second approach that Sleeter and Grant (1988) outline in *Multicultural Education* is *human relations*. Human relations is built on the premise that differences are a part of students' identities and we must instruct students on their differences and how to interact appropriately among groups who differ from their own identified groups. The hope is that through education, stereotypes will diminish and tolerance and acceptance will thrive.

In reality, however, acceptance in a group of individuals requires similarities that are recognizable and are noticed by children even before they come to school. Human beings construct their identity through interactions that allow them to sort individuals into their group or not into their group. The direct connection between identity and group membership is at such a depth that they cannot really be separated. Therefore, to belong to a different group or comply with the expectations of a different group, the student would need to abandon the construct of his or her identity as a human.

In this light, the human relations approach could be likened to a band-aid approach since it doesn't address the heart of the issue, which is the students' identity, validating that identity, recognizing its worth, and building that student's strengths in light of that identity. Human Relations, however, focuses on skills of communication and conflict resolution that work to address multicultural relationships when a problem arises. This approach ignores the current or past oppression of that group and is based on the premise that negative intergroup relationships are a given.

The third approach outlined by Sleeter and Grant (1988) is the *single group studies* approach. Steeped in the philosophy that there cannot be a completely neutral educational setting, single group studies hopes to encourage individuals to critically think about and investigate other cultures, and their own. As an approach, it is cumbersome and difficult to implement. It operates on necessary assumptions such as public education is a venue for instruction in critical thinking, and that cultures can be studied in isolation, and that individuals desire to think critically about culture and their identity as it relates to their culture. While the theory can be seductive, the actual application fails to affect actual change in perspectives or interactions.

Ultimately, the conflict created by this approach to multicultural education is the purpose of education. Since the beginning of public education, the role of the institution has been about more than imparting knowledge. At the heart of democracy is education and the heart of education is perpetuating our democracy. Challenging that purpose will be a monumental undertaking and is likely to hinder the benefits of the Single Group Study approach.

In addition to the strong tie between democracy and education, many of the structures and traditions of public education are designed to assimilate students into society. A dominant culture exerts a heavy influence on our society. Often the struggle of diverse students is about integrating into the dominant culture of school. While this seems to support the need for the single study groups, the critical issue is addressing the lack of a neutral culture in the school setting. The critical examination of cultures is a good beginning, but may not empower students to be successful regardless of setting or culture.

At the end of the day, the overall impact of the single group study approach on multicultural education can be summed up by Black History Month. While it is never a bad idea to learn more about diverse cultures and the heroes of that culture, limiting the focus of diverse cultures to a specific season of the year or containing culture study to a segment of time will likely have a limited impact in terms of how we address culture in education.

The fourth approach that Sleeter and Grant (1988) addressed is *multicultural education*. While this might seem confusing, as an approach, multicultural education is how many educators in this decade referred to an approach to multicultural education that promotes strength and value of cultural diversity, human rights, respect for others, and alternative life choices for people. This approach hinges on the concept of cultural pluralism and equal opportunity. Cultural pluralism is the state of equal coexistence of many different cultures without dominance or competition for opportunity working toward the common goal of democracy. Equal opportunity is the provision of opportunities without regard for race, gender, class, or handicap.

While these pillars of multicultural education seem to have been a part of society as a whole and legally imparted on education and other aspects of our lives, proponents of this approach argue that integrating these concepts at a compliance level is not sufficient for true multicultural education. In essence, it is not enough to merely state that all beliefs are allowed at school due to the separation of church and state, and then structure all holiday celebrations around traditional Christian beliefs. Moreover, to achieve multicultural education, equal opportunity in education must be more than stated, in fact it must be reflected in measurements of representation of diverse race, class, gender and religion in remedial programs such as special education or in enrichment programs such as gifted services.

In application, multicultural education is ambitious when considering that addressing multicultural education means addressing the pillars of cultural pluralism and equal opportunity on all fronts of education. This includes the curriculum, materials, instruction, and assessment of students in such a way that students have the opportunity to recognize, accept, and celebrate differences in cultures and individuals in the materials and concepts presented in class, the environment and structures, and even assessment questions. Considering how to honor, and more importantly remove any obvious and subtle biases found in everything from the content to the assessment requires reflection on the part of the teachers and administrators.

When seen in this light, it becomes obvious that multicultural education cannot be developed and marketed in a package style curriculum. This approach is more of a framework for planning, designing, and assessing instruction that builds practices of cultural pluralism and equal opportunity in teachers as well as students.

While this approach seems to really address the heart of the reason that there is a need for multicultural education approaches in the first place, it seems to disregard the fact that society continues to demonstrate a dominant culture and any multicultural practices are legislated only when reported. This approach does very little to empower students to create change in our society. Through this approach to multicultural education, students are not given skills to address continued bias or inequity in their workplaces, communities, and recreational activities in our society.

The final approach, and according to Sleeter and Grant (1988), is the most promising approach to multicultural education, *multicultural and social reconstructionist.* This approach is built on the ideology of conflict theory, cognitive development theory, and theory of culture. Conflict theory is the thought that behaviors among groups or cultural subgroups can all be tied to the advancement of their particular group in conflict with other groups. When examining group behavior such as racism or discrimination, they can be explained by the need of the dominant group to continue oppression to further advance their individual needs or the needs of the group. Conflict theory can also be called critical theory.

Additionally, this approach incorporates cognitive development theory developed by Piaget and Dewey and is based on the concept that understanding is constructed through experience. With this foundation, teaching must incorporate interaction between and among concepts and people with diverse cultures and experiences so that knowledge can be constructed to include a world that is both relevant and real in their lives. Students require rich interactions with various social groups in such a way that they develop into individuals who can critically think about societal constraints and social action. In this light, children must interact within key societal constructs such as democracy, citizenship, and economics.

The third aspect of this approach is the theory of culture which acknowledges that individuals make behavior choices based on behaviors learned through membership in social subgroups or cultures. Within society, cultures often have distinct norm behaviors based on the allocation of resources. Due to the interconnected nature of individual identity and cultural membership, separating behavioral responses of individuals from cultural background is impossible and can lead to inaccurate assumptions regarding cause. Membership in cultural subgroups develops an individual's concept of themselves in such a primal way, and therefore, individuals cannot be separated from their culture without disrespecting or dishonoring the culture.

When approaching multicultural education through the lens of these theories, a focus on practicing democracy, analyzing individual circumstances, and explicitly developing social action skills are critical. These practices must transcend cultural subgroups so that all students are valued and therefore value their own ability to impact the world around them. This approach will require adoption of common beliefs among educators with respect to critical theory, cognitive development, and theory of culture, and will elicit honest and open discussions challenging assumptions of society. This work is difficult and requires a commitment over the expanse of a student's career. Yet, without integrating social consciousness into mainstream curriculum, no real change will occur.

As a student growing up in the 1980s, I have personally participated in these approaches throughout my educational career. I can recall programs such as "Everybody Counts" and "Kids on the Block." As students, we openly discussed differences and witnessed programs designed to correct weaknesses of students in separate programs for special education, English language acquisition, and Title I mainly in programs designed to address the effects of poverty. Unfortunately, it has taken me pursuing doctoral level education before I encountered social reconstructionism as a student.

CRITICISM OF PRESENT PRACTICE

Some critics could propose that public schools serve students differently today. Sleeter and Grant (1988) identify significant gaps among social subgroups in our society. They highlight the economic and political effects of these gaps. "The unemployment rate for Blacks has remained about twice that for Whites since World War II" (p. 6). Disproportional unemployment directly impacts further economic factors such as access to housing, food, and health care. Additionally, subordinate subgroups, such as people of color, are incarcerated at a higher rate. Political positions are filled by White males significantly more frequently than by people of color.

Women continue to face oppression in the workforce as well. On average, women make about 70% of the earnings of men. "Women are given custody of children in about 90% of divorce cases and often must attempt to support the family on a low-wage budget" (Sleeter & Grant, 1988, p. 10). These wage inequities combined with the increased frequency of single mothers providing for families in most cases, begins to have a generational effect on students that can be demonstrated by the shrinking of the middle class. According to Sleeter and Grant (1988), "Children tend to grow up to occupy the same social class position as their parents" (p. 13).

There continues to be a very high cost to being disabled, as well. "Handicapped people as a group are still overrepresented in the rank of the poor, although they are somewhat invisible as an impoverished group, since statistics on their employment and income are not widely kept and published" (Sleeter & Grant, 1988, p. 10). Very low percentages of handicapped individuals are employed full time and their reliance on family support extends into adulthood, further impacting family member's resources. While this disproportionality has impacts on individuals, families, and cultures as a whole, it mimics what we see in school systems throughout our nation.

Educational impacts on achievement are significantly discrepant among subgroups. According to the U.S. Department of Education, schools with higher density of students of color often represent a higher level of students in poverty. Likewise, students of color, regardless of the density of the school perform with scaled scores of 25 points less than their White peers. Students often live in communities reflective of their culture and therefore attend schools that are reflective of the community. These factors impact the students' achievement and therefore have implications on earning potential across the span of student's lives. This comparison highlights the importance of significant action as many gaps remain between outcomes for subgroups and outcomes for the majority.

Additionally, critics may find fault with the work by Sleeter and Grant (1988) due to the lack of impact seen in multicultural education. Surface level multicultural education programs that are added on to existing structures in education are not going to influence the achievement gap. Educator preparation must include Mead's theory of self to highlight the depth of the impact that multicultural educational approaches can have along with the negative impact of the lack of multicultural educational approaches. Mead's theory is at play in every interaction among humans (Margolis & Catudal, 2001). This understanding must be incorporated in the work of educators despite prescribed programs in order to begin to educate for all. This task is monumental and crucial, causing a conflict for many educators about its possibility.

LESSONS LEARNED

Sleeter and Grant (1988) open a window for the profession of education to address the heart of education. Public education across the nation, as it currently exists, is under attack. The work of teachers and administrators is called into question regularly and our nation's academic performance when compared to other nations in our world, seems to be slipping to the middle of the pack. While I believe that public education has immense potential, the work of Sleeter and Grant provide us a window through which we can view the role of education for our society. Looking through the historical window of this work, we can see that the purpose of education might have been socialization, behaviorism, and indoctrination; but looking at the lessons of this work we can set our sights for designing a public education system that serves humans by equipping them to think critically, problem solve, and express their individuality without harm to their identity.

Education is an industry in change. Accountability measures, assessments, school choice, and teacher evaluation have all dramatically changed in public education in the last decade. Legislatures and other stakeholders continue to shape the foundations of education with legislation, guidance, funding, and media. Multicultural education is not immune to the pressures. Similar to the other aspects of education, the discussion has shifted to evaluating effectiveness of education by measuring outcome for students. Both at the state and federal level, educators have been challenged to prepare students for equal and integrated postsecondary outcomes for all students.

According to The Ohio Coalition for the Education of Children With Disabilities (2019), roughly 1 in every 7 students in the state of Ohio has a documented disability that negatively impacts academic performance. That means that just a little over 14% of students in Ohio have a learning difference. In Ohio, there are 13 categories under which students can qualify for special services. Some examples are specific learning disability, autism, orthopedically handicapped, visually impaired, and so forth. Of those 13 categories, only 2 of the categories impact the cognitive ability of the students. Those two categories combined represent less than 15% of the students with disabilities subgroup. This equates to approximately 2% of all of the students in Ohio demonstrating a limited cognitive ability which could impact the level of critical thinking or mental processing including memory. Shockingly, however, there is a 50% gap in achievement between students with special needs when compared to the total achievement of all students.

Despite the fact cognitive disabilities represent a very small amount of students, the impact of educational practices results in diminished academic achievement. This data leads to the assumption that an inequality of educational opportunities or resources exists for students who have been identified with special needs. Reaching students with learning differences in such a way that closes this gap is going to take a shift in paradigm (Ohio Coalition for the Education of Children with Disabilities, 2014).

The issue of equality in education is at the heart of the issue driving many of the accountability pressures in education. Early educational opportunities, or the lack thereof, can predict with stunning accuracy the outcomes for students. These results have effects long into adulthood. This is especially true for students from diverse cultural backgrounds and with various special needs. In order to effectively address these needs and provide equal access to opportunity, we must carefully examine the aim of education and shift the paradigms that limit educational opportunities for students.

While equality is the driving force, the funding surrounding education and the services that follow individuals with special needs such as learning differences or poverty, provides the fuel for the ongoing discussion regarding services and solutions to the inequality concerns:

> Perhaps as much as one-fifth of total current spending for slightly more than 10% of students-extraordinarily little evidence has accumulated about the effectiveness of special-education programs in raising achievement. Moreover, while evidence for New York and Texas suggests that special education programs may have crowded out regular-education spending, little evidence of the impact on achievement for non-special- education students exists. (Hanushek et al., 2002, p. 584)

Lessons learned through the work of Sleeter and Grant point to ineffective multicultural education approaches when they are implemented as separate or outside of the ongoing interactions of instruction.

According to the U.S. Department of Education, legislation governing and assigning funding for special education was first put into law in 1974 with the Individual With Disabilities Education Act (IDEA). At the time, the need for increased equity for students with disabilities was high. Students were spending lifetimes in institutions or labeled as non-educable and therefore excluded from school entirely. IDEA originally created space for students to be educated along with their typically developing peers and to be given the opportunity to access similar opportunities. Thanks to that piece of legislation, special education has made important impacts in the lives of students. "Special education programs on average boost the achievement of students provided this special treatment, and it appears that schools target services toward students who derive larger benefit" (Hanushek et al., 2002, p. 585). This type of funding practice occurs under

Title I funding which is designed to combat the negative impacts of poverty on education. Unfortunately, an achievement gap continues to plague students in the subgroups that receive this funding.

The struggle for educators implementing vaguely worded statutes is the lack of empirical evidence to help guide their decision-making processes. Without the guidance of educational research, educational practitioners must rely on the research of the medical, psychology, and scientific fields. This research has led to what is known as a "medical model of special education." According to Zaretsky (2005):

> Whether they recognize it or not, many educational professionals, including school administrators, have traditionally worked from a medical model of disability. Currently educational professionals appear to rely heavily on this knowledge base, generally considered stable, objective, and helpful knowledge in making decisions about appropriate programming and placements for students with disability. (p. 69)

The medical model identifies differences in ability in ways that distinctly value what is implied as "normal" while the disability is then implicitly assigned a lesser value. A medical model uses these value judgments to work through a procedure for a treatment or cure. Obviously when speaking about health, patients are pitied if their ailment cannot be cured or removed. This model permeates the instruction of students with diverse cultural backgrounds.

While the medical model meets the needs of the medical community, students and education would benefit from a different perspective regarding differences:

> Notions of normal and abnormal should also compel theorists and practitioners to interrogate unexamined value judgments used to represent what is right and desirable in special education programs and placements. We may be best served by being more accepting of multiple interpretations and ways of knowing than are presently embraced by more traditional forms of scientific study. (Zaretsky, 2005, p. 72)

In response to the medical model, education has attempted to tackle differences with a treatment approach. This treatment approach generally requires seeking a specialist removed from the classroom to be "cured" of an ailment. The flawed logic of the medical model leads to students waiting in segregated classrooms for a cure or disjointed multicultural lessons applied as a band-aid to heal the wounds of oppression and limited opportunities. This practice begins to limit educational opportunities over time for folks who are different. These segregated learning environments, which lead to missed educational opportunities, exacerbate the symptoms which lead to an increase in "treatment" or segregated intervention. This cyclical process over time has created the rather large achievement gap for students with disabilities.

NEW VIEW FOR EDUCATION

Utilizing a more integrated model for instruction which focuses on social reconstruction for the instruction of all students must be the approach we utilize if we are focused on equality for humans in school and society. The value of the medical model has created the need for more and more supplemental "cures." This has led to the assumption that students who differ from the dominant culture cannot achieve and can negatively impact the learning of others. While that assumption is widely held, the data does not support the claim. "Nevertheless, the evidence provides a convincing case that the special-education programs on average provide the intended benefits without reducing achievement for the non-special-education population" (Hanushek et al., 2002, p. 585). Several researchers have discovered that students with disabilities do not negatively impact the learning of the typically developing students. "The foregoing analyses indicate few notable differences in academic achievement among students in inclusion versus non-inclusion classrooms" (Daniel & King, 1997, p. 77).

Segregation in education has been addressed legally and found to be inappropriate. We would not consider segregation based on gender, religion, or race. How can we continue to segregate students based on perceived ability or performance when there is no evidence indicating that segregation improves achievement? This question is magnified by the understanding that research indicates that segregation promotes inequality. Hanushek and Woessmann (2006) compare the results of the international assessment PISA:

> The results consistently indicate that early tracking increases inequality in achievement…Across the estimates from the remaining samples (available from the authors), the most striking finding is that in no case do some students gain at the expense of others; both high and low achievers lose (or, in the one case of positive effect on mean performance, gain) from tracking. (p. C75)

This work is further supported by Hanushek in partnership with Kain and Rivkin (2002). The medical model has negatively impacted the assumptions of key stakeholders who make placement decisions for students who are unable to demonstrate success in our current education system.

Margaret Inman Linn (2011) writes, "In every society, a major goal of education is to transmit cultural values from one generation to the next" (p. 58). Based on the current practice of segregating students with special needs, as a society we value segregation of subgroups and that academic achievement is the only way for students to earn value. All students deserve the best of the public education system. As educators, our work is to ensure the highest level of opportunity as a result of the work that we do. If we continue to segregate students based on labels of disability or other subgroups, we will continue to limit opportunities for students. The choice is clear. We need to shift the emphasis in classrooms and school away from what students cannot do towards what students can do. The time has come for us to reconsider the use of strategies or approaches that cause segregation and separation of lower performing students and place the blame for failure on the student and not on the system tasked with instructing them.

"Personal meanings and intentions that individuals construct in their everyday lives should contribute to the knowledge base of special education. As the inclusion project has shown, we need to apply critical examination and reflexive methodologies education" (Zaretsky, 2005, p. 81). As our society shifts to a more global community the demands of the workforce are ever changing, therefore, we must continue preparing all students for competitive employment in jobs that might not even exist in the future. Student learning is essential to unlocking future opportunities. Instruction can make a measurable impact on the development of students. Hattie's (2015) research finds measurable positive impact on student learning with the use of strategies such as "not labeling students," "building student–teacher relationships," and "enlisting Piagetian programs." While these strategies have been compared to many other strategies across many studies and many students, Hattie's research does not delineate between strategies that are only effective for students with disabilities or for students without disabilities. Hattie's research would suggest that students with all abilities would benefit from these strategies. Following the medical model logic, if a cure for an ailment is known, yet withheld, there would be a negative consequence. In education, once we are aware of strategies that provide positive impacts, withholding them is inappropriate, unethical practice.

Rather than employing the medical model for addressing education, we should consider a more reflexive structure in educational environments. Classrooms should be places of safety for all students where their strengths are valued and challenges are addressed in an honest and specific way. Instruction should be tailored to individual identities and needs and presented using strategies with proven positive impact.

It is clear that there are several reasons to consider shifting our aim for public education. We typically address diverse populations of students by marginalizing them based on abilities, behaviors, or achievement levels that are deemed not "normal." Our system is set up to segregate students who demonstrate any difference or so-called abnormality that has been assigned a negative valuation by the adults in the public education system. The truest solution to this challenge is an engaging, relevant, respectful, and flexible classroom instruction model that addresses individual students with strategies for thinking critically, forming effective relationships within and among cultural groups, and communicating across cultural divides that have measurable positive impact on student learning. This is a challenging shift in the way educators design instruction, learning environments, and routine practices such as discipline, attendance, and extracurricular. This approach is called multicultural education that is social reconstructivist. It is about time we move in this direction. A shift is happening in education. Education professionals can choose to guide it. If we view this challenge through the curriculum window of Sleeter and Grant's (1988) *Multicultural Education* that is social reconstructivist, we can see hope for the success of all students and hope for the strength of our differences. When we lean on the lessons learned from our past, we can choose to educate individual humans to be citizens of the world and change educational outcomes for all students.

REFERENCES

Daniel, L. G., & King, D. A. (1997). Impact of inclusion education on academic achievement, student behavior and self-esteem, and parental attitudes. *The Journal of Educational Research, 91*(2), 67–80.

Hanushek, E. A., Kain, J. F., & Rivkin, S. G. (2002). Inferring program effects for special populations: Does special education raise achievement for students with disabilities? *Review of Economics and Statistics, 84*(4), 584–599.

Hanushek, E., & Woessmann, L. (2005). Does educational tracking affect performance and inequality? Differences-in-differences evidence across countries. *The Economic Journal 116*(510), C63–C76

Hattie, J. (2015). The applicability of visible learning to higher education. *Scholarship of Teaching and Learning in Psychology, 1*(1), 79–91.

Linn, M. I. (2011) Inclusion in two languages: Special education in Portugal and the United States. *Phi Delta Kappan, 92*(8), 58–60.

Margolis, J., & Catudal, J. (2001). *The quarrel between invariance and flux: A guide for philosophers and other players.* Pennsylvania State University Press.

Ohio Coalition for the Education of Children with Disabilities. (2019). *Ohio special education profile 2019.* https://www.ocecd.org/Downloads/2019%20Special%20Education%20Profile%20Report%201%202021%20(1).pdf?v=254

Ohio Coalition for the Education of Children with Disabilities. (2014). *Ohio special education Profile 2013.* https://www.ocecd.org/Downloads/Spec_Ed_Profile_Jan_2014_Update-Final.pdf

Sleeter, C. E., & Grant, C. A. (1988). *Making choices for multicultural education: Five approaches to race, class, and gender.* Merrill Publishing Company.

Zaretsky, L. (2005). From practice to theory: Inclusive models require inclusive theories. *American Secondary Education, 33*(3), 65–86.

CHAPTER 12

STAINED OR STAINED GLASS?

Multicultural Education for a Pluralistic and Democratic *Unum*

Nathan Warner

Author/Book studied:

Banks, J. A. (1997). *Educating citizens in a multicultural society.* Teachers College Press.

On a September Sunday morning in 1963, a bomb exploded at 16th Street Baptist Church in Birmingham, Alabama, killing four little Black girls, dressed in white, primping themselves in the bathroom before they would listen to that morning's sermon entitled "A Love That Forgives." Sara Collins, also in that bathroom, lost her sister, one eye, months to hospitalization and multiple surgeries, and, like the rest of her community, the one place that they were not forbidden to assemble. Who could measure the traumatic, terrible cost of the bombing or the significance and power it held, and still does, for civil rights?

Curriculum Windows Redux, pages 149–160
Copyright © 2022 by Information Age Publishing
www.infoagepub.com
All rights of reproduction in any form reserved.

One of the most powerful images from 16th Street Baptist Church bombing is that of a stained-glass window portraying Jesus as the Good Shepherd. After the bombing, the entire window remained intact save for the white face of Jesus. In its place was a blank space where the Good Shepherd's face had been busted out.

The imagery of that stained-glass window of the once white-faced Jesus stretching his arms over the black congregation, rendered faceless by a White supremacist bombing, remains a powerful metaphor in racial dialogue. Civil rights leaders, authors, and theologians offered interpretations of the image. Some spoke of the failure of the White church and its White Christ. Others found an invitation to redefine Christianity, for both Black and White.

The image is particularly powerful in consideration of what a stained-glass window really is: multiple colored panes of glass, each unique in shape forming one picture that may be subject to many interpretations. The idea is exquisitely beautiful and metaphorical. It reminds me of the motto of the United States, *e pluribus unum*; out of many, one.

James A. Banks (1997) writes in *Educating Citizens in a Multicultural Society* that the concept of *unum* is important in a pluralistic democracy. For a democratic and pluralistic society, certain questions regarding construction, inclusion, possession, and participation must be answered when considering unum. An unum is only legitimate and authentic when all its diverse groups, defined along the lines of race, ethnicity, gender, culture, and social class may fully participate.

Banks (1993) maintains that schools must be the institutions that help students acquire the knowledge, skills, and values needed to participate in being caring and socially active citizens who must make up a healthy democratic society. However, I believe it would be hard to produce evidence that this is the real day-to-day goal of most of our schools. In the stained-glass window of American education, it appears that our face has been busted out and needs repair. But what should that face look like? And who should decide the answer to that question?

In his "A Talk to Teachers" published not even a month after the 16th Street Baptist Church, James Baldwin (1963) wrote,

> The purpose of education, finally, is to create in a person the ability to look at the world for himself, to make his own decisions, to say to himself this is black or this is white, to decide for himself whether there is a God in heaven or not. To ask questions of the universe, and then learn to live with those questions, is the way he achieves his own identity. But no society is really anxious to have that kind of person around. What societies really, ideally, want is a citizenry which will simply obey the rules of society. If a society succeeds in this, that society is about to perish. The obligation of anyone who thinks of himself as responsible is to examine society and try to change it and to fight it—at no

matter what risk. This is the only hope society has. This is the only way societies change. (p. 42)

If Baldwin is right, American education is in trouble. In an education system dominated by accountability to standardized testing where third graders can be retained by a reading test score, diplomas are withheld from students without enough "points" from end of course exams to graduate, and half of teacher evaluations are tied to student performance on standardized tests, it seems that merely demonstrating knowledge of the "right" answers is the purpose of education. This leaves a democracy at-risk.

American education is not set up to advance a pluralistic democracy. Banks (1997) writes, "To prepare effective citizens for living in a democratic society, schools themselves must become democratic institutions that model caring, ethnic diversity, and effective citizen action" (p. 8). He further states,

> Our schools, as they are currently structured, conceptualized, and organized, will not be able to help most students of color, especially those who are poor and from cultures that differ from the school culture in significant ways, to acquire the knowledge, attitudes, and skills needed to function effectively in the knowledge society of the next century. (p. 11)

Banks maintains that our multicultural, democratic society needs a citizenry that can view history, culture, and current events from varying racial, political, ethnic, religious, and gender perspectives. To accomplish this great task, Banks holds that a multicultural education approach must be adopted in our schools and permeate every school environment in terms of curriculum, pedagogy, and relationships.

In keeping the imagery of the stained-glass window and the window metaphor, what follows are four "scenes" that I will use to illustrate Banks' most important ideas of multicultural education. I will attempt to use these scenes to tie my personal experiences to important concepts from Banks' work. While these experiences are used here to illustrate a point, they are also an important part of my journey as an educator, citizen, and individual in a pluralistic society.

SCENE 1: "TRUE COLORS, BECOMING A HAITIAN AMERICAN FAMILY"

When the "other" becomes part of you, your perspective changes. Two years ago, a 5-year-old Haitian boy became our son. His adoption was the culmination of 3 years of paperwork, meetings, interviews, fees, and travel. He has brought us great joy, and we are so glad and thankful that he is with us.

Throughout the process of his homecoming, we knew that this little boy would change our family drastically. It was never more evident than the first morning when I looked across the breakfast table at a wide-eyed, brown-faced boy who did not speak my language and was reluctant to communicate any more than a shaking of his head. I thought, "Ok, now what? Where's the manual?" In waves of joy and fear, the idea that we were suddenly a Haitian American family hit home in a new and fresh way.

In the couple of years that have followed that day, we have had many experiences, conversations, and thoughts that have deepened both our joy and our fear of being a "mixed" family. We have watched the reports of the killing of young Black men with horror and grief. We have, with frustrated, angry tears, read the articles and watched the news reports of the growing number of hate crimes against people of color. Like many Americans, we have struggled to find hope in an American society where racism can run so deep. These are not new struggles; but they are new to my family. For the "other" has become one of us and our perspective has changed. As our perspective has changed, it has impacted our actions and viewpoints as a family.

Banks (1997) argues for a changed perspective in American schools when he calls for an acknowledgement of the *e pluribus unum,* one out of many, in conceptualizing curriculum and pedagogy in schools. As our minority populations grow, and in many places become the majority, our schools are tasked with developing an increasingly diverse group of students with the skills, knowledge, and values that were traditionally reserved for an elite few (p. 6). However, it should be recognized that many of these students have been politically and socially kept on the fringes of American society. Change will require our schools to acknowledge that "we" look different and our schools "must become democratic institutions that model caring, ethnic diversity, and effective citizen action" (p. 6). American schools must be places that see and value differences in students; and our schools must structure the curriculum and the pedagogy in a way that respects and honors these differences as part of the idea of freedom and democracy.

Banks (1997) states that multicultural education is an education for freedom (p. 26). It enables an affirmation of ethnic, cultural, and racial identity. There is an allowance and freedom for students to also function beyond their own identities. Finally, it opens students' minds and develops their skills to function in a more national and global way that promotes social and civic change for the betterment of society. Banks writes that multicultural education

> maintains that all students should have equal opportunities to learn regardless of the racial, ethnic, social-class, or gender group to which they belong. It describes ways in which some students are denied equal educational opportunities because of the racial, ethnic, social class or gender characteristics. (p. 67)

Multicultural education seeks to promote democratic ideas of justice, equity, and freedom through curricular and pedagogical practices that consider the experiences and viewpoints of diverse people throughout the national and global community. Contained within Banks's (2004) conception of multicultural education are five dimensions:

1. *Content integration*—Teachers draw from various cultures for lesson content.
2. *Knowledge construction*—Teachers use various methods to help students understand and investigate the curriculum.
3. *Prejudice reduction*—Teachers adopt strategies to use toward democratic values and against prejudice and discrimination.
4. *Equity pedagogy*—Teachers modify instruction to facilitate the academic achievement of student from diverse backgrounds.
5. *Empowering school culture and social structure*—Educators structure schools in a holistic manner that attempts to meet the various needs of students.

It is these dimensions of multicultural education that set it apart from traditional practice. In short, Banks calls for a complete rethinking in our schools in matters of curriculum and pedagogy as those two concepts pertain to culture, race, gender, and ethnicity. Indeed, if we begin to see the "other" as part of us, it is our professional and moral responsibility to make sufficient changes in our operations to allow for our schools and societies to be inclusive of everyone.

SCENE 2: "NOT IN KANSAS ANYMORE"

Most Americans would recognize the famous line from the 1939 Wizard of Oz film where Dorothy looks around at her completely new surroundings and says to her dog, "Toto, I've a feeling we're not in Kansas anymore." I identified with Dorothy in my first year of teaching as I was hired at an urban middle school whose population was around 95% African American. It did not take me long to realize that I was in a completely different culture, and the reality that I had lived up to that point was not the reality of any of my students.

My personal history up to my hiring contained no interaction with people of color. This is not an exaggerated statement, but rather, a factual one. I attended a private Christian school, and my family was deeply embedded in a White, fundamental, evangelical community. There was a proverbial bubble around our existence, and that bubble did not include anyone who did not fall into the above description. To be clear, our culture was not one of overt racism, but it was certainly not inclusive or multicultural by any definition.

While it was the only culture I had ever known, I was never comfortable in it. So, as I entered my teacher education program, I knew I was heading toward urban education. I have never regretted the decision, but I have been humbled many times by the depths and reaches of my own White privilege and my lack of understanding of what being a person of color means in America. In those first years of teaching, it became increasingly obvious to me that my communication, treatment of subject matter, and pedagogy were going to need redefining if I was going to reach my students.

Banks (1997) writes that two of a teacher's most important functions are the selection of knowledge and the design of the pedagogy to teach that knowledge (p. 35). In this way, the teacher is in a place of power as the teacher has the opportunity to shape the minds of their students. For example, how a teacher approaches the subject of Western Expansion in light of the effects it had on Native Americans may shape a student's view of patriotism or concepts of American freedom and justice. Teacher choices here reflect ideologies that may be dominant in the culture of the teacher's own background, the school, or even the nation itself. Banks (1997) writes,

> Pluralistic democratic societies and institutions are often faced with decisions that involve conflicts in deeply held values, such as equality and academic freedom. They have to weigh and balance values that, as ideals, are equally important. These kinds of decisions create moral dilemmas that are difficult and complex. (p. 43)

Banks argues that, in a pluralistic and democratic society, children have the right to be educated in a manner that is considerate of their cultural values and respectful of their backgrounds. Not only this, but Banks holds that educators should be responsible for educating students in a manner that develops their ability to think critically about dominant and minority cultures.

Banks (1997) describes two types of knowledge: mainstream academic knowledge and transformative knowledge (p. 71). Mainstream academic knowledge can be thought of as what has been traditionally taught in schools. A major tenant of this knowledge is that there are objective truths, uninfluenced by human factors, to be found through research. Banks provides an example of mainstream academic knowledge through his discussion of the West paradigm. The West paradigm describes the frontier of the American West as an empty wilderness to be tamed and lacking a significant population and civilization. This paradigm also contains the idea of the importance and heroism of U.S. expansion without consideration of the cost to the estimated seven million Native Americans who already lived there.

Banks (1997) calls for educators to help students develop new perspectives on American history and society. Teachers should help students consider elements of history and society from a transformative academic knowledge which challenges mainstream beliefs and concepts by considering events from multiple perspectives and cultural experience for the purpose of expanding ideas of democracy and improving society. Reconsidering topics such as U.S. westward expansion and Indian removal, the role of slavery in the development of the United States as a superpower, and the suspension of individual rights of Japanese Americans in internment camps through the lens of transformative knowledge, helps promote ideas of democracy and expands the American perspective to be inclusive of diverse groups of people.

However, even when discussing "multicultural heroes" they can be contextualized within dominant culture (Carlson, 2003). Carlson (2003) provides the example of Rosa Parks and writes,

> Even those whose words and deeds represented a radical challenge to the dominant or hegemonic social order can be—and have been—incorporated within conservative narratives of national identity and progress. This is troubling to the extent that it means that even if progressives have succeeded in making the curriculum more inclusive, with a more multicultural cast of American heroes, there is no guarantee that these heroes will continue to serve progressive purposes once they are reworked within the dominant narratives of American history, which continue to be classist, Eurocentric, and patriarchal. (p. 45)

Carlson's point regarding multicultural education is that it is not enough to make curriculum more inclusive of various cultures. If multicultural education is to have an impact, it must also question how heroes and stories are being integrated within American culture and democracy. Carlson cites William Bennett's (1993) placement of Rosa Parks' story within his *Book of Virtues*. Bennett places Park's story among stories such as Chicken Little, Hansel and Gretel, and Jack and the Beanstalk, David and Goliath, and the defense of the Alamo. Carslon (2003) writes, "Bennett effectively incorporates Parks's story within an American narrative of expansionism that has participated in disenfranchising African Americans" (p. 48). Carlson provides an additional example of Martin Luther King, Jr., and writes that conservatives and traditionalists have turned him into "a universalistic symbol of nonviolence and a defender of a minimalist interpretation of civil rights as strict equality before a 'color blind' law" (p. 46). This criticism of the knowledge construction and integration elements of multicultural education is worth note and consideration.

An element of the culture in which I was raised was the development of patriotism to a country that was "under God." That the United States was founded by godly men who sought to develop a nation of religious freedom where the principles of Christianity would guide its citizens was not up for debate. My allegiance to a "good" and Christian government was quite expected.

As a boy, I was also fascinated by the stories of my Cherokee ancestry. My father would tell me how we were connected (very distantly) to the Cherokee nation, and it was cause for deep fascination and pride for me. However, as I grew to learn the fate of the Cherokee nation on the Trail of Tears at the hands of the government that was "under God" and required my allegiance, I remember, for the first time, thinking "something here is not right." This dissonance between my education of what America was and my realization of what my government actually did was confusing for me.

However, not all Americans have this dissonance nor believe these myths. Baldwin writes,

> The American Negro has the great advantage of having never believed that collection of myths to which white Americans cling: that their ancestors were all freedom-loving heroes, that they were born in the greatest country the world has ever seen, or that Americans are invincible in battle and wise in peace, that Americans have always dealt honorably with Mexicans and Indians and all other neighbors or inferiors, that American men are the world's most direct and virile, that American women are pure. (Korb, 2016, p. 1)

Nevertheless, Banks seems to applaud this dissonance. It is within dissonance that we begin to view our democracy critically and from multiple perspectives. It is here that democracy grows and becomes more inclusive as we acknowledge its shortcomings and push for its expansion.

SCENE 3: "THE SOMETIMES HIJAB"

"India" started wearing her hijab in October. The wearing of the hijab was something new for the seventh grader. She had not been wearing it in August or September, but she had now decided to begin to wear it on most days. Her father was Muslim, and her mother was Christian. She was moving back and forth between them and was exploring her identity. The student and I had talked about this previously as I wanted to strategize with her about how she might deal with any peer conflict. I did not think I had to prepare her for conflict with staff.

In the third week of October, India approached me about a conflict she was having with one of her teachers. At our school, we have a dress code, and she described that her teacher kept telling her she was committing a dress code violation because she sometimes wore her hijab and sometimes did not. I confess that I was somewhat taken aback by this report and hoped that the student had misunderstood or misrepresented something that the teacher had said. However, in my conversation with the teacher, I found that the student reported accurately. The teacher was adamant that the student was just wearing the hijab to "get around the dress code" because she should either wear it all the time or not at all. The remainder of our conversation touched on the student's right to be able to explore her own individuality and beliefs as well as her experience of being Muslim in our school, and it was our job to support her the best way we could. In the end, the teacher walked away still believing we were getting one pulled over on us, and I walked away astonished that I had even had the conversation at all.

All students, including students like India, need schools that are supportive of them. This should include support of them in relation to their race, gender, ethnicity, academic and intellectual needs, and their culture. This also includes the exploration of all of the above. Banks (1997) writes that a major tenet of multicultural education is equity pedagogy. He writes that,

> Equity pedagogy is teaching strategies and classroom environments that help students from diverse racial, ethnic and cultural groups to attain the knowledge skills and attitudes needed to function effectively within and to help create and perpetuate a just human and democratic society. (p. 79)

Doing this effectively means challenging the ideas and traditions of the dominant culture to become citizens who think democratically and critically about the society in which they exist. Simply employing culturally relevant practices does not constitute equity pedagogy if existing assumptions created by the dominant culture are not challenged. Characteristics of equity pedagogy include:

- strategies such as cooperative learning;
- generation of knowledge, construction of interpretations, and creation of new understandings vs. memorizations;
- identification and interrogation of knowers; and
- multiple solutions and perspectives to problems. (Banks, 1997, p. 80)

Equity pedagogy challenges almost every aspect of traditional education. Equity pedagogy affects assessments, teacher and student interactions, curriculum, and even the physical arrangement of the classroom.

Equity pedagogy has significant implications for teachers. It requires deep self-reflection on the part of the teachers as they must examine how current practices may be supportive or unsupportive of diverse groups of students. Banks (1997) calls for curricular interventions such as multicultural materials, vicarious experiences, role playing, and simulations to help students develop positive attitudes toward diversity (p. 96). It calls for teachers to tackle difficult ideas in hidden curriculum by asking questions that examine the meaningfulness of an assignment and identifying gaps in knowledge and readiness. Banks writes that to transform pedagogy, the adults in schools "must address social-class, racial, and ethnic inequalities imbedded in the differential support given to different classes and schools that are stratified by race, ethnicity, and class" (p. 82). This requires that teachers consider their students' experiences as valid and incorporate their lives and interests into the classroom in a way that is student-centered. Embedded in these ideas is that the teacher must take time to know the students and consider the classroom and the relationships within the classroom as a multicultural experience.

SCENE 4: CHANGE FROM THE INSIDE OF THE ROOM

My first few months as a new teacher were rough. With growing dread, I was realizing that my authority in the room was not given, it was earned. I had not zeroed in on the importance of developing rapport and relationship with my students, and it showed. One day, after one of my students had jumped up on my tables, ran the length of them, and jumped back off in a way that would make Spiderman proud, I went to see my principal. We talked for a while that day, but what I really remember him saying is this: "Nate, your name is on the outside of that door. What happens on the inside has your name on it. The change in your classroom has to come from the inside of the room." He was right, and I became better.

Banks (1997) makes the same point in his book. He outlines his ideas on how to bring multicultural education on track to make an impact on students growing in an increasingly diverse world. Overall, Banks calls for more scholarly educational leadership and a commitment to link scholarship with practice (pp. 115–116). More specifically, much of his thinking here revolves around teacher education programs and educational leadership. Banks calls for a teacher education policy that considers principles of multicultural education as it addresses how teachers acquire and demonstrate knowledge and skills that they will use in the classroom. Banks writes,

> Because teacher education students attained most of their knowledge without analyzing its assumptions and values or engaging in the process of constructing knowledge themselves, they often leave teacher education programs with many misconceptions about culturally and racially different groups and with conceptions about their national history and culture that are incomplete, misleading, and chauvinistic. Consequently, the knowledge that many teachers bring to the classroom contributes to the mystification rather than to the clarification of social, historical, and political realities. This knowledge also perpetuates inequality and victimization rather than contributes to justice and liberation. (p. 102)

Banks provides the answer to this issue in calling for teacher education programs to help students critically think about their own knowledge construction. Teachers should analyze their own paradigms in light of conflicting paradigms, values, and theories. In this way, teacher education programs would promote a deeper appreciation in students for multiple perspectives of various topics as they consider designing instruction and moving forward in their practice. Integrated into this practice is teacher education programs designing activities for teachers to grow in their own self-clarification. Self-clarification allows teachers to understand their own culture and ethnic identity better so that they might have a deeper appreciation and more positive attitudes towards other cultures and ethnicities.

Banks (1997) also advocates for schools to become places of multicultural education. Banks holds that an important goal of the school should be the development of appreciation of students' own culture and also the culture around them. This begins with the philosophy of self-transcendence (p. 136). Under this philosophy, students must first develop strong feelings of self-worth, valuing themselves and their own culture before they can then accept and appreciate another person's or group's culture. Schools committed to developing tolerance for diverse populations of students must recognize this and help foster this self-worth in their students. Banks' model contains two shifts in schools (Ngai, 2004). One shift is that curriculum leaders and teachers should help students to reflect on their own cultural heritage and then move to other "socio-cultural differences" (Ngai, 2004, p. 325). The other shift is that schools should commit to viewing concepts from multiple cultural and ethnic perspectives. Banks (1993) writes that the main goals of presenting different kinds of knowledge is to get students to understand that the construction of knowledge is influenced by the cultural and social context in which it is constructed. When students understand that knowledge is constructed within a sociocultural context, they can understand the need to think critically about education and the concepts they encounter and consider these concepts from multiple points of view.

Multicultural education has not been received without its own criticism. Banks (1993) writes that Western traditionalists want to retain the dominance of the traditional curriculum and see outside voices as a threat (p. 4). Pinar (1995) writes that traditionalists subscribe to the notion that everyone enjoys the opportunity to improve social and economic position (p. 326), and that there is not a need to change educational practices or knowledge construction within education. Cameron McCarthy (as quoted in Pinar, 1995) viewed multiculturalism as problematic and wrote that it was a "contradictory and problematic 'solution' to racial inequality in schooling" (p. 323). Finally, Pinar (1995) writes that approaches such as multicultural education that favor a "building bridges" approach to leveling the playing ground between marginalized groups and mainstream society undermines the great need for a collective minority identity campaigning for real change in education.

Despite its criticisms, multicultural education seems more appropriate now than ever. The FBI's latest report on hate crimes (FBI Department of Justice, 2016) identifies almost 6,000 cases of hate crimes involving over 7,000 people. These cases include everything from harassment to rape and murder. The victims were targeted for race, ethnicity, religion, and sexual orientation. Current political events also reveal a nation at odds with itself over matters of race, ethnicity, and cultural acceptance. Any notion of a post-racial America is laughable and naive. Educators should be at the front of efforts to fight against stereotypes, racism, bigotry, and discrimination. However, without focused and deliberate efforts, this fight will never have the power that is needed to change our schools and shape students' minds to be able to think critically about culture, race, ethnicity, gender, religion, and the construction of knowledge itself.

REFERENCES

Baldwin, J. (1963, December 21). A talk to teachers. *The Saturday Review*, 42–44.

Banks, J. A. (1993). The canon debate, knowledge construction, and multicultural education. *Educational Researcher, 22*(5), 4–14. https://doi.org/10.3102/0013189X022005004

Banks, J. A. (1997). *Educating citizens in a multicultural society*. Teachers College Press.

Banks, J. A. (2004). Multicultural education: Historical development, dimensions, and practice. In J. A. Banks & C. A. M. Banks (Eds.), *Handbook of research on multicultural education* (2nd ed., pp. 3–29). Jossey-Bass.

Bennett, W. J. (1993). *The book of virtues*. Simon & Schuster.

Carlson, D. (2003). Troubling heroes: Of Rosa Parks, multicultural education, and critical pedagogy. *Cultural Studies ↔ Critical Methodologies, 3*(1), 44–61. https://doi.org/10.1177/1532708603239267

FBI Department of Justice. (2016). *Hate crime summary*. https://ucr.fbi.gov/hate-crime/2015/resource-pages/hate-crime-2015-_summary_final

Korb, S. (2016, November 4). Baldwin in the Obama years. *Guernica*. https://www.guernicamag.com/baldwin-in-the-obama-years/

Ngai, P. B.-Y. (2004). A reinforcing curriculum and program reform proposal for 21st century teacher education: Vital first steps for advancing K–12 multicultural education. *Equity and Excellence in Education, 37*(4), 321–331.

Pinar, W. F., Reynolds, W. M., Slattery, P., & Taubman, P. M. (1995). *Understanding curriculum: An introduction to the study of historical and contemporary curriculum discourses*. Peter Lang.

CHAPTER 13

A RED, HARIBO GUMMY BEAR

Ashley Warren

Author/Book studied:

Britzman, D. (2003). *Practice makes practice: A critical study of learning to teach.* State University of New York Press.

I never thought a half, chemically destroyed gummy bear would land me in an ambulance with a student during my first year teaching, but it definitely shaped my identity as an educator. Halloween is a chemistry teacher's dream. A day filled with experiments: foaming columns of dry ice and acid-base indicators, an electric pickle, elephant's toothpaste, and my sparkling finale—the sacrificial gummy bear. What seems to observers as the easiest demonstration of all, the sacrificial gummy bear, is actually the most dangerous. With 10 minutes left in second bell chemistry class, I prepare discussing the chemistry behind the sacrificial gummy bear. In simple terms, the students are told that the liquid in the test-tube, a strong oxidizer, will oxidize the sugar in the gummy bear resulting in a production of sound,

Curriculum Windows Redux, pages 161–175
Copyright © 2022 by Information Age Publishing
www.infoagepub.com

light, and heat. In other words, the gummy bear is going to glow, smoke, and scream as if it's on fire. An amazing finale, right?

Just before dropping the red, sacrificial Haribo, a hand raises in the front of the room. Steve, a student who thrives on kinesthetic learning and who cannot stop smiling, poses to the class to consider what would happen if multiple gummy bears are consumed in the reaction. To quickly describe Steve, he is the type of person to ask for forgiveness rather than permission. Steve will smile through any and all situations, regardless of if he's in trouble or not. Hence, the name Smiley Steve. Not wanting to stifle Smiley Steve's curiosity, I tell him to drop four gummy bears in the test tube. His simultaneous hesitation and bigger-than-normal smile should have warned me, but I proceed to tell Steve to use the appropriate goggles, lab apron, and tongs. Steve excitedly drops the bears, and the reaction's allure has quadrupled in magnitude. Half mesmerized by the reaction myself, I have my body directed towards the class explaining how electrons are being transferred. During the explanation, students' mouths have dropped and there is silence in the room. In my mind I am ecstatic to think about how I am crushing this lesson! The student facial feedback was all I needed to feel that the class was a success. WRONG! In my moment of what I think is glory, a student just points to Smiley Steve. I turn around to see Steve staring at me, almost sweating.

> **Me:** [My immediate reaction is to ask] Steve, what did you do?
> **Steve:** Mam? [which he said every time he knew he did something wrong]
> **Me:** [in a louder tone] What did you do Steve?
> **Steve:** I just had the leftover gummy bear
> **Me:** What leftover gummy bear?
> **Steve:** From the test tube . . .
> **Me:** The test tube with the oxidizing agent in it? Steve, are you freaking kidding me?! Someone get the nurse! Someone call 911! Did you not see the symbol next to the bottle Steve? Kind of looks like it's dangerous! OMG!!!

For the record, the symbol looks like this:

Would you consume something if this were the first thing you saw? Yeah, I didn't think so. I can't begin to fathom what was actually processing through my mind as I realized that one of my students, a high school student, a student who I thought could use logical decision-making skills, ate something that contained a dangerous chemical. No amount of practical educational coursework would prepare someone for a situation like this. It was in this moment that I knew my chemistry expertise could only get me so far. My reputation as a teacher was over. I turn to help Steve, and of course, he's just smiling.

IDENTITY FORMATION OF AN EDUCATOR

What type of class would have helped me determine what to do in the gummy bear caper? Is there any amount of education that would have better prepared me for Smiley Steve's decision to ingest something from the laboratory? How did this experience change or shape how I taught future lessons? In *Practice Makes Practice*, Britzman (2003) believes that student teachers should be provided with a variety of opportunities during their postsecondary work to entangle themselves in diverse experiences to better determine one's identity as a teacher. Our current teacher education training is subpar at best, leaving students feeling as though they gain success as an educator through trial by fire. Is this a mindset we want to foster in our educators, or is there another more intimate way to teach future and current educators to reflect upon their craft?

WE VERSUS ME

Britzman's (2003) purpose of *Practice Makes Practice* is to elicit the struggle between educational dichotomies a student teacher battles during their experiences as a teacher and a learner. Do we rely on theory more or practice? Do we lean on the side of experience or knowledge? In our classrooms, we make choices based on these dichotomies. How do these choices mold our identities? What does teaching do to teachers? It is the tension that arises between the shaping of an educator and how the educator is shaping the classroom that will provide a deeper level of insight into the formation of a teacher.

Student teaching, the culminating experience where students can test whether or not they have the with-it-ness to maintain a classroom of their own, reflects the potential of what kind of teacher one could be as well as the reality of who one is currently as a teacher. Britzman's (2003) ethnographic analysis of two student teacher experiences, Jamie Owl and Jack August, elicited three common cultural myths teachers must question against as they establish and inquire their own educator role: teachers are self-made, teachers are experts, and everything depends on the teacher

(p. 223). The problem with assuming the truth of these cultural myths is that it limits the production of meaning in classroom experiences as stagnant or predictable. How often do teachers feel a loss of control in their classrooms? All the time! However, this loss of control could be a positive result of purposeful teacher planning. Personally, I knew I always wanted to be a teacher from the age of 6, but I always questioned whether I was good enough to have the elite status of "teacher" (I believe this mindset would be completely contradictory to how Britzman would expect teachers to view their roles, but I suppose I've always been an outlier). Despite these feelings, Britzman would imply that the thoughts teachers have about their career become stifled by the dominance of the lived cultural myths. Is a student teacher really going to fight for power in a classroom owned by another? Doubtful. Therefore, all stakeholders involved in education need to realize "classroom practices are produced, interpreted, and acted upon in multiple and contradictory ways" (Britzman, 2003, p. 215). Student teachers need to be given multiple opportunities to test who they want to become rather than what society has already dictated as essential.

How does one begin to process their own becoming as they are faced with constant contradiction? Pinar's reference to Whitson may initially get us started. Whitson's primary work of *bildungsprozess*, or coming to form, sheds light on the process of how society and its participants come to be (Pinar et al., 2006, p. 298). Through social negotiation, an individual is tasked with absorbing as much information about the world to challenge their innate intellectual abilities and conception of what it means to be human. Knowledge is a social practice, and while understanding all perspectives is imperative, knowing all of the dimensions hidden within oneself is equally important. The problem with *bildung* is the perpetual focus on society rather than the individual. Thus, leading us back to the problem with the three dominant cultural myths. If one is charged with reflecting for the purpose of making society better, then individual growth will remain stifled for the betterment of others. The propagation of the three cultural myths described by Britzman transmits the shattered lens of education. Through the current techniques and educational thought processes we use to "better" education, the only hope we have is to view education through the biggest broken piece of the lens. Rather than throwing away the broken pieces, we need to construct a new lens; a lens that is able to bend multiple light rays at just the right angles to merge the image we need to see: teaching learners and not teaching teachers.

How do we refract or distort contradictory and competing thoughts for a clear image? How does a teacher spend time focusing on the internal meanings they make while grappling with outside opinions? We must develop a "critical language that enables us to both identify ourselves and recreate ourselves as active subjects in history while distinguishing our real needs from manufactured [societal] desires" (Pinar et al., 2006, p. 305). Britzman's (2003) fascination with how others influence the student teacher's role as a teacher can also be reflected through the term *heteroglossia*, which insinuates the presence and stratification of conflict and coexistence between different ideas expressed by one person (Pinar et al., 2006, p. 299). Simply, as one reflects upon experiences, a heteroglossia mindset would incorporate conflicting opinions into the dialogue. How were students observing/creating meaning from the lesson? How do their meanings differ or relate? Did one class take away a completely different conception of knowledge than another? The possibilities of vantage point are endless, and while incorporating conflicting ideas is necessary, I believe Britzman still misses the mark.

Like an awning window, our scope of who we become as a teacher can only be stretched so far. We are pulled back by the hinges of society and how others view us. As educators, we are constantly asked to change ourselves based on the perceptions of others. Bildungsprozess and heteroglossia represent "another's speech in another's language" (Nikulin, 2006, p. 31). Before a student teacher, or any educator, challenges someone else's ideas against their mental framework/discourses, an educator must first face the personal, multifaceted, competing ideas within oneself. I move that true learning of oneself, or learning to teach, can only be initiated through a deep analysis of oneself. This analysis must break the hinges of the window, in order for it to allow all of the light in. Reflection is simply not enough.

Knowledge comes in several forms. "We do not see or feel an experience—we understand it. This means that in the process of introspection we engage our experience into a context made up of other signs [only] we understand" (Britzman, 2003, p. 218). According to Britzman (2003), "Experience becomes meaningful only after it is thought about" (p. 231). Reflection is seen as a personal journey, searching through an experience to provide a perspective for internal growth. However, reflection does not always lend us to view the various internal lenses that we harbor, that we may not recognize. Britzman suggests student teachers engage in a dialogic understanding, an exchange, where learners "move beyond conversation itself and attend to the conditions of its production" (p. 237). What enables or limits our educational discourses? How do these contributions change the meaning of the lived experiences in the classroom? How do these contributions effect the future teacher's critical voice and identity? "Because personal meanings are contingent upon context and upon the perspectives of others, they are always shifting" (Britzman, 2003, p. 37).

Only I can assign meaning to an experience. This means that at some point I've grappled with competing ideas or purposefully ignored others. However, those ideas are embedded and still schema present in my mind. Before I can assess the contributions others have made to these ideas, I need to internally assess the plethora of meanings I've assigned to the lived experiences under examination and why I have assigned them. Therefore, before a student teacher can effectively engage in dialogical understanding, one must first embrace a dispositional willingness to view and confront themselves in various positions such as a teacher, a learner, an observer, or even simply a participant in society. Others may be able to influence the amount of light that comes in through the window, but only I am able to break the hinges for complete insight into my own assigned meanings.

CHALLENGE ACCEPTED

Expressing my voice in education has recently not been an issue, but this was not always the case. Somewhere in student teaching I found my voice and creativity, completely lost it during my first few years of teaching, only to gain it back again adding to my recent success as an administrator. I never truly thought about what experiences led to the rise and fall of this critical voice. Britzman (2003) has inspired me in this work to do just that. Smiley Steve was one very pivotal moment in my first months as a teacher, but the following stories are three additional examples that first came to my mind in what shaped me for the role I play today in education. Why these particular stories? I'm not sure as I write this statement, but per my own advice, I plan to reflect upon my own meanings to determine how these experiences formed and challenged my identity as a teacher and researcher.

BURNING FLAMES

Two weeks. I had only been teaching an honors chemistry class during my first student teaching assignment for 2 weeks when I encountered my first true discipline issue. It was a Wednesday morning at 7:19 a.m. I was helping a student, Amber, with electron configurations and watching my students enter the room, secretly checking their answers with one another as if I wasn't paying attention. Next to our high school building was a Sonic Drive Thru, and it wasn't uncommon for students to bring in a Route 44 Slush and slurp it down to achieve their sugar high for the day. It's now 7:25 a.m., the bell rings, and students immediately settle. (Thinking back, I never questioned why my students early on respected me enough as their "teacher" to prepare for learning without me even prompting.)

"Good morning! Our focus today is to apply what we know about electron configurations by performing several flame tests. If you have any food or drink in the classroom, you will need to finish it now, grab your goggles, and head to the lab stations in the back." As my students shuffled throughout the room, I watched a few of them throw their cups and food wrappers away. I notice, however, one of my female students acting strangely with her cup. Holding on to it as if she has to finish every last drop, or almost worried that someone will take it. I turn away from her for a moment, to set up a lab station for a group close by, when all of a sudden I hear her loudly scold one of her friends in the class. Apparently, her Sonic cup spilled over when her friend was walking through the aisle of desks. "Sarah, it's not a big deal, just grab some paper towels and clean it up, please," I said in what I thought was the calmest tone. "Don't touch anything, Sam! I've got it!" Sarah says to the cup demolisher. I go over to help Sarah, and I immediately smell alcohol. Now granted, a majority of the room smelled like fire and alcohol due to our flame test demonstration, but with her odd behavior and the concentration of smell surrounding her, it was pretty clear she didn't want to be in trouble. "Sarah, after you clean this up I need to speak with you in the hall." "Why? I didn't do anything wrong!" "Sarah, I think you know why. This is not for discussion in front of others, I will meet you in the hall." "I'm not going out in the hall, and I asked you not to touch anything! I said I've got it!" At this point, Sarah puts the smashed Sonic cup in her bookbag, and throws the paper towels away in the trash can nearest to the door, but farthest from my desk. Why argue with me about this? Do I have "idiot" stamped across my forehead? While I was calm when I spoke with her, I remember just freaking out inside. I didn't read the code of conduct, so how am I supposed to deal with this? Where's my cooperating teacher at? Is abandonment really the way to teach me in learning situations like this? I stood by the doorway and patiently waited a few minutes for Sarah to meet me. After an intense stare down, which I won, she begrudgingly came.

"Sarah, what did you have in your cup this morning?" "Water! What are you trying to imply? Why would it be anything else but water?" "You and I both know it's not water. What I care more about is how did you get it and why do you think it's appropriate to bring that to school?" "I just told you it was water, and it's all gone now anyways . . . so I dare you to prove it now!" Ohhhh!!! To tell you how fuming I was would be the world's biggest understatement. I'm not quite sure what happened in the moments to come. It was as if I wasn't Ashley, the teacher, anymore, but a detective who was about to crack a case. Mr. Wilbur, my cooperating teacher walked down the hallway as I scurried back into the classroom to grab the paper towels from the trash can, a lighter, and paper towels soaked in water.

"Alright, Sarah, let's do an experiment. We can use science to explain a variety of scenarios, just like the one we are in right now. Since you're missing the flame test, let's do one of our own. Would water and alcohol burn at the same rate? What do you think? Well let's see." At this point I took the paper towel that I soaked in water and lit it on fire. And while it was burning, I took a video of it. I quickly took the paper towel soaked in the mess from her cup, and lit it on fire. I could barely get the video of it because it burned so quickly.

To this day, I will never forget the astonished look on her face as she realized this teacher wasn't messing around. Who she may have thought was her equal, was now an adult teaching her several lessons at once. I asked her to go back into the room, grab her backpack, and began to escort her to the office. As I turned toward the office with Sarah, I see Mr. W in the hallway. It wasn't until he asked Sarah to head to the office on her own, that I realized he was present for my personal flame test demonstration. My heart sank to my stomach. Crap! Was that something I shouldn't have done? Was I too mean? Should I have asked him to handle the situation? To my surprise he simply said: "Never in a million years would I have thought to do that. That was freaking awesome!"

I never gave this experience enough thought. Maybe because I wouldn't be able to replicate that in a million years, even if I tried. Thinking back now, I can smell the burning paper towel as if it were in front of us. I can also smell the confidence that this experience gave me due to my savvy, bold attempt to show a student that I wasn't falling for her deceit. It was one of the first moments that I didn't second guess what I was doing as the person in charge. Where did this confidence come from, though, out of the blue, and why?

Five to six years earlier, in my own high school, I watched kids get away with drinking at school daily. Some drank for attention from their peers, attempting to fit in with a crowd that they would later regret. Others drank because of mental demons they didn't want to come to grips with. School was the safe place and a drink in the morning calmed their anxieties to focus for their classes. Regardless of the reason, I watched idly. I knew this was a problem, and yet I silenced what I should have voiced. I think of Britzman's elicitation of the cultural myth: teacher as expert. The expert not only holds knowledge of content, but in my mind the expert should also contain the expertise of being aware of the surroundings: an expert of behaviors. In that moment, I was Sarah's critical voice for her. My fervent reaction was to show Sarah that she needed help and to also showcase to the class that my exhaustion of heat was simply for their safety as well as to exhibit my deep care for them because I know they were watching, if at the very least listening. I did not piece together until now the effect my prior experiences truly had on this rare incident. Jim Eison's article comes to mind when reliving this mental moment. Eison (1990) suggests the only thing truly needed for effective instruction is for a teacher to speak actively, teach actively, and care actively (p. 22). Oftentimes we fixate on what our students think of us, that we lose sight of what we think of ourselves. To speak actively, to teach actively, or to care actively, we must *think* actively. If I could go back, I would have walked back in the classroom and had a discussion of alcohol and the impacts on the body, especially the mental impacts. I would not have walked back in pretending nothing happened as I did. My confidence when proving my care for Sarah, was subdued for the uncomfortableness of addressing a bigger issue such as drugs and alcohol to an entire group of students. Lesson learned 9 years later.

SATURDAY SCHOOL

Teaching Advanced Placement (AP) courses is like raising a newborn. You're completely exhausted, walking around like a zombie, and you're lucky to remember what day it even is. You change lesson plans, labs, and activities as if they were diapers, and if anyone cries it's your job to immediately silence the tears by pulling out all the stops to encourage engagement and positivity. Yeah, teaching AP can be rough, but it is also so incredibly rewarding. During my first high school teaching job, I began an AP Physics B course because the students were not only capable, but also ready to engage in more challenging, scientific work. Around mid-November, half of my students indicated to me they were struggling and needed more help outside of class time. We were already working after school, but many had jobs or practice and could not consistently get enough help to improve their understanding. I proposed to the students a Saturday review/working session where the students could bring any of their homework problems to work collaboratively on with one another and me. My students were ecstatic, and even more so when they found out I would bring donuts each time.

Every Saturday for 2 months my students came to school at 9 a.m. until noon or 1 p.m. to work. I saw huge improvements in their physics conceptual understanding, and honestly I saw huge improvements in my own. Suddenly, one day in February, I was called to the office to discuss the purpose of my Saturday sessions with the principal. While I had (or so I thought) the support of my building, apparently there had been "complaints" from my non-AP parents that my relationships with my AP students were too close. I was instructed to stop holding the Saturday sessions because of "perception": "Perception is everything in education, Ashley. I completely believe you are helping our students, but we have to think of the community and how they are viewing it." I was demolished. How could anyone view these sessions as anything but going over and above for kids? Students are willingly coming in to get additional help and are seeing results and this is seen as a bad thing? Isn't my job to build relationships and engage students in ways to propel them towards career readiness? Half of my students were going into engineering, nursing, or pre-med. Did the community think that they wouldn't need this knowledge in college or for their futures? How was teaching students on a Saturday being too close to them? The conversation on that day destroyed my faith in my relationships with parents, with students and with administration. That night I couldn't sleep.

The next day, I told my AP students that we had to put an end to the Saturday sessions. They were irate to put it mildly. "Why are we being punished?" "Why are they doing this?" "They always stop things that are good for us!" "I'll fail the AP exam without these!" I had no explanation to give them other than I was instructed that we could no longer meet on Saturdays. I didn't think my feelings could get worse when I left school that day, but then something interesting happened. Both AP and non-AP parents began flooding my email inbox and phone. Apparently, my student's anger went immediately home, and parents were sharing their support for my work with their kids, thanking me for my dedication and baffled by the school's decision to shut down what they believed was a powerful motivator for their student's engagement in school.

I was approached the next morning for a meeting with the principal and the director of human resources (as if the first meeting wasn't intimidating enough). Both questioned why I blew the cancelation of my Saturday sessions out of proportion to students. They didn't believe that my only statement to the kids was that we were no longer allowed per a district decision. As I was listening to the HR director speak, I began thinking that this had to be something bigger than me, or bigger than what they were willing to share. Certainly, as educators, they see this conversation is absurd. Right? I couldn't quite put my finger on what was going on, and honestly, I was too scared to find out. The same day of this meeting, I received a bouquet of flowers from a mom of one of my AP Physics students. The card read: "Hang in there kid! Our kids are lucky to have an educator like you pushing them to new heights! Know that you are so loved!" Two hours after reading the card, I received another meeting request from HR and fast-forwarding to the meeting, the first question asked was why I received flowers with a card that told me to hang in there.

This teacher inquisition lasted another 2 months. During this time I discovered it was only one parent that had an issue with the Saturday sessions. A parent that didn't have a student in AP Physics. Why did this directly impact her? Her son had his first B ... in my academic level physics course. Moreover, it was also revealed to me that within those 2 months other teachers were targeted such as I had been. Not surprisingly from the same parent. Did I mention this parent held a powerful role in the district? Did I also mention that this parent called me in the group of parents that supported me earlier and made it seem like they supported me as well? It was at the end of this year, I was fortunate enough to find a new job in a district that would heal my wounds. On my last day at this high school, my principal stopped by to wish me luck. The very last thing he stated, "Keep going above and beyond for your students, kid! You're a really great teacher!"

If I was such a great teacher, why didn't I get support through what I would consider the most awful time of my professional career? These

4 months made me hate education. I found myself almost in tears every day coming to work and leaving work, believing that I would have another meeting about something that I believed I was doing right for kids. I was at my most vulnerable moment as a teacher and as a human being. I think what hurt the most was how my idea of help was misconstrued to be something ugly; the only reason a young teacher would want to host a Saturday session would be to hang out with her kids. My professionalism and my character were at question, and for what? For a pathetic B. One B.

I was aware of the role politics played in education, as I was a victim from someone's political agenda during my own high school career. Nevertheless, I would have never imagined the situation I endured would have actually happened. Why was the voice of one parent, regardless of their community stature, that much more influential than 50 others combined? Did those who should have been supporting me really agree with the tactics that were asked to be used? Why on earth would someone read a personal card delivered in a bouquet of flowers and use that against them when they were in the wrong for invasion of privacy?

This experience formed not only my identity as a teacher, but also my identity as a human. I put an inconceivable amount of stock in how others viewed me. I allowed others to make me question my own character and what I believed was right for students to succeed. As a high school student, I remember teaching Antonio, a first grader who was held back twice, how to read. I went through every method and strategy possible to engage him and he could have cared less. He had no trust in any adult because, to him, it felt like everyone had given up. It wasn't until I started rewarding him for the small accomplishments that he began to see that I cared. By the end of the first semester with him, he could read an entire book by himself and knew all of the sight words to move on to the next grade. He read our book to anyone and everyone, and even after I was finished with cadet teaching, I visited Antonio every year while he was in elementary school. While I didn't visit often, he remembered who I was and hugged me each time. Thinking of Antonio brings tears to my eyes. It was a time that my faith in education, in relationships, and in teaching was full. It was how I knew for certain that I wanted to be a teacher. I never knew that my first actual teaching job would have me question that feeling: that raw moment, or calling to the field.

Britzman (2003) discusses one of the common cultural myths: teachers are self-made. In my heart, I do believe teaching is a calling; however, it is the school's responsibility to grow teachers and make them into the professionals they should be. As educators, we are asked to always build relationships with students. We are told this is the key to success. How about the relationships between educators? If unity and morale is high, does that not trickle down to student relationships? If I cannot show respect for those that I work with, how on earth can I show respect for my students? If the

A-seeking parent would have individually talked with me about what her child could have done to improve their grade, there is no doubt in my mind that they would have ended up with an A. Why was this never an option? It was probably halfway through my fourth meeting that I realized that I would not be the quiet teacher they were so desperately seeking. This was really difficult for me. Just as teachers are thought to be the power-holders in the classroom, I think fundamentally teachers view administration as power-holders in the district. One wouldn't want to jeopardize their educational livelihood by challenging someone higher up the ladder. What did I have to lose though? A contentious workplace? An environment that I dreaded driving up to every morning? I did have students. I had kids that I absolutely adored and relationships with teachers that are still strong today. While this high school made me fearful of teaching in the way I believed was appropriate, it gave me insight into myself that I will thank them for. It allowed me to build up my nonnegotiables of teaching. It assisted me in wanting more from my administration. I gained confidence in myself, and even what was the darkest moment in my career, I would not have changed what happened. This incident made me question my career choice, but it propelled me in ways that I will be forever grateful.

SLITHERING FEARS

Parents in power are not the only thing that scares me. What's probably a million times worse: SNAKES! Where does this fear come from you may ask? It comes from a horrific incident in third grade when a teacher forced me to "conquer my fears" and pet this disgusting 16 foot, yellow python. Well, jokes on her because that snake got caught in my hair and I almost died! Okay, I didn't almost die, but to this day I believe any snake (even worm-size) is ready to unhinge its jaw to eat me. This is proof that educational experiences hold lifelong effects. This totally illogical fear is something I decided to share with my students during the first week of school every year I taught. I made this decision for two reasons:

1. I wanted my students to understand that I am a human being and that all educational experiences have an impact. This story also allowed me to connect a very real-life application to the chemistry of the brain, while simultaneously building relationships with my classes.
2. Probably the more important of the reasons, kids are the best at warning teachers about literally anything that is happening in the building.

Reason two really helped me out when a zoology teacher in the school decided to have a "Snake Week." My students came running in after every bell to inform me of the upcoming week. They gave me details about which student was bringing in snakes, what kind of snakes they were, and so forth. I lived in fear for the entire week! I kept the door to my classroom locked, and one student even crafted something for me to put under the door in case a slithering monster got loose and decided to make its home in my room.

While I believed I had prepared for anything that could have happened snake-wise during the week, what I did not anticipate was for my colleague to play jokes on the last day of Snake Week. Bob got to school early that Friday and hid 30 rubber snakes all over my room. Some of the hiding spots were more noticeable, while others I didn't find until the end of the year. Nevertheless, it was like having 30 mini heart attacks upon each discovery. To top this off, there was a note on my board that said one of the snakes in my room wasn't fake. There were no real snakes in my room, but as I walked into my room with my students, their reactions to protect me were unforgettable. During the last bell, my colleague came in with a snake wrapped around his arm. I, of course, had no idea. The kids in my room were speechless. I spoke with Bob for approximately 5 minutes, and towards the end of the conversation he inquired, "Can you really be afraid of what you don't know is there." At this point, my suspicion kicked in and I became hypersensitive to my surroundings. It was then, I zeroed in on the devil-created creature on his arm. I screamed, ran to the opposite side of the room, and began to tear up [now remember that I still had a classroom full of kids]. Is now an appropriate time to talk about the brain chemistry of fear?

Everything does not depend on the teacher. After I ran to the other side the room, my students came to my defense, got on to Bob for being a bully until he fled the room, and began asking AMAZING chemistry questions relating to what we were working on prior to Bob's dumb appearance. The kids held all of the power in that moment, and yet they respected me enough to engage in school. This story seems ridiculous to add as one of my pivotal moments in teaching, but it reiterated to me the power dynamics between students and teacher. Students only felt comfortable to take control in that situation because at some point, I have communicated with them that I am not the only one in power in the classroom. How on earth did I do this, and when? Was the snake story at the beginning of the year really the way that I introduced my status as a human?

The other reason this story stands out in my formation as an educator is the question that was imposed on me in front of my kids: "Can you really be afraid of what you don't know is there?" I wished now I would have taken the time to think this through with my class. I wished I would have shared with them how we never know how things will turn out; we cannot predict failure in the same manner as we cannot predict success. While I know these statements are true now, I wished I would have told them that it's okay to be scared, but not fearful, not afraid. Fear encourages us to hold back on our thoughts, our feelings, and asphyxiates the ability to dig deeper into emotions that we were unaware we were harboring. We are all fearful at times in our lives. As a young teacher who endured the AP Saturday session debacle, my voice was broken. If I talked with students about something as personal as fears, would it come back to bite me? Regardless of how others viewed me, I knew that I couldn't hold the weight of anymore "perception." Emotionally, I was drained, but what was I really afraid of? Failure? Losing my job? Not being able to answer tough questions? I thought less of my students and became selfish in that moment to protect myself. The girl that was so confident in what to do with alcohol in the classroom or the one to come to Steve's rescue, had some major internal introspection to get to who she is now.

CONCLUSION

If you're wondering if Steve is still alive today, rest-assured he is. Like my illogical fear of snakes, he has what I would consider a very logical fear of gummy bears now, and possibly the color red since I made him drink so much water that he got sick prior to the ambulance ride. What I thought would have ended my career in education, actually made me a stronger, more observant teacher. The stories above are only small pieces of my identity, but pieces that had a dramatic and lasting impact. Thank you Deborah Britzman. Your book inspired me to question my identity formation in terms of my own dispositions and meanings. Dialogue and communication are essential in meaning making, but the meanings I have assigned and harbor dictate the dialogue I share with others, and without looking further into my own meanings, I cannot continue to form my identity in the way I desire. "When teachers view their work as research, it becomes more difficult to take the dynamics of classroom life for granted" (Britzman, 2003, p. 239). Teachers are researchers. We hypothesize about ourselves, we collect data to reject or strengthen our theories of who we believe we are, and we conclude with the production of meaning assigned to experiences that tell us more about who we think we are. I boldly urge all educators to take this scientific frame of thought and to not only apply it to themselves, but to also encourage students to be willing to wrestle with their own conception of self. It may not have been an appropriate time for me to lecture or question Steve's actions during the ambulance ride, but while waiting for the doctor, I will never forget what Steve asked as he smiled: "Would the reaction be different if it were a green gummy bear?" I was envious! Steve's innocence, lack of fear, and complete focus for learning were untouched. Maybe I needed to eat some more gummy bears myself.

REFERENCES

Britzman, D. (2003). *Practice makes practice: A critical study of learning to teach.* State University of New York Press.

Eison, J (1990). Confidence in the classroom: Ten maxims for new teachers. *College Teaching, 38*(1), 21–25.

Nuhkulin, D. (2006). *On dialogue.* Lexington Books.

Pinar, W. F., Reynold, W. M., Slattery, P., & Taubman, P. M. (2006). *Understanding curriculum: An introduction to the study of historical and contemporary curriculum discourses.* Peter Lang.

CHAPTER 14

STICKS AND STONES

Kelly R. Wilham

Author/Book studied:

Paley, V. G. (1992). *You can't say you can't play.* Harvard University Press.

One day, my twin sister and I were walking home from elementary school talking and laughing. We lived less than a mile from school and were so excited that our parents finally allowed us to walk home. As usual, many of our neighbors also walked home and took the same path. A boy and girl that lived down the street were walking not far behind us. The boy and girl were having a conversation but somehow it quickly turned to picking up rocks and throwing them while yelling at my sister and me. Unfortunately, I was hit by a flying rock, so my sister turned around and said, "Sticks and stones may break my bones, but words will never harm me," and we ran home. At the time, our older sister would watch us until our parents would arrive home from work. We immediately told our sister what happened and she told us exactly what to do. "You go outside, cup your hand over your mouth, and yell 'b*@#!.'" I did exactly what my older, wiser sister told me to do.

Curriculum Windows Redux, pages 177–185

Now, as you can imagine, this is where the story gets hairy living in a small town! Within 5 minutes, the phone rang at our home. It was our mother saying she was on her way home from work and that she and dad would discuss what just took place! I really believed for a long time that moms and dads had secret radar because they heard and knew everything that went on! After our parents arrived home, and the interrogation was over, I clearly remember the shameful walk down the street to the neighbor's home to apologize. I really didn't understand why I was in trouble. My older sister told me to say it, and my twin sister was the one saying "sticks and stones" and I didn't throw any rocks! How many of us as children remember the saying "Sticks and stones may break my bones but words will never harm me"? I didn't pay that much attention to it until I was older and truly understood what the concept meant. Then, I just thought it was a bald-face lie!

Vivian Gussin Paley takes us on a journey back to kindergarten and the words and messages that children say to each other. Paley's (1992) book, *You Can't Say, You Can't Play*, is bursting with genuine conversations with children as well as stories woven throughout about a bird named Magpie. Her conversations and messages with students such as Angelo, Lisa, and Clara, are as profound today as they were when Paley's students shared their thoughts and feelings with her. Magpie lived in a magical world where all students were accepted. Thus, Paley introduces a new rule to her kindergarten students while having discussions with older students about the fairness of the rule and their opinions and sharing stories about Magpie. I choose this book to read because I am a veteran elementary principal and continuously look for ways to create an all-inclusive environment where all students are valued.

THE FIRST CURRICULUM

Numerous exceptional minds have contributed to the early education movement that also believed that child's play and storytelling were critical for children and were the basis of the first curriculums. "The kindergarten was developed in the nineteenth century by a German reformer and educator, Friedrich Froebel" (Berg, n.d., para. 1). His idea regarding the purpose of education was to develop the spiritual core of children in a prepared environment with a teacher facilitating the children's growth. This was achieved through self-activity and play, as well as imitation developed through songs, stories, games, gifts, and occupations.

> [Froebel] built upon the ideas of Johann Heinrich Pestalozzi, a Swiss follower of Jean-Jacques Rousseau's belief in the inherent goodness of children. During the 1830s and 1840s, Froebel made a case for the importance of music, nature study, stories, and play as well as symbolic ideas like children sitting together in the kindergarten circle.... In 1837 Froebel opened the first kindergarten

in Blankenburg, Germany. He also established a training school for women, whom he saw as the ideal educators of young children. (Berg, n.d., para. 1)

Maria Montessori understood child development and the importance of beginning with working with children as young as 6 weeks of age in an infant/toddler program. She believed that

> during the first three years of life, a child's brain absorbs more information from the environment than at any other part of his lifetime. Every sight, sound, touch, taste, and smell is taken in and processed. It is an amazing, wondrous period in a tiny, complete human being's life. (North American Montessori Center [NAMC], 2019, para. 1)

Montessori's infant/toddler environment provided a "safe, calm, carefully designed setting for optimal learning that nurtures the physical and spiritual being. Sensory, cognitive, language, social, and cultural activities address the natural tendencies of the child's developmental process" (NAMC, 2019, para. 2). Even at this early stage, a child is soon able to make choices for his own independence.

> Montessori's famous first class, the "Children's House," was actually a child-care center in an apartment in a poor neighborhood. Montessori refused to impose arbitrary tasks on the children. Instead she showed them ways to develop their own skills at their own pace, a principle she called "spontaneous self-development." Her classroom installed low cubbies where children could take out and put away their own supplies, child-size furniture, a garden and pets for them to care for, and assorted objects to encourage children to teach themselves. (Early Childhood Today Editorial Staff, 2000, para. 4)

In 1907, Maria Montessori opened Children's House in a low-income district of Rome. Children's House served children aged 3 through 6 years. Montessori wanted children in the program to have the opportunity to choose their own work within limits guided by skilled teachers or Montessorians. The environment was expected to be rich with developmentally appropriate and captivating learning materials. The fundamental concepts for children's learning at this age are the development of concentration, coordination, self-discipline, order, independence, and respect.

Before 1890, kindergartens were focused more on a child's socialization and not as much on a rigorous academic education or specific learning standards and benchmarks that needed to be met. There were no public funds from the government or department of education at this time. "Kindergarten was most prevalent in private institutions, including free kindergarten associations, social settlements, charities, parochial schools, and orphanages" (Berg, n.d., para. 4). Many of the 3- to 6-year-old children who attended the free, half-day kindergartens had immigrant parents who were of the working class (Berg, n.d., para. 4).

> In the late nineteenth and early twentieth centuries, the focus was on the whole child and their development which encompassed everything from their social, physical, and academic development, versus just focusing on core subjects such as reading, writing, and math. (Berg, n.d., para. 4)

All urban school systems in the United States had kindergartens that were open and funded by the public for 5-year-olds by the start of World War I. In 1920, an estimated half million 5-year-old children attended kindergarten. More children were attending public schools versus private ones by a margin of 19%. With a large number of children attending kindergarten, the public began to push for the focus to be on preparing the kindergarteners for first grade, which meant a more intense focus on academics and being socially prepared (Berg, n.d., para. 6). Before World War II, as kindergarten enrollments in the United States declined, many school districts cut back their funding even though other school districts simultaneously adopted the kindergarten programming. However, from 1940 to 1954, enrollment in public kindergarten increased rapidly. With this enrollment surge came the challenge of dealing with a large variety of class sizes. This led to some states deciding to pass class size laws in order to keep the class size no larger than 24 students. Other states dealt with inflated enrollment by increasing the age requirement to enter kindergarten (Berg, n.d., para. 8).

Vivian Gussin Paley, born in 1929, is a life-long learner, educator, and early childhood education researcher (Vivan Paley, 2019). She taught preschool and kindergarten, and did most of her research at the University of Chicago Laboratory Schools (Vivian Paley, 2019). Paley's research and findings made a significant impact on education with regards to storytelling and story acting curriculum. Let's be clear, Paley did not invent storytelling and story acting, "She is to be credited, however, with establishing them for the field as inseparable and regular classroom activities" (Cooper, 2005, p. 233). While teaching in the 1950s in New Orleans, Paley began to use her observations and reflect upon the rigidness of what was expected to be taught. Paley began teaching between the progressive functionalism and scholarly structuralism time periods; a period of time known as the developmental conformism (Vivian Paley, 2019). This was a time that may have been seen as a transition period. Our nation was "embroiled in a cataclysmic war and then recovering from it to find a cold war on its hands" (Glatthorn et al., 2012, p. 45). In 1957, the Russians launched Sputnik. This brought about great concern, doubts, and complaints about the United States educational system. People felt that there were not enough rigorous standards for the children, especially in the preschool and kindergarten programs.

In her own findings, Paley believed that storytelling and dramatization were critical with children (Vivan Paley, 2019). She began to write books in the 1970s about early childhood education. Paley would usually focus on one theme throughout her books. Her theme for this book focused on fairness and exclusion within the classroom while bringing in moral discussions and just plain human nature. Another theme, which she has carried out in many of her books is multiculturalism in the classroom and racially diverse classrooms. Paley's book also brings to light the hidden rules in our schools. Paley states that stories and story acting are just not adequate. She further explains, "Story is never enough, nor is talk. We must be told, when we are young, what rules to live by" (Paley, 1992, p. 110). How do we make all students part of the system? Paley went to great lengths to plan for the new rule. After discussing the creation of a new rule with the first through fifth graders, she would return to her classroom and share the summary of the discussion with her kindergarteners. The students would make comments and ask more questions about each grade level's responses. They were so excited to see what the older students were saying about their new rule. Paley made sure to plan with the students, talk about it, get opinions, think about it, and wonder how it will work (Paley, 1992, p. 56).

THE BAY WINDOW

I remember growing up and my parents getting new windows for our home. We had a huge picture window in the front living room where you could see everything. My parents made the decision to replace the window with a bay window. I must admit, my sisters and I were so thrilled! It became our special place to hang out. My twin sister and I would go behind the sheers, climb up onto the landing, and lie in the sun, and we would transform to another world. It was a world that each day when we came home from school we would meet, eat our snacks, discuss and reflect upon our day, and play. At times we would need to stop playing because the sun beaming in through the window would make it too warm to stay or our older sister would interrupt us. However, one day as we were playing, my twin sister noticed a "secret latch" on the side window. We immediately forgot what we were doing and became fixated on what it was and how to manipulate it. There was a matching latch on the other window as well. Eventually, we figured out that the new contraption we discovered would open up a "new world" for us. It was the secret to opening up the window and allowing the fresh air and sounds from the outside to penetrate in, and made our meeting place much cooler on sunny days! Somehow, as we let in the smells of our mother's lilac bushes and listened to the birds chirp, it made our world feel better and more open to views and differences of opinion as we grew older. It was our safe place to be genuine and real as a family. As all children do, we grew up! We became extremely busy with after-school activities, so we didn't meet as much at the window, however, we would somehow always make it there sometime during the weekend. Even through the years, our parents would come sit in the window to talk with us or make sure we were okay. As I reflect upon my meetings at the bay window, it occurs to me that I was never alone. I did not have to worry about being rejected as I always had someone to play with, talk to, and just be in the same room. Sitting or lying in our special window allowed me to look at issues and life through a different lens or someone else's perspective and to learn from it. What I learned at home, unfortunately some children don't get to experience until they arrive at preschool or kindergarten, and even then, they may not get to experience it. They don't have a bay window to crawl into to play and just be a kid.

PALEY'S BAY WINDOW

Just as the bay window allowed me to view life through a different lens, Paley masterfully creates a bay window for her students in her classroom to all be included, to tell stories, act them out, and to be accepted no matter what through her new rule. She shows her students the "secret latches" and teaches them the rules so that they can navigate through cooperative learning and play. She clearly articulates through her conversations with children from kindergarten through fifth grade, and the stories created by her kindergarten students that "Sticks and stones may break my bones, but words will cut right through you." Students such as Angelo have learned that they can share their stories through dramatization and the rest of their classmates have a better understanding of how other people feel when other students are mean to them. As Paley went to each grade level and discussed the new rule of "You can't say, you can't play," many insightful messages were shared. For instance, a fifth grade boy stated, "In your whole life you're not going to go through life never being excluded. So you may as well learn it now" (Paley, 1992, p. 22). He went on to share, "You won't be so down on yourself when you do get excluded" (Paley, 1992, p. 22). All students Paley spoke with from fifth grade to first grade discussed their many examples of being excluded throughout their years of schooling. One student suggested that if Mrs. Paley's rule would have been in place when she was in kindergarten, she would have really enjoyed school. Paley opened up a window for the student to also reflect and state that it is important to start with the students early in life with this rule, so it becomes automatic behavior to include everyone. Paley's book was delightful and an easy read. However, at times, the reader may have difficulty transitioning back and forth from the fictional Magpie stories to her story of the evolution of the "new rule."

As I read this book, it brought to mind many stories of exclusion of students over the years coming into my office and being so sad and distraught about not having any friends or someone to play with. I had a sixth grade student walk into the main office and ask to speak with the principal. I heard his voice and immediately went out to greet him. He had many challenges yet is cognitively gifted. However, some students could not see past some of his challenges and would not play with him. He told me what happened at recess when he asked a group of boys if he could play. There was a pause, and he began to sob. It shattered my heart for this wonderful young man to be so broken. The next day, I happened to be doing classroom walk-throughs and made a point of going into his math class. I asked the teacher if I could see if anyone could solve a math equation I was having difficulty trying to solve. I wrote a 15-digit number on the board and asked if anyone could help me. The young man immediately raised his hand and began sharing numbers with me as I wrote them on the board. I pulled my calculator out of my pocket and punched in the numbers to solve the equation. I then wrote the answer on the board. He was correct!!!! The other students went wild with amazement and excitement. The student asked if we could do another problem. So, I made another one up. Again, he was able to correctly solve the problem. He became an instant star in the eyes of his classmates. Students began to flock to him for help during math class and study hall. I wanted to do back flips for him! I continued to keep an eye on him as he finished out his days in my elementary school. He was never at a loss for a friend at recess for the rest of the year. Fortunately, I was able to open a new window for this student like Paley did for her students.

IS THE WINDOW CLOSING?

Is kindergarten the new first grade? Have we increased our expectations and rigor so much that our children aren't developmentally ready for it? Do the state testing system and reporting systems that are currently in place have any bearing on the increased expectations and rigor in kindergarten? Have we created an adverse systemic change in how we educate our children? As a taxpayer, should community members be angry that they are paying for early childhood programs that are not really meeting the developmental needs of the children and should politicians be held accountable for pushing the Common Core Standards? When I look at the future for the children, it saddens me greatly that we continue to push students when they are not developmentally ready nor have been developmentally prepared. I agree that it is a great expectation that all of our children will be reading on-grade level by the end of the third grade. However, you would then assume that federal funding, research-based programs, and the arts would increase significantly to support K–3 learning, and clearly, it is just not happening. I believe that all of these initiatives, laws, policies, and funded programs have the best of intentions to support schools and children from poverty.

Paley has made many contributions to early childhood education. With her research and analysis, she has clearly given proof of the crucial role of fantasy play in the psychological, intellectual, and social development of young children. From Paley's observations, she is able to show evidence of the limitless growth of young children who are allowed the time for fantasy play, storytelling, and story acting. Paley's research examines the developing logic and learning that allows children to construct meaning in their worlds, meaning that carries through into their adult lives. With the standardized testing and higher accountability for teachers and students, unfortunately this critical playtime, story time, and story acting is usually the first curriculum to go when mandates and other new curriculum arises. Many things changed with the No Child Left Behind (NCLB) Act of 2001, such as many legislative requirements for the early childhood literacy curriculum. NCLB was focused on direct instruction or teacher-led activities around five subareas of the reading process: phonemic awareness, phonics, fluency, vocabulary, and comprehension. Many outspoken legislatures believed that we were behind other countries and had a play-based curriculum that did not provide sufficient preparation for young children's early literacy development in these areas. However, when we mix in politics and negotiating power with our "best of intentions," things don't turn out the way they were planned. Unfortunately, the only people that are truly affected, lose, or get hurt, are the children. Is that the legacy that each of us are willing or wanting to leave behind? Do we want to close every window that is open to our children? Do we want to darken the lens so that they don't have the ability to work with all people whether they are alike or different? We all should be so fortunate to be able to have a bay window to look through and be able to see issues and people from many different lenses. Paley has a gift to be shared, in which all educators should create a classroom full of bay windows that our children can experience racial diversity, multicultural, fair, and all-inclusive classrooms where no child is excluded!

REFERENCES

Berg, E. (n.d.). Kindergarten. In *Encyclopedia of children and childhood in history and society*. http://www.faqs.org/childhood/Ke-Me/Kindergarten.html

Early Childhood Today Editorial Staff. (2000). *Pioneers in our field: Maria Montessori: A sensory approach to learning*. https://www.boyd.k12.ky.us/10/Content2/260

Glatthorn, A. A., Boschee, F., Whitehead, B. M., & Boschee, B. F. (2012). *Curriculum leadership: Strategies for development and implementation* (3rd ed.). SAGE Publications, Inc.

Cooper, P. M. (2005). Literacy learning and pedagogical purpose in Vivian Paley's storytelling curriculum'. *Journal of Early Childhood Literacy, 5*(3), 220–251.

No Child Left Behind Act of 2001, P.L. 107-110, 20 U.S.C. § 6319 (2002).

North American Montessori Center. (2019). *NAMC's infant/toddler Montessori diploma program.* https://www.montessoritraining.net/diploma-programs/infant-toddler-0-3

Paley, V. G. (1992). *You can't say you can't play.* Harvard University Press.

Vivian Paley. (2019, August 1). In *Wikipedia.* https://en.wikipedia.org/w/index.php?title=Vivian_Paley&oldid=908876757

CHAPTER 15

A GUIDE TO CREATING A DEMOCRATIC EDUCATIONAL COMMUNITY

How We Have Been Doing It All Wrong

Rebecca Wilson

Author/Book studied:

Kohn, A. (1996). *Beyond discipline: From compliance to community*. Association of Supervision and Curriculum Development.

Alfie Kohn's (1996) belief in progressive education is apparent in his book, *Beyond Discipline: From Compliance to Community*. Kohn questions current methods of classroom management as an effort to control and manipulate students into compliance in the classroom which prevents the development of caring, responsible, problem solvers. As a constructivist, Kohn describes the importance of students actively making meaning, rather than absorbing information which allows enhanced learning for students and educators

Curriculum Windows Redux, pages 187–193
Copyright © 2022 by Information Age Publishing
www.infoagepub.com
187

alike. Educators and students can work together to develop mutual meaning about how the classroom should work as well as work through adjustments to classroom functions as issues arise.

As a school social worker I hold a unique role within the education system. I am often the mediator between students, families, teachers, and administrators regarding a multitude of conflicts that arise on a daily basis. I have grown numb to the lack of basic communication and problem-solving skills that exist within school systems which echo the similar issues within our greater society. My days are filled with mediations, be it between students, teachers and students, teachers and administrators, students and parents, parents and teachers, parents and child protective services, and so forth. The list is long and ever changing as families and other governmental agencies become increasingly intertwined into the complicated system that education has become. Education's current behavioral system and norms leave little room for healthy and deep conversations.

While I often feel like an outsider looking in on a highly structured and stagnant education system, Alfie Kohn makes me feel accepted. Similar to the many awkward teens I work with on a daily basis, I want to fit in with fellow educators, but I struggle. I often disagree with the approaches educators utilize with students because they seem contrived and controlling. The educators desire for obedience and correct behavior/answers leave out creativity and critical thinking. Many educators attempt to impose their needs and desires on students instead of reflecting inward and adapting their behavior to influence student needs and their desire to learn. The lack of reflection occurs when educators are forced to teach a certain way and obtain student growth measures to maintain their employment. It only perpetuates a totalitarian way of thinking that restricts student growth. Instead of guiding students to be critical and creative thinkers, education overemphasizes compliance and obtaining the correct answer. By allowing students to question and shape their reality (aka, school) generates an educational system where students construct the environment they and we all need. Learning how to create meaning through problem-solving creates abilities that last a lifetime and open a window to numerous components of life as well as aids civilization by providing more individuals who caringly and responsibly contribute to a modern democratic society.

ALFIE'S WORLD

In order to promote academic excellence, educators need to attend to how children feel about school and about each other (Kohn, 1996, p. 103). When students enjoy school and being around their teachers and peers they are more open to learning. A child's attitude towards school helps to gauge their level of connection to an institution of learning and their first experiences with the democratic environment. When students feel judged and/or are afraid of embarrassment there is no space for creativity to grow. Instead students are focused on obtaining the correct answer and moving on to the next problem to complete the assigned task and eventually move on to what they would like to do or avoid criticism from the authority in the situation. Yet, creating a supportive environment allows creativity to flourish. The connection to positive feelings towards education and others promotes academic excellence (Kohn, 1996, p. 103).

Relationships with adults are a key strategy of Kohn's (1996) to transform classrooms into communities. Children are more likely to be respectful when important adults in their lives respect them, and they are more likely to care about others if they know they are cared about (p. 111). Respect is the foundation of any positive and successful relationship. Without respect there is little to no trust and learning relies heavily on trust between the teacher and the student. Students are better able to trust a caring person who is first and foremost a person (p. 111). It is important for teachers to relate to students on a human level instead of relationships similar to a prison guard and an inmate. Administrators, teachers, students, and families are all connected and reliant upon one another. In education, an emphasis on independence is not realistic when we are highly interdependent as a society. Interdependence requires cooperation, which elicits learning and caring about others. Teachers need to model how caring occurs and teach how the student might be with others (p. 113). Students are able to learn to care for others once they have been cared for outside of their home environment.

Once relationships are established with caring adults at school, students can begin to develop connections between one another. It is important for students to be linked to others around them. Interdependence on one another is better instead of independence (Kohn, 1996, p. 113). Society is strengthened by our connections and it is nearly impossible to excel on our own without some assistance from others. Our community rests on the knowledge of and connections among the people who are a part of it (Kohn, 1996, p. 113). Kohn (1996) emphasizes the importance of perspective taking to create generous, caring people. The focus on perspective taking or empathy is the foundation to creating a sense of community. When one is able to put themselves in another person's position and attempt to see the other perspective, personal and community growth occur.

To introduce students to a community away from their families is to create a community within the classroom. Kohn (1996) describes that classrooms are natural environments for students to work together towards common endeavors (p. 114). Focusing on the establishment of the classroom community only improves the relationships of students to educators and other students. A community may be formed through various activities and some as simple as class meetings where students are allowed to voice concerns or ideas that might improve the community. Allowing students to participate and develop the kind of community they desire within the school provides students with buy-in, ownership and pride in their community. Instead of the educator enforcing all the rules if the students and educators agree on community standards and regulations the students can hold one another and the educator accountable for the sake of the community. Engagement in the community process allows an empathic response to discipline as misbehavior is viewed as a person that needs help instead of a person who needs to be disciplined (p. 115).

Community assists in academic instruction as it can be utilized to promote the other when it is deliberately used by educators (Kohn, 1996, p. 117). When community is utilized purposefully by both educator and student, learning is deepened. Learning becomes a part of all academic endeavors as learning occurs and is strengthened in interactions with others. With community at the center of activities can be devoted to academic issues, academic work can be worked into other activities and academic study can be pursued cooperatively (Kohn, 1996, p. 117). Weaving academics into activities, topics, or discussions that students want to engage in enables students to learn from one another and the experience of working through the content. In order to enhance the sense of community and learning the curriculum can be selected with a focus on supporting social and moral growth which indirectly creates community as well (Kohn, 1996, p. 117). Allowing students to generate their own sense of the world and their place within it opens the potential for the students to learn to the best of their ability and to have some influence ever the environment they occupy. Yet, in modern schools, we assume we know what students desire without asking them and often rejecting their suggestions.

Developing a sense of community, within schools with the students, allows autonomy to grow and creates democracy (Kohn, 1996, p. 119). Schools provide an opportunity for communities, families, educators, and students to practice democracy that fits their values and morals. The democracy that is formed is able to be molded to fit the specific needs and desires of those involved and is ever changing as new community members enter and others exit. Dewey (2001) described how allowing students to create their own "miniature community" replicates real life and encourages students to consider living in the future (p. 13). Schools prepare the nation's youth for their future and there is no better way to prepare students for their future than to allow them to practice the skills necessary to participate in a democratic society.

Critiques of Kohn's work often identify that schools do not do enough to encourage students to learn for the sake of learning. Instead critics view that schools are too accommodating of student input which dumbs down the education system. Some consider that Kohn's "emergence of the self-indulgent, nonjudgmental, hierarchal classroom that—infusing radical libertarianism with radical egalitarianism—has resulted in the near to total collapse of standards" (Rochester, 1998, p. 168). The concern for the dumbing down of education actually is the result of a healthy democratic community. Pinar et al. (2008) states that schooling often reflects the culture of the dominant class, which allows the dominant class to stay in power. Rochester is allowed to criticize Kohn due to his ability to participate in a democratic society where he is a part of the dominant class. (Rochester is a university professor who lives in a wealthy neighborhood outside of St. Louis.) The freedom to express opposing views and ideas and learning to understand the other point of view are key components of Kohn's theoretical orientation. Encouraging individuals to question, discuss, work, and constantly evolve is a key component of critical thinking which enhances education and potentially the society at large. Society often seeks out advancements and change, yet, focusing on standards restricts our ability to improve and change when we are forced to all learn, think, and be all the same or similar.

While many in education feel more comfortable using behaviorist-based programs to control their classrooms, there is little supporting evidence that it works. Rewards and punishments do not assist students in becoming kind and caring people; instead, it teaches students how to manipulate others and behaviors in specific situations (Kohn, 1996, p. 34). How is it that educators continue to utilize these programs based on compliance and control that rarely provide the atmosphere they desire in their classrooms? The focus on the behavioral approach in teacher education neglects the full scope of the human experience. Many people enter the educational profession because they want to help, yet they are forced to become disciplinarians and "test-prep robots" which takes humanity out of the profession (Greene, 2016). Historically, educators are the most important representative of socialization for children; however, the humanity of the profession has been stripped away. Instead of fostering the positive side of human nature such as empathy, honesty, resolving disagreements, and so forth, they are focused on common core and teaching standards while future employers desire the aforementioned soft skills.

Considering teachers spend most of their day working with children and/or adolescents, they are not given much education about human development and how to effect change in the lives of those they teach. As a school social worker, I am trained with over 60 graduate course work hours on these topics as well as required to maintain education in these topics every 2 years to maintain licensure. While teachers are not trained like mental health professionals, they interact with children and adolescents enough to benefit from similar training before they enter the classroom. Most educators take one or two developmental psychology courses which only scratch the surface of the human psyche and how to assist these developing minds. Eisner (2002) describes that levels of mastery in education are individual and regardless of time with a focus on achievement for all students which enhances students' mental health and competence. The importance of going beyond a basic behavioral understanding of behavior, benefits students in many ways as well as their educators who will experience less exhaustion along with better understanding of their own psyches as well.

ALFIE MEETS MY WORLD

As a school social worker I am constantly looking for new methods and ways to engage students with adults and peers. A lot of the time it requires me to explore the interests of the students. In the last few years there has been an increase of interest among students in meditation (savasanah) and yoga. Initially I hesitated because I was concerned it was just students wanting to sleep at school. The more I explored yoga, meditation, mindfulness, sleep, and schools, the more I began to believe this would be an interesting exploration with students. After I took child and adolescent yoga training I began using it with students individually, in groups, and then in elective classes. A mainstay of yoga and mindfulness is to focus on the here and now not thinking about the past or future. However, I began finding myself dreading teaching my beginner boys yoga class. I felt that I had lost control of the class and the students were not taking it seriously as well as feeding off one another's negative energy. I tried correcting, rewarding, redirecting, assigned mats, phone calls home, and so forth. None of it seemed to work and I was becoming increasingly frustrated and not enjoying the class I highly enjoy teaching.

After some time and reflection I decided to try some of Kohn's advice and discuss my concerns and feelings with the students in the class. The class was organized with students sitting in a circle on yoga mats looking inward so there was a natural flow for conversation. When I shared my concerns with the students and explained that this was their class too and I wanted them to enjoy it, their reaction was surprising. Many of the students explained that they have not been asked how they would like the class to go since it was their class. The students repeated that they do not often feel like the classes they attend are their classes. I shared that this class was going to be different and their input was not only encouraged but desired. Students looked around at one another in disbelief as if they were waiting for Adam Kutcher to jump out from behind a door and shout out "you just got punked!" Once students absorbed this information they began to open up and share that they wanted to learn more poses, spend more time in savasana and for other students to respect that while they might find some of the content of the class silly they should respect those who want to learn. I was in shock. Students continued by elaborating that it is their job to encourage one another to try since they are all new to yoga and in order to learn more they need to encourage one another to listen and not talk while I am instructing or demonstrating. As a class, we agreed to these terms and if for any reason decided we needed to revisit others' concerns about the class, we could reopen the discussion at any time.

After the class meeting, the students slowly began to take it upon themselves to support one another and encourage each other to make choices for the benefit of the entire class. This really shined through when I missed a class due to a meeting and the substitute was impressed with how the students monitored one another. This was by no means a perfect transformation. There were times students did not follow their own recommendations and I would inquire if a class meeting would be necessary. There were a few times students shared their concerns or frustrations with a situation and we would all work together to attempt to resolve it. Overall, the students' engagement increased, my frustration decreased, and everyone's enjoyment went up. It takes time and effort to establish this type of community. I believe my role as the school social worker puts me at an advantage with the students because they have known me for many years where they only have their academic teachers for a year. However, I believe the effort is well worth the payoff and an opportunity to teach lifelong skills from which both students and educators can benefit. Learning is a process when educators and students alike work together towards common goals and understanding. Original, creative, and empowering ideas come from difficult conversations that take time and effort from everyone involved. Those who want to help others and improve the environment we currently live in and construct every day desire to build community over the compliance-based culture constructed for us.

REFERENCES

Dewey, J. (2001). *The school and society and the child and curriculum.* Dover Publications.

Eisner, E. W. (2002). *The educational imagination: On the designs and evaluation of school programs.* Merrill Prentice Hall.

Greene, R. (2016). *Lost & found: Helping behaviorally challenging students (and, while you're at it, all the others).* Jossey-Bass.

Kohn, A. (1996). *Beyond discipline: From compliance to community.* Association of Supervision and Curriculum Development.

Pinar, W. F., Reynolds, W. M., Slattery, P., & Taubman, P. M. (2008). *Understanding curriculum.* Peter Lang.

Rochester, J. (1998). What's it all about, Alfie? A parent/educator's response to Alfie Kohn. *Phi Delta Kappan, 80*(2), 165–169.

CHAPTER 16

CAN YOU FEEL IT? IT'S TIME FOR A CHANGE

Melissa Wipperman

> *Author/Book studied:*
> Fullan, M. (1991). *The new meaning of educational change*
> (2nd ed.). Teachers College Press.

Michael Fullan is significant in the field of educational reform because of his work in the areas of leadership, the educational change process, and roles within the change process. In *The New Meaning of Educational Change* (2nd ed.), Fullan (1991) "provides a detailed overview of how educational change works" (p. 8). In the first part of the book, numerous examples of change as it relates to elementary and secondary schools are described and Fullan (1991) seeks to " identify some guidelines for how change can be approached or coped with more effectively" (p. 10). In the remaining sections, Fullan deeply explains the roles of teachers, principals, students, district administrators, consultants, parents/communities, and finally governments in educational change. Fullan (1991) ends with reflection on the

Curriculum Windows Redux, pages 195–206
Copyright © 2022 by Information Age Publishing
www.infoagepub.com
All rights of reproduction in any form reserved.

educational change process and a call to action for educators to "approach educational change with the renewed respect that comes from the realization that it demands multilevel responsibilities" (p. 352). Using a thorough depiction of the possibilities for success and potential drawbacks to educational reform initiatives at all stages of implementation and process, Fullan arms readers with knowledge needed to anticipate and understand pitfalls of educational reform at the classroom, school, and district levels. Fullan (1991) suggests that "the only solution is that the whole school-all individuals-must get into the change business; if individuals do not do this, they will be left powerless" (p. 353).

Fullan's ideas about the process and roles of change in schools still resonate today. If his call to action was meaningful in 1991, it seems even more pertinent in 2017, as school leaders struggle to make a positive impact on students in a tumultuous era of state testing, teacher evaluation systems, and overall societal factors that may make student learning a challenge. By understanding the process and the important roles principals, district leaders, and teachers have in making meaningful change, educators in 2017 can drive student learning, school culture, and overall educational climate in a positive direction.

FEELINGS NEEDED TO MAKE CHANGE

My body usually lets me know when it is time to make a change. I have sleepless nights, my gums bleed when I brush my teeth, and there is a tightness that never leaves that small area just below my neck and between my shoulder blades. It is my body that creates change in my professional life, within my marriage or family relationships, and sometimes even gets me into the gym for a good workout. I imagine that if education has a body, it is feeling that tightness in the small area just below its neck and between its shoulder blades right now, and just like I need to make a change when I feel this way, education needs to make a change.

To completely and finally make a change, I need to live with my body's feelings for a bit, probably a bit too long. I struggle with options, think about what people around me might be judging me for, and what might happen if I ignore my body, and don't change. Education is in the same phase of living with and feeling the tightness, struggling through the judgments and what ifs. In my life, my body knows that I need to make a change before my mind knows that I need to make a change. Teachers, principals, students, and community members often know that there needs to be a change before change happens in educational settings. Right now within schools, uneasiness, sleepless nights, and stress are building to a level that may help enact meaningful change.

In reading Michael Fullan's, *The New Meaning of Educational Change*, I can better see the connection between the process of change and the way to make change happen in a field like education. If other educators are feeling like me—the tightness and our bodies are telling us it is time for change—it is most likely because the classroom really hasn't changed much since Fullan wrote this 2nd edition of his enduring book.

When Fullan published *The New Meaning of Educational Change* in 1991, I was a freshman in high school and I was required to take biology, gym, English, algebra, American history, and health classes. I sat in classrooms with rows of desks facing the front of the room where a teacher stood and lectured about topics that I would be forced to regurgitate on a multiple choice/short answer formatted test at the end of the week, again at the semester, and possibly once again on the ninth grade state proficiency test in order to graduate. Now, it is 2017, and I am a teacher of freshman students who are required to take biology, gym, English, algebra, American history, and health classes. For the most part, they sit in classrooms with rows of desks facing the front of the room where a teacher stands and lectures about topics that they are forced to regurgitate on a multiple choice/short answer formatted test at the end of the week, again at the semester, and once again on the state's end of course exam in order to graduate.

When looking through the window of a classroom in 2017, it is difficult to see any meaningful changes from when looking through the same classroom window in 1991. Written in 1991, this 2nd edition of *The New Meaning of Educational Change*, presents a detailed description of how people within learning organizations initiate, cope with, and lead change. District leaders, principals, teachers, parents, and students can still use Michael Fullan's research and wisdom to find meaning and purpose in the change process which *should* ultimately lead to meaningful changes in the classroom. The complex analysis of the change process that he presents in 1991 are honed and put into a strategic frame in the latest version of his perennial work—a 5th edition published in 2016. The most recent version gives context to and adds to the effectiveness of technical analysis of educational change. His work gives educators powerful insight into the reasons change initiatives fail or succeed in schools. Fullan admits that even leaders with an organized and thoughtful plan for change, may not succeed in terms of making progress. Fullan (1991) states the importance of asking this question when analyzing school reform, "What if the majority of educational changes introduced in schools, actually made matters worse, however unintentionally, than if nothing had been done?" (p. 15). Evidenced by the similarity of classroom structure, lesson delivery, student learning, and assessment, the educational changes that have been implemented over the course of the 26 years since Fullan wrote this edition of his book, it is possible that matters are worse. Many, many, educational programs have come and gone since he wrote the preface's first sentence:

> The issue of central interest in this book is not how many new policies have been approved or how many restructuring efforts are being undertaken, but rather what has actually changed in practice—if anything—as a result of our efforts. (p. xi)

Although many change initiatives have failed, have succeeded, and have already been forgotten over the course of these years, the view through the classroom window has remained unchanged. Has anything actually changed in practice? It is time that we revisit *The New Meaning for Educational Change* and Fullan's descriptions of the change process as we maneuver through current change initiatives at district, state, and federal levels of education. By keeping the focus on the meaning of change and how it affects the work we are doing at the classroom level, Fullan provides an opportunity to reflect on the reasons why the more things change, the more they remain the same.

TEACHERS AND PRINCIPALS NEED COLLABORATION TO CHANGE

In 2006, during my second year of teaching, I read the 3rd edition of Fullan's book as part of a class in educational leadership for a principal licensure program. At that time, when I read essentially the same Fullan ideas about educational reform, I remember feeling incredibly hopeful that change could happen in a classroom or school because at that time in schools, leadership had the capacity to make judgments about what was best for individual school cultures and for students. Implementation of innovative approaches when solving problems was commonplace. As I reread Fullan's ideas now, as a veteran teacher, I am no longer incredibly hopeful, but instead I am pessimistic about the possibility of the kinds of changes in education that he envisions. The possibilities for change are limited now because of how much oversight of daily operations has increased. Is my current level of cynicism because of my personal experiences in the classroom and with school leaders, or is this sense of negativity a result of increased governmental oversight, strict standardized testing schedules, and lack of leadership power at the local level in the current state of K–12 education? It has been interesting for me to consider the process of change at two very different junctures of my career and in differing climates of educational accountability and testing.

I think part of the reason why I am pessimistic about change goes back to that tightness that I feel just below my neck and between my shoulder blades, my body is telling me that it is time for a change. It is time for me to make a change in my professional career, to seek new challenges, and to recharge in a new environment. After spending the last 3 years as a traveling ESL teacher in an urban school environment, I need to become a part of a school community again, where I can more intimately see changes in students, teaching, and school culture. I need to be around good people doing good things for students every day, and I need to see some progress with my students in a meaningful and consistent way. It will require a lot of courage to try something new, but my body is telling me to make it happen. I owe it to myself and I owe it to the students whom I work with to cope with change, excel through change, and ultimately prepare them to successfully deal with their own changes.

I know that some of the pessimism I feel now is related to my current teaching assignment and some of my experiences with largely bureaucratic educational systems that make even small changes a difficult process, but I also think that the sense of pessimism that I feel is felt by many in all areas of education. We are sinking in it together. We are becoming complacent and we aren't listening to the messages our bodies are sending us. We are the people who have chosen education to be a fundamental part of our lives, and we have a responsibility to respond to the need for educational change in our society. As a teacher, I have a unique opportunity to be a part of the educational change process and Fullan discusses the important role that teachers can play in enacting educational change.

Fullan suggests that teachers are integral to the process of change and gives guidelines for how to respect their feelings, understand their limits, and encourage participation in the planning. He describes the change process from the vantage point of the teacher and makes it clear that teachers are a vital aspect to an initiative's success. According to Fullan (1991), "Educational change depends on what teachers do and think—it's as simple and as complex as that" (p. 117). He also suggests that "If educational change is to happen, it will require that teachers understand themselves and be understood by others" (p. 117). Fullan describes conditions in which teachers feel devalued, alienated, and suffer from high levels of stress during the time period in which he initially wrote. Unfortunately, teachers, including myself, still suffer from isolated and intense working environments.

In terms of school reform, he maintains that addressing the needs of teachers is essential before embarking on change initiatives. Fullan (1991) suggests that change can "worsen the conditions of teaching, however unintentionally, or it can provide the support, stimulation and pressure to improve" (p. 126). As a new teacher, when I first read Fullan, I felt that change initiatives had possibility and I regarded them as a support for what was going on in my classroom, something that would be best for kids and make an impact on their learning. When I read Fullan that first time, I saw change as an opportunity for collaboration, something that I longed for as a new teacher.

Now, as I read his work later in my career, I still find hope in his work but I am more realistic about the pace of change. I better understand that the culture of schools needs to change to reflect the importance of collaboration among teachers for change to happen. Fullan also notes the importance of a culture shift in education. Fullan (1991) states:

> Thus the meaning of change for a future does not simply involve implementing single innovations effectively. It means a radical change in the culture of schools and the conception of teaching as a profession. (p. 142)

Without an overhaul of school schedules and a better understanding by leadership at all levels of the innate purpose and value for teacher collaboration within the school day, systemic change will be slow to set in. I know that if a school community can have courage to work creatively against the testing climate, and make time for collaboration, change can happen. However, I feel that now I also know that in order for change to happen there is a need for strong leadership and structure at the building level. Unfortunately, a principal's ability to provide structure for change is often compromised by the pressing issues of daily responsibilities and district mandates.

Within a discussion of the role of principal in educational change, Fullan describes a phenomenon that is still very much alive in districts today and one of the reasons that change is slow or nonexistent in some schools. Fullan (1991) explains, "The expectations that principals should be leaders in the implementation of changes that they had no hand in developing and may not understand is especially troublesome" (p. 153). Because principals are often required to follow district programs and mandates when governing individual schools, programs are not sculpted to match the context of staff, student, and community needs. When this happens, it is challenging for principals to be innovative, to allow for creative practices in classroom instruction, and to participate in collaborative activities. According to Fullan, "It would not be unusual for a school district to be participating in 50 or more state or federally sponsored programs at any time, all of which have implications for the principal" (p. 164). It seems unfair to expect a principal to be able to make progress when there are so many competing elements within school improvement, instructional leadership, and daily responsibilities. Many principals are feeling that tightness just below the neck or suffering from sleepless nights, because it is time for a change.

Like teachers, many principals are also isolated in their daily work. Often, they do not have opportunities to collaborate or discuss situations with other principals and there may be an innate unwillingness for principals to confide in teaching staff in order to maintain the supervisory tone of relationship. Fullan (1991) proposes, "Without personal contact, there is no significant change" (p. 166). The isolation of principals, and teachers, is a cultural norm in schools that is severely limiting the possibility for change. Again, as in his description of the teacher role within change, Fullan points to the importance of self-reflection and self-understanding as leaders and facilitators of change initiatives. He says, "The starting point for improvement is not system change, not change in others around us, but change in ourselves" (p. 167). Lastly, Fullan summarizes two factors that make principals effective, being able to reduce the isolation of work, and even though it may be challenging, to make change a priority. According to Fullan, an effective principal "showed an active interest by spending time talking with teachers, planning, helping teachers get together, and being knowledgeable about what was happening" (p. 108). Principals that I work with today would love to spend time doing all of these things, but in fairness to them, they really don't have the opportunity based on the structures of school building and prioritized responsibility of district chain of command dictates. Again, it comes back to a need for culture shift and systems that promote collaboration at all levels of education in order to affect change at the school level.

DISTRICT AND GOVERNMENT LEADERS NEED COHESIVE VISION TO BUILD CAPACITY FOR CHANGE

In Fullan's *New Meaning for Educational Change*, there is a sense of urgency and call to action for educational leaders. He outlines some of the barriers to change and ways for leaders to approach change in a way that respects the necessity but also takes into consideration the difference between simply developing a new program and creating a culture that allows for change. Fullan (1991) suggests that "innovations that have been succeeding have been doing so because they combine good ideas with good implementation decisions and support systems" (p. 112). For districts to have meaningful change, there needs to be a vision and a strategic plan that matches the needs of staff, students, and community. In many districts, there is not a cohesive structure that aligns to action steps and goals. For district administrators, thoughtful planning needs to be prioritized. Fullan says, "The greatest problem faced by school districts and schools is not resistance to innovation, but the fragmentation, overload and incoherence resulting from the uncritical and uncoordinated acceptance of too many different innovations" (p. 197).

Even in a district where competent leaders are using a streamlined approach to make progress in areas like instructional practices, professional development, or student attendance rates, one of the ways for districts to be successful is to continue to cultivate a culture that is good at change and accepting of change. This requires teachers, principals, and leaders to be self-aware and cognizant of the importance of establishing norms that prioritize collaboration. Fullan (1991) illustrates this idea within his discussion of the role of district administrators in change process, "There can be no one recipe for change, because unlike ingredients for a cake, people are not standard to begin with, and the damned thing is that they change as you work with them in response to their experiences and their perceptions" (p. 214). Meaningful change is constantly evolving, and the people involved change with it. When sleepless nights happen, the stress builds, and the tightness won't go away, people will react to collaboration and opportunities and make a change.

At the district level, a barrier to change is related to the current climate of governmental involvement and oversight in public education. In his analysis of state-mandated reform, Fullan (1991) recognizes that it is an "active changing target" (p. 269). This may have been true when he published in 1991, but I feel that is even truer today. Expectations and test score thresholds that are in constant flux affect a school district's ability to effectively participate in educational change that is innovative and enhances student learning. In the most recent edition of *The New Meaning of Educational Change*, Fullan (2016) describes the importance for governments to "push accountability, provide incentives (pressure and supports) and/or foster capacity building" (pp. 209–210). The most important of these three is the capacity building piece, but this is also the part that is often weakest in government accountability-based programs.

Fullan (2016) uses the example of No Child Left Behind (NCLB) to demonstrate that "heavy-handed accountability systems omit or seriously underestimate capacity building" (p. 214). According to Fullan, "NCLB certainly has brought matters of progress and performance out in the open" (p. 214), but, the problem is that there was no strategy or capacity building included in the plan, which led to failed implementation and weak results, the effects of which we feel in schools today. There is a feeling of stress and pressure to change, but there is a lack of culture to facilitate it. Fullan (2016) contends that Race to the Top in 2009 suffered from similar issues in that it did not include "any lasting capacity building strategies" (p. 215). Both No Child Left Behind and Race to the Top have been recent government mandates that have dominated education reform efforts, and because they did not focus on building capacity or a school culture for consistent change as Fullan recommends, there is a stalled level of progress in schools today. It becomes necessary for school leaders and teachers to consider the impact of mandates on daily life in the classroom and the effects of testing culture on students. As experts, it is our duty to implement curriculum reform that keeps expectations for all students high, but also creates a culture of collaboration and a willingness to embody an organization that is amenable to change.

EDUCATION LEADERS NEED TO UNDERSTAND CHANGE PROCESS, BUT FULLAN NEEDS CONTEXT

The true value of reading Fullan's 1991 book in 2017 lies in the fact that the technical analysis of an individual's relationship to change can affect the ability for large-scale or group change is still relevant and can still serve as a guide for understanding why people react the way they do when faced with making a change. Michael Fullan's value as a researcher and in the context of curriculum is solidified by Pinar et al.'s (2006) inclusion of his ideas about change implementation and the role of individual for successful curriculum implementation in *Understanding Curriculum: An Introduction to the Study of Historical and Contemporary Discourses*.

In terms of how the change process is related to each individual, Fullan begins with the way change is presented to the group and how each person is included, or not included, in the change. Fullan notes that an important aspect of educational change is the meaning making process.

> We have become so accustomed to the presence of change that we rarely stop to think what change really means as we are experiencing it on the personal level. More important, we almost never stop to think about what it means for others around us who might be in change situations. (Fullan, 1991, p. 31)

If schools can change into places where collaboration frequently occurs, the meaning and purpose for change will become shared and this will make permanent and consistent change more likely. In addition, he indicates that in school reform there is a need for complete understanding of "both the change and the change process" (Fullan, 1991, p. 46). Educators today can benefit from examining the way change happens at the individual level to understand how to manage reform efforts.

The goal of educational change is to improve outcomes and in order to show growth, teaching practices need to change. According to Fullan (1991), the goal of shared meaning and collaboration is to bring about changes in practice, and "change involves learning to do something new, and interaction is the primary basis for social learning" (p. 77). When implementing new programs, it is essential to build in time for interaction and practice with others. Fullan (1991) states:

> Innovators need to be open to the realities of others: sometimes because the ideas of others will lead to alterations for the better in the direction of change, and sometimes because the others' realities will expose the problems of implementation that must be addressed and at the very least will indicate where one should start. (p. 96)

For change to be successful, this collaboration and sense of purpose will make a difference in longevity and sustainability of initiatives. Part of what makes Fullan's work relevant to education today is the notion that input from many sources is valuable and a worthwhile step in the implementation process. Differing perspectives often lead to better ideas for daily life in schools. According to Fullan (1991), " It is easier—more tangible, clear and satisfying in the short run—to concentrate on developing a new program than to enter the conflict-filled, ambiguous, anxious world of seeing what others think of the idea" (p. 112). Because it is difficult, this input stage is often not included at the beginning of the change process. It seems that only, often, after a district level initiative is mandated, the feedback begins, and often results in limited buy-in from staff.

In his analysis of the change process and how it is used in an educational setting, Fullan considers and explains the roles of all involved parties in reform, which is useful, especially with a multitude of real life examples, in that it gives the reader perspectives of leaders and even the government in terms of their role in curriculum and reform. However, a weakness of Fullan's text is his repetition of the same ideas throughout all sections. Fullan tends to discuss overlapping trends when discussing the roles of teachers, administrators, and government leaders. This repetition can be cumbersome. Another flaw in Fullan's work is his habit of stringing abstract ideas together into long quotations without clearly connecting them to real-life examples. When he wrote *The New Meaning of Educational Change* in 1991, his focus was on theory and the process of change, and he does not offer much strategy or planning resources. In the latest edition, Fullan has recognized the disconnectedness of his ideas and has made an effort to include action steps and better related examples. Many of Fullan's ideas are theoretical and intangible for education leaders in the context of daily life in schools. If the only thing educators were working on was change, his plans may be easily implemented. However, schools are not just focused on change initiatives, so the circumstances of leadership, learning, and possible systemic aversion to change impact school reform efforts. Some factors of Fullan's model are still relevant today, but others may not be applicable in today's culture of testing and Common Core State Standards.

In 2009–2010, when the Common Core State Standards initiative started to emerge as the mainstay of accountability in public education, educators, students, and community members reacted in various ways. This large-scale change created situations in which teachers were coping with, trying to understand, and hoping to see the value in such a dramatic shift in curriculum in a relatively short period of time. Through the lens of Fullan's change theory, leaders can analyze how implementation and the need for building capacity for change will be required to continue progress that has started with this standards initiative.

When Fullan's ideas about change are examined alongside of Eisner's (2002) perspective in *The Educational Imagination on the Design and Evaluation of School Programs*, insight into the purpose for unified standards and the relationship to public's perception on American public education, a leader's understanding of the community's role in educational change intensifies. Eisner (2002) suggests that a "reason standardized test scores and grades have become the basis for judging educational quality is that we have not provided the public with alternatives" (p. 188). Essentially, because leaders in education have not been thoughtful about the change process in the context of parents and community members, the current trend of testing has persisted. Fullan, although written in 1991, reminds us of the importance of involving parents and the community in the process in order to create change. Fullan (1991) says, "If teachers and administrators who spend 40 to 60 hours a week immersed in the educational world have trouble comprehending the meaning of educational change, imagine what it is like for the parent" (p. 227). As the era of standardized testing persists and instructional practices continue to evolve to meet the demands of high stakes tests, it is necessary for educators to involve families in discussions about student learning.

Fullan also devotes significant discussion to the role of students in change process. This provides educators with a reminder to maintain focus. According to Fullan (1991), "Educational change, above all, is a people-related phenomenon for each and every individual. Students, even little ones, are people, too. Unless they have some role in the enterprise, most educational change, indeed most education, will fail" (p. 170). Fullan's chapter on students is particularly unique in that he suggests that "effective change in schools involves just as much cognitive and behavioral change on the part of students as it does for anyone else" (Fullan, 1991, p. 189). For educators today, this is the advice that is most meaningful and gives credibility to the endurance of Michael Fullan's *The New Meaning of Educational Change*.

By using Fullan's ideas in conjunction with curriculum reform, educators today can learn through the book's multiple perspectives on motive, explained failed attempts, and descriptions of how people approach the same situation in different ways. At a time when so many educators, parents, and students are feeling like it's time for a change, it is useful to return to Michael Fullan's *The New Meaning of Educational Change*.

As I begin another year of teaching, I can feel some of the tension in between my shoulder blades starting to subside. I am experiencing less sleepless nights and I find myself looking forward to starting a new position in a new district. The next few months will provide me with many opportunities to be a part of change and to react to changes around me. Michael Fullan's perspective on change, in particular how important collaboration and a focus on growth is to success in a school community, will be in the forefront of my mind as I build relationships with new colleagues.

REFERENCES

Eisner, E. W. (2002). *The educational imagination: On the design and evaluation of school programs* (3rd ed.). Merrill Prentice Hall.

Fullan, M. (2016). *The new meaning of educational change* (5th ed.). Teachers College Press.

Fullan, M. G. (1991). *The new meaning of educational change* (2nd ed.; with S. Stiegelbauer). Teachers College Press.

Pinar, W. F., Reynolds, W. M., Slattery, P., & Taubman, P. M. (2006). *Understanding curriculum: An introduction to the study of historical and contemporary curriculum discourses* (Vol. 17). Lang.

CHAPTER 17

CAGED IN

Systematic Oppression and the School-to-Prison Pipeline

Elaysha N. Wright

Author/Book studied:

Laura, C. (2014). *Being bad: My baby brother and the school-to-prison pipeline*. Teachers College Press.

This is my truth and these are my feelings. You will hear my voice more than you can see it. Emotions are real and during this process they have become even more real. To think for so long I was dehumanized in a place that was seen as my only ticket to win the race to the "American Dream." The dream to get a good education, to go to college, and get a great paying job. Meritocracy seemed to be real. To know what I know now in education, I was living a lie. I played the game to get to where I am. I almost lost myself. I am not sure why I am in the process of teaching my young scholars that same game that I once played. I needed education for more than just going to college; I needed education to help me and my family walk over the cracks that so many of our community members have slipped into.

This is a wake-up call to those who are from communities similar to my own. I am not sure why Black faces on R.I.P. T-shirts have become so normalized. I am not sure why the majority of my male family members have become incarcerated and taken away from their families while nobody has questioned the system. Yet, we continuously blame our Black men for doing wrong. Why are we not concerned about losing our Black children to the streets and to the system? We scream, "BLACK LIVES MATTER" but do they really hear us? Do we really hear ourselves? These are the questions I continuously ask myself. These are questions that I am so desperately trying to figure out in this journey to an open window.

CRYSTAL T. LAURA'S BOOK, *BEING BAD*

Crystal T. Laura (2014) is the author of *Being Bad: My Baby Brother and the School-to-Prison Pipeline*. Dr. Laura sits in the county jail as she searches her brother's brain for answers. She wonders and questions what led him down this path from his neighborhood school into the prison system. Her brother Chris takes her down memory lane as he breaks down his educational journey. In school, Chris was seen as a hyperactive child. He was disengaged from traditional learning styles. Chris eventually gets diagnosed for his challenges but his mother was against it. His mother was his biggest advocate and resisted all labels until she learned that it could potentially get him more help. Their mother wanted what was best for her children, especially Chris because his challenges made the school feel as though they could not work with him. As much as their mother worked for Chris, the school system all the more tried to push against them and push them out. Eventually, Chris ended up in the county's jail for robbery and assault. One thing you must know is Crystal T. Laura's goal in this piece is not to prove her brother's innocence but to prove that there is a correlation between schooling and who ends up in our prison system.

Crystal T. Laura (2014) framed the book through the voice and story of her little brother Chris, but her goal was to inform readers of wider, systemic issues. Dr. Laura wanted to raise awareness on the unfair treatment of our Black males in school. She approaches the zero tolerance policy and the school-to-prison pipeline through her research and the voice of her baby brother.

Crystal T. Laura preaches love and compassion as a change strategy for justice. Dr. Laura (2014) believes, "When people get caught up in the school-to-prison pipeline, it means they have been poorly educated, prepared for dead end jobs, the streets, and permanent detention; they have been systematically screwed" (p. 7). This systematic racism has followed us down the road to the school-to-prison pipeline, which started from zero-tolerance policies. Zero-tolerance policies have done more harm than good to our Black students and communities.

ZERO-TOLERANCE POLICIES

"The term *zero tolerance* was first employed by President Ronald Regan's administration when it launched its War on Drugs initiative in the early 1980s" (Zero Tolerance, 2005). At this time teachers decided to use harsh punishments with harsh consequences even when they did not have to. After 1980, schools expanded zero-tolerance policies to include a wide variety of actions such as fights, drugs, and alcohol. It eventually started to encompass dress code and petty acts.

Smaller scaled acts were worded into real extreme behaviors: Pushing and shoving was renamed "battery," taking headphones is theft, and talking back is now disorderly conduct (Advancement Project, 2010). These minor incidents cause more school suspensions to occur for incidents who do not typically threaten school safety (Skiba & Peterson, 1999).

Although not originally intended, zero-tolerance policies are denying education due to suspension and expulsion. Students who are being pushed out do not go to programs that are good learning alternatives for school. There is no one going into houses to make sure the student who is suspended or expelled is getting the help that they need to still succeed in school. There are lower test scores and higher dropout rates for students who follow the school-to-prison track. Everything goes downhill for these students because schools do not reaccept them all of the time. Students who go through this tend to lose interest in the school and those same students receive labels that will hurt them for the rest of their lives. Once a student drops out of school the chances rise for them to go into the system and go deeper into the juvenile system. Even when students do not drop out and try to do better, their record comes back up when they are applying for jobs, colleges, and scholarships. The effects of the zero-tolerance policy often extend past a student's teenage years (Heitzeg, 2009). Many individuals affected by zero-tolerance policies flood into our prison systems.

SCHOOL-TO-PRISON PIPELINE

Education was never made for Black and Brown people in America. Education is doing what it was intended to do. It is closing windows for Black and Brown people from the inside since it can no longer close its doors and windows from the outside due to *Brown v. Board of Education* (1954). The window has been closed since the day Black and Brown children stopped building their own schools from the ground up. Hope is what our children, educators, and families used to have and hope is what they called their schools.

The pipeline to prison begins when inner city youth are being disciplined too harshly and controlled too much in their schools due to zero-tolerance policies. Zero-tolerance policies are leading children into the criminal justice system (Heitzeg, 2009). What happened to students being disciplined at school? What happened to the days of school personnel working with students instead of against students to correct student behavior? I am starting to think that some teachers are becoming more and more afraid of the children they are teaching. There is a disparity in terms of which children are affected by the pipeline to prison. "The school to prison pipeline disproportionately impacts the poor, students with disabilities, and youth of color, especially African Americans, who are suspended and expelled at the highest rates" (Heitzeg, 2009, pp. 1–2). This is not a coincidence. Some teachers who teach these students often do not understand their culture even if they try. I think their cultural norms are drastically different from their teachers and their teachers assume that everything they do is bad but in reality their behavior is normal behavior for people within their culture. It is time for us to understand the children in our classrooms better before we as teachers are allowed to start disciplining children for no justifiable reason. "Children from low income areas get cheated. They do not have a fair access to educational resources, quality teachers, high quality curriculum, and no advanced level courses than their more affluent white peers" (Wald & Losen, 2003). Culturally relevant teaching is important.

Children need to have more mentors in schools and help services. Discipline policies penalize and remove students instead of providing support for them and facilitating positive growth (Tuzzolo & Hewitt, 2006). In more privileged schools, students have more resources and services that help students before they get in trouble. If we know inner-city youth struggle emotionally, we need to put quality in their communities or in schools to help children out before they get themselves into trouble. I am not in support of the idea that schools can become safer when you remove "bad" children. This is just as bad as the eugenics movement. Schools are starting to try to rid themselves of all of the children that they believe are not fitting into their perfect idea of a good school. Children do not come out of the womb defiant; they simply become products of their environment. Therefore, it is up to the child's systems that they are in everyday to help shape and mold the child to fit into society.

There is no proof that increasing school discipline leads to improved student behavior and when students get suspended from school frequently their grades suffer which leads to a decrease in students grades (Dow et al., 2003). Teachers and administrators can help children escape from this so-called pipeline to prison by building stronger relationships with them, helping to change students' attitudes and social emotional competence, contributing to conditions for learning and figuring out why their children are behaving the way they are by talking to the children more (Coggshall et al., 2013). Educators need more training on how to deal with youth they consider to be troubled because the reality is they may not be troubled at all; they may just need someone to listen to them. Re-entry to school is critical in the pipeline (Wald & Losen, 2003). Students need services when they are out of school for so long to make sure they can stay ahead of their work. People need to care more about the children that are in their schools.

Crystal T. Laura breaks the school-to-prison pipeline up into three different metaphors: schoolhouse-to-jailhouse track, cradle-to-prison pipeline, and school prison nexus. The schoolhouse-to-jailhouse track is the track that most of us are more familiar with. Dr. Laura believes that mostly poor students of color will fall through the cracks. This track moves students from the academic and work path into our prisons and jails. In K–12 education, Black boys fall behind their other peers academically. Black students are not enrolled in gifted or AP classes (Laura, 2014). Metaphor two is the cradle-to-prison pipeline. This is the area that we really need to pay more attention to. Our Black children have been counted out since the womb. "So many poor babies in rich America enter the world with multiple strikes already against them" (Laura, 2014, p. 31). We do not have many alternatives to help students in low-income communities stay out of trouble. "Some children are born on the path to prison. They aren't derailed from the right track; they haven't been given a fighting chance to get on it in the first place" (Laura, 2014, p. 31). The last metaphor is the school-prison nexus. This metaphor makes us aware that many low-income schools are structured to look and feel like a prison.

RACE AND RACISM

Racism in America is still happening in and outside of many institutions. Race is only a social construct, but somehow we in America have turned it into so much more. White supremacy has loomed over our heads since the founding of our country. Internalized racism occurs when Black people see the world through the lens of White supremacy (hooks, 1992).

Public education has been structured the same since it began. When is it going to change to include our Black, Brown, and minority students? Most students want to get a good education. Why are we holding them back?

There was a point in time where one teacher stopped recruiting students to work with him by reviewing their test scores. He did not believe that tracking students by test scores would put students in programs that were best for them (Hillard, 1995). Jaime Escalante, believed the class cut-ups were often the most intelligent, but were bored with poor teaching. The school that he taught at did not want test scores for troubling students to go up because the school wouldn't get Title I money (Hillard, 1995).

No matter how much money is lost or gained, Black and Brown students need to believe that people care about their education. We need to have higher expectations for our minority students in school. Higher expectations will increase students' scores and their opportunity to learn. The passion that was had before teachers entered the classroom needs to be the same passion they use every day. They need faith, love, hope, energy, time, and a personal investment/commitment to their students and their families. We need to believe all students can achieve, no matter the color of their skin, and no matter what challenges their behaviors might bring to them. If we believe that all students can, then they will!

Teachers who want to do more for their students must be willing to commit to the following: The teacher must be willing to be a member of an intellectual learning community. The teacher needs to understand the importance of being a stakeholder in the community that they are serving. The teacher is an active community advocate. A teacher must also be willing to set goals that are achievable and attainable for their children and communities (Hillard, 1995). Our children are more intellectual than the standardized test or disability test makes them out to be.

CRITICAL RACE THEORY

Crystal T. Laura's brother Chris is not the only Black/Brown child to face the school-to-prison pipeline. There are many others who are suffering through it right now. We need to use our voices and open up about this issue. As a critical race scholar, I do believe racism is normal and it will never go away. Just because we know this, it is not okay to operate in a racist system. We need to hear stories and counternarratives of Black people who have been affected by the system. If we hear more stories, maybe active change could happen.

Many Black inmates believe it's fully their fault that they are where they are so they never think that anybody else understands them. They believe they are alone in the system. I often question: If Black people are on a path to jail, how can we change jails to become a place of growth? Slaves are reproducing slave machines, which essentially are helping the American capitalistic society.

THE CHARGE: CULTURALLY RESPONSIVE TEACHING

It is time to meet children where they are. Standardized tests for years have been tailored towards the majority and they have not represented the lives or the realities of our minority children. Imagine teaching what is relevant to every child in the classroom. Think about how much more interested children would be if they saw people who looked like them in textbooks and in stories they read in their examples. Culturally responsive teaching focuses on the strengths of an individual instead of their weaknesses. This is what Black students need, but teachers teach to the White culture. McIntosh (1990) says, "I can be sure that my children will be given curricular materials that testify to the existence of their race" (p. 7).

Ladson-Billings is a world famous teacher educator who explores culturally relevant pedagogy. She believes that with a history that includes the denial of education; separate and unequal education; and regulation to unsafe, substandard inner-city schools; the quest for quality education remains an elusive dream for the African American community (Ladson-Billings, 1994). True American education is simply a dream and a dream that most African Americans want to achieve and be good at but they are not always given a fair chance at it. African Americans/Black students are behind White students on all academic measures (Ladson-Billings, 1994). *Brown v. Board of Education* (1954) was supposed to rule out the segregation of schools, but that ruling did not change as much as the Black community had hoped it would. Black people are still in schools that are indeed separate and unequal. W. E. B. Du Bois assumed the quality of education was poor in the segregated schools but what he did not see was the future, where this is still true today. African American men have a greater chance at being murdered then they do going to any college or university (Ladson-Billings, 1994).

We need more after-school programs and student-led projects so teachers can learn the interest of their students so they all can truly engage. According to Gay (2013), teachers need to learn their audience and learn to teach to different backgrounds and through different experiences because not everyone can relate to the teachers' backgrounds. Schools need to be filled with teachers who actually care, who will stop at nothing to make sure every child they have can learn. What would education programs look like if students were not allowed to fail? Failure in education should not be an option. Black teachers who were in Black schools were dedicated to their students; they would not let them go down bad paths without attempting to intervene. The teachers were well trained, and they were very personal with their students (Walker, 1996). It takes a village to raise a child.

When Vanessa Siddle Walker (1996), the author of *Their Highest Potential: An African American School*, went to visit a school, she saw that the African

American/Black students were invisible. They were invisible during all academic/classroom time but they were very visible outside of the classroom when "learning" was not taking place (Walker, 1996). This is not to say that these students goof off and they play around in school and they don't want to learn. This goes to show us that students of color are not engaged in our classrooms and that is the fault of our systems and our teaching.

The idea of community is what keeps us going. Where is community when it comes to education? We need to rebuild our community centers and create our own resources within our own communities. We seek so much help from the outside world that we are not self-sufficient.

We need to remember our foundation and put back in schools some of the things that are home in our culture. If we look at school discipline structures in schools, they count Black and minority children out before behavior can be corrected. The old school discipline system of spanking kids and being firm and harsh on the spot might have made more sense to Black and minority cultures, but now it is taken out completely. Our system allows students to be kicked out because we as teachers are afraid to deal with the student him/herself. "Culturally, the community also held common beliefs about children. Children were expected to obey their parents and knew that they would be spanked when they were disobedient. Moreover, children were taught to obey any adult with whom they were in contact, whether at church or at school. The community did not consider it inappropriate to discipline another's child; in fact, it was expected that any adult who saw a child behave inappropriately would reprimand the child and report his or her behavior to the parent" (Walker, 1996, p. 213). Our Black/Brown children are losing their sense of respect that has been deeply embedded and important to their culture.

I am sure many Black/Brown people have thought about resegregating our schools again to give minorities a chance to grow, but when we look closer at this we are already there. The reality is our public schools are where most of our minority children attend school. Those schools are already failing, with a high population of Black/Brown people within them. What's next? We need to take ownership and help our students learn and grow. We need to figure out what we have to do and not always rely on resources that the White schools have. We see this as a problem but why can't we create our own curriculum and build our schools from the ground up? We know the schools are unequal, so why drown in that reality? Our Black and Brown students need to see more people that look like them. We need more Black and Brown people to become more educated in their fields to take control of teaching their children. There is power in culture.

MY LIFE AGAINST THE BRICKS

Education and the hope for change for all has not changed much. Systematic racism has not changed much. For years I listened to my mom and g-ma talk about racism and start off every sentence with the cliché "Back in my day." Growing up, I compared their stories to famous slaves or popular historical Black or African American people I learned about during Black History Month. I was naive enough to think that racism only happened back then and it no longer existed because I lived the dream that Dr. Martin Luther King Jr. spoke about in his famous "I Have a Dream" speech. I held the hands of my White classmates and I played with them on the playground. Well, at least in elementary school, and only at school. My school was predominately White but my neighborhood was 100% Black, so I lived two different lives.

When the doors opened to my first day of middle school, I had a culture shock. Those 3 years made me feel as if I had a time machine that traveled back to the 1950s and 1960s. All of a sudden the color of my skin mattered, the braids and hairballs on my head mattered, and the 2400s in Skyline Acres where I grew up, mattered.

A mixture of sadness and pride overwhelmed me daily. The same girls that I thought were my friends in elementary school would not sit next to me in the cafeteria. When I walked around with my free and reduced lunch tray trying to find somewhere to sit, the only available seats were with the people who looked like me. At those tables in the back, people welcomed each other with open arms versus putting a purse or another item right there to show they did not want me to sit. The cafeteria was very segregated. It was during that time that I questioned why we had to bubble in our race on the test. I became very curious, I opened my eyes for the first time to the world around me. Why did my teachers yell at only the Black kids for going to the bathroom in groups but not the White kids? I was always confused when they would get mad when I asked if they were racist.

My seventh grade year had to be the worst year of my life. I had the opportunity to try out for the cheerleading team but rumors surfaced about my school not picking Black girls. I searched pictures high and low and realized there were always 0–1 Black girls that made the team every year. What were my odds of little me making the team? I feared rejection. I didn't even want to try, but my mother motivated me to step outside of myself and do what I had to do for our race. She let me know that I had her support. She told me, "I know a lot of Blacks don't make it and we don't have money to give to the Boosters but you have real talent and you just have to be great." She made me think back to the days when I saw one Black cheerleader at the high school on Friday nights. She wanted me to be that guiding light just like that other cheerleader was for me. My mom motivated me and I got through it, and made the team. According to the Black parents whose sons played football and basketball, I was special. I made them proud and I gave their children, other little Black girls, hope. I felt proud but handling the racism really should have made me quit. I was always by myself, they thought I was poor, they never came to my house, and they asked the most ignorant questions. What hurt the most was the fact that my Black friends stopped supporting me and called me the token Black girl. I was over being everyone's token or the girl who played the game to get where she was. I remember doubting myself. I questioned why I wanted to subject myself to so much daily hatred. I remembered what my mother told me and I pushed through the words because of the little Black girls standing in front of the gate trying to take pictures with me. They made me remember for whom I was doing it. This is the first moment in my life I had to stop thinking about myself and start thinking about the world around me.

As I continued to play the game I found myself being molded into the person the school wanted me to be instead of being the person that I could really identify with. When I tell you I lived two different lives, that was the truth. I really lost myself in this space of confusion. My only hustle was to make it. My friends from the 2400s block in Skyline Acres were not put into the same classes that I was put in. Most of the kids, especially the Black boys, were put into special education/behavior classes. I did not understand how the same kids that I grew up with and raced cars with drifted away from me in middle and high school because they were not willing to conform to the schools cultural codes. My little brother was also an example of this. He was tracked and had an IEP and similar to Chris's mother, my mother refused to fall for him being just another label. We as a family fought hard as a team to keep my brother afloat in all of his classes.

I was a student who had straight A's and one B in my whole middle school career but somehow the school only put me in advanced classes in high school instead of honors courses. They told me they did not want me to take the honors and AP courses because I would probably drop down anyway. My mom came in and put her foot down. I made it into those classes and I worked so hard to prove them wrong and keep my grades up. I exceeded the school's expectations, my family's, and even my own. I set my own goals based on my White classmates. They came to school on a track that was going to guarantee them several college acceptance letters. I was just trying to play keep up and navigate the system on my own because I had no clue.

It is so sad. I was that little Black girl that broke stereotypes and barriers. I was able to slip through the cracks. I never became a product of my environment like the school thought. For the longest time I thought it would be easier for my skin to be white. When I graduated from one of Ohio's public ivies I felt myself fly. It was at that moment when I realized who I was. I took so much pride in being Black. I even coached that same middle school cheerleading team that caused me so much pain. I am who I am today because of that same Black girl who wanted to conquer the world who lived in Skyline Acres, 2400s block.

I know you are reading this and think there is some type of hope out there. I am glad and I am hopeful but as I sit here and write I have so many flashbacks. I hear the screeches of cars in the streets, the gunshots that pierced my uncle in his chest, and the blood that painted the grass where he fell, and I hear the tears of all of my uncles crying right outside of my window. My uncle died on the corner of my house in 1999 and then my cousin Brianna lost her life to the hands of another man in 2017. I am praying, someday, we will be healed from the bullets that pierced their hearts. I am that person who saw so many family members get incarcerated for selling drugs or writing bad checks for trying to put clothes on their kids' backs and food on the table. I am tired of losing my people to the streets and to our jail system. Homes are being broken and I always wonder how better education that is culturally inclusive would have prevented this turmoil. People tell me all the time I made it, but did I really? This pain I feel haunts my whole community and my family daily. The injustice that served and still serves my community precedes us.

It amazes me that still to this day nobody is helping our community fight to have the same resources as the other community with the "nicer" houses. We thought having the community center open was helping change the lives of children who had nowhere to go after school or in the summer, but somehow we did not bring in enough money for the nicer community center/YMCA on the other side of town to keep us open. I cannot describe this indescribable pain. My heart hurts for all of us in this struggle. What are we really saying? I am one person out of an entire generation of family members. We have to do better. It is time for more people to take responsibility for why our families and communities are broken up. We cannot keep blaming ourselves because we have bigger, more systemic issues at play.

CONCLUSION

We are trapped in. The room is foggy and there is no escape or way out. Systematic oppression precedes us. The window that we want so badly to open is glued shut. We are forced in and swallowed by the rivers of our daily tears. For those of us who have managed to break the window, we know of the struggles that our brothers and sisters on the inside are burdened with. We need people on the outside to help dismantle the pieces to the window. We need to restore and rebuild the bodies that lay lifeless in fear of such a hopeless system that we have been a part of for so many years. Crystal T. Laura made me realize that we as Black and Brown people blame ourselves for entering into the prison system when in reality it is time for others to take responsibility for this injustice as well. Our path was created for us, therefore, our visitations and limited world access lies before us.

Once a real window is able to be cracked open, we can start on a mission to create path-changing classrooms for our Black and Brown students. We can stop kicking students out of school as a way to enforce a punishment. We can learn to deal with and understand the children we are supposed to teach. We can open up a window to allow a community centered approach to help each individual child succeed in our educational system. This shift of focus can help individuals involved in a child's life open up their mindsets in order to become reflective on the child's environment and the systems that are in place for the child to potentially misbehave. When people become educated they need to reach back and help their communities out instead of leaving their communities to fend for themselves. One educated person can help many more people become educated. We must remember it is our responsibility to educate each other because nobody else is going to care enough to do it. We need to have personal investment in our schools. It is time for us to own up to our part in the school-to-prison pipeline.

REFERENCES

Advancement Project. (2010, March). *Test, punish, and push out: How "zero tolerance" and high-stakes testing funnel youth into the school-to-prison pipeline.* https://www.justice4all.org/wp-content/uploads/2016/04/Test-Punish-Push-Out.pdf

Brown v. Board of Education of Topeka, 347 U.S. 483 (1954). https://supreme.justia.com/cases/federal/us/347/483/

Coggshall, J., Osher, D., & Colombi, G. (2013). Enhancing educators' capacity to stop the school-to-prison pipeline. *Family Court Review, 51*(3), 435–444.

Dow, G. Feggins, R., Rausch, M., Simmons, A., Skiba, R., & Staudinger, L. (2003, May 16–17). *Consistent removal: Contributions of school discipline to the school-prison pipeline* [Paper presentation]. School to Prison Pipeline Conference, Boston, MA.

Gay, G. (2013). Teaching to and through cultural diversity. *Curriculum Inquiry, 43(1),* 48–70.

Heitzeg, N. (2009). *Education or incarceration: Zero tolerance policies and the school to prison pipeline.* http://files.eric.ed.gov/fulltext/EJ870076.pdf

Hilliard, A. G. (1995). *The maroon within us: Selected essays on African American community socialization.* Black Classic Press.

hooks, b. (1992). *Ain't I a woman: black women and feminism.* South End Press.

Ladson-Billings, G. (1994). *The dreamkeepers: Successful teachers of African American children.* Jossey-Bass.

Laura, C. (2014). *Being bad: My baby brother and the school-to-prison pipeline.* Teachers College Press.

McIntosh, P. (1990). *White privilege: Unpacking the invisible knapsack.* https://psychology .umbc.edu/files/2016/10/White-Privilege_McIntosh-1989.pdf

Skiba, R., & Peterson, R. (1999). The dark side of zero tolerance: Can punishment lead to safe schools? *The Phi Delta Kappan, 80*(5), 372–382.

Tuzzolo, E., & Hewitt, D. (2006). Rebuilding inequity: The re-emergence of the school-to-prison pipeline in New Orleans. *The High School Journal, 90*(2), 59–68.

Wald, J., & Losen, D. (2003). Defining and redirecting a school-to-prison pipeline. *New Directions for Student Leadership, 2003*(99), 9–15.

Walker, V. S. (1996). *Their highest potential: An African American school community in the segregated south.* University of North Carolina Press.

Zero Tolerance. (2005). In *Encyclopedia.com.* https://www.encyclopedia.com/topic/ Zero_Tolerance.aspx

CHAPTER 18

HOW HIGH IS THE WATER?

Debra Amling

Author/Book studied:

Duckworth, E. (1987). *"The having of wonderful ideas" and other essays on teaching and learning*. Teachers College Press.

Isn't that the question you should always ask before jumping in feet first? Don't we all want to know if we will be in over our head or just ankle deep? How deep is too deep? Can we handle it if it is knee deep? Waist high? Up to our neck? Or high enough we can barely breathe? And what do we do if it is over our head?

So how high is the water in education? Do we know? How can we find out? What can we do about it? I think most people agree that the state of public education is beyond ankle deep. As we delve into the educational waters, we find so many initiatives, issues, and ideas. With so many changes in the world of education in the last 50 years, educators find themselves dealing with new challenges every day. If we desire to keep children at the center of education, we need some wonderful ideas.

Eleanor Duckworth's (1987) book, "*The Having of Wonderful Ideas" and Other Essays on Teaching and Learning,* explores the relationship between Jean Piaget's theories of child development and classroom practice. Combining those with Duckworth's background as an elementary educator allows her to draw parallels from Piaget's work to the classroom. Her essays provide a glimpse into the theories, and she then delves into the classroom complete with recommendations for teachers. She has a passion for the professional development of educators. Her essays clearly demonstrate that passion with her easy to read and inspiring words.

Duckworth's book was written in the late 1980s. At this point in the educational landscape, *A Nation at Risk* (National Commission on Excellence in Education [NCEE], 1983) had already been released and was characterized by its authors as "an open letter to the American people." The report called for elected officials, educators, parents, and students to reform a public school system that it described as "in urgent need of improvement" (p. 31). Holly (2000) discussed the impact of the report by noting it made the front page of almost every major newspaper and was the featured story on evening news of the three major television networks (p. 421). *A Nation at Risk* (NCEE, 1983) focused America's attention on the plight of education unlike never before and this scrutiny resulted in tighter constraints and higher expectations. Educational historians, Tyack and Cuban (1995) reported that in response to *A Nation at Risk,* states enacted more educational laws and regulations than they had in the previous 20 years (p. 78). Duckworth's (1987) book full of "wonderful ideas" was in stark contrast to those political legislation reforms.

In addition to understanding the educational climate at the time of the release of Duckworth's (1987) book, it is also helpful to examine the work of her mentor, Jean Piaget. Piaget examined the development of children's reasoning through interviews with children. Brainerd (1996) in his article, "Piaget: A Centennial Celebration," describes Piaget's work as "without parallel as a source of ingenious experimental techniques for unlocking the mysteries of children's thinking" (p. 195). He further describes the Piagetian measures such as "class inclusion, conservation, deferred imitation, egocentric and socialized speech, horizontality, perspective taking, object permanence, subjective and objective moral judgment, and transitive inference, to name only a few, have each produced thousands of studies by investigators around the world" (p. 195). Duckworth's (1987) first encounter with Piaget was as a graduate student in his philosophy class on the development of spatial notions in children (p. xi). Despite the profound impact of Piaget's work on Duckworth (1987), she discusses her relationship with Piaget by stating: "It was a struggle of some years' duration for me to see how Piaget was relevant to schools at all" (p. 1). Five years after working with Piaget, Duckworth (1987) began work in elementary science curriculum as a staff member of the Elementary Science Study, whose approach to science education was to engage teachers and children and aid in children's intrigue of science (p. xii). Ultimately, Duckworth discovered she could use Piaget's theories as a framework for thinking about learning and that the use of Piaget's model of working closely with one child at a time, provided her with a sensitivity to individual children in the classroom (p. 4). This framework also allowed Duckworth to realize "children can ask the right question for themselves if the setting is right and once the right question is raised, they are moved to tax themselves to the fullest to find an answer" (p. 5). It was in the science curriculum position that Duckworth began to explore the relationship between education and Piaget's teachings of intellectual development (p. 5). The clear connections drawn by Duckworth in her book between learning and children's intellectual development were an attempt to remind educators of that time to keep children at the heart of education.

One of the major themes in Duckworth's book is the importance of the role of learners in constructing their own knowledge. As a progressive educator, I believe strongly in a child's participation in its own learning. The works of John Dewey, Lev Vygotsky, and Jean Piaget define my pedagogy as an educator. My first introduction to Piaget was an undergraduate student enrolled in a required child psychology class. I recall being amazed with the stages of development and wondering about their accuracy. As time passed in my life as an educator, I learned to appreciate and understand how the stages applied to a child's development and the direct correlation to my teaching. When I became a mother, I was fascinated to see my children's intellectual development from infancy. I have vivid memories of watching my oldest daughter, Caroline, as an infant play peek-a-boo with me and realizing that she truly didn't understand that I was behind the blanket each time until I revealed myself and said "peek-a-boo." Watching my own child develop object permanence, as defined by Piaget, helped solidify my belief in Piaget's stages of intellectual development and the need for children to have an environment that allowed them to develop at their own rate. Being a mother and having the opportunity to watch my children construct their own learning had a profound impact on my role as an educator. I realized the importance of creating the "right setting" that Duckworth mentioned.

A powerful example of the "right setting" is shown in Duckworth (1987) when she relayed her experience with conducting one of Piaget's classic interviews:

> I had cut 10 cellophane drinking straws into different lengths and asked the children to put them in order, from smallest to biggest. The first two 7 year olds did it with no difficulty and little interest. Then came Kevin. Before I said a word about the straws, he picked them up and said to me, "I know what I'm going to do," and proceeded, on his own, to order them by length. He didn't mean, "I know what you're going to ask me to do." He meant, "I have a wonderful idea about what to do with these straws. You'll be surprised by

my wonderful ideas." The having of wonderful ideas is what I consider the essence of intellectual development. (p. 1)

How do we as educators allow for this type of intellectual development? Are our learning environments set up for this type of learning? Educators often talk about their role in the classroom. We focus on our questioning techniques and our responses to students. In Duckworth's example, it wasn't what she said that helped Kevin to develop his wonderful idea; it was what she didn't say and the environment that she created. For the last 15 years I have taught kindergarten as part of a progressive program in a public school. The program is based on many of the works of early 19th century educational philosophers and theorists like Jean Piaget and Lev Vygotsky.

Jean Piaget and Lev Vygotsky emphasized that the growth of human intelligence is embedded in the process of children co-constructing their learning with their social and physical environments. The educational implications of these theorists have been clear and challenging: classroom environments should model democratic communities that foster children's learning through engaging, purposeful experiences that honor the children's interests and are authentic to the outside world. (Upper Arlington Schools, 2022, para. 3)

Our program has 10 principles, which serve as a guide for developing the classroom community as well as designing our learning environment. Two principles specifically address the role of the student in their own learning.

We engage in thematic studies and foster authentic and emergent learning experiences.
We structure experiences that actively engage children in the process of learning and guide child choice and decision-making. (Upper Arlington Schools, 2022, para. 8)

Educators need to encourage the wonderings and curiosity that exist naturally in children. I have traditionally used the inquiry approach to help develop these emergent learning experiences and to create a classroom that engages children to construct their own learning. The inquiry-based approach to learning is a concept I consider as part of the foundation of my pedagogy. I begin a new unit of study by asking children what do we know and what do we want to know about a particular subject. I use their answers to help guide my direction for the study and help design our learning environment. Near the end of the study, I follow up by asking what did we learn? This self-reflection process is a vital step in the learning process. It serves as confirmation of a child's own learning.

It is not only the setting that allows for the "having of wonderful ideas." Duckworth (1987) states, "There are two aspects to providing occasions for wonderful ideas. One is being willing to accept children's ideas. The other is providing a setting that suggest wonderful ideas to children" (p. 7). The role of the teacher is vital in a child's intellectual development but not for teaching and the talking but for the experiences that we provide and the opportunities for children to experience them at their own rate. As a primary teacher, I have often conferenced with parents who had concerns about their child's academic progress, often wanting to compare their child to a sibling or classmate. Many times, I have used the analogy of learning to walk in comparison to acquisition of learning to read or write. I remind parents that all children don't start walking on their first birthday and that pediatricians share that there is an acceptable range of time for children to learn to walk. As parents, we provide children with the opportunities to learn to walk by holding their hands as they try out their wobbly legs, or putting them in toys that let them safely attempt walking or by letting them hold onto furniture as they practice balancing on two feet. We accept all attempts. We let them fall and help them back up and we encourage them to try again. We need to be reminded of our role in these experiences as children develop in school settings. These are the lessons for parents and teachers much more than they are for children.

These lessons are difficult to keep in the forefront of education. What can today's schools do to reclaim the focus of education on children? As a progressive educator in a public setting, I struggle daily with maintaining an environment focused on students without getting distracted by outside influences. I want to spend my time learning about the needs of my students: emotional, physical, social, and academic, and providing them with experiences and time to learn, but the pressures from outside sources often creep into my classroom. I find myself, as an educator, constantly feeling the push to make learning happen faster. The state testing occurs in the spring before the end of the school year, yet the assessment focuses on learning that has sometimes yet to happen. How do I ensure that all learning has happened prior to the assessment? How can I speed up the process? Parents often ask the same question, in an attempt to further their child's learning and they request that their learning be accelerated, sometimes in a single subject or sometimes by advancing an entire grade level. This request for more, sooner and faster, fills teachers and students with a great deal of apprehension. Duckworth (1987) refers to her mentor, Piaget for support with this request. "Piaget referred to this as 'the American question.' For him, the question is not how fast you go but how far you go.

How could it be that going fast does not mean going far" (p. 70)? I appreciate this question. As an educator, whose focus is on children, we need to continue to think about our motivation for grade acceleration. Will children actually go farther if they go faster? Duckworth says "no." In her section of "Productive Wrong Ideas," Duckworth (1987) discusses what a child gains by staying in her learning longer. "If a child spends time exploring all the possibilities of a given notion, it may mean that she holds onto it longer, and moves onto the next stage less quickly; but by the time she does move on, she will have a far better foundation—the idea will serve her far better, will stand up in the face of surprises (p. 71). If only parents could be convinced of this idea.

Another major theme in Duckworth's book (1987) is the "development of broad views of curriculum and finding ways that such views might be reflected in evaluation" (p. xiii). In looking at developing a broad view of curriculum, Duckworth expertly defines curriculum with a teacher's viewpoint in mind. Duckworth (1987) describes the task for the teacher to provide situations for children at all levels to participate (p. 48). This understanding of curriculum was an idea I developed early in my career. After 3 years of teaching, I interviewed and was hired to teach at a new alternative elementary school in my district. The concept of the elementary school was centered on multi-age education. I taught one class of three grade levels. I had 27 students: seven first graders, seven second graders, and seven third graders. Early on in my first year, I had visions of determining individual needs and teaching throughout the day in small groups of children grouped with common needs. I quickly discovered that I didn't have enough time in the day to meet all their needs through this instructional method. I found that by creating very simple and straightforward tasks for children, they were all able to locate their own entry point and create their response. In the beginning of the year, I tried to create writing response opportunities for children with requirements appropriate to their grade level standards and to their ability level, but then I realized that journal writing as a class was a more developmentally appropriate approach. When I asked children to write about their weekend on Monday mornings, each child would write the story in the way that made the most sense to them. My younger students would write a sentence and draw a picture and my older students would write a page or more with details and a complete story. I didn't need lengthy prompts or individual expectations, children naturally told their stories, oftentimes surpassing my initial expectations. Duckworth (1987) talks about practical situations, which correspond most to children's natural activities, are the best kinds of learning situations (p. 49).

I quickly found that developing personal narratives allowed children success with being highly engaged in their own learning and allowed me opportunities to meet children where they were with their writing development. Science and social studies themes, however, were problematic in a multi-age classroom. Duckworth (1987) quoted educational philosopher, David Hawkins: "David Hawkins has said of curriculum development, 'You don't want to cover a subject; you want to uncover it'" (p. 7). Just as I found an entry point with writing, I soon found that by creating experiences for children around science and social studies allowed children to uncover the curriculum at their own level. That, it seems to me, is what schools should be about. Teachers can help to uncover parts of the world that children would not otherwise know how to tackle.

It is not only children that need to uncover the world but teachers too! Throughout my reading of Duckworth's book, I kept going back to a phrase that Duckworth (1987) designated as a personal touchstone, "I need time for my own confusions" (p. 82). She elaborated by saying, "All of us need time for our confusion if we are to build the breadth and depth that give significance to our knowledge" (p. 82). A classroom needs time for confusion, time for learning, and time for reflection, and then time for it to happen all over again. A clear reference for this type of learning is Duckworth's (1987) sharing of an encounter that Piaget had:

> You may recall Piaget's account of a mathematician friend who inspired his studies of the conservation of number. This man told Piaget about an incident from his childhood, where he counted a number of pebbles he had set out in a line. Having counted them from left to right and found there were 10, he decided to see how many there would be if he counted them from right to left. Intrigued to find that there were still 10, he put them in a different arrangement and counted them again. He kept rearranging and counting them until he decided that, no matter what the arrangement, he was always going to find that there were 10. (p. 4)

The persistence and reflection in this anecdote can be reflected in a classroom environment as long as teachers allow for the time that it takes for it to happen, but beyond the time, is to allow for the development of the perseverance needed in students. Students need to persevere through the confusion and have faith in their abilities to try and try again. Those confusions are part of the setting that teachers need to provide for students. Duckworth (1987) wrote, "Exploring ideas can only be to the good, even if it takes time. Wrong ideas, moreover, can only be productive" (p. 71). Time is necessary for the wrong ideas to occur. Adults and children understand a concept at the deeper level when they have had time to consider all the options and the reasons behind the success and failures. In today's age of instant gratification, it is not always an easy task to create an environment where children not only can, but also want to, succeed and fail. Duckworth (1987) made an interesting observation that teachers need to develop in students: "Having confidence in one's ideas does not mean 'I know my ideas are right; it means I am willing to try out my ideas'" (p. 5).

The role of the teacher is crucial in developing the environment and setting expectations for students. Duckworth's (1987) passion for teaching and learning extends beyond children into the realm of teacher education.

> Much of my work with teachers includes helping them acknowledge the complexity in what seems like simple things they thought they understood, or helping them realize the details of their own understanding and appreciate that their own ways of understanding are valid. In the course of taking seriously their own ways of understanding, the teachers also come to take seriously others' ways of understanding. Thus they come to take seriously the thinking and feeling of the children they teach. (p. 116)

Duckworth (1987) writes in depth about her love of teaching teachers. She references two main reasons why she loves to teach teachers; "Teachers are interested as I am in how people learn and that I always learn from them in return" (p 122). As an instructional leader in my district, it is often my role to facilitate the learning of teachers. I, too, love teaching teachers. I love the interest they have in the why behind what children do. I am fascinated by the conversations they have with each other around children. When I am in the role of teacher in a professional learning environment with other teachers, I keep in mind Duckworth's thoughts about learning. Duckworth (1987) believes that teachers should have a chance to watch themselves learn. As adults, we don't spend as much time as children in situations where we can experience the learning process. We need to push ourselves to be in environments where the productive struggle is real in order to help us to relate to our students.

It is important for teachers to remember to keep children's thoughts and feelings at the heart of the classroom in order to model for them their place in the world. Duckworth believes strongly in the role of the student in his or her own learning. It is the responsibility of the teacher to set the stage for this type of learning to take place. Duckworth (1987) believes that there are two aspects involved in constructing individual's knowledge:

> The first is to put students into contact with phenomena related to the area to be studied—the real thing; not books or lectures about it—and to help them notice what is interesting; to engage them so they will continue to think and wonder about it. The second is to have the students try to explain the sense they are making, and, instead of explaining things to students, to try and understand their sense. These two aspects are, of course, interdependent: When people are engaged in the matter, they try to explain it and in order to explain it they seek out more phenomena that will shed light on it. (p. 123)

Again, a simple understanding of education by Duckworth but one worth understanding. Most people will agree that once they experience something, they understand it better. And if they can teach it to someone else, they increase in their mastery of the subject. This basic concept in education is a foundation in my development as a progressive educator. It is a child's ability to explain the why that helps me to know what they know.

Learning is more about what children know and can explain than what I can possibly teach them. I find this a difficult concept for new teachers to grasp. It is hard for some teachers to give up control of the environment, to let the students guide the learning and come to conclusions that are their own. Duckworth (1987) references the idea that children coming to terms with their own ideas is not difficult, the difficulty "is that teachers are rarely encouraged to do that—largely because standardized tests play such a powerful role in determining what teachers pay attention to" (p. 69).

In helping students develop their own ideas, I attempt to keep my questions focused on the why and the how and make sure that they are doing more of the talking than I am. Andy Kaplan (2013) in his article says, "The child creates meaning through experimenting with materials and conditions that lead inward as well as outward. The child seeks not just to know but to be able to communicate that knowing" (p. 123). I agree with Kaplan, I do think that children want to communicate their thinking and learning. As a teacher it is my role to set up an environment that allows for that to happen. I believe allowing for the conversation isn't enough; it is about building on these conversations on a daily basis. Children need to draw connections between their learning on a regular basis. As the teacher, I help facilitate this learning and aid them in comparing and contrasting their previous learning and understanding to what is happening in the present through questions and conversations. As a recent classroom teacher of young children, I see the need for oral language in today's classrooms more than ever. Children today are often pacified with a device of some type. I see this in restaurants, grocery stores, and car trips of every length. Parents of the 1950s and 1960s and beyond were often cautioned about the use of the TV as entertainment because it had the potential of being addictive. Now that same "TV" can travel everywhere with a child and rarely does it inspire oral communication. As classroom teachers, we need to be aware of the changes in society and the effect that they can have on children's development. I return again to Duckworth's (1987) plainspoken words that ring true to any classroom, "Wonderful ideas do not spring out of nothing. They build on a foundation of other ideas" (p. 6).

One of Jean Piaget's most well-known child development theories is the theory of conservation. In the task, a child is comparing the level of water in multiple containers to determine which contains the most water. A child looking at this task might first be struck by the depth of the water in one container in comparison to another and immediately decide on a strategy for solving the problem.

One of my colleagues gleefully showed me an essay written in first grade by 6-year-old Stephanie. The children had been investigating capillary tubes, and were looking at the differences in the height of the water as a function of the diameter of the tube. Stephanie's essay read as follows: "I know why it looks like there's more in the skinny tube. Because it's higher. But the other is fatter, so there's the same." (Duckworth, 1987, p. 2)

Duckworth (1987) commented on Stephanie's essay, "Nobody asked Stephanie to make that comparison and, in fact, it is impossible to tell just by looking. On her own, she felt it was a significant thing to comment upon. I take that as an indication that for her it was a wonderful idea" (p. 4). Why did Stephanie feel compelled to make this observation? Was it the time that she was provided to construct her own learning? Was it the setting that the teacher created that allowed her to feel that her ideas should be shared? Stephanie wanted to know how high the water was. She felt compelled to share her learning. She had confidence in herself and her ideas. How can we be like Stephanie as educators? Can we construct our own learning about education? I believe we can. We just need wonderful ideas! And we can start with Eleanor Duckworth's!

REFERENCES

Brainerd, C. J. (1996). Piaget: A centennial celebration. *Psychological Science, 7*(4), 191–195. https://doi.org/10.1111/j.1467-9280.1996.tb00357.x

Duckworth, E. (1987). *"The having of wonderful ideas" and other essays on teaching and learning*. Teachers College Press.

Holly G. M. (2000). Defining education: The rhetorical enactment of ideology in "A Nation at Risk." *Rhetoric and Public Affairs, 3*(3), 419–443. https://doi.org/10.1353/rap.2010.0069

Kaplan, A. (2013). Reconstructing progressive education. *Schools: Studies in Education, 10*(1), 122–133. https://doi.org/10.1086/670004

National Commission on Excellence in Education. (1983). *A nation at risk: The imperative for educational reform.* https://edreform.com/wp-content/uploads/2013/02/A_Nation_At_Risk_1983.pdf

Tyack, D. B., & Cuban, L. (1995). *Tinkering toward utopia: A century of public school reform.* Harvard University Press.

Upper Arlington Schools. (2022). *What is progressive education?* https://www.uaschools.org/ProgressiveEd.aspx

CHAPTER 19

A WINDOW OF POTENTIAL

Michelle Banks

Author/Book studied:
Whitehead, A. N. (1929). *The aims of education and other essays.*
The Free Press.

Is there a "window of potential" that might open to an educational world where imagination and experience coexist? Of this, I hope! If we are to unite theory and practice, or even create intentional overlap, we must create a window of potential, a view of the possible. As playwright and critic, George Bernard Shaw expresses, "What we want to see is the child in pursuit of knowledge, and not knowledge in pursuit of the child." Often, we as educators find ourselves stretched between this reality of daily practice and the hope found in theory. If we can open this window of potential to a world where children seek knowledge and understanding through inquiry and discovery, guided by the parameters set by the standards and curriculum objectives, perhaps Shaw's call to bring learning to life will reflect Alfred North Whitehead's (1929) hope for education as described in, *The Aims of Education.*

Curriculum Windows Redux, pages 231–240
Copyright © 2022 by Information Age Publishing
www.infoagepub.com

Whitehead's collection of essays provides a glimpse into the "what" and the "why" of promoting educational aims beyond inert ideas and dead information. He explains that

> theoretical ideas should always find important applications within the pupil's curriculum. This is not an easy doctrine to apply, but a very hard one. It contains within itself the problem of keeping knowledge alive, of preventing it from becoming inert, which is the central problem of all education. (Whitehead, 1929, p. 5)

I believe that Whitehead's concern with keeping knowledge alive is the critical pursuit necessary to open this window of potential in classrooms today and in the future.

In the world of K–12 education, we are challenged by this potential of keeping knowledge alive while we are bound by current state standards and curriculum. Whitehead's essays create a sense of urgency in me to respond to the call for ideals and aims far nobler than our current standards and assessment practices. Indeed, a common theme we as educators like to tout is that we are committed to not just teaching the standards, but educating "the whole child." Whitehead's essays provide, perhaps, a glimpse into this window of potential of how we consider the whole child. In fact, he calls us to look through this window into past practice to see that "every intellectual revolution which has ever stirred humanity into greatness has been a passionate protest against inert ideas" (Whitehead, 1929, p. 2). If I were to join an intellectual revolution, it would indeed be connected to seeking what is best for students. Whitehead's call for education to be alive, not inert, is one challenge for current educators; it feels like a revolution might just be necessary to move toward this reality in schools.

If we believe that what is best for students includes problem-solving, creativity, and active learning, Whitehead's intellectual revolution opens this window of potential. Finding the window of potential which opens to a world where imagination and experience coexist, creates in me the hope of current educators impacting curriculum and instruction in the 21st century classrooms! Can we embrace the belief that "imagination is not to be divorced from the facts: It is a way of illuminating the facts" (Whitehead 1929, p. 93)? Can we choose to impact the educational landscape by developing creative, meaningful, alive learning experiences for children, in fact, through the lens of our standards? As Whitehead (1929) implored, can we, "Let the main ideas which are introduced into a child's education be few and important, and let them be thrown into every combination possible. The child should make them his own, and should understand their application here and now in the circumstances of his actual life" (p. 2)? As Whitehead implores us, "The pupils have got to be made to feel that they are studying something and are not merely executing intellectual minuets"

(p. 10). This drive for understanding is explained by Whitehead: "He is studying it because, for some reason, he wants to know it. This makes all the difference" (p. 11). Through this window of potential, we catch a glimpse of the possibility that children and teachers recognize the standards as simply the parameters and develop a sense of longing for greater understanding and real application to their world.

Might we consider another educational giant, John Dewey, who alongside Whitehead in 1929, contributed to the world of education his book, *The Sources of the Science of Education?* In this book, Dewey's thoughts resonate with Whitehead's as he begs us to consider how educators might integrate the theoretical and curricular constraints with the potential to inspire, enlighten, and bring life to learning in the classroom. Dewey (1929) asks,

> What are the materials upon which we may and should draw in order that educational activities may become in a less degree products of routine, tradition, accident and transitory accidental influences? From what sources shall we draw so that there shall be steady and cumulative growth of intelligent, communicable insight and power, of direction? (pp. 9–10)

It is here that we see such similar calls from Dewey for learning to be alive and applicable in the lives of students and teachers, void of the inert ideas that attempt to persist even now in our educational system.

In addition, Dewey's (1929) work supports Whitehead's desire for a child's education to be comprised of few or important ideas. Dewey describes the process of education as a system, a science, that within allows the educator to integrate and correlate the curriculum ideas into the practical life of the classroom. He describes these as connecting principles that help a teacher to "see more relations, more possibilities, more opportunities... that (with) his ability to judge being enriched, he has a wider range of alternatives to select from in dealing with individual situations" (Dewey, 1929, pp. 14–15). This is a compelling argument to allow science and system to drive the art of creating connections and deeper understandings within the walls of an imaginative classroom environment.

In his essay, "The Rhythm of Education," Whitehead (1929, pp. 15–28) appeals to those in education to consider the social and emotional well-being of students. Just as educators in 2018 often strive to honor the child, Whitehead in 1929 also called us to consider asking what is best for the child. He describes this as the rhythm of education, where acknowledgement is given to the differences in how children learn in a more cyclical nature rather than through a uniform advancement. Whitehead (1929) beautifully describes this rhythm as "meaning essentially the conveyance of difference within a framework of repetition. Lack of attention to the rhythm and character of mental growth is a main source of wooden futility in education" (p. 17).

When considering the standards and curriculum set forth in the United States in 2010 with the Common Core and the following state standards which reflect them, we are struck by the lack of attention to this rhythm of learning. Instead, we find standards which address objectives to be achieved with students ranging from age 5 to 18, in the uniform progression of vertical alignment, seemingly tailor-made for an educational system. Upon reflection, however, might we ask whether another perspective on these standards should be considered? Perhaps these standards provide, rather than narrow the opportunity for students to sway within this rhythm? Perhaps a window of potential emerges here: The vision of these standards being navigated in such a way as to allow for children to experience this rhythm of stages in learning which Whitehead called the stage of romance, the stage of precision, and the stage of generalization.

If we agree that "the dominant note of education at its beginning and at its end is freedom, but that there is an intermediate stage of discipline with freedom in subordination" (Whitehead, 1929, p. 31), then perhaps we can investigate how the standards and current curriculum are woven into this intermediate stage specifically. Perhaps here, in this stage of gaining precise knowledge, educators can skillfully and artfully design learning environments and opportunities to support the ongoing love of learning.

It is inspiring to watch the unfolding of Whitehead's claims that "without interest there will be no progress" (p. 31). He describes the importance of keeping students engaged and passionate about gaining this precise knowledge by giving them adequate time to experience the freedom of the first stage of romance where inquiry and interest abound. He describes the stage of romance as the background for the stage of precision. I appreciate and value the idea that when the stage of romance has been properly guided, then another craving naturally grows within the child . . . the ability to retain precise knowledge, which then ushers in the stage of precision.

With Whitehead (1929), I agree that the art of teaching is to "discover in practice that exact balance between freedom and discipline which will give the greatest rate of progress over the things to be known" (p. 35). He goes on to claim that the formula for success is this rhythmic sway from freedom to discipline to greater freedom. He suggests that for progress, greater emphasis should be on freedom in the stage of romance and, then, "definite acquirement of allotted tasks" should be emphasized in the later middle stage (p. 35). Finally, the third stage, the stage of generalization, is described as the stage of shedding details in favor of the application of principles. In this stage, students move back toward romance, pursuing through interests the application of this new knowledge and learning.

Within these stages we find the flexibility that Dewey (1929) described when an educator understands the constraints and parameters of a system but recognizes that "his practical dealings become more flexible. Seeing more relations he sees more possibilities, more opportunities" (p. 15). It is our ability, as educators, to see the system and its standards and yet develop our vision through this window of potential in designing, igniting, and inspiring joy in the classroom and space for children to cycle through these stages of growth and understanding. It is Whitehead's balance of freedom and discipline leading to the greatest progress!

The window of potential in educating the whole child invites us to consider how educational practice, from the 1920s until now, claims to agree that various subjects and courses should be taught at times that match the developmental stages of a child, and yet, practice shows that we don't always consider this thinking. We see the disconnect between theory and practice. In fact, the Common Core and State Standards have designed a curriculum path that doesn't necessarily consider the research surrounding developmentally appropriate time periods of a child's life, or at least account for the differences, strengths, and weaknesses of each child's development. Similarly, nor do the publishing companies and assessment vendors, who have dominated the educational world and drive much of our children's curriculum, assessment, and support in school systems. The theory of balancing freedom, and discipline, and the rhythmic stages, seemingly fades in light of the practices driven by these realities of our times.

In regard to assessment, in particular, even in 1929, we read that Whitehead (1929) refers to external assessments, which measure a child's ability to memorize "all the questions likely to be asked" (p. 5). He points to the ongoing challenge of keeping learning and knowledge alive, not simply measured by a test of rote memory. He suggests that "no system of external tests which aims primarily at examining individual scholars can result in anything but educational waste" (p. 13). As Dewey (1929) warns,

> It is very easy for science to be regarded as a guarantee that goes with the sale of goods rather than as a light to the eyes and a lamp to the feet. It is prized for its prestige value rather than as an organ of personal illumination and liberation. It is prized because it is thought to give unquestionable authenticity and authority to a specific procedure to be carried out in the school room. (p. 15)

What a profound thought that Dewey had almost 90 years ago that still remains the reality of our day! How often we find that the focus on data and accountability leads to this prestige value rather than the love of learning and the development of a learning community where complex thinking and creativity are of value.

With the influx of vendors and publishing companies since the time of Whitehead and Dewey's books, we have been inundated with outside assessments and benchmarking tools to help educators measure their students' ability to respond to questions regarding curriculum and other seemingly inert ideas. It is here, in this educational environment, that we might exert our energies in this intellectual revolution. Perhaps teachers might refuse to simply teach standards as dead knowledge to be learned, but instead find ways to bring the deeper understandings of those standards and develop passions and interests in classroom practice.

I stand with Whitehead's (1929) premise that "all practical teachers know that education is a patient process of the mastery of details, minute by minute, hour by hour, day by day" (p. 6). It is by walking through this educational landscape that we can help students see, not missing the wood for the trees, but "seeing the wood because of the trees" (p. 6). When we are able to recognize the deeper understanding and application in our world, this is indeed using the trees to help us see the wood.

Ernest L. Boyer (1997), a renowned education expert and former president of the Carnegie Foundation for the Advancement of Teaching, gave a speech at the Annual Conference of the Association for Supervision and Curriculum Development in Washington, DC. Perhaps he could see this window of potential as he embraced the possibility of keeping educational thought and learning alive. He described this window of potential, even with a disclaimer:

> I know how idealistic it may sound, but it is my urgent hope that in the century ahead students in the nation's schools will be judged not by their performance on a single test, but by the quality of their lives. It's my hope that students in the classrooms of tomorrow will be encouraged to be creative, not conforming, and learn to cooperate rather than compete. (Boyer, 1997, p. 117)

Can we, some 25 years after Boyer and 89 years after Whitehead and Dewey, still see through this window of potential? Can we too embrace the call to protest against inert ideas? Can we work to develop the main ideas as few and important, creatively designed in many combinations to promote growth and understanding? Can we view the potential?

Similarly, in this current time of accountability and measurement, vendors and publishing companies push the use of assessment and student achievement into teacher evaluation methods. Hauntingly, Dewey claims back in 1929 that

> there is a strong tendency to identify teaching ability with the use of procedures that yield immediately successful results, success being measured by such things as order in the classroom, correct recitations by pupils in assigned lessons, passing of examinations, promotion of pupils to a higher grade, etc. For the most part, these are the standards by which a community judges the worth of a teacher. (p. 15)

The familiarity of this description is undeniable in nature. Perhaps this call for an intellectual revolution has resurfaced again for us as educators but with a greater understanding as we dig into the past.

In the first chapter of *The Aims of Education and Other Essays*, Whitehead (1929) suggests that to avoid mental atrophy, we should "enunciate two educational commandments, 'Do not teach too many subjects,' and again, 'What you teach, teach thoroughly'" (p. 2). It is here that we as educators are challenged to this development of main ideas, ideals, and potential for learning! It is here that perhaps the standards themselves provide the opportunity to teach thoroughly and with depth.

Looking to Whitehead's (1929) description of the present is both inspiring and convicting. He calls us to an understanding of "an insistent present... the only use of a knowledge of the past is to equip us for the present... the present is all there is... it is holy ground; for it is the past, and it is the future" (p. 3). He describes teachers as those who "evoke into life wisdom and beauty which, apart from his magic, would remain lost in the past" (p. 98). As we narrow our focus through the window of potential, how might we see the present as our opportunity to bring theory and practice into an aligned view? To view the "what" and "how" of teaching as our playground for the revolution against inert ideas? Can we agree with Whitehead that imagination is contagious and "can only be communicated by a faculty whose members themselves wear their learning with imagination?" (p. 97). This calls us as educators to be more than givers of information to joyful, creative learners ourselves. How might we develop classrooms full of joyful and imaginative learning? Can we narrow what we teach so that we can truly teach it thoroughly? Is this where we might use the standards as the priorities and as catalysts to newly engaged, fresh learning among teachers and students?

This call to view education through this window of potential has reminded me of a book I read over 20 years ago while completing my master's degree at The Ohio State University. I was introduced as a reader to a popular speaker and educator, Parker Palmer (1983), in his short book, *To Know As We Are Known*. Within the pages, I found the words, the common language to express my longing for the aims of education to be far greater than inert ideas and dead information. Palmer called me to a deeper understanding of myself, the community of education, and to the possibility that schools could resemble this communal discovery of truth and knowledge.

Palmer (1983) claims that "what good teachers have always known—is that real learning does not happen until students are brought into relationship with the teacher, with each other, and with the subject" (p. xvi.). He refers to the images of community consistent with "the aims of education... knowing, teaching and learning" (p. xii). He calls educators to develop the idea of community and recover the meaning of community in light of education and educational goals: knowing, teaching, and learning.

Palmer's description of education as a communal enterprise points toward the Deweyan language of connecting principles and curriculum to create deeper relationships and greater understandings. In fact, Palmer (1983) says that such an educational experience "would help students develop the capacity for connectedness that is at the heart of an ethical life" (p. xix). Does Palmer see this window of potential in his search for authentic educational communities where knowing, teaching, and learning are part of this connected nature of learning? For Whitehead (1929), it is the solution he urges, "to eradicate the fatal disconnection of subjects which kills the vitality of our modern curriculum" (p. 6). For Dewey (1929), as an educator finds greater continuity in understanding connecting principles, "his practical dealings become more flexible. Seeing more relations he sees more possibilities, more opportunities" (p. 21).

And yet, this connectedness stands in complete opposition to the competitive nature of our current educational systems. Systems that over time have grown more competitive, more regulated by outside forces such as vendors, legislatures, and publishing companies. Whitehead (1929), almost 90 years ago, points to "external assessors" who report on curriculum and the performance of students, who push educators away from curious and joyful exploration in learning and instead lead them to, "with good discipline, pump into the minds of a class a certain quantity of inert knowledge" (p. 5). And for Palmer (1983), this version of pedagogy

> persists because it conveys a view of reality that simplifies our lives. By this view, we and our world become objects to be lined up, counted, organized and owned, rather than a community of selves and spirits related to each other in a complex web of accountability. (p. 39)

I agree with Palmer (1983) that often, perhaps in part because of the nature of our educational landscape and system,

> We want a kind of knowledge that eliminates mystery and puts us in charge of an object-world. Above all, we want to avoid a knowledge that calls for our own conversion. We want to know in ways that allow us to convert the world—but we do not want to be known in ways that require us to change as well. (pp. 39–40)

Palmer goes on to claim that "we find it safer to seek facts that keep us in power rather than truths that require us to submit" (p. 40). I find these challenges to be personal and targeted. If we believe that the connectedness of curriculum, pedagogy, child development, and ultimately truth lie at the heart of educational aims, I find myself coming full circle, asking whether an intellectual revolution is indeed necessary and if so, what next steps must follow?

If educators are committed to not just teaching the standards, but educating "the whole child," perhaps, a glimpse into this window of potential of how we consider the whole child is where we begin our revolt. Might we start with what Whitehead (1929) said in his "Rhythm of Education" essay, "a statement so bald as to exhibit the point of this address in its utter obviousness?" He describes the importance of stating the obvious because he did not believe that this "obvious truth had been handled in educational practice with due attention to the psychology of the pupils." And in today's language, we would say that Whitehead was truly asking what is best for students, when making such an obvious but needed statement. His claim was that "different subjects and modes of study should be undertaken by pupils at fitting times when they have reached the proper stage of mental development" (Whitehead, 1929, p. 15).

His suggestion, however, was not to simply ask students to do easy things first and then work toward the difficult. Instead, he states that "some of the hardest must come first because nature so dictates, and because they are essential to life" (Whitehead, 1929, p. 16). It is here that current educators might embrace the strength and continuity that the standards create. By harnessing the power of the vertical alignment established by the standards, we connect this curriculum to the development of children.

Whitehead's extremely effective example is the infant who faces his first intellectual challenge, that is, acquiring spoken language. While seemingly daunting, it is necessary, as dictated by nature. It is here that we see postponing difficulty is not necessarily what it means when we seek to do what is best for students; instead, as Whitehead (1929) encourages, we might allow for children to progress through these stages as a normal part of the learning cycle: from the stage of romance where inquiry and exploration are novel and new connections are made, to the stage of precision where the acquisition of new knowledge is added and assimilated into prior discoveries, to the final stage of generalization where understanding is applied and demonstrated. The continuous repetition of this cycle in learning becomes "the rhythmic character of growth" (p. 27).

Might we see this rhythmic cycle as a way to embrace the whole child? The daily practice of allowing a child to discover, imagine, create, develop, assimilate, and apply new learning perhaps begins to open this window of potential, letting in the light of hope, joy, and community into our classrooms. Classrooms might join this intellectual revolt that Whitehead (1929) claims is essential, for "every intellectual revolution which has ever stirred humanity into greatness has been a passionate protest against inert ideas" (p. 2). May our passion for seeking what is best for children empower us to throw back the curtain which hides this window of potential where we might then indeed see our children in pursuit of knowledge rather than knowledge in pursuit of our children.

REFERENCES

Boyer, E. L. (1997). *Selected speeches, 1979–1995.* The Carnegie Foundation for the Advancement of Teaching.

Dewey, J. (1929). *The sources of a science of education.* Liveright.

Palmer, P. J. (1983). *To know as we are known.* Harper.

Strauss, V. (2015, February 12). What's the purpose of education in the 21st century? *The Washington Post.* https://www.washingtonpost.com/news/answer-sheet/wp/2015/02/12/whats-the-purpose-of-education-in-the-21st-century/

Whitehead, A. N. (1929). *The aims of education.* MacMillan Company.

CHAPTER 20

MULTICULTURAL EDUCATION

Theory and Practice

Jason A. Fine

Author/Book studied:

Bennett, C. (1986). *Comprehensive multicultural education: Theory and practice* (3rd ed.). Allyn & Bacon.

Imagine waking up one morning and being uprooted from life as you knew it as a homeless child and relocated into a multimillion-dollar home with a potential adoptive family. What could go wrong? The odds of winning a lottery jackpot are one in 292.2 million, but a student I'll refer to as "Monica" recently had this dream turned into a reality... or nightmare depending on how you characterize the situation. All too often, lottery jackpot winners are perceived by the general public as lucky, but there are enduring tales of anguish with lottery winners who regret falling into fortune and have a desperate aspiration to return to life as they once knew, because of maladministration of resources.

Curriculum Windows Redux, pages 241–252
Copyright © 2022 by Information Age Publishing
www.infoagepub.com
All rights of reproduction in any form reserved.

Monica is a 15 year-old, African American student who had previously attended the largest public school system in the state. Her mother was incarcerated and her father was living in the homeless shelter and deemed unfit to provide appropriately for Monica. A family friend took Monica under his wing and worked with one of the highest performing school districts in the state to enroll Monica, which I have the distinct pleasure of serving as a principal. We have many great attributes in our district, but an area of concern is our lack of diversity and conceivably, cultural understanding. White, non-Hispanic students make up 86.6% of our building's population and close to 97% of our teachers fall into the same category. Monica stands out in our hallways not only because she is one of only four African American students in our building, but most important because she is an eighth grader who is 6'3." She is athletically gifted, but came to us as an ineligible student-athlete because she had surpassed the number of years the state allows students to compete at the middle school level. Monica had been placed into a foreign environment with her lottery ticket in hand and the only prerequisite for cashing it in was to conform to our culture seemingly overnight. Our curriculum's lack of cultural understanding appeared to subjugate Monica as she struggled every day to fit into our culturally deficient community. Monica does not have access to an appropriate curriculum that meets her individual needs and she refused to conform to our "White" interests and curriculum. As a result, Monica chose to leave the apparent lottery ticket and the perceived life of luxury on the table. She chose to return to the shelter to live with her father after just a few short months in an attempt to take back her education and take control of her own purpose.

As a bystander to this scenario, I envision myself sitting on one side of a two-way observation mirror with so-called experts in the field of education by my side. On the other side of the two-way mirror I imagine Monica all alone trying to navigate her new world, seemingly thousands of miles from anyone that understands her actual needs. On my side with the educational experts and countless resources, the two-way observation mirror is as clear as a freshly cleaned window and it allows the educational experts to freely peer into Monica's world. Sadly, her side is simply a reflection of her fragile being and it shuts her off to those purportedly trying to support her in order to properly provide her with a fair and leveled learning experience in conjunction with her peers.

As we sit just feet away and observe Monica, she appears uncomfortable and uneasy about her situation. She is stranded and appears duty bound to conform to requests that are foreign to her and she has never been prepared for this type of environment. She is being asked to sit quietly in each of her classrooms. She is being asked to learn from a curriculum that alters her history and never tells "her" story. She is forced to participate in activities that all of her classmates are asked to participate in without consideration of her cultural needs. Her teachers appear preoccupied with the work she is not producing rather than the stress she is producing for being different. She looks as if she is on the brink of catastrophe and she is confused by the behavior and expectations of those around her. She wants to simply shatter the two-way mirror in order to become an active member of her education and we need to help her make that a reality. This "curriculum window" is shutting Monica off from her support because it is only transparent from one side. It is imperative that we find a way to demolish this "window" to see Monica's world from her perspective and find a way to reverse the process and put us on her side of the glass. By allowing both sides to see and communicate with one another we can work in conjunction to provide a voice to both the students and the educators producing and delivering the curriculum while moving forward together.

Comprehensive Multicultural Education Theory and Practice by Christine Bennett (1986) brings to life the inadequacies of past and current curriculum practices in education. While the book attempts to tie in curriculum with authentic facts about culture, it is clear that change is necessary. *Comprehensive Multicultural Education* is thought-provoking and provides cutting edge information on how to tie our ever changing and vast curriculum with authentic facts about culture in the 1980s and is certainly still relevant today. I am a firm believer that it is no coincidence that this book found me at this specific moment in my life because of the scenarios I am finding myself in at work and in my personal life. I am a building principal in a district that is determinedly moving forward in an enlightened manner with regard to cultural competency and we have undergone intense training that has produced positive results. The work is in its infancy stages in both my professional and personal life and we all must strive to triumph when it comes to gaining this important education. I have continuously functioned with the mindset of treating everyone with respect, but the literature I have been exposed to and the intense training I have embarked on tells me that I have more work ahead. It has been a fascinating journey as I have shifted my mindset from "it's not my problem" to perhaps "I am the problem."

Christine Bennett has authored 18 books and is a pioneer in multicultural education. She has focused on racial inequalities, culture and climate in desegregated schools, and these impacts on our society. Her approach has left a profound footprint on education, as her ultimate goal was to achieve an empathetic equality for all. Bennett's (1986) work is still in progress and she defines multicultural education as "an approach to teaching and learning that is based upon democratic values and beliefs, and seeks to foster cultural pluralism within culturally diverse societies and an interdependent world" (p. 13). In other words, we are seeking to find a utopian society among all nations, characterized by "equity and mutual respect among existing cultural groups" (p. 13). Bennett continues by stating, "educational excellence in our schools cannot be achieved without educational equity. Equity in education means equal opportunities for all students to develop to their fullest potential" (p. 16). All students deserve the same opportunities afforded to other classmates in America, regardless of differences. Our students come to us each day from a wide variety of backgrounds. Bennett states, "30 percent of this society's school-age children are ethnic minorities" (p. 18) and therefore, we must be able to adequately meet the needs of all students.

Teachers are often the determining factor in the success of a child. A major theme from Bennett (1986) is the certainty that if teachers are expected to have a positive outlook for all students from various races they must comprehend the differences in culture that often exist in classrooms with multiple cultures contained in it. Educators need appropriate professional development to adequately prepare them to discern and understand culturally distinctive behavior. Such professional development can eliminate assumptions that are often associated with certain racial clusters (Bennett, 1986). "Many teachers, administrators, and students who are racially prejudiced can develop the kinds of understanding required to become less so and this is the major goal of multicultural education among adults" (p. 29). Bennett shares that educators must be void of racial prejudgment and ethnocentrism if they are to be successful with a classroom of children with dissimilar cultural, ethnic, and socioeconomic circumstances. Teachers must have fewer preconceived judgments than the average person in order to properly support a classroom in today's society (Du Bois, 1935). Bennett (1986) believes that "a multicultural society requires educational programs that are multicultural, in design. Most students in every ethnic group can achieve the basic requirements in school under the proper conditions" (p. 35). The time is now for us to stop fantasizing as a society that we don't see color in our colleagues and our students. If we are imprudent enough to believe that we treat everyone the same way regardless of race, religion, sexual orientation, and so forth, then we are not being culturally responsive to the needs of those around us. We have a responsibility to see our students for who they are and acknowledge and celebrate the different experiences they bring to every situation, while fostering an environment of inclusion, understanding, compassion, and love.

Monica's needs and background experiences are unlike anything that her teachers have ever seen before. She doesn't look like anyone in most of her classes, including the teachers, and her background story is difficult to comprehend for most. However, that doesn't mean that we can't support and provide her with the type of education she deserves and craves. Currently in the United States, a crippling issue has a stranglehold on culturally diverse populations of students and this is known as cultural racism. Bennett (1986) defines cultural racism as the use of authority by Whites to "perpetuate their cultural heritage and impose it upon others, while at the same time destroying the culture of ethnic minorities" (p. 49). Cultural racism combines ethnocentrism, the view that other cultures are inferior to the Anglo-European, and the power to suppress or eradicate manifestations of non-Anglo-European cultures (p. 49). Unfortunately, all across the United States the legacy of cultural racism can be found in the formal curriculum—in tests, media, and course offerings (p. 49). It also rears its ugly head in the hidden curriculum, which is also known as the informal curriculum, when nonminority educators maintain low expectations for minority students, the evolution of myths and stereotypes held by key players, and an unforgiving and unsympathetic school environment that is not supportive of all children (Bennett, 1986). It is critical that educators shift this mindset of racial superiority as they work with students and deliver the curriculum to all children.

It is also vital that we challenge the curriculum that is delivered across the nation and to look at reform. According to Bennett (1986), "The traditional curriculum in most schools in the United States is a classic example of institutional and cultural racism" (p. 49). Each one of us that attended elementary school was taught by our teachers to sit "Indian-style" or as we moved deeper into our education, the fallacy that certain races were tied to lower or higher IQ differences. As a result of much of this racial stereotyping, schools have unintentionally or intentionally nurtured the conviction in White supremacy (Bennett, 1986). "School texts and educational media have presented negative myths and stereotypes about most of our ethnic minorities, have overlooked important contributions, and have presented a distorted view of past and current history that reinforces the doctrine of White supremacy" (p. 50).

Along the same lines, we use words in our English language that delineate good versus evil and they revolve around representations of Black and White value. Bennett references a pamphlet that was published in 1841 that described the use of many words used in our language, such as blackly, blackguard, blackjack, black sheep, and so forth, to describe negative properties of a situation (Moore, 1841). Children learn at an early age through the English language and in schools that black oftentimes represents evil and white represents good. We need to be mindful of the subliminal messages we are sending to students in classrooms when participating in this type of conversation and relaying to students that it is acceptable to compare the two in this manner.

In order to support marginalized students, we have to acknowledge the need for change and must have a better understanding of cultural differences in the classroom. Bennett (1986) uses Longstreet's (1978) definition of ethnicity, which is

> that portion of cultural development that occurs before the individual is in complete command of his or her abstract intellectual powers and that that is

formed primarily through the individual's early contacts with family, neighbors, friends, teachers, and others, as well as with his or her immediate environment of the home and neighborhood. (p. 65)

Bennett identifies five properties of ethnicity that afford educators with strategies for identifying possible areas of misinterpretation in multicultural classrooms. Properties identified are verbal communication, nonverbal communication, orientation modes, social value patterns, and intellectual modes as areas of possible concern (Longstreet, 1978). In American schools, students are expected to speak the English language. However, we need to examine the "cultural conflict many children experience in schools that ignore or repress the language they have known since birth" (Bennett, 1986, p. 67). Bennett states,

> All the pre-primers available on the market assume a level of development in oral languages that the Mexican American child has not reached at the beginning of first grade. Phonologically speaking he neither hears nor discriminates certain sounds. Accustomed as he is to hearing Spanish mostly at home, he hears Spanish in the classroom instead of English and tries to decode accordingly. The result is frustration and awareness that he is failing at something [while] the other children are succeeding. (Benitez, 1973, p. 7)

Bennett (1986) continues by sharing that in the 1980s a group of elementary teachers noticed as early as first grade, that Black students were surpassed by Whites. Until the teachers listened to "tapes of black students speaking, they were oblivious to the distinct Black dialect. They then realized that asking many of these children to read only the available materials was like asking Whites to begin reading Old English" (p. 68).

Another noticeable cultural difference is the classroom management expectations of our students. Different cultures may approach the learning process differently and what may appear to come off as disrespectful or disengaged to the learning process may simply reflect cultural differences. Bennett points out the differences in specific cultures and their expected behaviors in a classroom when sharing that cultures may prefer to follow the "you-take-a-turn-then-another-takes-a-turn" approach, while other cultures prefer to express their thoughts in a loud, spontaneous, heated discussion. This can oftentimes be perceived negatively by differing cultures and this misunderstanding can lead to additional prejudices (Longstreet, 1978).

Nonverbal communication, according to Bennett, also plays a large role in many of our daily interactions (Longstreet, 1978). Bennett (1986) shares that within the dominant White culture, we equate good eye contact with good listening skills and engagement. We also attribute characteristics such as honesty and integrity with someone that is using direct eye contact with a speaker. However, within other cultures, not looking another person in the eye is a sign of respect and admiration. This type of cultural misunderstanding can create a hostile environment for both the classroom teacher and the student perceived as being disrespectful to the macroculture (p. 71).

With regard to orientation modes, Bennett (1986) describes the differences of cultures with regard to time. She explains that some cultures encourage society to tackle things one step at a time in a linear fashion. They expect people to be on time and ready for the activity ahead of time. Other cultures may have different expectations and encourage people to approach the activity in a spontaneous manner, while operating on an individualized schedule. Although different cultures have different expectations for approaching time, the bell schedule of the building typically dictates the life of a child in most school settings. This can have a negative impact on certain students who prefer to approach time in a polychromic manner (p. 73).

Social values are essential to how we are perceived by others. Bennett (1986) defines values as "beliefs about how one ought or ought not to behave or about some end state of existence worth or not worth attaining" (p. 73). Many children from the dominant culture learn best when challenged individually and they are expected to seek assistance from an adult when they are in need. These children typically prefer competitive structure and tend to thrive from it. Learning is often individualized, for these students and educators typically model learning from games and other competitive forums. These students are often rewarded with stickers, stamps, rewards, and opportunities. These preferences are oftentimes reversed in other cultures. In these cultures, the learning or outlook on learning is often more collaborative and less individualized. Students frequently find themselves relying on their classmate or peer and less on the teacher. However, a common cultural misunderstanding by teachers is often overlooking a typical preference to seek out assistance from a peer rather than an adult as an act of defiance, dismissive socializing, or possible cheating (Bennett, 1986).

Bennett's (1986) final guideline for understanding cultural differences is in the area of intellectual modes. This refers "both to what types of knowledge are valued most and to learning styles, or how learning takes place within an individual" (p. 75). Bennett discusses the positive outcomes that may come from the understanding that not all students learn in the same manner. This understanding can be a celebration, but can also produce dangerous results. The celebration comes from the understanding of teachers that they must alter their instruction for a classroom to be more responsive to the needs of all students contained in it. Danger lies in the prospect of educators producing new ethnic stereotypes while reinforcing old ones, such as "Asians excel in math"; "Blacks learn aurally"; "Mexican American males can't learn from female peer tutors"; and "Navajos won't ask a question or participate in a discussion" (p. 76). A common misconception is that educators should treat all students the same and this is the problem students like Monica face each day. By treating students the same, we may be unintentionally stacking the deck against them. Bennett believes that "when teachers misunderstand their students' cultural behavioral styles, they may underestimate their intellectual potential and unknowingly misplace, mislabel, and mistreat them" (p. 183). Often, teachers will misdiagnose a child's needs and will alter their instruction at the expense of the child. "Thus we see that it is not the learning style of the child that prevents the child from learning; it is the perception by the teacher of the child's style as a sign of incapacity that causes the teacher to reduce the quality of the instruction offered" (p. 183).

Monica was often heard telling students or teachers that she wished people would stop caring so much about her in this new environment. She came to us with minimal records from her previous schooling experience and was reading at a second grade level upon enrolling. She showed little interest in the supports provided and refused much of the assistance offered. She quickly qualified for special education services and we provided a one-on-one multisensory reading approach that showed success, once Monica began to trust the adult delivering the service. However, in the larger settings, Monica continued to struggle with classroom expectations. Grades were a frustration point for Monica and she ignited anytime students would become competitive and would ask her how she did on an assignment or assessment.

Also, Monica was continuously told to take her sweatshirt hood off of her head because the teachers felt she wasn't engaged and was lacking eye contact during the lectures and discussions. She showed excitement when she knew the answers to certain questions and would continuously call out answers or shout out off topic knowledge without raising her hand. Monica socialized with her peers multiple times throughout a class period and would text message her friends much of the time. On multiple occasions she was observed answering phone calls during class, which would result in consequences. Monica was frequently late to class and on occasion she would get up and leave the classroom without permission because this type of behavior was accepted in her old schools that she attended. She struggled with adults monitoring her every move and she desired to be left alone. Eventually, she became so frustrated with the perceived stalking from our students and staff that she told a classmate that she would "take care of all of these White people." Monica boasted about how acquaintances in her old neighborhood would take care of a situation like this, which resulted in a lengthy removal from school.

Bennett would argue that most of these behaviors are part of Monica's cultural upbringing and our lack of cultural understanding caused unnecessary anguish. Clearly through her experiences that challenged these characteristics, she was crying out for help because of the incongruous expectations she felt on a daily basis (Longstreet, 1978).

The biased curriculum historically available to students and educators in the United States is another large impediment that many of our students face on a daily basis. Therefore, the need for a multicultural curriculum is necessary to support our students. According to Bennett (1986), a multicultural curriculum "is one that attends to the school's hidden curriculum— for example, teachers' values and expectations, student cliques and peer groupings, and school regulations" (p. 300). In order to move forward with a multicultural curriculum, we must develop and acknowledge the numerous historical perspectives free from our current White biases. The White majority conceived many of the topics taught in schools across America and our textbooks often represent this type of thinking. As a result, many of the essential historical concepts, such as slavery or the discovery of America, are told from the perspective of the White majority. These dangerous practices have isolated ethnic groups and cultures for years. The need to take back our nation's curriculum and bring about a new ethnic perspective is a challenge that teachers must be compelled to convene.

Bennett (1986) suggests that teachers start small and focus on one or two ethnic groups that hold a special meaning to the students, the community, and the building leader. The entire community must become educated about the group's perspectives by diving into the literature and media of the groups. The educator should identify and connect with local resources in order to gain an appropriate familiarity and find a way for them to become involved with the students. Resources must be examined for any bias and a list of primary source resources should be used to present the lesson to your students. "It is important to remember that we run the risk of stereotyping when we seek the perspective of a particular nation or ethnic group" (p. 311).

In order to support students like Monica, we must develop intercultural competency and this can be achieved, regardless of your stage of life. Bennett (1986) defines intercultural competence as "the ability to interpret intentional communications (language, signs, gestures), some unconscious cues (such as body language), and customs in cultural styles different from one's own" (p. 313). We must demonstrate qualities of compassion and communication if we want to be successful in this aspect. Bennett states that this goal "recognizes that communication among persons of different cultural backgrounds can be hindered by culturally conditioned assumptions made about each other's behavior and conditions" (p. 313). It can be incredibly difficult for one citizen who has only been subjected to norms of his/her individual culture to recognize and appreciate a communication based entirely on a different set of standards. Bennett believes that "once people understand how their own language, experience, and current modes of cognition relate to their own culture, contrasts may be made with the cultural experience and modes of cognition of culturally different others" (p. 314).

Additionally, it is up to educators to take action to battle all forms of discrimination. "Combatting racism, sexism, prejudice, and discrimination means lessening negative attitudes and behavior which are based on gender bias and misconceptions about the inferiority of races and cultures that are different from one's own" (Bennett, 1986, p. 320). The goal for schools is to "develop antiracist, antisexist behavior based on awareness of historical and contemporary evidence of individual, institutional, and cultural racism and sexism in the United States and elsewhere in the world" (Bennett, 1986, p. 321). Teachers can aid by factually educating our students on the concepts of race and biological make up shared by all humans. Teachers across all curricular areas can support students by educating them on how to distinguish bias in resources distributed in schools. It is also vital that we educate all students on the racist practices of our past, including our redlining practices of many of our communities, including the community Monica found her new life in. Educators must provide diverse students an opportunity to work cooperatively with one another to achieve a common purpose to foster shared admiration and gratitude. Primarily, we must acknowledge and own our racist past and current present practices (Bennett, 1986).

Monica seemingly had it all . . . a new house, an outpouring of affection from new friends, teachers who cared profoundly about her, and a new lease on life. However, she didn't feel connections to her new environment and couldn't relate to those around her because of a lack of cultural understanding on our part. Soon after she enrolled, Monica began to lose the spark we saw in the first few weeks of meeting her. The school connected her to counseling within the school day to support her emotional needs and provided countless resources to her and her guardians. During this strong start she connected with several students who were also athletes. She built a trusting relationship with the counselor and many of the teachers and administration. However, after the first quarter, Monica's attitude about school began to change and she began to spiral. As the workload and behavioral expectations increased, Monica's desire and determination began to diminish.

Monica started missing assignments even when she had several adults working with her in a one-on-one setting to ensure the work was completed. She found herself getting in trouble in class for calling out and for being perceived as disrespectful more frequently. She began missing class more frequently and became more withdrawn from her classmates and teachers. Her grades started dropping and she seemed to show little concern for how she was performing. Four months later, her temporary guardian contacted the school to let us know that Monica had chosen to leave their home to go back to live with her father in the homeless shelter. We were all puzzled by the sudden change in performance by Monica, but why were we so shocked? We expected Monica to conform to our society and never altered our instruction, our expectations, or our curriculum to fit the needs of this student or any of her classmates. She was crying out for help with her disengagement and outbursts. We often find ways to shrug off our responsibilities by blaming others, complaining about others, or defending our ineffective actions. We often blame the horse that has been led to the water for not drinking . . . but what if the water we are asking the horse to drink from is polluted?

School systems must rethink how we distribute content to our students. We owe it to people of all nations and religions to give them a voice and it is no longer acceptable for the educational experts to create their story for them. The practice of placing students on the other side of the two-way observation mirror and out of reach of the indispensable resources that every student deserves must stop immediately. Instead, we must stand united with locked arms with our students and take the necessary risks to ensure that the next Monica receives the equitable education she deserves. Unfortunately for us, the two-way observation mirror and "curriculum window" couldn't be opened in time for Monica. She left a lasting impression on the educators in our building and we continue to fight for her to come back to us. We expected Monica to abide by our laws while we ignored her practices. We worried too much about the content we were delivering to her, when in fact, the most important lesson learned was the one she was teaching us. Monica taught us about the needs of humanity.

As I finalize my reflection on Monica's story I unexpectedly find my own self in an empty room that is separated by another two-way observation mirror. I am surrounded by silence and encumbrance. I realize that I have my own biases that I have to unpack and address when it comes to Monica and the rest of our students. I found simplicity in blaming Monica's perceived failures on the "educational system." What has my role been in Monica's experience? I realize that the other side of the two-way observation mirror is bursting with all of my former and current students and families and they are challenging me to address my own biases that I may unsuspectingly bring with me every day. These biases must be challenged in order to smash the two-way observation mirror with understanding and knowledge of these predispositions. Who am I to say that attending my school is a better alternative to living with a child's father, regardless of perceived living conditions? We've all heard the horror stories of lottery winners losing everything, but I am now confident that Monica truly hit the jackpot by finding her way back to her father.

REFERENCES

Benitez, M. (1973, March 25–27). *A blueprint for the education of the Mexican American [Paper presentation].* Annual Convention of the Comparative and International Education Society, San Antonio, TX. https://files.eric.ed.gov/fulltext/ED076294.pdf

Bennett, C. I. (1986). *Comprehensive multicultural education theory and practice.* Allyn and Bacon.

Du Bois, W. E. B. (1935). Does the negro need separate schools? *The Journal of Negro Education, 4*(3), 328–335

Longstreet, W. (1978). *Aspects of ethnicity: Understanding differences in pluralistic classrooms.* Teachers College Press.

Moore, R. M. (1841). "Racism in the English language" [Pamphlet]. The Council on Interracial Books for Children.

CHAPTER 21

ESCAPING POVERTY AS A MOTIVATOR FOR ACADEMIC SUCCESS

Jeremy L. Froehlich

Author/Book studied:
Gagné, R., & Perkins Driscoll, M. (1988). *Essentials of learning for instruction* (2nd ed.). Prentice Hall.

There are many different philosophies and approaches when it comes to establishing, executing, and evaluating a particular curriculum for use in primary and secondary education in the American education system. Countless books and research have been presented for all to consume in an effort to choose or follow a particular curriculum path or strategy. The purpose of this volume of the Curriculum Window series is to provide its readers with a window into how curriculum scholars of the past felt about the curriculum arena, and this chapter in particular will provide a window into Robert M. Gagné and Marcy Perkins Driscoll's (1988) book titled *Essentials of Learning*

Curriculum Windows Redux, pages 253–264
Copyright © 2022 by Information Age Publishing
www.infoagepub.com
All rights of reproduction in any form reserved.

for Instruction. I hope to open a window by relating my personal experience as a student and, in particular, describe what motivated my desire for academic success; provide some background on the authors and their contributions to curricular and pedagogical practices; highlight how the authors' views at the time of their writing now connect to current curricular practices; and finally explore through personal experience other areas in which I believe educators can promote learning that are not mentioned in this text.

To start this chapter, I would like to relay my personal experiences and challenges I faced growing up in poverty in a small town located in central Ohio, and how these challenges shaped my attitudes toward school. I was born in early April of 1977 to a mother that was a little over a month short of her 16th birthday and to a father that was 17 years old. My mother was a sophomore in high school who had not yet got her driver's license, and my father was a senior who had just graduated a semester early from high school to prepare for my birth by getting a job at a local bus manufacturing company as a mechanic. My mother and father decided to get married prior to my birth despite the urgings of my grandparents, on both sides, suggesting that adoption might be the better choice given the situation facing my parents.

In preparation for my arrival, my parents moved into an attic apartment in a low income part of their hometown. My mother initially struggled finding a job that would accommodate the schedule she had to keep now that she had an infant and not enough income to afford child care. Things were incredibly tight, but my parents made ends meet for the first 2 1/2 years of my life. They even welcomed a baby girl 2 years after I came along, giving us a family of four. Shortly after the birth of my sister, my father was laid off from the bus manufacturing company. My father struggled to find employment in the early 1980s, so my mother who dropped out of high school as a sophomore began to look for a job to help keep the family afloat. She would work for minimum wage doing menial jobs at a local nursing home.

Just as things were beginning to go south for our young family, my father began fighting various ailments that his doctors were unable to diagnose. My father was first diagnosed with and treated for pneumonia. This treatment program would not yield any benefit, and the doctors would later abandon the pneumonia diagnosis as other organs, in addition to his lungs, began to shut down. His appendix would burst around this time, and his kidneys began to shut down. My father would lose 50% of his body weight with no diagnosis or plan of treatment. He would have his appendix, part of his lung, and a kidney all removed as the doctors tried desperately to address his organ failure for which they were unable to identify the source. The stress of the medical issues as well as the financial shortcomings during the time led to the end of my parent's short marriage. With the doctors not being able to put their finger on the cause of my father's medical condition, he was given a short time to live and would move back in with his parents following the divorce and being released from the hospital. My father would later make a miraculous recovery (a story maybe for the next chapter I write), but the divorce was inevitable and the illness kept him from being able to work and provide financial support to our family for the next few years.

My mother would work her minimum wage job at the nursing home for the next couple of years. She would struggle to provide the basic necessities for my sister and myself including child care, rent, and food. It was about this time that I became very aware of our financial situation. I can remember very clearly from the time I was three or four asking what is for dinner some nights and being told that we would have to wait until tomorrow's paycheck before we would be able to eat our next meal. It is a very chilling feeling being hungry and not being able to do anything about it as a child. We lived just a quarter of a mile from the local McDonalds, but I would not get to eat there until much later in my life. I know now that my mother needed help, but she was very proud and did not want to ask for what she felt was a handout at this time in her life. So my grandparents who lived fairly close, but advised her to not get married and to give me up for adoption, were never called or asked for help at this time.

I had just turned five when my mother began to work on earning her general education diploma (GED) in hopes of bettering our situation. My mother earned her GED the summer following my fifth birthday, and in an effort to begin saving money, we moved into a camping tent on my grandparent's property. So, despite living in a camping tent, this was the first time that my sister and I had food every night since my grandparents could help with meals when needed. I was also able to crudely equate an improvement in educational level to improvement in one's lifestyle. It was not winning the lottery, but my mother had passed her high school equivalency tests and our living situation had improved. We had a new relationship with our grandparents, we had dinner every night, and my mother was able to begin saving a little money.

After about 4 months of living in a tent on my grandparent's property, my mother was able to purchase a mobile home, and we finally had a place of our own. This happened as I began attending kindergarten. My mother, now with her GED, was able to get a job as a nurse's assistant at the same nursing home she had worked before. The pay was not much better, but the job was more meaningful for her and led her to begin thinking about going to nursing school. It was late in my kindergarten year that I had my sixth birthday party. I was excited to invite some of my baseball teammates to my house to play games and eat a red velvet cake that my grandmother had made for the occasion. I was too embarrassed to invite them over when we were living in the tent, but I was excited to show off my new home with this party. The party was going well, my friends seemed to be having fun, and my mother had just let me know that as a surprise she was going to take us to Pizza Hut for lunch. I had never eaten at Pizza Hut, and I was super excited as a 6-year-old to make this trip. As my friends and I loaded up in my mother's rundown mid-1970s Chevy Nova (painted in that awesome pea baby food green color we all remember from that era) with ripped seats and the headliner hanging from the car ceiling, one of my friends said, "Man, you are really poor. I thought your house was bad, but your car is worse. I told my mom not to leave me here." As I mentioned earlier, I was aware that my family was not well off, but I did not know any different. This was the first time that I realized I was different, and that people looked at me differently, because my family was poor. My friend's comment, which I know was just an innocent comment that young kids are known to make, has stuck with me to this day. I made it my goal from that moment to better my situation when I could.

That experience I had at my sixth birthday party would change how I would associate with my friends for a long time. I was now uncomfortable at school. I grew increasingly concerned with the clothes and shoes I wore, and I would try just to blend into the background and try hard not to draw any attention to myself. I would not invite a friend over to my house again. Even as my family's circumstances would change as I will share later, I would go to my friend's house instead of inviting them over to my house. School no longer was a place that I liked to go. I thought everyone was judging me because I could not afford the same things everyone else had. A quick story I vividly remember from this time was getting a new pair of Nike tennis shoes. My mother was so excited to get these and give them to me because I had always wanted a pair of Nikes like my friends had worn to school. She had found them on sale and thought she was going to make my day. I proudly wore my new Nike tennis shoes to school the next day only to be made fun of because the light teal blue Nike Swoosh looked like girls shoes. My mother went to her room crying that night when I told her why I would never wear those shoes again. I was again, in my mind at least, singled out for being unable to afford the things my schoolmates could afford.

I was blessed, however, that the academic part of school was very easy for me. I do not know if I could have managed the anxiety of going to and staying at school with the added difficulty of not understanding the academic material. I never had the experience of connecting with a teacher as a student in elementary and secondary school. As I look back, I think my intentionally avoiding being the center of attention and doing very well on my academic work kept the teachers from feeling the need to build a relationship with me. In their mind I was progressing just fine, and their focus would be better served on the students that are struggling with the academic piece of school.

Just as I started fourth grade, my mother would finally decide to enroll at a near-by technical college to try and earn her licensed practical nurse (LPN) degree. This would prove to be a difficult task for my mother as she worked full time to support us while also going to school full time to earn her nursing degree. This would be the first time she would take formal classes since she was a sophomore in high school nearly 9 years earlier. During this time, I was expected to get myself and my little sister up, make sure we got ready for school, make and serve breakfast, and get us on the school bus. My mother made the commitment to go to school, but we still could not afford childcare and that responsibility fell on me as she had to work the early shift at the nursing home to make time to attend classes in the evening. This was, however, the first time in my life that an emphasis was placed on education. My mother did not preach to me that education was important, but she did set an example for me with the sacrifice she was making to go back to school full time while working full time. In just a few years, my mother went from high school dropout to college educated!

Having completed her LPN degree and earning her nursing license, my mother would apply for and earn a position as a full-time nurse at the nursing home she began at 6 years earlier as a minimum wage worker. This job would pay better than minimum wage and for the first time we, as a family, were able to have a little discretionary money. We were able to go to Hearts or K-Mart to do back to school shopping for clothes and supplies. We did not have to do our clothes shopping at The Salvation Army Store as we had always done before. I finally got to go to the McDonalds that was down the street from our first apartment for lunch. My mother also began looking at homes to purchase at this time. I was starting to make the connection that education was the answer to combating poverty. As my mother progressed in her education, we, as a family, were also becoming more financially stable.

To close the story on my mother's journey, she would soon purchase a home. We went from a mobile home to a three bedroom, two bathroom home on three acres. My mother would later go back to school to earn her registered nurse designation while I was in high school, which would lead to a new job opportunity at another nursing home as the head of nurses. By the time I had graduated high school, my mother went from single mother and high school dropout to a college educated nurse who was in charge of the entire unit of nurses in the nursing home in which she worked. She went from what looked like the start of generational poverty to becoming fairly affluent. I was able to take my mother's example of using education as a way to improve her life, and I used her example as motivation for myself to further my education. My mother has not stopped with her educational progression. She has since earned her master's degree in nursing and was recruited to be the director of nursing at a hospital in a city in Southern Florida, and she is now working on her doctorate in nursing. The window I hope to open in a later section of this chapter is in reference to Chapter 4 titled "Learner Motivation" (Gagné & Driscoll, 1988), which discusses student motivation and ways in which to tap into these student motivators. However, before I move onto opening that window into learner motivation, I will use the next sections to provide a little background on Gagné and Driscoll and a quick synopsis of their book.

ABOUT THE AUTHORS

In this section, I would like to provide a brief background on the authors, and then in the following sections provide a brief synopsis of other parts of Gagné and Driscoll's (1988) book, and then finally connect my introductory story to Gagné and Driscoll's chapter on learner motivation. Both Gagné and Driscoll approach curriculum through the lens of the psychology field. Marcy Driscoll, according to her academic vitae, earned her bachelor's degree from Mt. Holyoke College, master's degree from the University of Massachusetts, and doctorate from the University of Massachusetts all in the field of psychology. She has, also, authored, refereed, and edited countless articles and books in the field of educational psychology to go along with these degrees. In addition to the previously mentioned accomplishments, Driscoll is currently the dean and director of University Teacher Education at Florida State University (Driscoll, 2019). Robert Gagné earned his bachelor's degree from Yale University and doctorate from Brown University, both in psychology. According to his obituary, "Gagné was one of the great bridge builders between laboratory and practice" (Rothkopf, 2002, para. 1). Gagné's work covered a wide range including studying the conditional responses of rats to a certain stimulus in the laboratory to the understanding of what motivates a child to learn in his research with Driscoll. Pinar et al.'s (1995) book titled *Understanding Curriculum* mentioned that the six factors in education that Gagné developed would be used as foundational blocks for curriculum planning and design going forward (p. 167).

SYNOPSIS OF THE BOOK

This book provides other introductory theory into how students learn, in addition to the area of student learner motivation for which I will discuss later in this chapter, including how "the responsibilities of planning and delivering instruction obviously require...knowledge of the process of learning" which are important for new teachers to understand and develop (Gagné & Driscoll, 1988, p. 2). Gagné and Driscoll (1988) provide a model of the learning process that provides a simple visual representation of how the learning process works, from reception to performance, allowing one to see how a student takes and processes the instruction a teacher provides (p. 23). "As a manager of instruction, it is the teacher's job to plan, design, select, and supervise the arrangement of the external events, with the aim of activating the necessary learning process" (p. 39). They move from the theory of learning, to the process of learning, and then next to the outcomes of learning. In this section, Gagné and Driscoll explain the five different learning outcomes that they believe exist in student learning which are verbal information, intellectual skills, cognitive strategies, attitudes, and motor skills (p. 65). The next section is motivation, which is the overarching focus of the chapter I am presenting and will revisit in a later section of this chapter, and following motivation they then move to conditions of learning which guides new teachers on how to provide the optimal learning environment for their students.

Gagné and Driscoll's (1988) concluding three chapters focus on planning strategies, learner strategies, and delivering instructions. These chapters were all relevant to current practices in that they relate closely to the areas of emphasis on our current teacher evaluation rubrics. Planning instruction is a major part of Ohio teacher evaluation rubric. The section on learner strategies focuses on knowing one's students and understanding how they best learn so that the instructor can meet them where they are. This relates closely to how a teacher can individualize their instruction for the varied students that they instruct, and it mirrors what is current practice as one designs individual education plans for our students in our special education departments. Finally, the last section focuses on instruction delivery, which deals with the current curricular emphasis placed on differentiating instruction. It is not only important to know how your different students learn, but then the teacher must deliver the instruction in a way that is accessible to all students. Differentiation is a huge focus on our teacher evaluation rubric and is an expectation for our teachers that instruct our students with disabilities.

OPENING A WINDOW: STUDENT MOTIVATION

Gagné and Driscoll's (1988) book is an excellent resource or text for any undergraduate student interested in pursuing or studying the field of education. The concepts that Gagné and Driscoll present are interesting, but they are mostly presented as foundational skills and principles for future teachers. Chapter 4, "Learner Motivation," however, really caught my attention as an educator who is fascinated with student motivation. The window I would like to open regarding this text has to deal with student motivation.

Chapter 4 of *Essentials of Learning for Instruction* begins with Gagné and Driscoll (1988) explaining how student motivation and learning are related. They say:

> Learning takes place in people who are motivated. It is difficult to imagine someone who is completely unmotivated; we normally think of each person as experiencing wants for something, however trivial, every minute of the day. The most fundamental motivation for a learner is a desire to enter into a learning situation, and we make the assumption that learners have already been motivated to place themselves in learning situations when they attend class, view television, or read printed pages. (p. 63)

I agree wholeheartedly that student learning occurs only when students are motivated to learn, and I will relay the authors' thoughts on student motivation as I open this window for the readers of this chapter. The student motivations or ways to motivate students in this chapter all deal with motivation by and for academics, and I will close this section by providing my personal thoughts on student motivation, which I believe are not always academic in nature as I hope my introductory story showed.

Chapter 4, "Learner Motivation," is divided by Gagné and Driscoll (1988) into three different sections: first, sources of motivation for learning; second, a model of motivation; and finally, motivating the learner. I will start by relating that the focus of the first section was "sources of motivation." Gagné and Driscoll (1988) say that "the motives of human beings arise from basic physiological conditions called tissue needs (hunger, sex), from the action of various physical stimuli of the environment (heat, cold, shock), and from emotionally tinged cognitive states within the person" (p. 64).

Gagné and Driscoll (1988) extrapolate this concept to human knowledge, and they list three sources of motivation, which are curiosity, achievement, and self-efficacy, that are the keys to a student gaining knowledge (p. 64). Curiosity is mentioned as an important source of student motivation in this section especially in younger students. It is also noted that since there are fewer surprises for students as they get older their curiosity will diminish with time, and thus curiosity will be less of a motivating factor for students as they advance through their educational process (p. 64). Gagné and Driscoll (1988) next mention achievement as a source of "strong motivation relevant to learning" (p. 65). Students being able to accomplish something or see their performance improve (achieve) as a direct result of learning is a powerful motivator as it pertains to student learning (p. 65). Finally, self-efficacy is listed as a student learning motivator. Self-efficacy as a motivator means that students are likely to perform in direct correlation to how they perceive they will grasp or understand the material. For instance, if a student has performed well academically in the past, she or he would be more motivated to take on future learning, and on the contrary, if a student performed poorly in the past, she or he would be less motivated to take on future learning (p. 65). When students are motivated, they are willing to expend the mental effort necessary to achieve knowledge through the assigned learning tasks (p. 65).

Gagné and Driscoll (1988) use the second section of learner motivation to present their A.R.C.S. (attention, relevance, confidence, and satisfaction) motivation model (p. 68). They use this model to explain what conditions are necessary to have a motivated learner. To have a motivated student, Gagné and Driscoll argue that there are four main conditions that are required to be met (p. 68). First, an instructor must gain the attention of the student, and this is done by capturing and maintaining the student's interest in a manner that is appealing to the student (p. 69). Second, the instructor must prove to the student the content is relevant, and the instructor must appeal to the student's personal interests (p. 69). Third, the instructor must be able to convince the student that she or he can accomplish the assigned task or learning objective by building confidence in her or his abilities to understand and digest the lesson (p. 70). And finally, the instructor must provide her or his students with adequate feedback to let the students know they have accomplished the task correctly, or that they are on the right path, to provide the student with a sense of satisfaction in their learning (p. 70). Gagné and Driscoll propose that when the conditions of their ARCS model are met the instructor will have an optimal environment for student learning as the students will be properly motivated to learn (p. 71).

The final section of Chapter 4, "Learner Motivation" (Gagné & Driscoll, 1988) is motivating the students. In this section, Gagné and Driscoll (1988) use the motives and model they presented earlier in the chapter to provide techniques for implementation, which can be used for motivating student learners. Gagné and Driscoll talk to the reader about differentiating instruction, using relevant and concrete examples, and using various instructional techniques with student learners (p. 72). The techniques they present to assure relevance for student learners are to develop consistent routines so that new material looks familiar, to show how student learners can employ tasks now, and to show student learners how this information can be valuable in the future (p. 74). To ensure student learners have confidence, Gagné and Driscoll argue that an instructor needs to provide clear learning objectives, scaffold tasks so that they move from easier to more difficult concepts, and to also provide the students with some control of their learning (p. 76). Finally, Gagné and Driscoll teach that an instructor can create student learner satisfaction through providing timely and relevant feedback and encouraging the student to apply the tasks they have learned across their various content areas (p. 76).

I do not believe anyone would argue the value of student motivation as it pertains to student learning and to the success of the instructor. Teachers will be rewarded handsomely if they take the time to figure out what motivates their students to want to gain knowledge and academic success. The criticism I would make in regard to student learner motivation is that not all students are going to be motivated by academic means. In this chapter, Gagné and Driscoll's (1988) model and motivators are all found in an academic setting. The point of the introductory story I shared about my circumstances growing up was to show that motivation can come from outside the classroom or schoolhouse. Schoolwork was easy for me, and it would have been easy to not come to school due to the anxiety I experienced while at school. I might have done just fine academically in this scenario, but I was motivated to do well and attend school regularly primarily because I saw how my mother's financial situation changed for the better as she progressed educationally. I mentioned how I never had a teacher try to build a relationship with me beyond what was necessary for them to provide grades to report to the district. I can only imagine how I would have made it through school if I struggled with the academic content without having the security of a strong positive teacher relationship to carry me through that struggle.

It has been my experience that many teachers get into the profession because they liked school, they worked well within the constraints of the classroom, and they earned good grades while they were students. They may not know what some of their students are going through, and therefore, they may not be able to readily motivate their students that do not like school, do not see the value in school, and/or do not thrive within the same constraints in which the instructor thrived because they cannot relate to that feeling. I believe many teachers may not see the value in building relationships beyond the academic confines of school with the student that struggles because of texts, like *Essentials of Learning for Instruction* (Gagné & Driscoll, 1988) that only focus on academic student motivation. I often wonder if my anxiety about going to school would have been lessened if a teacher would have gotten to know me and my situation, and not just seen that I scored highly on all my assessments and assumed I was doing just fine. I have, however, used my personal experience with being a student to guide how I approach different students in my school. I try to give all students the benefit of the doubt and realize that not all students enjoy or will be successful in school as it is currently constituted. I do my best to make these students' experiences at school as positive as possible, but a teacher has infinitely more access to positive relationship building with students than does a building administrator.

I really enjoyed Elliot W. Eisner's (2002) chapter in his book *The Educational Imagination: On the Design and Evaluation of School Programs* titled "On the Art of Teaching." He makes it clear that there is not a routine prescription for instructing and motivating students. In fact, Eisner (2002) says, "Teaching is an art in that teachers, like painters, composers, actresses, and dancers, make judgments based largely on qualities that unfold during the course of action" (p. 156). Eisner argues that teaching ends are found not through preconceived notions of instruction but rather through the interactions an instructor has with her students on a daily basis. The theory of student motivation that Gagné and Driscoll (1988) present is not in of itself bad, but it is important that a good teacher views the idea of student learner motivations from varied perspectives and not just the one presented by Gagné and Driscoll (Eisner, 2002). Academic motivators are extremely important, but the necessities of life must first be met, such as making sure a school is a safe space for its students, before a student will respond to purely academic motivators.

To close this section, I think it is important that teacher education programs teach the prescribed model of student motivation as it is found in *Essentials of Learning for Instruction* (Gagné & Driscoll, 1988) as all future teachers need to know how the majority of their students may be motivated. I struggled with the structure of school because I felt like I was all alone being a son of a single mother and living in poverty in a community in which this was not commonplace. I did not have a teacher that could empathize with my situation and make me feel like school was a safe place. I was lucky that I had my mother who was an example to me, which kept me focused on achieving academically even if it was not by academic means. It was this example of her sacrifice to continue her education and to show me that through her increased educational levels, our life could be improved as well that provided me with the motivation to attend school and to continue to do well while I was there. Teachers should "provide a climate that welcomes exploration and risk-taking and cultivates the disposition to play" (Eisner, 2002, p. 162).

CONCLUSION

Robert Gagné and Marcy Driscoll's (1988) book, *Essentials of Learning for Instruction*, is a good resource that is still applicable in today's curriculum structure, and its principles would be well served as a foundational text for teachers. I feel Gagné's background in applied psychology, and specifically as it relates to education, can be particularly useful for new teachers in that it sets the stage for future teachers understanding how and why different students may learn differently. I would like to conclude this chapter by providing the reader a few other key takeaways I gleaned from the text *Essentials of Learning for Instruction* and provide the reader with some final thoughts on this book as it relates to current curriculum practice.

Gagné and Driscoll (1988) provide a sterile and clinical approach to learning and instruction that is still useful and beneficial to any future teacher. I particularly like the fact they emphasize student motivation as an important aspect of student learning. However, even though I find no fault in the motivators they provide in this text, I believe a criticism of this text, and many others, is the lack of identifying motivators or barriers that exist outside of academics. As I hope my introductory story illustrated, there are important motivating factors beyond the academic ones mentioned in most teacher preparation texts. I, for instance, was motivated by my fear of continuing in poverty to attend and do well in school.

I have had the opportunity to work with some great students who were motivated to do well in school by factors outside of academics. I would like to relate one final personal experience I have had as an educator. I had a student that was motivated by the opportunities that athletics afforded him. This student was sitting with a 0.0 GPA following his freshman year of high school, he was in danger of not being eligible to participate in extracurricular activities, his brother had been shot in an act of gang violence, his mother was incarcerated, and his grandmother was asked to raise him and his brother. This student was not motivated by curiosity, achievement, or self-efficacy, as Gagné and Driscoll (1988) suggest all learners are, but he was motivated by the relationship he built with his football coach and the prospect of escaping his rough circumstances through earning a football scholarship and a potential professional football career. This student would end up graduating high school with a GPA of 3.2, he earned a college degree, and he would live out his dream by playing in the National Football League. Through this external motivator, he was able to improve his lot in life as well as set the stage for his family to follow in his footsteps. Being an educator is an incredibly rewarding job and curriculum design and planning are certainly important, but I hope all future teachers remember that not every one of their students is as excited about going to school as they were when they were in their students' shoes.

REFERENCES

Driscoll, M. P. (2019). *Curriculum vitae.* https://www.fsu.edu/cvdb/MDRISCOLL.rtf

Eisner, E. W. (2002). *The educational imagination: on the design and evaluation of school programs.* Prentice Hall.

Gagné, R. M., & Driscoll, M. P. (1988). *Essentials of learning for instruction.* Prentice Hall.

Pinar, W. F., Reynolds, W. M., Slattery, P., & Taubman, P. M., (1995). *Understanding curriculum: An introduction to the study of historical and contemporary curriculum discourses.* Peter Lang.

Rothkopf, E. Z. (2002, September 12). In appreciation: Robert Mills Gagné (1916–2002). *Association for Psychological Science.* https://www.psychologicalscience.org/observer/in-appreciation-robert-mills-gagne-1916-2002

CHAPTER 22

STILL CHASING GHOSTS

Louis Hacquard III

Author/Book studied:
Schubert, W. (1980). *Curriculum books: The first eighty years.*
    University Press of America.

KEEP ON LIVIN'

*Sometimes you gotta go back to actually move forward. I don't mean going back
to reminisce or chase ghosts, I mean going back to see where you came from. Where
you've been, how you got there, see where you're going. I know there are those
who say you can't go back. Yes you can. Just have to look in the right place.*

—Matthew McConaughey

Think what you may about the ever-changing personality phases of actor
Matthew McConaughey. However, much like the world of curriculum, his
career, as well as his thought provoking monologue from this 2014 Lincoln
commercial, are indications that curriculum is not something that can be
studied as an isolated area of academic focus. Much like the newest phase of

Curriculum Windows Redux, pages 265–272

McConaughiac depth, curriculum is existential, transcendental, and above all, it is cyclical. So therefore, in order to have any chance at developing a curriculum for the scholars of the future, it is essential for us to go back and "look in the right place." Perhaps *Curriculum Books: The First Eighty Years* by William Henry Schubert (1980) is this "place."

THE SCHUBERT FITS

Prior to his retirement in 2011, William H. Schubert worked at the University of Illinois at Chicago (UIC) for 36 years. Schubert served as the chair of the Department of Curriculum and Instruction, as well as several other leadership roles in route to receiving the College of Education Distinguished Scholar-Teacher Award (International Academy of Education, n.d.).

In *The Phi Delta Kappan*, David L. Silvernail (1982) reviewed *Curriculum Books: The First Eighty Years* and wrote:

> "Educators will find this clear, concise overview of curriculum history a valuable addition to their professional libraries. The book helps readers to better understand the evolution of the curriculum in recent decades," adding that "I applaud Schubert for chronicling the evolution of the curriculum. He took on a monumental task and performed it admirably." (p. 423)

Of course, not every scholar digs transcendentalism. However, even the practicality of Schubert's work can be influential. In *The Journal of Educational Thought*, Harro Van Brummelen (1983) commented:

> It is worthwhile adding Schubert's book to one's personal library, as I have done. The summary overviews of the development of curriculum thought are helpful, succinct statements. The lists of books are useful both for finding books by specific authors or on certain topics, and for getting a feel of the types of books published during various decades. For curricularists, it is a book that on occasion will save several hours of library searching. (p. 272)

Schubert's work provides a comfort and consistency to a profession that feeds off change. Necessary, unnecessary, or somewhere in between, the search, the "itch" for an improved way to educate and measure achievement has an interesting eighty years of documentation.

WE DIDN'T LIGHT IT

Staying consistent with the cyclical nature of our overall theme, I, too, want to take a glance back. Long before I was a doctoral student at Miami

University, planning a successful run in the curriculum game, I spent my undergrad years studying education in Southeastern Ohio at the University of Rio Grande. During my time at Rio, my most interesting collegiate friends were on the soccer team, and many had traveled from various cities throughout the United Kingdom. They were a fun group of guys, and I had become to the Rio Grande soccer team what Jack Nicholson had been to the Lakers: a consistent presence on the sideline.

As a true fan should, I usually make a trip to campus in late summer to watch a few preseason practice sessions. It was always fun to visit and hear about the 2 months of vacation that the boys spent back in the UK, aggressively making up for lost time. Anyway, when the team reported to campus early, they were assigned to a dorm on a temporary basis. This leads to dozens of somewhat irresponsible college students picking a room, and basically throwing their possessions into a massive pile. Unfortunately, the doors to these rooms were usually unlocked.

Well, the summer before my junior year, one of the players had brought his entire CD collection with him to help make the dorm life of preseason a little less grueling. The dude probably owned 70 compact discs, all of which ended up getting stolen but one: *Billy Joel's Greatest Hits* (1985). It was the only album that the thief purposefully chose not to steal. The irony is that was the only one of my friend's albums that I would even consider to be worth stealing, and all I could say to him was, "Hey, we didn't start the fire."

Much like my reaction to the stolen (and awful) music collection, I have the same sentiment when it comes to the current state of public education. Many scholars may believe that the present world of curriculum is a hot mess. That is a matter of opinion. But whatever one's outlook may be, this current state of affairs is not a recent development. Reading *Curriculum Books: The First Eighty Years* (Schubert, 1980) was a firm reminder that we most definitely did not start the fire.

For the sake of adding some context, in October of 1989, Billy Joel released the album *Storm Front*. The biggest hit on the record repeated the lyrics: "We didn't start the fire. It was always burning since the world's been turning." The story behind the song was shared in a 1994 interview that Joel gave in Oxford, England. Apparently, two upcoming musicians were appalled by the political chaos they had been witnessing throughout their youth. He had agreed with their sentiment, but the duo sort of dismissed Joel's empathy because they felt his younger days were probably uneventful. Joel then explained to the young men about the events of the 1950s and 1960s, creating the motivation for what would eventually become "We Didn't Start the Fire."

In regards to the constant search for a perfectly crafted, unbreakable era of curriculum, the same scenario that Billy Joel shared in his anecdote could easily take place on a weekly basis in teachers' lounges across

America. Educators may view the present state of standardized tested, data-driven public education as chaos. But it is nothing new; not even close.

THE WORLD GOT STILL

Well the good ol' days may not return. And the rocks might melt,
and the sea may burn.

—Tom Petty and Jeff Lynne, "Learning to Fly"

Schubert (1980) organizes his book by decades and describes the beginning of the 20th century as "a time when arts, sciences, and other scholarly activities flourished with a special fervor" (p. 13). The most impressive feature of the book might be its format. Arts, culture, history, and all of the other events within each decade are included in the overall explanation of the evolution of the decade's curriculum books. It actually reads quickly, the creativity being the primary reason. So, although it is a book about books, it is ultimately much more than that. Schubert (1980) emphasizes the connectedness of the world and our education and summarizes it very well where he writes, "Although it is impossible to draw direct lines of cause and effect between the activities described . . . and educational developments in the same decade, it is certain that the latter were influenced by many combinations of the former" (p. 15).

A CHEAP PAIR OF SNEAKERS > A NEW SET OF SPEAKERS

"You're complicating Pacman; eat the dots, avoid the ghosts."
—Trace Hacquard

After comparing and contrasting decades of ideas, Schubert's book is proof that different approaches to curriculum can be successful. I think we forget that in this era of standardization. There is not one specific curriculum algorithm that has been scientifically proven to predict success. There is more than one way to grill a steak. For example, the 1985 Chicago Bears would tell you that defense wins championships, but the 1999 Rams, a.k.a. "The Greatest Show on Turf," would probably disagree. The point I am trying to make is that there is not one single approach to curriculum that should be considered as the ultimate standard of excellence, and we should not want there to be. It seems like we are complicating something that should be simple: teaching and learning.

So, as Schubert has beautifully documented, things impact each other; they are connected, and it is no different with curriculum. This era of differentiation and data-driven policies is a phase that some claim is here to stay. We are often asked to "trust the numbers." Of course, there are some of us who have heard this before. And so we give the request an appropriate level of professional courtesy, knowing that this mathematical phase could be yet another snapshot in our educational scrapbook. It is our biker jacket, our disco, our acid-washed jeans. It is our "Rachel" haircut. So although change is cyclical, it is also gradual. We often are unaware that it has happened until we take a look at that scrapbook. However, this approach to curriculum, or life for that matter, is not for everyone. Some may be looking for a permanent solution. But old school or new school, it's still rock and roll to me. And after reading Schubert's work, I believe he would concur.

DESIGNED CHAOS

Those of us who have dedicated our professional lives to education understand the intensity of it all, the nonstop process of self-evaluation. We begin with an interesting idea, creating goals and objectives. We then apply these ideas and goals to learning experiences, sometimes applying them to varieties of content. Often, our judgment and evaluation lead to the continuation of our original idea, and sometimes we need to adjust it. Regardless of the outcome, we learn from it and move forward. As much as we would like to pretend that there is some sort of map that guides us to our destination, there simply is not. We build our curriculum within our profession using our best judgment.

Ultimately, there can be an extremely thin line between profession and perfection. And so, we grind away somewhere within that gray area. As we are seeking to move further toward a level of excellence, we often find ourselves back to where we started: that original, interesting idea. However, this cannot be interpreted as some sort of failure. Failure would be allowing fear to prevent us from trying new things, from tweaking, adjusting, and spicing up our ideas over time. You *can* go back.

As I have mentioned, Schubert used moments in culture and history to help the reader grasp the curriculum trends within each decade. Decades move along, and ideas move through the peaks and valleys of academia. The events of the world inspire growth, intellectual thought, and perhaps most importantly, creativity. In fact, Schubert (1980) inspired me to explain what I am calling "Hacquard's three C's of creativity," which are: curriculum, cola, and (ice) cream. I feel as though the need for creativity in curriculum will be more apparent after the other two are explained. The reader will see how sometimes good ideas are bad, the bad ideas are good, and some of the best consequences and results are unintended.

Let's start with cola. Specifically, Coca-Cola. Whether it is the genius be-hind the 1979 commercial where "Mean" Joe Greene trades his jersey to a kid with a bottle of Coke, or in the 1971 ad where "a camera pans across faces of all shapes, colors, and ethnicities, as they sing from a hilltop in Manziana, Italy, 'I'd like to buy the world a Coke'" (Andrews & Barbash, 2016, para. 2), Americans have a history of appreciating the marketing of this product. And they like to drink it, too.

Coca-Cola knows all about making its way back to where it started. As popular as the beverage was, the urge for improvements amidst competi-tion can lead to mistakes. Arguably, one of the greatest marketing blun-ders in history. On April 23, 1985, the 99-year-old Coca-Cola company an-nounced it was moving on from its original formula to a sweeter version that, in taste tests, consumers were preferring over Pepsi.

To the traditional thinker, the company drastically underestimated America's attachment to the brand. Maybe the fear of Pepsi clouded their judgment? And so, after being "flooded with phone calls, 40,000 letters and reams of bad press, the company backtracked 3 months later, announc-ing the return of Coca-Cola classic" ("Top 10 Bad Beverage Ideas," 2019, para. 1). In an interesting twist, sales for the original Coca-Cola skyrock-eted. So paradoxically, what was bad for business was good for business. And lessons were learned.

Perhaps standardized test-driven, fear-based curriculum design may be the valley that is necessary for the peak that Schubert could detail in his next book. Regardless, ideas and creativity are not formulaic. And as math-ematical scholars are trying to design and measure a solution to a complex problem, maybe the answer to curriculum is to go back to some fundamen-tals. The "classic," if you are a Coke drinker. And if you are a snacker? Well, here is literally some food for curriculum thought.

For the past 3 decades we have witnessed a massive surge in snack food types, and varieties of those types. People have been getting more and more options to relieve their cravings. And while this does not pose any threat to curriculum scholars, it does strike fear into the more primitive snacking industries. Specifically, ice cream.

As a fan of the original Coca-Cola, reading, and writing, I am a believer in the beauty of simplicity. And so years ago, I was appalled when I first saw a concession stand selling a product called Dippin' Dots. Their marketing slogan was (and is) that they are "the ice cream of the future." But they are not. And in my opinion, they were never intended to be.

I do not love going into conspiracy mode, but after learning about the Space Race, I cannot resist. My theory is that a committee within the ice cream industry created Dippin' Dots, an inferior product to traditional ice cream, to heighten the awareness of the real thing. Yes, Dippin' Dots, in my judgment, was originally a fear tactic. They made consumers realize that if these little frozen pellets were the ice cream of the future, then they had better enjoy traditional ice cream while it lasted.

As I traveled across the country watching baseball games, it appeared that the manufactured panic was a success. I noticed people consuming more ice cream than ever, or so it seemed. And so perhaps the dairy industry's Machiavellian tactics helped muscle their way to the top of the overly competitive world of snacking. The simple beat the complex at their own game. However, with this strategy came an unforeseen flaw: Dippin' Dots was interesting enough to a cult of snackers. Sure, they were inferior to ice cream, but not inferior enough to be forgotten almost 30 years later. You see, certain snackers find these Dippin' Dots quite tasty in a sci-fi sort of way. And as hard as the ice cream industry has tried to keep the self-proclaimed ice cream of the future in the past, they have failed miserably.

So maybe the last 5 or 6 years have been a designed era of awfulness to help us realize what is important in education? Maybe the "New Coke" was designed chaos. I do not know. But what I do know is that we often end up back where we started, and if that was a good thing, then it will always be there when we need it. As for Dippin' Dots, they were and are a creation that manufactured a fear of the future, for the present, to revert to the past. Their irony is their unintended reality: They still exist. And maybe they always will. Just not as ice cream. Just as planned. Except that it wasn't.

RIGHT BACK WHERE WE STARTED FROM

Curriculum can be practical and vocational, much like small towns, pinks houses, and many other Mellencampian things. However, it can also be thought-provoking and abstract, like Dali's melting clocks. The sooner our profession grasps this mutual respect, the sooner we will be able to remove the stigmas that can often be associated with various types of academic pursuits. One's position on this may depend on how much you want your mechanic to know about Shakespearean sonnets or your lawyer's appreciation level of Monet's early work. However, the world would be far less interesting if we decided to mold students that were one-dimensional.

And so, the recurring theme in Schubert's writing is that curriculum is a reflection of society. We change as the world changes, and the curriculum we design and prioritize adjusts accordingly. A modern example would be the carnivalization of society as well as the carnivalization of curriculum. Years ago, a group of children might go to a baseball game to watch a pitcher or center fielder. Today, the game is more likely to be the background music for the interactive, family-themed activities available in the Fun Zone just beyond the outfield. I mention this not to sound curmudgeonly, but to acknowledge that adjustments are a part of all of this. In the Billy Joel cycle of chaos, we are long past the entertainment value of Davy Crockett and Elvis Presley. Our students deserve three-dimensional printers and drones; we must adapt accordingly.

Make no mistake, the profession, as well as the curriculum it continues to search for, is a serious matter. Here's the thing: The song is titled "Hold on Loosely" (Barnes et al., 1981). Yes, the one by 38 Special that includes the lyrics, "Hold on loosely, but don't let go. If you cling too tightly, you're gonna lose control." My analysis could be way off, but perhaps many of us in the profession are clinging a bit too tightly. In this era of pseudo-accountability, it seems like we are searching for some elusive concept that will solve our problems. It is the idea that there is some sort of answer waiting for us at some modern-day version of the Oracle of Delphi. Ultimately, the dust doesn't settle until it settles, and time will tell how this era will be remembered. Perhaps our answers will eventually be discovered by our inner-McConaughey leading us to the right place.

REFERENCES

Andrews, T. M., & Barbash, F. (2016, May 17). "I'd like to buy the world a Coke": The story behind the world's most famous ad, in memoriam its creator. *The Washington Post*. https://www.washingtonpost.com/news/morning-mix/wp/2016/05/17/id-like-to-buy-the-world-a-coke-the-story-behind-the-worlds-most-famous-ad-whose-creator-has-died-at-89/

Barnes, D., Carlisi, J., & Peterik, J. (1981). Hold on loosely [Song]. On *Wild-Eyed Southern Boys*. A&M.

International Academy of Education. (n.d.). *William H. Schubert*. http://iaoed.org/index.php/fellows/item/31-william-h-schubert

Joel, B. (1985). *Greatest hits volume 1 & volume 2* [Album]. Columbia.

Joel, B. (1989). *Storm Front* [Album]. Columbia.

Petty, T., & Lynne, J. (1991). Learning to fly [Song]. On *Into the Great Wide Open*. MCA.

Schubert, W. H. (with A. L. L. Schubert). (1980). *Curriculum books: The first eighty years*. University Press of America.

Top 10 bad beverage ideas: New Coke. (2019). In *Time*. http://content.time.com/time/specials/packages/article/0,28804,1913612_1913610_1913608,00.html

Silvernail, D. L. (1982). A solid introduction to U.S. curriculum heritage. *The Phi Delta Kappan, 63*(6), 423. https://www.jstor.org/stable/20386382

Van Brummelen, H. (1983). Curriculum books: The first eighty years by William Henry. *The Journal of Educational Thought, 17*(3), 269–272.

CHAPTER 23

EQUITABLE EDUCATIONAL INPUTS = SOCIAL JUSTICE FOR ALL

Kimberly K. Halley

Author/Book studied:

Darling-Hammond, L. (2010). *The flat world and education: How America's commitment to equity will determine our future.* Teachers College Press.

Just on the edge of Ohio's Appalachian region, my first administrative job allowed me to serve 835 elementary students, most of whom were growing up in rural impoverished homes. The school received government-assistance Title I funding due to the high percentage of students living below the federal poverty level. Nearly half of the students qualified for free and reduced lunches. Many others met the criteria, but family pride prevented the submission of documentation forms to school personnel. Maintaining the status quo was deeply ingrained in the community culture, both from

Curriculum Windows Redux, pages 273–284
Copyright © 2022 by Information Age Publishing
www.infoagepub.com
All rights of reproduction in any form reserved.

families and school district staff members. It seemed it had not occurred to most of the multigenerational residents of the district that rising above a lifestyle of poverty and making a "better life" for self through education, were options they could actualize. Despite the fact that my middle-class, working family resided in the surrounding geographical area less than 10 miles away from this community, the life of many residents was a different world to me as a new principal.

During my principal role, I observed families crippled by poverty. As I witnessed the lives of children negatively impacted by destitution, I began to understand their financial predicament was often caused by a series of unfortunate circumstances. A few instances of bad luck devastated homes with families living paycheck-to-paycheck to stay on top of the monthly bills. Caring school personnel did their best to support the impoverished children by donating resources from their personal wallets. School staff members often provided additional basic necessities as a way of helping families get ahead of expenses, such as gift cards at Christmas, socks and undergarments, warm clothes during the winter months, and additional food on the weekends or holidays. It was disappointing to the school staff when the caregivers of some children squandered the additional resources, however, we continued to fill the gap for basic survival needs.

I observed the negative impact on the lives of children in my school. Initially, I judged the resulting actions and the values of the parents and adults living in poverty. In time, I gave up judging the motives of the parents to provide for their children. Author Brené Brown (2015) captured my attitude transformation when she stated, "All I know is that my life is better when I assume that people are doing their best. It keeps me out of judgment and lets me focus on what is, and not what should or could be" (p. 113).

As a result of serving a school situated in an impoverished community, my leadership values became forever imprinted with a deep commitment to advocate for the education of poor and under-resourced children. I realized that an equitable and excellent education is the only hope to leave a life of poverty for some kids. My sense of urgency to equip every child for a future of prosperity continues to be fueled by that initial administrative experience over 10 years ago. My leadership approach continues to be propelled by this drive to provide an excellent education for all children today.

Throughout my career, my administrative roles and responsibilities have continued to expand to larger and more diverse districts in the state's capital city. My passion for equity in education has enlarged to encompass student groups beyond the economically disadvantaged. Leadership positions in central office administration afforded me opportunities to advocate for students from all marginalized groups, including English learners, students of color, and students identified in special education. Despite the fact that the barriers from students' homes vary in rural, suburban, and urban districts, the need for an equitable education remains the same for all school-aged children in the United States. Therefore, a book about equity and the U.S. education system by Linda Darling-Hammond was appealing to me.

THE AUTHOR'S ARGUMENT—EQUITY, ACCESS, AND OPPORTUNITY

In *The Flat World and Education: How America's Commitment to Equity Will Determine Our Future,* Linda Darling-Hammond (2010) advocates for the advancement of all children by way of a better U.S. education system. During her nine-chapter book, she weaves together research findings and statistics to challenge the past and present American educational reforms. The author provides a bipartisan critique of the educational policies birthed from both major U.S. political parties. An alarming possibility is surfaced by Darling-Hammond: that the current United States educational system actually perpetuates discrimination of race and ethnicity through "our continued comfort with profound inequality" (p. 8). This thought is disturbing to the reader. She goes on to argue that current U.S. educational policies and reform efforts enacted at the federal, state, and local government levels actually disadvantage the students they are intended to protect.

Darling-Hammond (2010) uses facts and figures to portray an educational crisis in the United States, much like the 1958 Soviet Union's victory in the Space Race with Sputnik was utilized to stir panic among citizens. The author leverages America's fear of the country's diminishing global power to strengthen support for education policy reform. She makes an argument that the U.S. educational system is stagnant while other developed countries accelerate student learning as measured by international assessments, such as Program of International Student Assessment. The influence of the Tyler rationale on standardized achievement tests, credited to traditionalist Ralph Tyler during the 1940s and 1950s, continues to linger as nations measure the learning of students on written assessments (Pinar et al., 2006).

Darling-Hammond (2010) utilizes a social justice platform to lobby for children from marginalized groups by way of an equitable education system. During the last 2 chapters, she details the ways in which the current U.S. educational policies and structures can be overhauled to provide equal opportunity for learning to all students. In return for drastic change of our current system, the author defends that education can be the mechanism for creating a more equitable society for all young people in the United States.

The author argues that our entire American society will be strengthened when we ensure that each student's *right to learn* is upheld. She believes political discourse heavily influences educational policy, schooling structures, and curriculum decision-making in our country. As a result, she places heavy blame on the country's legislators who maintain the status quo and refuse to equalize the American educational system. Darling-Hammond (2010) argues that the United States has the financial means to provide educational experiences that level the playing field for disadvantaged students. Her intended outcome of the text is to "motivate policy makers and practicing educators to act decisively and thoughtfully" (p. x). The author lobbies for a complete reinvention of American school reform.

Darling-Hammond (2010) addresses the widespread perception that U.S. schools are failing in quality and jeopardizing the future vitality of America. A startling statistic worth noting is that American students of color and low income children are more than three times as likely to be taught by educators who are less-qualified, inexperienced, ineffective, and not fully licensed. The current system of school funding creates many reasons that expert educators elect to be employed in schools with less diverse student populations. Accomplished teachers and principals are drawn to schools with wealthier communities which can afford higher salaries and other luxuries. Local dollars supplement state and federal education funds which result in appealing perks for teachers, such as higher competitive salaries and health coverage, more current teaching materials, and better physical facilities. The fact is that if a child is Black or poor in America, the likelihood is high that he/she will be assigned to an unskilled teacher. Darling-Hammond skillfully informs the reader about this unfair situation: The learning of students of color and low-income students is negatively impacted when they do not have access to proficient teachers. How can U.S. citizens allow this dismal reality to continue in our schools? The reader feels compelled to action for the correction of a long overdue injustice.

FINANCIAL MEANS

According to the author, lack of financial resources is not the barrier that prevents the U.S. education system from dramatically enhancing the learning of its students. She uses powerful statistics that are difficult to defend and contextualizes the impact of mediocre schooling on the larger society. She assigns a dollar amount paid by society when current school funding mechanisms allow high school drop-out rates to soar among certain groups of students. For example, we learn that our country has wasted more than $200 billion in wages, taxes, and social costs due to dropouts. Incarceration results in $50 billion lost wages and prison costs. MacInnes (2009) is cited for discovering that tens of billions are wasted each year on reforms that fail, fads that don't stick, unnecessary teacher turnover, avoidable special education placements, remedial education, grade retention, summer school, lost productivity, and jobs that move overseas. (pp. 61–62)

Furthermore, "States that would not spend $10,000 a year to ensure adequate education for young children of color spend over $30,000 a year to keep them in jail" (Darling-Hammond, 2010, p. 24). She seems to agree with the old adage "spend it now or spend it later." Our society could choose a more socially just manner in which to spend tax dollars. A greater portion of the United States federal and state tax base could be devoted toward educational inputs for children on the front end of lives. If this educational allocation were to occur, our society would significantly diminish the expenditure of prison costs later for the same young lives.

As spending ratios of schools are compared within the United States, we see it is common for the wealthiest school districts to outspend the poorest districts by 3:1 in the same state (Darling-Hammond, 2010). As a former principal of a Title I funded school, it seems unbelievably unjust that our country allows that statistic to be accurate. Our nation possesses the financial means to prevent this inequality from occurring. The schools who serve students from impoverished home environments need *more* resources to overcome deficits the children bring to school with them—not three times less.

COMPARISON TO OTHER COUNTRIES

In return for dramatic transformation of education, three small countries have enjoyed significant increases in student achievement over the last 30 years. Despite their many differences to the United States, the nations have dramatically improved multiple education measures, such as increased rankings on international assessments, higher graduation rates over 90%, and accelerated college admissions. The systematic strategies used by Finland, Korea, and Singapore are similar in the following ways:

1. Created equitable funding with incentives
2. Eliminated examinations that limited access
3. Revised national standards and curriculum
4. Developed national policies to promote teaching
5. Enabled ongoing teacher learning
6. Sustained long-term reforms

The nations cited as examples have dramatically altered their educational policy, teacher training systems, and resource allocation to ensure equitable access to learning opportunities. Darling-Hammond (2010) compares the faulty reform approaches utilized in the United States during the last decades with those used in other countries and nudges the reader to consider the possible impacts for the United States. When compared to other countries, the U.S. investment in education is "one of the most unequal in terms of inputs" (p. 12). In Chapter 7, she conducts a global contrast of investment in teacher quality between the United States and that of other developed countries.

ACCOUNTABILITY SYSTEMS

Darling-Hammond (2010) is critical of the testing regime in the United States and the "unintended negative consequences" that are produced with federal and state accountability systems (p. 97). She calls for a move away from the current testing system consisting of basic recall and multiple choice questions, in exchange for a more meaningful and authentic assessment to measure 21st century thinking skills. There is a detrimental impact in measuring student learning through single achievement tests alone. Darling-Hammond argues that high-stakes state tests consisting of low-level questions result in a low-level curriculum in the classroom. Precious learning time is wasted when teachers feel pressured to expose students to test preparation activities of reading short passages, filling in blanks on worksheets, and answering fundamental comprehension questions. To compound the pressure, some districts value student performance on state assessments to the degree that individual financial incentives are offered to educators who produce improved results.

Furthermore, state accountability system sanctions are issued for results that fall below state passage rate expectations. As a result, schools implement teaching and administrative practices which produce negative effects. In exchange for the desire to perform well on state assessments, school districts in my region of the state have become motivated to "play the numbers game." Unfortunately, educators have been found guilty of cheating, changing student test answers, deleting student enrollment records, and making decisions that help their passage rates appear higher. Schools have elected to scam the state accountability system rather than investing in teacher recruitment, retention, professional development, and training. Administrators and teachers have had their state-issued educator licenses revoked by the Department of Education, served jail time for criminal offenses, and shamed their communities by way of local media sources. The unintended consequences are all for the sake of earning higher scores on state assessments.

INPUTS, NOT OUTPUTS

Darling-Hammond (2010) argues that the current U.S. accountability system measures the outputs of the educational system. She appeals for the elimination of this unfair practice. She challenges our country to refrain from using student performance data to label low performing schools, to apply sanctions, and to issue compliance requirements that take precious educator time and effort. Most important, Darling-Hammond believes our country should stop punishing the children who become the collateral damage in a broken system. When schools withhold high school diplomas for unmet graduation requirements, students are unfairly punished for the result our country's educational system caused. Instead, U.S. policy should ensure equitable inputs into all school systems across the country. Schools which serve students from disadvantaged home environments need additional resources to enhance the educational experience. Darling-Hammond advocates for a complete redesign of U.S. education policy, rather than the stale and ineffective tactics currently utilized in American schools.

QUALITY EDUCATION

One of Darling-Hammond's (2010) strongest arguments is that the United States has the financial capacity to drastically improve the quality of education for all students. National and state funding are available to guarantee that all students in American schools have the essential elements for a 21st century education. She underscores the critical nature of deploying excellent teaching practices to all children in all communities through the development of excellent teachers. Darling-Hammond believes districts can deploy resources for robust teaching when there are "serious state efforts to develop strong preparation programs, systems of mentoring, and focused (teacher) performance assessments" (p. 233).

As I read Darling-Hammond's (2010) recommendations to improve educational quality in all American schools, I was reminded of a text by Ladson-Billings (2004). In *Landing on the Wrong Note: The Price We Paid for Brown*, she cites the problems with the 1954 *Brown v. Board of Education* decision. One critical misstep of the Supreme Court "separate but equal" ruling was not addressing the issue of the quality level of education needed in integrated schools and all schools. In support of equitable quality of schools, Ladson-Billings (2004) argues that "the only way to ensure more school desegregation is to disconnect schools altogether from local property taxes and reconstitute students as citizens of states, not merely residents of particular communities" (p. 10).

In my current role as a curriculum specialist and educational consultant to school leaders, I appreciate the emphasis Darling-Hammond (2010) places on equalizing the quality of education. Unfortunately, I have seen too many educators seek "the magic bullet" to school improvement efforts. They search for a new educational program or textbook series to purchase for a quick fix that will solve all of their student performance problems. On the contrary, Darling-Hammond's approach aims to improve education by strengthening teaching and learning across the country.

She argues that all students need a quality education in which classroom teachers refine their instructional craft over time. This practice should not be exclusive to school districts that have the local means to provide a rich learning environment for teachers. For teaching refinement to occur, ongoing and embedded professional development services are required. Time during the professional workday is needed for teacher reflection and collaboration with colleagues and specialists. Additional components of a quality education include current technologies and appealing learning materials for students. Physical environments that are safe, comfortable, and attractive are needed for robust learning to occur. Most importantly, food stability is required in order to optimize student concentration on complex learning activities. The school funding mechanism is broken in the United States and education policy is the lever that can begin to circumvent the current gridlock.

PROPOSED SOLUTIONS

The author's lingering question of the text is "What will it take to secure a constitutional right to equal educational opportunity for all the nation's children?" (Darling-Hammond, 2010, p. 98). She develops her thinking around policy system changes that are needed in five specific areas. She uses the success of other countries that have effectively improved their educational systems to identify five key elements that must be redesigned in the United States:

1. Meaningful learning goals
2. Intelligent, reciprocal accountability systems
3. Equitable and adequate resources
4. Strong professional standards and supports
5. Schools organized for student and teacher learning

For the above measures to become a reality in the United States, school funding must be centrally and equally funded from federal and state dollars. Currently, local financial resources supplement and enhance the learning that takes place. There is large economic disparity across communities in this country. As a result, students from wealthy communities experience greater opportunity for rigorous learning than others. Rather than allowing the current funding formula to continue, there must be an equitable investment on the important aspects of the country's educational system.

I concur with the author in wishing for an educational system in which all of the resources currently invested on state accountability systems could be reallocated to improve teaching and learning. If we put a dollar amount on resources currently spent on "test preparation" our country would realize a significant amount available for our vision of quality education and school improvement. There is an exorbitant cost to tutoring salaries; test prep materials and workbooks; the purchase of state testing materials and vendor scoring; and the instructional minutes devoted to increasing test scores before, during, and after school.

CRITIQUE TO HER ARGUMENTS

As an experienced school administrator, I have learned that people react to change from different perspectives. Some feel motivated to change because they view it is an ethical obligation, it is simply "the right thing" to do. During most of the text, Darling-Hammond (2010) stokes the ethical spark and relies on the audience's passion for social justice to make her argument. Readers who view change through this lens quickly agree with her plan to redesign schooling environments in all U.S. schools.

However, one critique to her argument is that not all readers will hold this stance. Therefore, I anticipate some readers will defend the current system and develop excuses for our country's inability to radically alter schools. I expect that some dissenters believe the United States cannot overcome the current challenges and will cite barriers due to the unique and diverse nature of our country. One likely argument will be that the United States has a diverse population and citizens possess a wide range of economic circumstances. Democracy promotes career choice, options, and economic stratification. Due to the nature of our democratic society, some will believe it is impossible to diminish the effects of the economic disparity of individuals and communities.

A frontrunner of excuses given will be the national expense to correcting the current method in which schools are funded. For central and equitable educational funding to occur, more resources will need to flow from national and state funds. In order for the disparity among school communities to be diminished, little to no local funding will be utilized. It is likely that the "haves" will not appreciate their share going to the "have nots."

A second critique to the text is the comparison of educational solutions and reform efforts utilized by other countries. Many readers will struggle with deploying the solutions in America that were enacted in nations dissimilar to us, such as Singapore, Finland, and South Korea. The reform efforts implemented in other countries that produced compelling results of higher student achievement on international assessments may not be appropriate or effective in the United States.

The third critique of Darling-Hammond's (2010) plan is based on recent failed attempts to transform U.S. schools on behalf of our diverse student populations. Among her list of five elements that must be redesigned in U.S. schools, she includes meaningful learning goals and intelligent, reciprocal accountability systems. However, the United States has attempted to implement both of these elements in reform initiatives to "close the achievement gap" during the last 2 decades.

The national learning goals determined in No Child Left Behind (NCLB) were aspirational and right-minded. It is difficult to criticize aspirations that all children in the country will read well and have appropriate mathematics skills. One component of the accountability system illuminated the achievement of our country's most vulnerable learners. For the first time in U.S. history, there was an emphasis on the learning of subgroups of students, such as economically disadvantaged, African American, and English language learners. Accountability systems established high learning expectations for all students, measured specific data points, and monitored results. Schools that did not meet the achievement expectations were issued punitive consequences. However, as the United States learned during the early 2000s, establishing meaningful educational goals without proper funding will not produce the results for which we strive.

The Common Core State Standards (CCSS) is another version of a recent failed attempt at national education reform in the United States. Much like Darling-Hammond suggests in the 2010 text, content experts and educator committees crafted ambitious curriculum statements. CCSS articulated what students should know and be able to do in English language arts and mathematics in Grades K–12. State consortiums were developed, called PARCC and Smarter Balance, to create assessments to measure the skills generated by addressing the Common Core State Standards. These assessment results served as the basis for state and federal accountability systems. However, these efforts churned political resistance from virtually all stakeholder groups in the United States. Educators, parents, and citizens were unified in their disdain for CCSS and the accompanying assessments. Despite their varying reasons for disapproval, the groups spoke loudly and clearly to U.S. state legislators. State policy makers quickly abandoned their commitment to CCSS and the revised assessment efforts.

As our country moves forward with the recent adoption and bipartisan support of Every Student Succeeds Acts (ESSA), there is a sense of renewed hope for educational reform. Perhaps ESSA will be different than the previous attempts to strengthen learning goals and accountability systems in the United States deployed through NCLB and CCSS. ESSA has the potential to implement additional elements from the 2010 plan of Darling-Hammond in *The Flat World and Education*.

PERSONAL CONNECTION

As I consider my experiences as a practicing administrator alongside the perspective of Darling-Hammond (2010), I fundamentally concur with most of her thoughts. Ethically, I stand for equality for all students in our country. Educational opportunity to engage in meaningful learning should be afforded to all children in our country, and "all" means all. Our country perpetuates discrimination when we allow impoverished and under-resourced communities to bear the financial burden of schooling. My earliest principal experience demonstrated that the children of high-poverty communities receive less than their portion for an excellent educational experience.

Many critiques of the U.S. education system ask the reasons that previous reforms did not effectively elevate learning for America's students. As a former building principal, central office leader in a large district, and regional educational specialist/consultant to many school systems, I can simply say the reasons are vast and complicated. To underscore the perspective of Ladson-Billings (2004) cited previously, the *quality* of education must be addressed to ensure an equitable education for all students. Simply "throwing money at the problem" is not the solution. Equitable funding alone will not relieve the pressure felt at the building and classroom level. In addition, complete educational systems and structures need to be enacted to develop the expertise of teachers and active leadership. An effective system of recruitment, training, and retention of educators is needed. The support of education stakeholders must be leveraged to address the political dynamics in the United States. We learned this critical lesson through the country's previous educational reforms, specifically NCLB and CCSS. My leadership experiences have taught me that large change initiatives need to provide a delicate balance of support and accountability for the educators implementing the enhancements.

CONCLUSION

Darling-Hammond (2010) adeptly convinces the reader that "the United States needs to move much more decisively than it has in the last quarter century to establish a purposeful, equitable education *system* that will prepare *all* our children for success in a knowledge-based society" (p. 2). She details out her thoughts on a plan to operationalize this vision. She lobbies for radical changes in educational inputs, such as educator recruitment, teacher preparation programs, ongoing professional development for active practitioners, and retainment in the field.

To summarize, "dismantling the institutionalized inequities that feed the racial, socioeconomic, and linguistic achievement gap will require substantive policy changes in redesigning schools, developing teachers and principals, expanding our conceptions of curriculum and assessment, rethinking funding strategies, and reconceptualizing accountability" (Darling-Hammond, 2010, p. 277). The mountainous challenge issued by Linda Darling-Hammond (2010) has a steep incline, but the view at the top of the slope will be worth the hard work required to make the climb. She believes in our country's will and capacity to create an educational system that appropriately serves the current and future learning needs of all our young people. America's impoverished and marginalized student groups are depending on us to change the system on their behalf.

REFERENCES

Brown, B. (2015). *Rising strong.* Spiegel & Grau.

Darling-Hammond, L. (2010). *The flat world and education: How America's commitment to equity will determine our future.* Teachers College Press.

Ladson-Billings, G. (2004). Landing on the wrong note: The price we paid for Brown. *Educational Researcher, 33*(7), 3–13.

MacInnes, G. (2009). *In plain sight: Simple, difficult lessons from New Jersey's expensive effort to close the achievement gap.* The Century Foundation.

Pinar, W. F., Reynolds, W. M., Slattery, P., & Taubman, P. M. (2006). *Understanding curriculum: An introduction to the study of historical and contemporary curriculum discourses.* Peter Lang.

CHAPTER 24

THE GRASS ISN'T ALWAYS GREENER ON THE OTHER SIDE

The Fraud and Corruption of Charter Schools and the Corrosion on the American Dream

Mindy Layne Jennings

Author/Book studied:

Fabricant, M., & Fine, M. (with Foreword by D. Meier). (2012). *Charter schools and the corporate makeover of public education: What's at stake?* Teachers College Press.

We have all been there at one or more times in our lives. We want the American Dream. We want the best that we can obtain. And when it comes to our children, we are no different. In fact, some would argue to say parents will do

Curriculum Windows Redux, pages 285–296
Copyright © 2022 by Information Age Publishing
www.infoagepub.com
All rights of reproduction in any form reserved.

anything to make sure their children can have the opportunities they were not provided while growing up in their generation. As parents, we want our children to get the best education they can. We want them to have the best opportunity of building their own lives one day and living their own American Dream.

Once the traditional public school system was accused as having failing schools across the nation, the charter school movement began (especially for profit, private charter schools). Charter schools brought the promise to do a better job than the traditional public school system. By providing a choice where children can attend school, parents had the ability to eliminate the barrier of only one choice. Parents could now withdraw their children from their home school and enroll them in a charter school. Charters also promised to decrease marginalization of minority youth and offer equality in education. With the hope and promise of providing a better education, many parents jumped through the window for their child's chance of greener pasture.

I will admit I was disappointed when Dr. Poetter assigned this particular book to me. There were some really good books that I wanted to read and reflect upon. Instead, I was given a book that was #9 on my list of 15 books he shared with us that evening in class. I was shocked. I couldn't believe this was the book he had chosen for me. I looked the book over some more that evening. *Charter Schools and the Corporate Makeover of Public Education,* written by Michael Fabricant and Michelle Fine (2012), with a Foreword by Deborah Meier. The only thing I could get excited about were the authors, which included a social worker and social psychologist. I kept thinking the entire night, "What in the world am *I* going to do with this book? I am a psychologist. I deal with mental health diagnoses and learning problems in kids every day. What in the world do *I* have to contribute to a book about business and charter schools?"

I decided to think about how I would become engaged in this assignment. After all, I was extremely excited about being a part of this cohort journey in publishing a book. So how was I going to make the best of what I was given? I know from reading Dr. Poetter's article on this project that he puts a lot of thought into what books would be included and who would be assigned each book in the collection (Poetter, 2018). I talked about the book choice to others. That didn't help, as no one had any interest in the topic, either. Some colleagues didn't even let me finish the title of the book before they shared their displeasure in the topic and didn't want to hear anything about it. I then told myself that it should, at least, be a semi-easy read. Maybe I would learn something about the negativity behind charter schools and become well informed in its history. As a result, I would actually be able to debate the topic with knowledge. This would certainly be a positive, since it would allow me to debate with facts, rather than the normal negative phrasing heard from others within the traditional public education system.

After sitting down at my local Panera Bread, I spent the better part of my Saturday that weekend reading the book from cover to cover. I have to admit, I learned quite a few things about the birth and process of charter schools. The book was definitely a lesson learned in the history of how charter schools came to be, what their original intent or purpose sought to accomplish, and where they are now. The book additionally provided the inception of politics and corporations into the charter school movement and how this has affected the charter school's initial purpose. I came to respect the original intent behind the charter school movement. I could understand and have empathy with why it appeared to be a logical answer to so many schools failing to provide an equal education to all. However, despite my respect for the charter school movement's genesis, I realized just how much had changed from the initial purposes of the movement, and how much greed had come to prey on the American people.

THE BEGINNING

Charter schools were originally born out of the release of the 1983 federal government report: *A Nation at Risk* (National Commission on Excellence in Education, 1983). *A Nation at Risk* documented the proposed weaknesses of the failing American public school system. The public-school side of the grass instantly became less green. The report caused major damage to the once green grass in the public-school system's window. Charter schools promised a greener pasture to the American people. They promised change, and maybe a better alternative. If you lived within a failing school district, you no longer needed to uproot your family and move somewhere else to provide your children with a good education. The place where you live should no longer determine the type of education your children would receive. If the grass wasn't greener where you lived, you could enroll your child in a charter school. Charter schools proposed competition and innovation as providing parental and community choice to public school education with the hopes that competition would instigate the failing public schools to do better (Gajendragadkar, 2006).

Charter schools also promised an alternative to parents who did not want their children to be subjected to statewide assessments and their consequences. Charter schools were going to help parents take back control of their child's education from the government. Education decisions needed to be placed back into the hands of the community, youth, and parents. It needed to encompass small areas to create stronger school systems.

Curriculum in public schools have historically chosen to leave out pieces which were not favorable to the European American. When history is provided in pieces, specifically leaving out parts which make up our identity, an impairment in our intelligence, informed action and functional competence occurs. As curriculum in the traditional public school system honored European Americans and did not include many instances in which they would be considered less favorable, they also left out many of the pieces of history contributing to the development of African Americans. As a result, the distorted and incomplete views created a marginalization on African Americans and their contribution to the history of creating America (Pinar et al., 2008). Charter schools proposed being able to decrease the marginalization of poor, Black communities that public education had failed to eradicate (Fabricant & Fine, 2012). By proposing the ability to decrease marginalization within the poor, Black population, the charter school was going to provide these families a better choice for education. The charter schools were going to give these families their greener pasture.

In the beginning, charter schools began receiving an average of 20% less funding than traditional public schools. Beginning charter schools built smaller schools and enrolled fewer students, with the hope that students could receive more direct support in the learning environment. However, Charter schools quickly realized the amount of funding they were receiving was not going to be nearly enough to operate their facilities. To help with funding, they turned to philanthropists and corporations. Although this more often provided Charter schools with funding that exceeded the expenditures in public schools per student, it also came with a hefty price. With this funding came greed and the need for those supporting the Charter schools with funds to begin controlling the day-to-day operations. They began dictating who they could accept in the school and how many students the school would enroll. With larger enrollments, more funds could be at their disposal.

Once charter schools began to increase their enrollment numbers, their performance began to decline and oversight of capacity grew more and more relaxed (Fabricant & Fine, 2012). More students would bring in more and more money. What once started with good intentions to do better than the traditional public school system in the best interests of all children, soon reflected the very things charters promised the public they would change and do better.

From this onset of greed from corporations, the education of children and their best interests began to fade away (Fabricant & Fine, 2012). Along with the private money came corporations' own rules and regulations, resulting in a bigger need for greed than the need to help in educating young minds.

THE LAND OF OPPORTUNITY

It did not take long for opportunistic individuals to realize there was money, and a lot of it, to be made off of the charter school industry. And like a wolf in sheep's clothing, they swept in for the prey and fed off the parents' desires to provide a better education for their children. The wolf's only agenda, though, in nearly every case, was to maximize profit. The corporate education wolf guides the parents to the window to look at the lush green grass. It is much more appealing to the eye. The sun is shining, and all of the opportunities are there for the land to grow and prosper. It offers the opportunity of a better education than that of the traditional public school that is failing their children. The wolf makes the case that the grass does not grow equally across the field and creates unnecessary hurdles for their children to overcome. Once he has gathered his flock and begins to gain money from each enrollment, the wolf sits back and collects what he has earned.

THE MONEY TRAIN KEEPS ON COMING

During the 1990s, the federal government began to financially support the charter school movement. The Public Charter Schools Program (PCSP), enacted by Congress in 1995, allocated 6 million dollars for the initial start-up of charter schools. By the year 2001, this amount had grown to 190 million dollars annually (Gajendragadkar, 2006). Charter schools now receive more than 9 billion dollars per year in public funds (DeJarnatt, 2011). The Department of Education also became involved by aggressively allocating funds to conferences and studies (Gajendragadkar, 2006). With this large amount of money and general lack of funding oversight, there is a lot of room for corruption and fraud.

Charter schools are operated by a governing board. They are also funded largely by taxpayer money. Charter school boards frequently consist of the founder and members who have a strong relationship with the CEO (Dejarnett, 2011). Subcontracting a for-profit education management organization (EMO) or a nonprofit charter management organization (CMO), is another option frequently chosen by the charter school board. The subcontracted responsibility can vary. They range from payroll to running the entire school (Fabricant & Fine, 2012). Both options expose a business interest, instead of an educational interest. And in many cases, board members have multiple interests and interests shared with each other. Sharing multiple interests leaves the charter school system open to a high risk of conflicting transactions and making decisions which are not in the best interest of their school (DeJarnett, 2011). One common example includes board members who are also the landlord and the tenant (DeJarnett, 2011). When board members have dual interests, they may find it hard to adhere to their duty of care and loyalty to their charter school. Instead, they make decisions based in the best interests of their personal finances (DeJarnatt, 2011). Because the school organization is run like a business, the public is not aware these practices are not always in the best interest of educating their children. What's even more deceptive are the commercial, radio, and billboard advertisements, which lure the public into thinking the education provided in a charter school is the better option. The advertisements build the deception of making education better than what their children can have in the traditional public system. All of this adds to the wolf's ability to promise the parents the lush and greener grass through the charter school window. The wolf's interests, however, revolve around his personal financial gain.

Ohio, like many states across the United States, did not incorporate regulations limiting the number of charter schools that could open within the state or provide oversight on regulations. Therefore, there were no requirements and no credentials needed to own and operate a charter school in the state of Ohio. Many charter schools were owned and operated by individuals with no educational history. Many were opened solely for the purpose of making money, often at the educational expense of children.

THE FIGHT FOR CHANGE

Greed found its way into city wide tragedies. After Katrina hit New Orleans and so many of the public buildings were destroyed, the wolf swooped in again with the promise of improving education in a city known for its supposedly failing school system. However, with privatization, came more segregation, pushing families out of New Orleans, particularly those of color and poverty. Many of these families could not return to New Orleans in the wake of Katrina, due to their public school being destroyed and the charter school not accepting their children at enrollment. They promised better education, but what they really promised were more segregated schools, enrolling students that were White and not low income. Eventually, laws were made to regulate charter schools, which soon outnumbered the public schools in New Orleans, to accept at least 10% of their students from marginalized populations (students of color, students living in poverty, students with special needs). However, without proper oversight, these charter schools continued to do business as usual (Fabricant & Fine, 2012).

SEED schools such as those in Washington, DC, which were highlighted in the documentary *Waiting for "Superman"* (Guggenheim, 2010), have been reported as retaining, suspending, and expelling students excessively (Fabricant & Fine, 2012, p. 50). Additionally, once this decline spirals and the student leaves, the charter school students are not coded as "dropouts." When students are coded as "dropout," it is negatively reflected on the school's data report. Many of these students then return to the public school system (Fabricant & Fine, 2012), where they (public school) will be held accountable for the growth and outcome of these students. If the student does drop out of a public school, it is reported within their building and district public data system. In the public school system, there is not an option when a student withdraws to drop out of school. It must be coded as such, resulting in the negative impact on the district reporting system.

Many charter schools also require parent participation with volunteering and also signed contracts with specific requirements which may include a grade point average minimum, hours of weekly reading at home, and so forth. If the parents do not comply or refuse to sign the contract, the student is not accepted and/or is withdrawn and forced to go back to the public school system (Fabricant & Fine, 2012).

With these types of practices in place revolving around behavior and academic consequences, the charter school can then retain the top students and therefore the charter schools' academic success appears better than it really is. The public school does not have the option of turning away students, regardless of their race, gender, socioeconomic status, special needs, or other "less favorable" differences from the "typical" highest achieving students. Thereby compounding the negative look of the grass on their side of the window. Is the public school system really the one that should be blamed in these cases? Where is the responsibility and the data to demonstrate the lack of appropriate education by the charter school which gave up on these students? The charter school grass, instead, grows greener with results from their selected "typical" highest achieving students.

As you can see, charter schools have found a way to keep the deception alive by choosing their population to teach. In the traditional public school, leaders cannot keep certain students from enrolling. The traditional public school must record all "dropout" and "expulsion" numbers. The traditional public school must provide education, regardless if the child is passing, attending regularly, or has a disability which may affect the outcome of their report card. If the traditional public school system were reporting on only their top students who come to school every day with motivation, dedication, no significant disabilities or mental health illnesses, no trauma induced behaviors, living at home with all of their needs met, feeling safe in their home, and having both parents within the home, the traditional public school system's report card would look much more appealing to the citizens in their community. The grass would look much greener from their view through the window.

Chicago also fell victim to the greed of philanthropists and large corporations and politicians over what was in the best interest of children. Public schools deemed as "failing" were closed and charter schools were opened in their place. However, many neighborhood students were not allowed in the new charter schools. Students from closed public schools were also significantly less likely to attend summer programs and also were subjected to a higher chance of transferring to a third school. The poorest communities were facing gentrification and were in mostly African American communities. In this process, educators, community members, and parents are left out of the decision-making process about which schools are to be closed and who can and should attend the reopened charter schools (Fabricant & Fine, 2012). This was another promise not kept by the charter school initiative and proving again that they are no longer in the best interest of every child's education. They are no longer doing a better job at educating youth and providing equality among all students.

These consequences have not only hit the larger cities. Recently in Ohio, the state was forced to shut down the state's largest virtual academy charter school. Electronic Classroom of Tomorrow (ECOT) created a highly publicized scandal, being exposed for fake enrollment numbers, which largely inflated the amount of money it was receiving in funding. And with state politicians being paid campaign funds from the ECOT CEO, no one required ECOT to produce its enrollment records for several years. Ultimately, ECOT was forced to close once it was mandated to give back $60 million in funds collected fraudulent for false enrollment. It could no longer afford to stay open and pay for teachers' salaries and other necessary bills to stay operational (Kilpatrick, 2017).

Teachers were left without jobs and students were left without a place to obtain an education. Charter schools do not have teachers' unions, so the released teachers had little recourse when let go. Unfortunately, these teachers were left to look for new employment in the middle of the school year, at a time where there are not many immediate openings.

Additionally, due to the overnight applications being submitted from students who attended ECOT, some of these students waited for weeks or longer to be accepted. Some returned to their home district, which occurred immediately, due to obligations mandated to the local school district. Charter schools are not mandated the same in this area. Charter schools are not mandated to enroll a student as soon as they arrive. Students are left in the mercy of the charter schools timeline. If a charter school is not staffed well and is experiencing an increased flux in applications, it can take weeks, or even months, for the student to start receiving school services. And with their increase in admittance, these charter schools will now have to hire staff as well. However, charter schools are also not under the same staff to student ratio as traditional public schools. The amount of students in each classroom can double that of the union negotiated ratio in a public school system. A ratio which is kept within appropriate guidelines for optimal learning environments. These high numbers in the classroom result in the students having less and less instructional time and direct time with the teacher when needed. And what happened to the ECOT students that weren't going to ECOT regularly? Where are they? And who is keeping track of where they are? Speculation would lead you to believe that a percentage of the ECOT students are not in school anywhere.

HOW ARE CHARTER STUDENTS PERFORMING ACADEMICALLY?

With lax policy and therefore a lack of oversight in place, research studies have proven that traditional public schools are outperforming charter schools. National evaluations and studies have documented, over more than a 10-year period, the outcomes of performance across the United States comparing charter schools to traditional public schools. While charter enrollment almost always offers parents a choice to have their students not be subjected to annual statewide and high stakes testing, it would appear that charter schools' curriculum most commonly incorporates a lower standard of learning. We also know that a significant number of charter school students either leave on their own after 2–3 years or are not allowed to return to the charter school due to their inability to adhere to the guidelines at the school. Once students go from charter schools back into their public school, the children most often have skill sets below the grade level placement and the skill sets of their peers. This creates often debilitating consequences for socialization, social emotional well-being, and makes it more difficult for the students to be ready for life beyond high school.

As a licensed and practicing school psychologist in the traditional public school system since 2000, I have also experienced many challenging outcomes due to the general failure of the charter school system. One of the major challenges is providing the correct support for students as they reenter the traditional public system, typically two to three grade levels behind their grade placement. Many of the students are marked for intensive intervention after benchmark assessment results report former charter school students as being the lowest performing in their grade level. Many of the students I have experienced coming back, will often have the same academic skill set as when they left. Students who may have been a few months behind, now are years behind their peer academic development. The public school immediately begins intensive intervention. However, due to significant delays in student growth over time, it is very difficult for students to ever close the academic gap. As they grow academically, their peers are also growing. As a result, many students left behind are eventually referred for an evaluation for special education eligibility. While many may be found eligible for special education services due to their academic gaps being below their ability and grade placement, the majority of them most likely do not have a specific learning disability, but rather have an assessment profile much like those who do. Due to their skill set being years below, they need the most intensive direct instruction they can receive. There are many obvious negative outcomes and numerous questions in these situations. As we all know, there is a negative impact emotionally with being diagnosed with a disability. When this could have been avoided, it is that much more troubling to know identification must proceed. Additionally, federal funding is provided for those students with disabilities. Are we really allocating these funds to children with disabilities? Or are we allocating funds to help with teaching children who received a lack of good instruction by charter schools? Is the charter grass always greener, as promised by the wolf? Are the students receiving a better education? Are the charter schools having more success than the public school system?

MARGINALIZATION IS BECOMING WORSE

Charter schools, with the entrance of corporate greed, have created greater marginalization in poor Black communities, resulting in the opposite effect of their original goal. Charter schools had the ability and opportunity to decrease segregation and racial isolation by offering no boundaries enrollment, something public schools could not provide. Unfortunately, over the years, with the involvement of donations from large corporations and philanthropists, the hopes of being able to improve segregation and racial isolation, have become less and less achievable (Gajendragadkar, 2006). Additionally, charter schools increase racial isolation due to White charter school students being less likely to attend schools with large minority populations. Furthermore, minority students in charter schools are more likely to attend charter schools with a majority of other minority students, while White students tend to be exposed to other White students (Gajendragadkar, 2006).

WHERE DO WE WATER THE GRASS?

Many scholars have noted over history that the "fabric of society frays when we invest unequally or disinvest in public education" (Fabricant & Fine, 2012, p. 90). Inequality has lasting effects on everyone in a society (Fabricant & Fine, 2012). Instead of watering what we have, we jump to the other side, only to find out that it also has its weaknesses. What we are left with is both sides looking the same, instead of one side actually being greener. If we invest in our public school system instead and water our side of the grass, we can make major improvements.

Such is the case in New Jersey and California. It has not been easy and has evolved over a period of time, but these states are seeing real results in closing the academic gap and decreasing marginalization in African

American and Hispanic populations (Fabricant & Fine, 2012). Another interesting bit to their success has occurred with strong teacher-unions within their state. Since the inception of the charter school reform, supporters belittle teacher unions and see them as being a great evil among the failure of public-school systems (Fabricant & Fine, 2012). New Jersey has proven that we need to support our teacher unions and trust that our teachers can be part of the reform within the traditional public school system to shape solutions and strategies to build better public-school education for all students (Fabricant & Fine, 2002).

WHERE DO WE GO FROM HERE?

There are so many opportunities to make the grass greener on our side, if we didn't annually have over 9 billion dollars being funneled out of the system into the charter schools. Our grass could grow and be greener than either side. Provided with more funding, the traditional public school system can afford to place counselors, social workers, and school psychologists at every grade level to help with social and emotional needs. We could focus on the whole child to improve the quality of education overall. We could afford to provide students with real life experiences exposing them to field trips with academic connections, instead of asking for the funds from the PTO which collects money from fundraisers that children and parents work at raising. We could afford a low classroom ratio of students to teacher and lower number ratios so that they may have more time to meet the needs of each child on their caseload. We could incorporate more professional development to grow as a staff and incorporate research effective programming into our day. There are numerous opportunities to make our grass grow greener. Why take money away and give it to charter schools that are not educating youth any better and sometimes courting fraud, broken promises, and corruption? We all look through that window and see and perceive that someone else is doing better than we are. We could possibly jump through the window and have the best there is for our children. If only the American Dream could be achieved by jumping through a window and landing on the greener grass on the other side.

While charter schools are not required to administer statewide assessments, they are still held accountable for providing evidence of the results they have promised. If the charter schools are failing, local school boards, school districts, and other governing agencies can eliminate the charter school (Gajendragadkar, 2006). Funding would then follow students back to the district.

There appears to be no easy answer. But one thing is for certain; if charter schools are here to stay, they need more provisions, and the goal and purpose cannot be a financial gain. Instead of creating charter schools, there is a need to invest in the traditional public school and continue to make improvements for all children.

REFERENCES

DeJarnatt, S. (2012). Follow the money: Charter schools and financial accountability. *The Urban Lawyer, 44*(1), 37–83. http://www.jstor.org/stable/41638068

Fabricant, M., & Fine, M. (2012). *Charter schools and the corporate makeover of public education: What's at stake?* Teachers College Press.

Gajendragadkar, S. S. (2006). The constitutionality of racial balancing in charter schools. *Columbia Law Review, 106*(1), 144–181. http://www.jstor.org/stable/4099463

Guggenheim, D. (2010). *Waiting for "Superman"* [Documentary film]. Walden Media; Participant Media.

Kilpatrick, M. (2017). *Troubled charter school ECOT becomes focus of Ohio attorney general's race.* http://www.cleveland.com/open/index.ssf/2017/10/troubled_charter_school_ecot_b.html

National Commission on Excellence in Education. (1983, April). *A nation at risk: The imperative for educational reform.* https://edreform.com/wp-content/uploads/2013/02/A_Nation_At_Risk_1983.pdf

Pinar, W. F., Reynolds, W. M., Slattery, P., & Taubman, P. M. (2008). *Understanding curriculum: An introduction to the study of historical and contemporary curriculum discourses.* Peter Lang.

Poetter, T. S. (2018). *Opening curriculum windows: Curriculum pasts interpreted today by tomorrow's scholars.* Miami University.

CHAPTER 25

LOOKING THROUGH A KEYHOLE

Attempting to Shift the Paradigm

Kristine T. Michael

Author/Book studied:

Delpit, L. (2012). *"Multiplication is for White people": Raising expectations for other people's children.* The New Press.

We may be uncomfortable talking about race, but we can no longer afford to be silent. We have chosen a profession that—like parenting—requires us to put our comforts second to those of children.

—Jamilah Pitts

I was assigned Lisa Delpit's 2012 book, *"Multiplication Is for White People": Raising Expectations for Other People's Children.* In it, the author examines the previous several decades' attempts at education reforms and their many failures. Prior to this assignment, I was not familiar with Lisa Delpit. The

---

Curriculum Windows Redux, pages 297–306
Copyright © 2022 by Information Age Publishing
www.infoagepub.com
All rights of reproduction in any form reserved.

author has divided her book into sections surrounding birth, elementary years, adolescence, and university. At some points I found myself feeling defensive while reading what she had to say. While I am often very aware of gender differences, especially as a female administrator, I was not as aware of the racial issues that Delpit surfaces. As an educator, I try to be very aware of my privilege as a White educator and honor and respect all cultures. I refocused my reading with the lens of looking for the window that the author was helping me to look through.

The stories the author shared of her own daughter did not necessarily resonate with me as much as I would have expected. Her stories reminded me of a board member who makes all their decisions for a school district based on their own child's experience, rather than reflecting on all children within the district. Yet on the other hand, while reflecting back on previous doctoral coursework on critical race theory, perhaps the author is not wrong. As a White educator with White children, I believe that the author would see me as unable to view racism from the inside, but only as one on the outside looking in, almost as if through a keyhole, even though I am straining to see what is inside. Perhaps I am unable to see as I live and work in an environment that are both very homogeneously White.

A certain line jumped out from the first chapter: "One reason for the lack of African American academic success in schools is that many poor African American students are simply not being taught" (Delpit, 2012, p. 8). The author goes on to explain how there is no academic achievement gap at birth and that preschool is not an inoculation for lack of achievement. This made me think about the research paper I wrote for Dr. Saultz on early childhood education, specifically Head Start and publicly funded preschools. Those research studies in favor of publicly funded preschool cited other studies that didn't focus on race as much as they did socioeconomic levels. Those research studies presented results that demonstrated a positive gain from publicly funded preschool for all children, but specifically students from lower socioeconomic families.

I've been thinking hard about how to hook my reader with a window metaphor. I've decided to settle on the metaphor of a keyhole as a type of window that allows you to look through a narrow opening from the outside in or the inside out. I believe this keyhole metaphor captures the author's assertion that one challenge in education is that the majority of U.S. students are a minority, while the teaching force is overwhelmingly White. I can't remember if it was the author or another who would have called me "Teaching While White."

I believe a keyhole is a type of a window. I believe while I can learn and reflect on my own teaching practices, I am not an African American so I am on one side of the door looking through a keyhole into the lives of the African American students that I am teaching. The author, an African American, is looking at education through the keyhole of her own race.

Delpit (2012) uses Beverly Tatum's comparison between smog and racism. To paraphrase, Tatum says that just like people who live in LA breathe smog without even being aware of its existence, White Americans are breathing in racism, power, and dominance with almost no awareness of it. Just like the majority would not want to breathe in smog if they were aware of the smog, the majority would not want to breathe in racism. Yet, just like a city with smog, racism is present and often invisible. As a White educator participating in Miami's doctoral cohort, I have had many opportunities to look at my own practices through the lens of critical race theory, a frame of which I was previously not aware of. My family now accuses me of seeing racism everywhere, which in turn has led them to feel defensive. As a family who believes strongly in equity and one who spent a year living in Africa, it is hard for them to see the things I am pointing out as examples of invisible racism. It's as if they are unaware of the smog surrounding them. In an attempt to be able to have a small glimpse of the window in which Delpit views the world, we moved to an environment that was as different from our homogeneously White "bubble."

DAKAR, SENEGAL—AUGUST, 2012

Stepping off the plane, we were a very few dots of white in a sea of black. More than anything, excitement welled inside of me at the opportunity that lay in front of us. I had done it. I had ripped off the mantle of being afraid and made a jump across a vast crevasse from the White side of the Atlantic Ocean to the Black side of that same ocean. I was tired of being afraid. I did not believe being afraid was a reasonable reaction to being surrounded by people whose skin was another color than mine, but it was the one being hammered into not only me, but my children as well, by the media.

I had a deep desire to expose my children to life outside the White bubble we live within. While as a family, we did not seek out a White bubble to live within, we live in the same small college town that my husband and I grew up in. You'd think the presence of a liberal arts college would be enough to help the community diversify, yet it has not had that effect. Minority children make up less than 8% of the student body, with African Americans a mere 2.5%. Those numbers have held firm for more than the 3 decades since my husband and I graduated.

Trying to raise tolerant children is different than raising children who understand that they are a part of the cultural power apparatus, not just economically, but simply by the hue or color of their skin. I believe my children are very tolerant and will verbally defend any student who is being made to feel "less than," due to the color of their skin, their special education identification, or socioeconomic status. They do not hesitate to challenge their classmates if they do or say something that they feel is intolerant of "others." I wanted something more for us. I sought the opportunity for us to be the "others."

THE HISTORY OF LISA DELPIT

Lisa Delpit is a professor at Southern University, in her hometown of Baton Rouge, Louisiana. The Baton Rouge, Louisiana, of her childhood was a pre-integrated one. She went on to attend Antioch College in Ohio, known then and now for its radicalism. As a student there, Delpit learned progressive teaching strategies, which she took with her into the classroom in her early teaching experiences in Philadelphia, with a class that was 60% poor African American and 40% wealthy White children. It was there that Delpit came to the conclusion that her students did not learn in the same ways. It was these experiences that led to the well-known essay, *The Silenced Dialogue: Power and Pedagogy in Educating Other People's Children* (Delpit, 1988). Delpit went on to obtain her master's and doctorate at Harvard University with a focus on urban education and the connection between culture and learning. Awarded the MacArthur "Genius" Fellowship 1990 for her work, Delpit is viewed as an expert on teaching and learning in multicultural environments.

The title of Delpit's 2012 book *"Multiplication Is for White People": Raising Expectations for Other People's Children*, refers to an incident a colleague described occurring with a student she was tutoring in math. The student wanted to know why the tutor was bothering trying to teach him multiplication since adding and subtracting is for Black people and multiplication is for White people. This starkly illustrates an unintended curriculum that the student had perceived from schooling. In *The Educational Imagination*, Eisner (2002) describes the intended or explicit curricula, which is the content that schools intend to teach, or believe they are teaching, and the implicit or hidden curriculum, which reflects how students are socialized as a result of the school's structure.

"The upper and middle class send their children to school with all the accoutrements of the culture of power" (Delpit, 1988, p. 283). Delpit witnessed occasions in both her own classroom and in the many observations she has conducted in classrooms across the United States that capture a disconnect between what the teacher believes he or she is teaching and what the children are learning. "Success is predicated upon acquisition of the culture of those who are in power" (Delpit, 1988, p. 283).

COLOR WAS NOT THE ONLY DIFFERENCE

What I did not realize until we were firmly entrenched within the expat community, was that despite being a racial minority, we were still the ones who held the economic power. I was expected to employ several local people to work within my household and pay them a "fair" wage. Fair represented a salary that was higher than what they would earn if they were working in the local economy, but certainly not what I would consider a living wage.

We had a housekeeper named Martine. We paid her the equivalent of $300 a month. She worked 8 hours a day, 5 days a week, and did all our cleaning, shopping, and cooking. She also kept me alive while I was deathly sick with malaria. In addition to her salary, she was "afforded" the opportunity to shower each day before leaving for home. I also chose to pay her grandson's school supplies and $100/quarter to attend a private Catholic school as the local schools were extremely subpar and had over 70 children per classroom. The Catholic school education would not be comparable at all to the education my children were receiving at the international school where I was a curriculum director. Her grandson came to work with her when he did not have school and I told her to eat anything she wanted while she was in the home. She very infrequently did so, instead choosing to bring a baguette to work from the bakeries that provided the government subsidized bread at $.50 per loaf. She would buy it on her walk to work, from any number of vendors. It usually came wrapped in newspaper.

Mountaka was our day guard. We paid him $200 a month. He worked from 7 a.m. to 7 p.m., 7 days a week. If he needed a day off, he would substitute with the night guard or enlist another guard to fill his spot. Our home did not have an outdoor toilet or shower for his use as many homes did. He had to walk to the nearest mosque to use the bathroom. Mountaka started his day walking my two dogs for me and then moved on to washing the car each day. While I felt a daily washing seemed unnecessary, it was a very dusty environment with the majority of roads being without tarmac or pavement. Black guards around the city could be seen washing cars every morning, not just of the White expats, but of all those who had the means to employ a guard.

Sevryn was Martine's husband. He was our night guard. He worked from 7 p.m. to 7 a.m. He would often come early to work so that he could eat dinner as I would create plates of left overs for both Mountaka and Sevryn. It killed me everyday that I was inside eating the dinner his wife had prepared us while they were outside. Yet if I had not made plates for them, they too would have eaten the government subsidized bread.

As Pinar et al. (2008) points out, "Race is a complex, dynamic, and changing construct. Like gender, race is not a biological given, and the cultural weight it has been made to bear is out of all proportion to any biological or morphological differences among groups of people" (p. 316). I went to Africa expecting that the change in the majority of race from White to Black was going to change things. I had not accounted for the cultural weight that would still exist due to socioeconomic differences. In the 2017 Denevi and Chandler-Ward's (2017), *Teaching While White* podcast, the hosts state that, "White privilege is a system of advantage based on race." I would argue that we need to look into the complicated relationship between not only race, but that of socioeconomic power, which is where the theoretical framework of critical race theory comes into the conversation. Within that framework, multiplication would also only be for well-off children, not for those living within poverty. Perhaps the keyhole through which Delpit (2012) peers is too narrowly defined by her own race and should expand to include socioeconomic inequalities. In that way, the keyhole allows race to look through from each side of the door, but also allows for socioeconomic power to be on either side of a door as well.

> When we speak of the "white race" or the "Black race" ..., we speak in biological "misnomers," and more generally in metaphors. Those metaphors and "misnomers" not only have resulted in massive suffering and oppression but have also been used to organize the "white" world, including the American school curriculum and the curriculum field. (Pinar et al., 2008, p. 316)

I believe Delpit would encourage all of us in education to be more aware that those differences are entrenched in American schools and that in order to help eradicate them, we must make some shifts in how we are teaching our students.

Some people have generalized Delpit's work too much saying, for instance, that Delpit is opposed to the writing process and believes in skill-based instruction. When you read the actual texts she wrote and listen to interviews with Delpit, you'll find that what she is opposed to are practices such as whole language. She believes whole language practices do not give minority children what they need to be successful in mainstream society. Occasionally, Delpit is used to demonize writing work such as Donald Murray's, yet I believe that interpretation is a very narrow view of what Delpit was concerned with when it comes to educating students from the marginalized cultures. "Teaching children who are not a part of the culture of power in a school setting which is part of the culture of power is teaching across cultures" (Delpit, 1991, p. 541). Delpit herself has come out and stated that she is "definitely not against writing process or writing process theory. My focus is constantly on starting where kids are" (p. 543).

As Anderson's (2017) article points out:

> If you're in an advantaged position in society, believing the system is fair and that everyone could just get ahead if they just tried hard enough doesn't create any conflict for you ... [you] can feel good about how [you] made it. [...] But for those marginalized by the system—economically, racially, and ethically—believing the system is fair puts them at conflict with themselves and can have negative consequences. (para. 5)

This gets to the heart of what Delpit is trying to get across and I strain to see through the keyhole. To quote Pinar (1975), the goal of the self-examination process is to explore the question: "What has been and what is now the nature of my educational experience?" (p. 2).

"During this time, the student has been immersed in a culture that is so naturally a part of our way of life, that is it is almost taken for granted. In that culture called schooling, there are certain publicly explicit goals: teaching children to read and write..." (Eisner, 2002, p. 87).

CAN WE SEE OUR WAY THROUGH?

As Eisner (2002) states, "It is important to realize that what schools teach is not simply a function of covert intentions; it is largely unintentional. What schools teach they teach in the fashion that the culture itself teaches (p. 93). Delpit not only struggles against a system, but also against society whose "Recognition of the impact of the hidden, implicit curriculum is relatively new" (Eisner, 2002, p. 93). I believe that I would still argue with Lisa Delpit (2012) that there are so many contributing variables to the lack of school success for not just majorities, but also for those who are identified as socio-economically challenged; that education as a whole needs to focus on using instructional practices that go beyond barriers. Educators need to have an awareness of the multilayered challenges that they face including "the exclusion of third-world literature from school literature courses reveal[ing] the political aspect of canon formation" (Pinar et al., 2008, p. 315), as well as to the existence of the null curriculum.

> What schools do not teach may be as important as what they do teach. I argue this position because ignorance is not simply a neutral void. It has important effects on the kinds of options one is able to consider, the alternatives that one can examine, and the perspectives from which one can view a situation or problems. (Eisner, 2002, p. 97)

The position a person with perceived power (rather it be race or economic status) takes is as important as the awareness of the stance so that it does not come off as posturing. As my children and I quickly discovered, it was not enough to live in a society that reversed the order of racial make-up. It was not enough to be aware of the economic disparity that existed within our Dakar life. Pinar et al.'s work (1995) with curriculum, as autobiographical and biographical text, might help both Delpit and me be able to understand how our view of curriculum is colored by our very personal experience with curriculum.

The *talibé* are Muslim boys who are found all over Dakar. They had been sent by their families to a *daaras*, or "boarding school" in the city to study the Quran with a marabout. The marabout, in turn, sends out the boys to beg for a daily quota of money or rice. Dirty, without shoes, these boys, who could be as young as four, would approach with an empty tin or small bucket, begging for money. Dirty noses, dirty clothes, the word was that the marabout would not allow the boys clean clothes or to bathe as the more dirty they appeared, the more likely they were to be successful begging. *Talibé* who could not meet their quota were harshly disciplined. Living in large communes of hundreds of boys for one marabout, hunger and physical abuse were the norm. Outside every store we went to, the boys would be waiting with their pails upraised. Often at crowded traffic areas, the boys would thread their way through cars looking for a handout.

Gaucher was the physical education teacher at the international school of Dakar. Gaucher was a large Black man, tall in stature and large in personality, who grew up in Dakar, Senegal. When he first obtained his position as a teacher, he wanted to be able to give back to his community. He decided he was going to purchase shoes for all the *talibé* boys who lived in his neighborhood. At great personal expense, Gaucher proudly bought dozens of pairs of tennis shoes and distributed them to the boys. The very next time he saw the boys, there were no shoes. When questioned as to where the shoes had gone, the *talibé* boys explained that the marabout grew very angry and beat the boys for having the shoes. They were not to have anything that the marabout had not provided himself. The shoes were confiscated to be resold to bring in additional money into the *daaras*. Gaucher was devastated. Even being on the same side of the metaphorical door was not enough for Gaucher to be able to cross the divide.

Our solution was to purchase extra bread to give to the boys as it could be eaten and not turned over to the marabout. Yet, I would often find myself slipping coins to the youngest of the boys as I could not stomach the idea of them not making their quota. There were a few women who were well known in the city for making huge batches of porridge or soup to feed the boys breakfast every morning. Being aware of the situation and being able to provide a solution for the issue were two very different things.

> It becomes clear that what we teach in schools is not always determined by a set of decisions that have entertained alternatives; rather, the subjects that are now taught are a part of a tradition, and traditions create expectations, they create predictability, and they sustain stabilit. (Eisner, 2002, p. 105)

Schools have a long way to go to even create the awareness in their teachers of the disparity that exists among racial, as well as socioeconomic groups and how the curricular decisions we make are often unwitting accomplices in continuing to maintain the status quo. Unfortunately, today's political environment with a president who has gained power by drumming up a following by fanning the flames of reverse racism and pointing out how "others" are taking away from those he deems worthy, has made the jobs of educators even more difficult. How to open the conversation to greater awareness is difficult in the best of times, as many educators have lived within the smog of racism for so long, they are unaware of its existence.

McCarthy argued a neo-Marxist position that "schools as apparatuses of the state, both legitimize racial differences in society and reproduce the kind of racially subordinate subjects who are tracked into the secondary labor market" (Pinar et al., 2008, p. 318). I agree with Lisa Delpit that schools have a long way to go before they are as equitable as they should be in providing education and opportunities for students. Based on us being on opposite sides of the same door, trying to see through the keyhole, I believe we will have very different ideas about how we should go about attempting to accomplish this work. Despite our varied views, neither side of the door can afford to give up the struggle to see through the keyhole in our struggle to do what is right for all students.

LESSONS FROM DELPIT

A big takeaway from Delpit is the idea that teachers can alter what happens in the classrooms for their students, but that it will necessitate a shift in how the predominately White, middle-classed women educators of the United States view both their own existence in an environment where many of the children they teach do not look like them or come from backgrounds with which they can relate. Our African experience pushed us to view our experience through not just a lens of different races, but of the impact socioeconomic conditions also plays in opportunities afforded different groups of people. The main thing I draw from Delpit is the need to look at the environment on my side of the door and recognize that it is quite possible for me to not recognize barriers for some of the students. It is also possible that even if I am looking very carefully and diligently, the lenses of my eyes might not be enough to recognize anything other than the privileged background in which I experienced my own education. Through continued work, people on either side of the keyhole might succeed in opening up the door.

REFERENCES

Anderson, M. D. (2017, July 27). Why the myth of meritocracy hurts kids of color. *The Atlantic.* https://www.theatlantic.com/education/archive/2017/07/internalizing-the-myth-of-meritocracy/535035/

Delpit, L. (1988). The silenced dialogue: Power and pedagogy in educating other people's children. *Harvard Educational Review, 58*(3), 280–299. https://doi .org/10.17763/haer.58.3.c43481778r528qw4

Delpit, L. (1991). A conversation with Lisa Delpit. *Language Arts, 68*(7), 541–547.

Delpit, L. (2012) *"Multiplication is for white people:" Raising expectations for other people's children.* The New Press.

Denevi, E., & Chandler-Ward, J. (2017). *Episode 3: Whiteness visible: Part 1* [Podcast]. Teaching While White. https://www.teachingwhilewhite.org/podcast/ 2017/9/29/whiteness-visible-part-1-1

Eisner, E. W. (2002). *The educational imagination: On the design and evaluation of school programs* (3rd ed.). Prentice Hall.

Pinar, W. F. (1975, April). *The method of "currere"* [Paper presentation]. Annual Meeting of the American Research Association, Washington, DC.

Pinar, W., Reynolds, W., Slattery, P., & Taubman, P. (1995). Chapter 10: Understanding curriculum as autobiographical/biographical text. *Counterpoints, 17,* 515– 566. http://www.jstor.org/stable/42974926

Pinar, W. F., Reynolds, W. M., Slattery, P., & Taubman, P. M. (2008). *Understanding curriculum: An introduction to the study of historical and contemporary curriculum discourses.* Peter Lang.

CHAPTER 26

TO CHANGE OR NOT TO CHANGE

A Cautionary Tale for the Educational Chameleon

Tanya Britton Moore

Author/Book studied:

Hunter, M. (1982). *Mastery teaching: Increasing effectiveness in elementary, secondary schools, colleges, and universities.* TIP Publications.

Extra, Extra, Read All About It! It has been discovered, finally, the latest and greatest way to increase student growth and performance. Guaranteed to increase the proficiency level of your students just by implementing this new, innovative program!

How many times have we heard this in the educational community? Over and over again, new strategies and new curriculum innovations flood educational news as the final solution to improving student learning. And no,

---

this is not a recent trend, this has been going on for at least 100 years. Don't get me wrong, there have been excellent ideas and strong contributions to the education field during this time, but readily changing programming to jump on the latest bandwagon can have its consequences. As curricularists, it is always essential to keep well informed of the latest research and the newest ideas, but it is equally important to realize that there is not just one way to teach students; each student is different. What works for one may not work for another. So then, why do we as educators jump into new ideas with the misguided hope that all of our educational problems will be solved with these new innovations? We jump so often that we become educational chameleons.

EDUCATIONAL CHANGE RESEARCH

According to the Foundation for Critical Thinking Press (2007), educational fads tend to last 7–10 years (p. 4). The list of educational fads over the past 100 years is lengthy and would be cumbersome to produce. However, block scheduling, Bloom's Taxonomy, character education, emotional intelligence, and multiple intelligences are just a few examples of fads that have trended over the past century (Foundation for Critical Thinking Press, 2007). All of these trends bring powerful ideas to enhance education. However, not a single one of these ideas solves every problem. Each of these innovations contains snippets that can be implemented into a well-rounded program with the intention of increasing learning, while many of them are just upcycled ideas.

A 4-year, eight volume study led by the RAND Corporation, known as the Change Agent Study, was completed to determine what does and what does not work in changing education (Bracey, 1991). Bracey (1991) examined their work to determine which findings from the original study were still valid. While he found all of the findings to still be valid, he stated that some just needed to be revised, for instance, change continues to be a problem in the smallest unit; policy cannot mandate what matters; and local variability is the rule while conformity is the exception (Bracey, 1991). Bracey also identified takeaways from the study that need revisions. For example, the original study stated that initial motivation is crucial, though it only looked at voluntary programs. The study also claimed that reliance on outside consultants causes programmatic failures, unless the consultants work hand in hand with those in the building for a seamless relationship (Bracey, 1991). There were other outcomes of the broad study, but for the purposes of this paper, those are the most relevant to the discussion of educational change.

With educational fads having such a short life span, it is not often that a fad grows exponentially to create an educational celebrity, though it does happen from time to time. One of the most followed and acclaimed innovations to improving student learning came from a "revolutionary educator," a "true maverick" during the 1980s (Folkart, 1994). Madeline Hunter earned the nickname as a world-renowned researcher that claimed teachers were the "primary influence on learning skills," not the environment or heredity (Folkart, 1994). From a clinical psychologist at a children's hospital to a public-school principal, Hunter held a variety of positions throughout her career in her path of developing a clinical teaching method (Folkart, 1994). During her principalship, she began her own form of action research in her own environment. She began researching to challenge the previous-held beliefs that poor and broken homes produce poor learners with low IQs. "We have yet to find a student who won't learn (when taught properly)" (Folkart, 1994, para. 8).

Hunter wrote *Mastery Teaching* in 1982 as a guide for quality teaching. Through her research, she came to emphasize that teachers were not born to be teachers, but rather, teachers could be made. Teachers did not need to be intuitive, they just had to have the right recipe when planning lessons. Just as a master chef gathers, measures, and mixes each ingredient for a delicious cuisine, a teacher can also follow a recipe to ensure student growth and learning. The perfect recipe for such effectiveness was created by Madeline Hunter. Or was it just another fad?

As a soon-to-be director of curriculum, I want to caution others and myself regarding educational fads and educational change, in general, along with the dangers they bring to the integrity of our educational system. Please don't think that I am taking the stance that nothing in education should ever change. My stance is quite the opposite. I believe change is needed when necessary and warranted. I believe in continuing to expand our thinking as we learn more about how our brain works, how students learn, and how the world is changing. I also believe in thorough understandings, research, and questioning before implementing change. This essay is intended to examine the success of Madeline Hunter through the lens of educational change in hopes of providing a cautionary guide to current and future curricularists. Let's first take an in-depth look at Hunter's clinical teaching method.

MADELINE HUNTER AND MASTERY TEACHING

The 1980s was a difficult time in the United States for public education. *A Nation at Risk* was published in 1983 and directed the spotlight towards the U.S. educational system and its flaws. There came new demands for an overhaul of the educational system as it existed. "In demanding an overhaul, these reformers echo an old American theme: a longing for a new country, a new life, a new structure, a new faith, a new solution, a new invention, a new technology, a new self" (Senechal, 2010, p. 4). People began glorifying new ideas as being innovative and outside the box, when in reality, the new ideas were not necessarily new nor were the old ideas obsolete (Senechal, 2010). While districts were scrambling to figure out what to do to combat the darkening views of education, Madeline Hunter appeared at just the right time with an answer.

She promoted that understanding what is being taught and why it is being taught will inevitably increase student learning. Hunter (1982) stated that "teachers must be able to read signals from students and assess the learning situation so necessary adjustments can be made" (p. 3). In order to do this, she highlights a multitude of step-by-step directions to assist teachers in structuring their learning environment. She termed this approach *mastery teaching*. Hunter's version of mastery teaching presents a model of mastery learning that addresses the methodology that is used when planning and presenting a lesson. Hunter (1982) states throughout *Mastery Teaching* that her model has been proven to increase effectiveness, though the proof is missing. The book itself has 17 chapters to guide teachers or groups of teachers through modules towards increasing instructional effectiveness.

She begins the guidebook by discussing the various decisions made within the teaching profession. She identified three categories of teaching decisions and stated that if errors are made within any of those categories, student learning can be impeded (Hunter, 1982, p. 3). Some of the other key points of her clinical teaching method focus on student motivation. Hunter (1982) stated that "motivation is a learned behavior" (p. 11). She also discussed preparing students to learn and the importance of not wasting time on meaningless activities (Hunter, 1982). She had strong beliefs on providing effective information to students through organization, presentation, and modeling. She believed in teaching to both halves of the brain and also focused on extending the thinking of students, dignifying errors to promote learning, and using time effectively (Hunter, 1982). She was not a believer that practice makes perfect; instead she believed that the teachers' lesson plans and objectives laid the foundation for information retention (Hunter, 1982). She ended the guidebook by discussing teaching for transfer. She emphasized the importance of teaching so that past learnings are able to influence acquired new learning. She went so far as to say that "transfer is more of a predictor of speed of new learning than is IQ" (Hunter, 1982, p. 107).

Everything that Hunter promoted was logical and sound. She made a lot of money on her system and it was adopted in schools throughout the world. Teachers were expected to follow Hunter's model with integrity and in many schools. It was used as an evaluation tool for teachers. Thousands of teachers went through professional development trainings to prepare for this new wave of teaching. There were opportunities for growth within the mastery teaching model for teachers to be teacher leaders as well.

The widespread growth of the mastery teaching model took the education world by storm. After all, this was the solution to everything that was wrong in education. This was the answer that everyone was looking for. If this was the case, why then did schools and districts abandon Hunter's model, some more quickly than others?

AN ANALYSIS OF MASTERY TEACHING

The philosophical and clinical approach to education proclaimed by Hunter (1982) seemed like the answer to many districts and state departments and they immediately jumped on the Hunter bandwagon. However, "Hunterizing" teachers did not necessarily have the outcomes that were expected (Coulombe, 1994, p. 337). Though Hunter experienced great personal success from her model, she had to defend it from the attacks it was receiving from educators.

In 1985, Hunter published an article titled "What's Wrong With Madeline Hunter?" In this article she aimed to debunk all of the false claims and myths made against her model. Some of the myths that she chose to address included that the model stifled creativity, that its intention was to serve as a teacher evaluation model, that there has been no research to support the model, and that the model is mostly effective for direct teaching (Hunter, 1985). She stated throughout the article that people were using the model incorrectly, and that parts of the model were to be only considered when planning, not implemented rigidly in practice (Hunter, 1985). "She concluded that, by and large, what was wrong was that a number of myths had been built up around her model of teaching, and that a number of problems with implementing the model had been ascribed to faults in the model itself" (Bracey, 1988, p. 378).

Richard Gibboney (1987) looked at Hunter's model through the perspective of John Dewey. According to Gibboney, Hunter did not produce research evidence to support her claim for improved learning. She also did not provide support for her claims of higher achievement (Gibboney, 1987, p. 47). These would have been a huge concern for John Dewey had he still been alive during the Hunter era. John Dewey held that a finding might be scientific in psychology or in sociology, for example, but that it is not scientific in education until it has been tested in educational practice (Gibboney, 1987). Dewey also viewed the primary aim of teaching is to cultivate thought whereas Hunter did not unite the elements of her teaching model with thinking (Gibboney, 1987). Though looking at Hunter through a Dewey perspective provides additional criticisms of Hunter's model, it is also interesting to hear claims from actual teachers in the field that implemented Hunter's model in their classroom.

Based on a study completed in Pennsylvania of more than 200 teachers who were involved in the Hunter-style programs, some good news and some bad news emerged (Garman & Hazi, 1988). In terms of the bad news, there was a consensus of uneasiness among the teachers. They felt like they were playing a game to keep their administrators happy (Garman & Hazi, 1988). The teachers who did not jump on the Hunter bandwagon and attempted to implement ideas of their own felt rejected. All of this ended with anger and hostility towards each other and the profession in general. In terms of the good news, though frustrated by implementation, teachers also were happy that there was additional attention being focused on teaching. Educational conversations with colleagues were happening and a common language was being developed (Garman & Hazi, 1988). Doors opened for opportunities for teachers to become trainers and the teachers who were committed felt distinguished. Though all of these good aspects of the model were realized, it wasn't enough to keep the teachers focused and committed to the Hunter model.

Another critique of Hunter's work is in regard to a conceptual shortcoming. Larry Davidman (1988) points out that Hunter "presents her theory as an educational concept which stands apart from or transcends the curriculum" (p. 84). He states that her model for professional development for teachers focuses attention on the instructional aspect of teaching and learning rather than the curricular side (Davidman, 1988). He claimed that there is no depth or content discussion within her model. Though it could be said that the content comes after a solid plan, many would argue just the opposite. Instruction and content need to go hand in hand and the connections need to be clear to the staff. Professional development that is one sided may not be enough to carry an initiative to success.

A perfect storm occurred during this period in public school practice. Hunter provided a model at just the right time. However, educational fads fade in and out and even tend to come back under different conditions. As educators, how do we know what to trust and what not to trust? Is jumping on each bandwagon, becoming an educational chameleon, helping our students succeed? How does educational change affect the integrity of the educational system as a whole? These are all questions that I hope to answer as I look at the role of educational change in our world currently and historically and what we can learn from "Hunterization."

A REFLECTIVE CHAMELEON

Thinking back on my educational journey, I can create a list of many fads that I bought into throughout my teaching—those of my own doing and those due to a district initiative. Educational change is inevitable; however, throughout my career, I was not always clear as to what led to particular changes. Really, all of the ideas, strategies, and programs that I learned seemed like amazing ideas. In my classroom, I was always willing to be a risk-taker and try something new. I am not sure that I ever thought these ideas would solve all of the problems facing my students, but I did think that if I utilized these strategies, then I had to be doing something right. I wonder how much time and money a school district spends just to keep up with the latest and greatest trends.

It is easy to become an educational chameleon and change on a whim and to continue chasing a solution for a problem that doesn't have just one solution. "The only reasonable solution to raising the quality of education is in-depth thinking based on a substantive concept of education" (Paul & Elder, 2006, p. 12). As I reflect on my past experiences as a teacher, I am determined now as an administrator to have a sound plan for analyzing and promoting educational change and to promote the belief that there are many solutions to problems.

Today, public schools are yearning for the best report card data and student growth data. Education is the center of many political debates and has gained so much more public attention in the past 20 years as the accountability era has reached a heightened level. Many students are leaving the public education realm to attend private schools, online schools, or charter schools because there is a belief that public education is failing. The constant struggle to implement new strategies that can potentially help fix a broken system is ever present. So, when these innovative ideas come along, how do we as professionals discern the quality of the idea, the feasibility of implementation, and then progress monitor to determine the idea's effectiveness?

Determining the Quality of the Idea

In order to determine the quality of an educational innovation, information regarding the company or person promoting the strategy must be investigated. Paul and Elder (2006) outlines a series of questions that can be used to analyze new trends in education before implementing. These questions all center around the organization's concept of education, the intellectual traits desired, and the fundamental goals of teaching (Paul & Elder, 2006). It is an integral part of the process to have a clear mission and vision and to ensure that any new innovative idea has a decodable mission to determine whether or not it aligns with that of the organization.

In the case of the mastery teaching model, it is important for potential followers to understand her background. By having a clear understanding that her model is a clinical teaching method, her model looks at education as non-intuitive. Coming from a medical background, Hunter viewed teaching as a prescribed science. It is not the teacher or the student who guides the learning, rather learning is enhanced by using an effective lesson planning method (Wagschal, 1974). For districts contemplating adoption of the Hunter model, it would be important to analyze her background and philosophy of education before implementation. For instance, did schools of that period understand that the Hunter model is far less child-centered and is more mechanistic and structure focused? Did they know that while her model may work for some schools, it might not work for others?

I am currently the principal of a fourth and fifth grade elementary school of about 650 students. While I am a fan of much of what Hunter researched and compiled, I would not adopt her mastery teaching method based on the quality. I have personal beliefs that teachers matter. Teachers are intuitive and make decisions based on their student needs. I do not believe there is one correct formula to teaching. As an administrator, I empower my teachers to take ownership over their teaching and to be risk-takers. I support new ideas, but do not typically let the school jump into any one idea that is instructional based. I make suggestions for improvement and adopt building curriculum, but instruction is left up to the teachers.

Examining the Feasibility of Implementation

Second, the feasibility of implementation must be examined. All programs advertise how easy it is to implement them and how quickly test results will improve. However, understanding the professional development needed to implement a new innovation with integrity needs to be determined. It is essential for there to be teacher and administrator buy-in when implementing something new and in order for there to be buy-in, a clear understanding of the implementation process along with reasonable goals must be developed. Even though a program may come with easy-to-use guides, a certain amount of success comes from teacher attitude and presentation.

Teachers enjoy the creative options and intuitive nature of this career field, for the most part. Mastery teaching prescribes a rigid guide for teachers. Gaining buy-in with a system that limits their creativity and threatens their autonomy will be difficult in any setting. Though there are incredible ideas throughout her system, the feasibility of adopting such a model that is so rigid and rigorous may make it difficult to retain staff and may induce more stress in the long run, especially in today's accountability era. Beyond having teaching buy-in, ensuring correct implementation is key to any initiative success. This can be very difficult to do, depending on teacher interest and administrative support.

As an administrator, if asked to implement the mastery teaching model, I would struggle with the feasibility of implementation. My staff understands my expectations, and while I might suggest Hunter's model as a resource, I would never make it a mandated program. First, I know that teacher buy-in would not be present because there is no administrator buy-in. Second, I believe that our scores would actually decrease if implemented. While there are some parts of her model that we integrate throughout our current instructional practices, I do not believe that her model provides opportunities to reach all students where they are on the learning spectrum. Finally, in regard to feasibility of implementation, there are far too many restraints on teacher creativity and too much time spent on a process rather than providing students instruction at their individualized level.

Planning for Progress Monitoring

Progress monitoring and timelines must be determined. In order to collect accurate data on any programmatic implementation, a substantial amount of time to study the results and outcomes of the program is essential. In order to calculate growth data for students, years may be needed before determining effectiveness. In the absence of careful assessment, it becomes easy to be that educational chameleon and "change colors" too quickly. Another part of this process is having an efficacy checklist to ensure that the program is being implemented the way that it was intended. Wagschal (1974) writes about his experiences as an educational consultant. He discusses that during his follow-up visit after his various trainings, he notices that the correct innovative words are being used, but for all practical purposes, nothing has changed (Wagschal, 1974). "Teachers and students still behave pretty much the same way they used to: the content and process of day-to-day teaching has survived virtually unscathed by my own innovative efforts" (Wagschal, 1974, p. 333).

Madeline Hunter made many claims about her model and its effectiveness. These claims were accused of being unfounded and measured inaccurately. However, if a district chooses to implement a program such as Hunter's, collecting appropriate and long-term data would be needed. Every day there is a new idea, or a reinvention of an old idea; determining how long to stay on one initiative must be decided before beginning. Hunter made claims that the reason people did not agree with her program or see the expected results is because they were not implementing the process correctly (Hunter, 1985). An initiative is only as successful as its implementation. This is where the real danger of becoming an educational chameleon rears its head.

In my reflections of my current position, there have been times when we have jumped on a curricular bandwagon. I have been that chameleon as a leader. I have jumped my building from one math program to another and from one vocabulary program to another. Always these jumps were made with good intentions, but was enough time allowed to truly determine their effectiveness? As I am transitioning into my new role as a director of curriculum, I am currently tasked with leading the charge on a new math program adoption. Making a curricular decision is difficult. One of the characteristics of a program that I think is critical for a new program is if it allows for creativity and stretch within the curriculum. Rigidity and scripted lessons do not allow teachers to do what they do best, which is teach. I feel the same about the instructional strategies that Hunter's model promotes. I would love to see true data from other districts or schools who have implemented her model and how they progress monitored for effectiveness before making a decision to adopt. But I realize that data did not exist then, and that often doesn't exist now, no matter the change. However, I plan to progress monitor, whatever our new math curriculum, and use that process and data to coach teachers and improve student learning.

MY CAUTIONARY GUIDELINES
FOR EDUCATIONAL CHANGE

Teachers are working overtime to keep up with the changing field of education. They are wavering on ways to break away from traditional teaching and embrace new ways of teaching. However, with the daily hustle to keep up with all of the new fads, have we forgotten what good teaching looks like? "We will never reach perfection, but the more we strive for it, learning from history as well as experience, the closer we will come" (Senechal, 2010, p. 16).

My advice through all of this research and learning from the Hunter era is three-pronged. Change is good when some guardrails are put up. First, do not fix something that isn't broken. Second, do your research. Third, if you do decide to implement a new initiative, ensure it is being implemented with integrity and according to the specific protocol and monitor implementation for a significant amount of time.

Just because there is a new idea, it does not mean that the current or old idea is bad. Unless there is a problem with the current method of teaching or the curriculum, then do not try to fix them. Though I always think that professional development is necessary and there are new ideas to incorporate, when it comes to teaching strategies and instruction, there is no clear recipe to follow. I caution the current and future curricularists to always have a gauge of how things are progressing both anecdotally and quantitatively. Look for pockets of regression and make changes there. In the case of Madeline Hunter, I can think of ways in which her model would be useful for some of my teachers, but definitely not for all. Know the needs of your building or district and give teachers many tools for their tool belt, not just one.

When contemplating implementing a new initiative, know the background and the true data behind the research. Research is essential. Unfounded claims can be made by anyone to sell their product. Research not only the philosophy behind the initiative, but talk to previous implementers, while also knowing that just because something works for one school or district, does not mean it will work for all schools or districts. This is especially true when dealing with teaching and curriculum.

Implementation with integrity is essential. When it comes time for educational change, whether small scale or large scale, implementation is key. Understanding the true expectations of any program from an administrative side is key in helping increase effectiveness. Professional development and coaching are also extremely important to success. Bracey (1991) notes in his commentary on education change that sole reliance on outside consultants will cause an initiative to fail. One study completed in Napa County on the implantation of the Hunter model and its effects did show growth in students and teachers who used the process (Stallings, 1985). However, one key feature of this study is that going through the Madeline Hunter model is not nearly enough. It is necessary to have ongoing training and a long-term process of implementation (Stallings, 1985).

THE FUTURE OF EDUCATIONAL ADMINISTRATION

Educational change is not going away, nor should it. New ideas and new innovations will continue to be highlighted and promoted. The important part of change is to follow the guidelines outlined in this cautionary tale. Implementation of change will always continue to be difficult. It is essential to realize that there is no fix-all solution for all educational concerns.

All in all, there is a lot to learn from Madeline Hunter. She was smart and combined learning from both her worlds, medicine and education. Even though I may not agree with her model in its entirety, she brings up many good instructional considerations. Beyond the instructional side, however, I think we can learn a lot from the Hunter era in education. It is key to not let the era of accountability guide the process.

Implementing change at the expense of every other consideration jeopardizes the entire educational process. Programs may sound good, especially during the dark times when failure seems to be all that is discussed, but my advice remains constant. Do not rush into things. Do not be an educational chameleon.

REFERENCES

Bracey, G. (1988). What's right with Madeline Hunter? *The Phi Delta Kappan, 69*(5), 378–379.

Bracey, G. (1991). Educational change. *The Phi Delta Kappan, 72*(7), 557–558.

Coulombe, G. (1994). Remembering Madeline Hunter. *The Clearing House, 67*(6), 337–338.

Davidman, L. (1988). On improving the conceptualization and implementation of the Hunter Model. *Teacher Education Quarterly, 15*(4), 83–90.

Folkart, B. (1994, January 29). Obituary: Madeline Hunter. *Los Angeles Times.* https://www.latimes.com/archives/la-xpm-1994-01-29-me-16521-story.html

Garman, N., & Hazi, H. (1988). Teachers ask: Is there life after Madeline Hunter? *The Phi Delta Kappan, 69*(9), 669–672.

Gibboney, R. (1987). A critique of Madeline Hunter's teaching model from Dewey's perspective. *Educational Leadership, 44,* 46–50.

Hunter, M. (1982). *Mastery teaching.* SAGE Publications.

Hunter, M. (1985). What's wrong with Madeline Hunter? *Educational Leadership, 42*(5), 57–60.

Paul, R., & Elder, L. (2006). *A critical thinker's guide to educational fads: How to get beyond educational glitz and glitter.* The Foundation for Critical Thinking.

Senechal, D. (2010). The most daring education reform of all. *American Educator, 34*(1), 4–16.

Stallings, J. (1985). A study of implementation of Madeline Hunter's model and its effect on students. *The Journal of Educational Research, 78*(6), 325–337.

Wagschal, P. (1974). Following the bouncing fad. *The High School Journal, 57*(8), 331–334.

CHAPTER 27

BAJO LA LUPA, UNDER THE MAGNIFYING GLASS

Erica Lynn Mitchell O'Keeffe

Author/Book studied:

Sears, J. T., & Carper, J. C. (1998). *Curriculum, religion, and public education: Conversations for enlarging public square.* Teachers College Press.

"Now, if it is not enough to have your own view fairly presented as one of several points of view, then there is no possibility of having public schools consistent with the Constitution," Michael W. McConnell.

—Sears & Carper (1998, p. 34)

Does curriculum influence society and society influence curriculum? Take a thought journey with me. Humans perceive the world through their personalized experiences. Some of the most crucial years of learning and defining one's identity takes place during the school (K–12) years. During these years (5–18), your brain is a sponge, wiring and networking what you

---

Curriculum Windows Redux, pages 319–332

learn and what you experience. What if what you see, hear, touch, smell, and taste (what you experience) lacks diversity?

Think back to your school years and envision the pictures in your textbooks, the stories you learned, the movies you watched. Who wrote those stories? Have you ever wondered why you were taught evolution and not intelligent design? Which books did you not read because the board of education prohibited them? Communities have fought over textbooks, the banning of books, a teacher who said they were a Christian in class, abstinence versus teaching safe sex, transgender bathrooms, and on and on. Ask yourself why? Communities fought because they do not want their children taught certain curriculum that goes against their value system.

Why did you learn what you learned? Who influenced what you were taught? How we interact with the world is very much attributed to what we learned in our homes and schools. Does curriculum influence society and society influence curriculum? In my opinion, curriculum is a massive and distinctive power—it can encourage social justice and stir up controversy simultaneously. It is a silent power, often underestimated by the general population. It goes unnoticed until an esteemed community member finds the curriculum contrasting with his or her ideals. Mostly, parents are preoccupied with daily life. They have a desire for their children to go to school, learn, graduate, maybe obtain a scholarship for college, and become more productive and successful than them. Therefore, by and large, the general population is unknowingly influenced by curriculum.

In 1993, James T. Sears, a professor at the University of South Carolina (USC) experienced firsthand the curricular influence. A letter of discontent regarding his new course, "Christian Fundamentalism and Public Education" was sent to the president of USC, a public university sitting in the Bible Belt of America. This letter contained the signatures of 45 out of 124 members of the House of Representatives, threatening to cut university funding if this course was not canceled.

> Conservative lawmakers don't trust the university's assurances that the seminar was appropriate for doctoral-level students and would espouse no ideological agenda. One of Walker's biggest concerns is with the instructor, James Sears, who is an acknowledged homosexual. "I don't see how someone in his position can be objective about Christianity," he said. (GoUpstate, 1993, para. 2)

Why were these politicians concerned with ideologies and the sexual identification of the professor? Clearly, they feared what doctoral students were going to learn in his class. Did this class misalign with their values and threaten the downfall of society? Were these doctoral students incapable of discerning the course content? Communities, influence the enacted curriculum and in this case, inspire controversy. In contrast, could this curriculum have the power to broaden minds and encourage social justice? Is social justice what these politicians feared? Either way, this course's curriculum was going to transform society.

James T. Sears, writes about his USC experience from 1993 and examines the influence of society on curriculum and curriculum on society, as co-editor of the book, *Curriculum, Religion, and Public Education: Conversations for an Enlarging Public Square* (Sears & Carper, 1998). Furthermore, he declares the necessity for using dialogue as an integral component of the enacted curriculum to transform the American educational system.

Divided into seven parts—(a) "Foundations for Conversations"; (b) "Textbooks: Whose Stories Are to Be Told?"; (c) "Values in the Public Schools: What and Whose Values Should Be Taught?"; (d) "Sexuality Education: What Does Teaching Sexual Responsibility Mean?"; (e) "Outcome-Based Education: Who Should Set the Standards?"; (f) "Science: Who and What Are we?"; and (g) "A Concluding Conversation Among Education Scholars"—this book unites thoughtful deliberations from varying perspectives, political and religious affiliations, by magnifying the need for curricular transformation. "These contributors make sure that the utilitarian and pragmatic models of educational philosophy, often disguised as a neutral and unbiased pedagogy, do not go unchallenged. Nevertheless, this book neither downplays nor exaggerates the dangers of sectarian motivated curriculum reform" (Davenport, 2000, p. 871).

James T. Sears, a man of history and intellect, is a PhD scholar of curriculum studies and higher education. Moreover, he attained master degrees in secondary education and political science. He was born in 1951 in Tipton, Indiana. Sears has held professorships at several well-known universities such as: The University of South Carolina, Trinity University, University of Southern California, and Harvard University. Additionally, James T. Sears is widely known as an author of numerous books regarding lesbian, gay, bisexual, and transgender (LGBT) historical accounts, including: *Rebels, Rubyfruit, and Rhinestones* (Sears & Brown, 2001); *Growing Up Gay in the South* (Sears, 1991); *Lonely Hunters* (Sears, 1997); *Behind the Mask of the Mattachine* (Sears, 2006); *Gay, Lesbian, Transgender Issues in Education* (Sears, 2005); and so forth.

Curriculum, Religion, and Public Education: Conversations for an Enlarging Public Square (Sears & Carper, 1998) intrigued me the moment Dr. Poetter said something to the effect of,

> This book was not chosen by the last cohort and that is a shame because it raised quite the controversy. It brought topics such as: sex education, homosexuality, religion, science versus creation, textbook wars, and other imperative issues to light. It is a strong book, I hope someone picks it.

I was sold. We had the opportunity to choose our top three book titles. This was my number one choice and I won it. I knew I needed to read it in order to overcome my own personal biases before embarking on my dissertation journey, knowing that queer and feminist theories would be a large part of my research. Little did I know that part of my teaching career paralleled Sears' story. Thus, this essay will convey my story, supported by works from *Curriculum, Religion, and Public Education: Conversations for an Enlarging Public Square* and James T. Sears' professional yet controversial experience.

"A Shameless Moonbat," indeed, that was my new title. The public named me without a cause. Apparently, this happens in the realm of education. In the blink of an eye, my school email became inundated with scowling, hurtful remarks sprinkled with death threats from all over the nation. "Others were less kind, suggesting that those involved with the project should hang in the public square for treason or be sent to Mexico to live in the streets" (Zachariah, 2007, pp. A1–A4). Michelle Malkin, a well-known national conservative, selected stories from the blogs, "Anti-Liberal Zone" and "Moonbattery," and posted them to her nationally prominent website, and presented them as factual. These blogs claimed that I told kids to swim the Rio Grande and taught them communistic lesbianism, among other things. Malkin wrote (2007), "Alright. Now, let's see the teacher require her pupils to put themselves in the shoes of murdered Newark students (insert names here) and gain a balanced understanding of the full consequences of open borders. Class dismissed" (para. 7).

Herewith, I was hurdled into the middle of a culture war because of a school immigration project. Is American education founded on the notion of assimilating young minds to the American ideals and society? If so, how does history, comprised of politics and societal standards (current and past), influence schools and the curriculum in the 21st century? Is American society still caught up in a culture war and therefore, are schools as well? One may ascertain that what is taught and not taught in the American public schools often is inspired by politics, controversy, history, and/or societal viewpoints. Richard John Neuhaus, "a theologian who transformed himself from a liberal Lutheran leader of the civil rights and antiwar struggles in the 1960s to a Roman Catholic beacon of the neoconservative movement of today" (Goodstein, 2009), marched with Dr. Martin Luther King Jr. and served as an advisor to President George W. Bush, has an authoritative perspective on cultural wars. Neuhaus proclaims,

> It is a strange thing in our culture that politically we still have people on all parts of the political spectrum who view the "social issues"—abortion, school prayer, homosexuality—as some kind of alien invasion into the political project. (Sears & Carper, 1998, p. 25)

Furthermore, Neuhaus asserts,

> The concept of culture war also suggests a mindset that suspends all of the rules of civility. That is a real danger, especially if one ups the ante and declares that we are engaged in a religious war in this society. (Sears & Carper, 1998, p. 26)

Throughout his essay, Neuhaus affirms the impact of culture wars on American education, "The myth of the little red schoolhouse and American democracy was by no means entirely a myth. It was seen by many astute social observers as being one of the most important institutions in the American 'melting pot'" (Sears & Carper, 1998, p. 26) because it taught citizens how to behave in American society, also known as acculturation. Perhaps these culture wars elucidate some reasoning to the wild public reactions to two parallel curricular stories.

As if negative publicity to my teaching career was not enough, bloggers decided to post all of my school district's board member's email addresses, my personal information, and advocated for my removal. Where did these random bloggers find out about the immigration project I had been implementing for the past five school years in suburbia? *The Columbus Dispatch* article titled "Students Struggle as Immigrants Do" (Zachariah, 2007b) highlighted this project as a positive and inspirational learning experience for students. Michelle Malkin, the bloggers, and other participants who commented unconstructively on this project, did not have any factual information. Yet, they turned this eloquently written story into a damaging farce by inserting words and phrases such as: indoctrination, communism, wasted, breaking the law, ramrodding, and more. Next thing you knew, my project and I were listed in the Drudge Report, making national and international headlines.

How could America, the land of the free, believe such atrocities? According to Davenport (2000), "The fine line that distinguishes indoctrination from education is often difficult to establish. The heated debates in America over public school curriculum serve, if nothing else, to remind us of this difficulty" (p. 870). I was never interviewed and I was not permitted to respond because anything I said could have been twisted into more lies. Moreover, because Michelle was a trusted national source of "truth," The American public took these people at their word in ignorance, which in of itself, proves why teaching people how to think for themselves and conduct authoritative research on topics should be pertinent educational endeavors, all the while improving democracy and our society.

As best stated by John Dewey (1897/2010) in *My Pedagogic Creed,* "I believe that education is the fundamental method of social progress and reform" (p. 31). Additionally, Dewey describes democracy as, "A society of free individuals in which all, through their own work, contribute to the liberation and enrichment of the lives of others, is the only environment where any individual can really grow normally to his full stature" (Sears & Carper, 1998, p. 50).

My story is much like James T. Sears' experience with his course "Christian Fundamentalism and Public Education" in 1993 at the University of South Carolina. "Upon learning about this seminar, religious groups, along with many of the state's politicians and its conservative citizenry, voiced their concerns—amplified through the news media—to university administrators and the board of trustees" (Sears & Carper, 1998, p. 36). Sears received hate mail, death threats, was named "Satan of the University," and the public threatened his career and university funding. Why? Because he was teaching a course, never taught before, in the Bible Belt and he identified as homosexual. Pundits misinterpreted and passed judgment on his values, wisdom, honor, and educated mind. He, too, found himself smack in the middle of a culture war.

This tumultuous public outrage and humiliation inspired his book, *Curriculum, Religion, and Public Education: Conversations for an Enlarging Public Square* (Sears & Carper, 1998). Therefore, alongside James C. Carper, he explored the several historical and societal perspectives impacting American schools. This book is an anthology of respected educators and philosophers providing opinions, reflections, history, and perspectives regarding social influences on curriculum. What are teachers permitted to teach? Which textbooks can a school system adopt? Is sex education a subject that schools or parents should teach? These are just a few of several questions thoughtfully investigated throughout this book.

As a Spanish teacher, it was my job to instruct students in the foreign language standards through a cultural lens. The theme of immigration and empathy were embedded in the national and state standards as well as in district curriculum. Empathy is best taught through experience. Therefore, I created an "immigration project," where students obtained their individualized pseudo identity from a Latin American country. This project emulated the entire process of immigration, immersed students in the Spanish language, and afforded new cultural perspectives only found through Latin American country websites. "Ms. Spanish Teacher promised them that the process—even in make-believe—would frustrate them. But they would gain, she hoped, an understanding of what is one of the most important political and humanitarian issues facing the U.S. government today" (Zachariah, 2007b, pp. B1–B2). Once students completed their research, they participated in a gallery walk of their work where they presented their learning to community members (e.g., parents, staff members, central office personnel, peers, etc.).

Why did this project cause such controversy? What values do our American citizens employ and how do those values infiltrate the American curriculum?

> Values, particularly in America, proliferate, and these values find their educational expression in the ways in which schooling, curriculum, teaching, and evaluation are to occur. Curriculum ideologies are defined as beliefs about what schools should teach, for what ends, and for what reasons. (Eisner, 2002, p. 47)

Immigration, homosexuality, and religion are culture wars found all throughout the nation and American history. Nonetheless, they are real-world issues that impact everyday people. Particularly, immigration evokes mixed emotions; conservative and liberal factions exist, both hidden and uncovered in American society. Should we open the borders to everyone who wants to enter the United States? Do we have enough land and resources to support such an influx of people? How do we handle the people who come here illegally? Only the fit and educated should be allowed entry, right? Why should "they" have rights? They were not born here and now they are going to live off the government and add to existing poverty. What about the illnesses they bring? And so on, and so forth. But... "they" just want to live the American Dream like the rest of us who were fortunate enough to be born in the United States of America. Right, wrong, or indifferent—immigrants are people, too. Almost a decade after my project and 2 decades after Sears' course, these culture wars continue to course throughout society in 2018.

According to Sears and Carper (1998):

> These reflect a disturbing phenomenon: the tribalization of America. Here complex issues become reified into simplistic slogans (e.g., "Abortion Is Murder," "The Christian Right Is Neither," "When Guns Are Outlawed Only Outlaws Will Have Guns") as a variety of ideological and theological positions get reduced into competing binaries: us/them, right/wrong, win/lose, sinner/saint, left/right. (p. 40)

Examining this immigration project from 2007 through a magnifying glass with more wisdom and perspective gleaned, I do not claim to have the answers nor did I when teaching the curriculum. However, I do agree that I taught this subject with added zeal because of my personal beliefs, values, and experiences. Eisner (2002) reveals this awareness:

> Because education is a normative enterprise, it cannot be approached value free. Such a position would leave educators with neither rudder nor compass. Any normative enterprise is, by definition, guided by certain beliefs about what counts. These beliefs, in one form or another, constitute an ideological view. (pp. 52–53)

I, the Spanish teacher, influenced curriculum and inspired student thought regarding a social justice topic. And, society influenced my curriculum—what I taught and what students learned. Although, foreign language education experts, textbook companies, and I agreed that immigration was a cultural and linguistic imperative for student learning, I had to eliminate it due to the controversy. Does curriculum influence society and society influence curriculum?

As educators, should we ignore certain aspects of teaching due to contentiousness or should we open dialogue in the classroom and explore reflective thought and problem-solving processes?

For me, immigration was close to my heart. An entire "secret society" exists within the American immigration system. I should know, I experienced the entire legal process with a Mexican immigrant in 1999. It taught me several lessons: Even in government offices one experiences racism, sometimes the legal route makes it so difficult that it forces people (due to survival) to dabble in the illegal, there is an entire underground society of undocumented immigrants, and much more. Please do not misinterpret my words: I do not agree nor condone illegal notions; however, I have gained empathetic perspective as to why one might be in the position of "illegal immigrant status." Maxine Greene details my sentiments of the importance of teaching youth to think and speak for themselves:

> Many of us who are teachers are eager to provoke questioning from young people who traditionally would have been silenced in the classroom as they were taught to internalize the values and the icons of the dominant culture. We hope to release more and more students for a pursuit of meanings that will deepen and diversify what we conceive to be American. (Sears & Carper, 1998, p. 29)

My immigration experience as a White, middle-class, female born and raised in the United States of America, suddenly classified as a Mexican immigrant due to the man I had married, taught me awareness and empathy. With curriculum in mind, some might say that my personal experience encouraged a new set of ideologies, a newly acquired set of values that I chose to incorporate into my classroom as explicit curriculum. True or not, it continues to demonstrate the profound power of curriculum. The immigration process was an eye-opening experience that exposed a dimension of society that many never witness. As an educational leader and teacher, I value the imperativeness of teaching students' empathy, global citizenship, how to think critically, and how to make sound decisions through searching for truth. The impetus of teaching the immigration project was for students to look through the worldly window as an immigrant and see what they see, through their eyes.

Throughout teaching this project, I kept my personal political opinions regarding immigration to myself. As a matter of fact, it would have surprised all of the conservatives who claimed I was a liberal that I was raised by intelligent, truth seeking, fundamentalist, Christian Baptists, after all. To the

American public, because I taught and spoke Spanish, I must be a democrat Mexican. These claims were as outlandish as the claims made about Sears not being able to stay objective during a Christian course because of his sexuality. It is for these assumptions that exist in society that demonstrate the need for teaching students a diversified curriculum. Nevertheless, one of my students, on December 19, 2007, in response to the article "Moonbattery," (2007) and several other posts, combatted these unrealistic notions:

> Guess what…it's another Spanish V student responding to your very own brainwashed self; this was the most difficult but amazing project ever. I have never learned so much in my life and especially about such an important issue. "Ms. Spanish Teacher" should only be receiving praises for pushing us to discover the truths about immigration for ourselves. Prof never once revealed her own beliefs on the issue and to this day I still do not know her own opinions. Rather she made us formulate our own views based on the reality of going through the actions…My opinions were not swayed, rather unlike your own uninformed bias, I have intelligence behind my view.

This was for the students to decide. They, themselves, after researching and "experiencing" immigration, had to formulate their own opinions, values, and ideologies regarding their political standpoints. Another student, responded:

> Our Spanish teacher in no way told us which opinions to have—instead, she provided us with the information to develop opinions on our own. For the first time in my high school career, students are debating what they think is right or wrong. To be honest, I couldn't tell you how my teacher feels about illegal immigration. But I could tell you how 9 or 10 students in my Spanish 5 class feel about it. Our teacher has not forced her opinions on us—instead she has given us the opportunity to have opinions of our own. This is one of the most educational projects I have ever completed in my high school career, and it's the hardest I've ever worked. I am now fortunate enough to have an opinion of my OWN when it comes to illegal immigration. And I can promise you that it is not the same as any other students in my class. We haven't conformed to one person's views—we have found our own! So, thank you Profe for giving us that opportunity.

In the words of Michael W. McConnell, "The best kind of curriculum, I believe, would be one in which the children would be introduced to a multiplicity of points of view, including those that are expressly religious" (Sears & Carper, 1998, p. 34), or in this case political. I believe these Spanish V students would agree with McConnell as they discovered their own voice through experiential learning. Furthermore, the conversations elicited deep thinking and uncovered varying perspectives on immigration;

"Walking a mile in someone else's shoes," had a whole new meaning for these students.

Similarly to Sears and Carper (1998), after all of the media hype surrounding his "Christian" course and once it had been taught to fruition, his students, like mine, supported him:

> Interestingly, The State, which had originally intended to run a "pro" and "con" set of articles, could find no one who had completed the course with anything negative to say. By the end of the semester, even some of my harshest critics praised the course, and following a three-month delay, the board approved all 35 promotions. (p. 39)

Often the people with bias are not the ones teaching. In the United States, most teachers have to undergo several years of college education, pass examinations, and then undergo an apprenticeship, called "student teaching," prior to being permitted to enter a classroom and teach America's youth. I believe the American public should look inwardly at their own biases through a magnifying glass before passing judgment on our schools. Due to the misinterpretations of curriculum, I encourage Americans to read this enlightening book—*Curriculum, Religion, and Public Education: Conversations for an Enlarging Public Square*—by Sears and Carper (1998) because it affords in-depth insight into why certain Americans react without knowledge regarding public education; it details how history, politics, money, and religion influence curriculum.

Why would some Americans react to the immigration project as they did? Sears and Carper might proclaim, because of our history. For example, "When the common school movement was started by Horace Mann and others in the 19th century, there was no question whatsoever that it was a movement to acculturate a large number of immigrants and to Americanize Aliens" (Sears & Carper, 1998, p. 26). Americans have viewed schools as a place to assimilate a variety of people and cultures into one American society. Thus, education has been a place, not for critical thinking or learning, but rather a place to teach people how to believe and how to act. Furthermore, one could argue that during this time period, many people felt that immigrants, bringing forth their unique identities, were inherently a "bad thing," especially if education was trying to erase those identities and replace them with a new one. Could this be considered dehumanization of immigrants? And are we not more than a century past these ideals?

> The extension of the concept of ideology into the general sphere of cognitive theory, linguistics, philosophy, and deconstruction is advanced here because it is an arguable case that the most influential ideologies are not those formally acknowledged and publicly articulated, but rather those that are sub-

liminally ingested as a part of general or professional socialization. (Eisner, 2002, p. 51)

Eisner ascertains that ideologies form the curriculum that educators implement and that society permits. Does this begin to explain why people from all over the nation respond with such passion and fervor of both hatred and compassion to the immigration project of 2007 and to Sears' course, "Christian Fundamentalism and Public Education," in 1993? Is it partly due to the fact that American schools were set up to acculturate our immigrants and children? Accordingly, by teaching them (immigrants and our children) the truths and realities of both empathy and America's secrets, we might "mess up" or "dissimilate" our American society? According to Eisner (2002), "Thus far I have described ideologies largely as a function of acculturation and as an inherent part of the psychological structures—languages and theory—that we acquire as members of a culture" (p. 51).

In concert with Eisner, Richard John Neuhaus affirmed, "The public school has become the cockpit for the playing out of the culture wars" (Sears & Carper, 1998, p. 26).

> Although in some societies ideological commitments can be both uniform and powerful, it is not the case that in pluralistic societies uniformity among ideologies is the norm. More often than not, ideological positions pertaining to curriculum and to other aspects of education exist in a state of tension or conflict. In pluralistic societies, a part of the pluralism emerges in competing views of what schools should teach and for what ends. These competing views prevail or succumb in a political marketplace. (Eisner, 2002, p. 51)

While the immigration project was a strong assignment acclaimed to be sound by several foreign language educators, 2007 was the last year for the teaching of the immigration project.

Ending this project, or controversy, was in the best interest of the school district. Neuhaus confirms, "Schools are already distracted from this goal (educating children) and will be even more distracted by all these great societal battles that people will try to fight out on the public school turf" (Sears & Carper, 1998, p. 27). Immigration would still be taught, but students would not attain the learning as once before. The theme of immigration took a back seat to other themes found within cultural contexts of the Spanish curriculum. Eisner (2002) summarized this phenomenon well:

> Because schools and school districts are subject to the vicissitudes of local and national expectations, changes in schools based on the prevalence of a particular ideological view may last for a short time. As the social and economic conditions of a community change, as its political climate alters, as staff come and go, it becomes necessary for schools to make adjustments and to accom-

modate to these newly emerging conditions. What this means at the level of practice is the continual readjustment of programs and priorities, even if one wishes to maintain the direction the school has taken prior to those changed conditions. Educational practices and priorities reflecting ideological commitments need modification in order to survive, just as a tightrope walker must correct for movement in the wire if he or she is to remain on it. (p. 53)

Joseph L. Mas, chairman for the Ohio Hispanic Coalition on Saturday, December 29, 2007, published his commentary in *The Columbus Dispatch*:

Thank you, "Ms. Spanish Teacher," and thank you, "Mr. Principal." Not for your advocacy of the undocumented community, for that is not what you did. But thank you for your courage and insight in teaching your charges a perspective often missing from the public discourse. A perspective, one might add, not unlike that shared by the vast majority of our ancestors.

After this experience, I could not wait to lose my former last name, to forgo part of my identity, so that I could escape public scrutiny in the educational realm. I was tired of being *bajo la lupa* (under scrutiny). Prior to attaining my educational leadership administrative position, I hurried and changed all of my transcripts and diplomas pertaining to my old name, "Ms. Spanish Teacher." I ran as far away from this immigration project as I could, never looking back and not mentioning it until now. It is extremely difficult to undergo unwarranted humiliation that defames your reputation as an educator, even when everything was honorable and right.

Now, I, too, am liberated. Thank you, James T. Sears—you liberated me through your story. You reminded me that I am not alone and I should be proud for inspiring a nation of people to embark upon critical, humanitarian conversations for world improvement. The immigration project experience is an integral part of who I am today. James T. Sears and I made history. The American public stared into a magnifying glass and saw a variety of perspectives regarding American society. Even the haters had to take a look inward. My students learned a great many things, most importantly, they learned how to think for themselves and make informed decisions.

One student became an immigration lawyer and another student recognized me as his most memorable teacher from MIT because of this project. Another student learned of her adoption from Russia and how immigration was an integral part of her identity. I am now a stronger, braver, and a more courageous educational leader. Eleven years later, a principal of curriculum and instruction, I define myself as both the lioness and the lamb. I am empathetic and kind, yet a great warrior for truth and love. I encourage all to respectfully stand up for what is right, search for truth, and work towards making the world a better place, one person at a time. This can only transpire by looking through the magnifying glass at one's personal biases, ideals, values, and belief systems. Once we understand ourselves, we are able to begin to understand others. As educators, we model and teach the future citizens of our democratic way of life. It is my belief that education is one of the most vital, if not the most essential professions, existing within our nation.

> Those who choose to cross territories risk the wrath from all sides along the border. Just as it is dangerous for a Cambodian youth flagging his colors to cross Chicago's Broadway Avenue, so, too, it is difficult for an evangelical Christian embracing a Bible to enter a public university classroom of an "avowed homosexual." Without these border-crossers, though, our public square dwindles. (Sears & Carper, 1998, p. 40)

Thus, embedded in curriculum exists society's values; cultural norms; historical perspectives; ideals regarding gender, religion, sex; and more. Curriculum is knowledge to be gained: it is the context, content, and skills that we teach our children from the early age of three when they enter preschool all the way through high school graduation. The federal government has left it up to states and local communities to decide what curriculum is taught in their school districts. Typically, the curriculum taught in schools contains the cultural values found within the community. Ask yourself, is there or will there ever be a true curriculum that is equitable for all types of learners when what we teach and learn depends on the value system and financial backing of the community in which we live? One can ascertain that curriculum is knowledge which is power. The curriculum we enact has the power to influence our society, for better or worse, through the American youth.

REFERENCES

Davenport, D. R. (2000). Reviewed work(s): Curriculum, religion, and public education: Conversations for an enlarging public square by James T. Sears and James C. Carper. *Journal of Church and State, 42*, 870–872.

Dewey J. (2010). My pedagogic creed. In D. J. Simpson & S. F. Stack (Eds.), *Teachers leaders, and schools: Essays by John Dewey* (pp. 24–33). Southern Illinois University Press. (Original work published 1897)

Eisner, E. W. (2002). *The educational imagination: on the design and evaluation of school programs* (3rd ed.). Pearson Education, Inc.

Goodstein, L. (2009, January 8). Rev. R. J. Neuhaus, political theologian, dies at 72. *The New York Times.* https://www.nytimes.com/2009/01/09/us/09neuhaus.html

GoUpstate. (1993, June 3). *Christian right conservatives pressure USC to drop class.* http://www.goupstate.com/news/19930603/christian-right-conservatives-pressure-usc-to-drop-class/1

Malkin, M. (2007, December 17). *Open borders 101.* The Unz Review. http://michelle malkin.com/2007/12/17/open-borders-101/

Mas, J. L. (2007, December 28). Teacher gives her students perspective. *The Columbus Dispatch.* https://www.dispatch.com/story/opinion/editorials/2007/12/29/teacher-gives-her-students-perspective/23700401007/

Sears, J. T. (1991). *Growing up gay in the South.* Routledge.

Sears, J. T. (1997). *Lonely Hunters.* Westview Press.

Sears, J. T. (2005). *Gay, lesbian, transgender issues in education.* Harrington Park Press.

Sears, J. T. (2006). *Mask of the mattachine.* Harrington Park Press.

Sears, J. T., & Brown, R. M. (2001). *Rebels, Rubyfruit, and Rhinestones.* Rutgers University Press.

Sears, J. T., & Carper, J. C. (1998). *Curriculum, religion, and public education: Conversations for an enlarging public square.* Teachers College Press.

Zachariah, H. (2007b, December 15). Students struggle as immigrants do. *The Columbus Dispatch,* B1–B2.

CHAPTER 28

COGNITIVE DISSONANCE OF LEADERSHIP

Jennifer M. Penczarski

Author/Book studied:

Sergiovanni, T. J. (1982). *Supervision of teaching.* Association for Supervision and Curriculum Development.

In 1982, the Association for Supervision and Curriculum Development published the book *Supervision of Teaching.* The chairperson and chief editor of the book was Thomas J. Sergiovanni. I was very excited to have the opportunity to read Sergiovanni for the first time. His work was recommended to me on several occasions by colleagues, and at first glance, it appeared to be a good fit given my current role as a superintendent. The book, however, was not what I expected. This was my first experience reading a yearbook around a given topic, and I struggled with connecting all of the different authors' thoughts.

Over the past few months, I found a personal connection with Thomas Sergiovanni that will help me continue to challenge my core values and

Curriculum Windows Redux, pages 333–344

beliefs about educational leadership and supervision. By using the cognitive dissonance theory lens, I can see the personal disconnect between my values and beliefs about leadership and my attitudes, behaviors, and actions as a leader. In this chapter, I will share my personal struggle and tension with the concepts of supervision, leadership, and evaluation, and examine Eisner's struggle with the word "supervision" and Sergiovanni's revisioning of leadership over time. My purpose is to open a window of leadership that embraces the dissonance and encompasses balance and harmony among the ideas and practices of supervision, leadership, and evaluation.

COGNITIVE DISSONANCE THEORY

In 1957, Leon Festinger proposed the theory of cognitive dissonance. He proposed that everyone strives for internal consistency in order to function in the world. Essentially everyone needs consistency between their expectations of life and the existential reality of life. Dissonance is defined as the result of a person performing an action that contradicts their core values and personal beliefs, or when new obligations create a discrepancy. When this inconsistency occurs, something must change in order to eliminate the dissonance (Festinger, 1962, p. 93). This can occur by reducing the importance of the dissonance, increasing consonant beliefs so that they outweigh the dissonants, or modifying the dissonance so it is no longer an inconsistency (Festinger, 1962 p. 95). This theory can easily be applied to education and the theme of supervision because leaders are in constant dissonance with themselves as mandates often do not align with personal core values. Festinger received the Award for Distinguished Scientific Contribution from the American Psychological Association for his work on cognitive dissonance theory.

Supervision of Teaching

Supervision of Teaching (Sergiovanni, 1982) is the 1982 yearbook of Association for Supervision and Curriculum Development (ASCD,) and is broken up into five parts consisting of 13 chapters written by eight different authors. Sergiovanni hopes to bring about a comprehensive understanding of supervision that can guide new directions and pathways for education by challenging leaders to think differently. In the introduction to the book, he gives an overview of the parts and chapters. He describes the activities of an administrator who has an impact on instruction as helping teachers and working in classrooms with students (Sergiovanni, 1982, p. vi). He also identifies the embedded concepts of supervision as being "supervision as authority stemming from superordinate relationships" and "supervision as quality control" (Sergiovanni, 1982, p. vi). When thinking about his career and work in leadership, coupled with the timing of this publication, I believe this yearbook was the beginning of Thomas Sergiovanni opening a window of understanding about the difference between leadership as a process and leadership as substance.

Part I, "The Genesis of Supervision," is a timeline of the evolution of supervision in the United States. The author uses different lenses to help the reader understand the different perspectives and viewpoints of supervision. The three major eras discussed in the chapter are the common school era, the progressive era, and the depression. Part II, "The Many Faces of Supervision," looks at the theory of supervisory practice. Chapters 2, 3, and 4 examine the scientific, artistic, and clinical approach to supervision while Chapter 5 focuses on the culmination of all three approaches to improve instruction. These approaches are stronger when fused together as one strategy than if applied individually (Sergiovanni, 1982, p. vi). Part III, "The Human Factor in Supervision," dedicates the next four chapters to examining the human impact on supervision through the various lenses of personal growth and professionalism. These chapters begin to explore the impact of organizational structure and bureaucratic requirements on schooling. Part IV, "The Hidden Dimension in Supervision," describes the impact of curriculum, bureaucracy, and society on the process of supervision, while Part V, "The Future," identifies potential developments and possibilities of what is to come with supervision and evaluation (Sergiovanni, 1982, p. vii).

I can appreciate Sergiovanni's work in melding the ideas and themes of the eight authors into one comprehensive yearbook around a given topic. Over the past 4 years, I have worked to bring together superintendents from five small school districts to design a comprehensive educational directional system for our county. Each district has its own core values and beliefs, but each district's uniqueness brings about new ideas that help pave the pathway for the future of education for our students. The five districts also share many commonalities but have struggled over time to reveal these common attributes. This struggle has changed our thinking and made me a stronger leader.

AUTHOR AND EDITOR

Thomas J. Sergiovanni was a key scholar in redefining the role of the principal in educational leadership. At the time the book was published, Sergiovanni served as a professor and chair in the Department of Educational Administration in the College of Education at the University of Illinois at Urbana–Champaign. In 1984, 2 years after the book was published,

Sergiovanni was named professor at Trinity University in Texas. He was known for his work with the Center for Educational Leadership, the Trinity Principals' Center, and the International Schools of the Americas in San Antonio, Texas. Sergiovanni was remembered for his innovative rethinking about principal leaders and community. Thomas Sergiovanni died at age 75 in Dallas, Texas.

ELLIOT W. EISNER'S DISSONANCE WITH SUPERVISION

Throughout Chapter 4: "An Artistic Approach to Supervision," Elliot W. Eisner questions the connotations of the word supervision. This is a word I have struggled with my whole career because when used to describe a task of principal, it seems very managerial in nature. Eisner writes that the word supervision implies

> a supervisor is supposed to have a super vision. The relationship between the supervisor and the teacher is hierarchical and while hierarchy will never be absent from human relationships, in the context of supervisor/supervisee relationships it suggests that the former has the right to prescribe to the latter how the job is to be done. (Sergiovanni, 1982, p. 54)

This is the first place in the book where I could clearly identify the cognitive tension and connect to Eisner's concern about hierarchical relationships.

In my third year of a principalship, I was given the challenge of transforming a low achieving middle school into a high achieving middle school. People shared that most viewed this as the most challenging building in the district. This was not something new, I have heard this about middle schools in general throughout my career. These schools are often seen as the dumping ground for ineffective staff. This was not the case of the school I was to lead. The middle school was full of talented people who cared about students and had the potential to be great curriculum designers: However, I quickly realized that the way they had been supervised had limited their ability to do what they believed was best for students.

I was invited to hold a staff meeting prior to the end of the school year and before the start of my tenure in order to formally introduce myself and share my vision, or "super vision" according to Eisner. I had attended many staff meetings as both a teacher and principal over my career, but I had never walked into a meeting quite like this. All of the teachers were sitting at desks arranged in straight rows, in silence, in a middle-school classroom. The soon-to-be former principal stood at the front of the room near a podium and signaled me to come forward to speak. She walked to the podium and introduced me, the teachers applauded, and then the room became dead silent once again.

Throughout my career I have been anything but traditional both in my instructional practices as a band director and my leadership style as an assistant principal. My style would best be described as high energy, motivational, and people-centered. Many people refer to me as their personal cheerleader, but at this moment in time I was stifled. The setting was not one where I could begin to build relationships with my new staff, but rather one where I could merely define the hierarchical chain of command. It was the first time I felt what a culture of supervision looked like in education. I spent the next 2 years breaking free from the established organizational structure and creating a culture that embraced leaders and learners. I never prescribed how to teach, because like Eisner, I believe teaching and supervision is an art, with each individual having his or her own unique approach to instructional practices. The meaning of artistic supervision, according to Eisner, is

> using an approach to supervision that relies on the sensitivity, perceptivity and knowledge of the supervisor as a way of appreciating the significant subtleties occurring in the classroom that exploits the expressive, poetic and often metaphorical potential of language to convey to teachers or to others whose decisions affect what goes on in schools what has been observed. (Sergiovanni, 1982, p. 59)

Supervision not defined within these parameters is nothing more than management. I believe Eisner was working to change the dissonant beliefs in the traditional definition of supervision by redefining the parameters and providing more constant beliefs that align with his values about supervision.

SERGIOVANNI'S SEARCH FOR A THEORY OF PRACTICE

In Chapter 5, "Towards a Theory of Supervisory Practice: Integrating Scientific, Clinical, and Artistic Views," Sergiovanni (1982) searches for meaning by using the domain of inquiry. The domain of inquiry can be defined by three question areas:

1. What is going on in this classroom? How does it work? Can it be explained and predicted? What laws and rules govern behavior in this context? How can I accurately and vividly describe classroom events;
2. What ought to be going on in this classroom? What cultural imperatives should determine action? What values should be expressed? What qualities of life should be in evidence? What standards should be pursued;
3. What do events and activities that comprise the "is" and "ought" dimension of classroom life mean to teachers, students, supervisors

and significant others? What is the cultural content of the class-room? What implicit education platforms exist? What values are suggested by actual behavior and events? What are the meanings implicit in discrepancies between the espoused and in use theories? (pp. 72–74)

During my master's program in educational leadership, I had a professor who insisted that if we walked away with nothing else from his teaching, we would know the secret to be a successful educational leader. In his experience as a superintendent, the secret to being successful lay simply in knowing the difference between what is happening and what is really going on. Although it had been 15 years since I took his class, I have never forgotten what he said, and the concept came full circle again for me after reading this chapter. Sergiovanni's underlying theme of identifying what is and what ought to be in the classroom caused me to think about strategies to ensure the evaluation process provides a window for the teacher and a window for the evaluator to see what is really happening with classroom from different vantage points.

My first administrative position was as an assistant principal in a high school of about 1,200 students. Although the majority of my day was spent addressing disciplinary infractions, the greater part of my interactions with teachers centered around the evaluation process. Teacher evaluation was one of the scariest things I had to do as a principal because my experience in the general education classroom was very limited. Prior to becoming a principal, I was a band director for 8 years. My classroom did not function as a general core curriculum classroom. I was assured by my mentor that I knew what good teaching looked like, and I had the skill set to provide feedback to improve teaching. I also relied heavily on my perceived strength of knowing the difference between what was happening in the classroom and what was really going on. The greatest barrier was simply my confidence, as I would be evaluating teachers who had been mastering their craft in the classroom for decades. Drawing on what I came to later understand as Thomas Sergiovanni's domain of inquiry, what is and what ought to be, I was able to provide valuable feedback around improving teaching and student learning.

Two memories of teacher evaluations from my first year of evaluating teaching jumped out of me as I read this chapter of the book. The first was one of an exemplary educator, and the second was one who struggled with opening the window of student learning. Both caused me dissonance as a leader, and both allowed me to open a new curriculum window making me a better evaluator of staff.

My office was located across the hall from one of the best loved and respected staff members in the building. He was one of those teachers everyone knew in our community, and one most students looked forward to having as a teacher. He had the reputation of having high expectations and producing high levels of student learning. This teacher allowed me to experience firsthand what student engagement looked like and felt like during a 47-minute period. This was one of the only observations I asked to redo. For this observation, I took my seat in the back of the room to observe a junior level language arts class. From the preconference with the teacher, I knew the lesson would be about the puritans. My approach to evaluation was to take very descriptive notes about the experience. This would define what is going on in the classroom. From those notes and my experience during the class period, I could make judgments about what ought to be going on and identify any gaps.

My notes started off like any other observation with a detailed account of everything I was seeing and hearing, but about half-way down my first page of notes, the context changed. I began to write down information about the puritans and literature. The teacher completely engaged me in the lesson. For the first time, I forgot I was doing an observation and evaluation. This was one of those magical teaching and learning moments I will never forget. I was lost in the lesson, I actually caught myself trying to raise my hand, near the end of the class, to answer a question. This was a classroom I visited often over the next 2 years to watch a master artist at work. I needed to learn about and see more instructional strategies in action, so I could share this art of teaching with others in the future.

On the flip side, I also experienced teachers who had a disconnect between what they thought was going on in the classroom and reality. Unfortunately, high school teachers are often characterized by being more concerned with teaching content than with student learning. Although I do not believe this is always the case, I did encounter a teacher, my first year, with no understanding of what was really going on. Her viewpoint was clouded, and she could not step outside of her classroom role as teacher to see the impact of her teaching practices on learning. She was not able to look through the window from a student viewpoint. I spent a great deal of time and energy working to help the teacher understand the gap between what she thought and what ought to be happening in the lesson. Until her window was opened, she did not understand or acknowledge that there was a difference.

My focus at the time as a leader was to make her effective vs. building a relationship and understanding of her viewpoint. It was easier to write a poor evaluation with an improvement plan than deal with the cognitive dissonance between wanting to understand and see instruction from her viewpoint, and building a relationship, providing coaching to help her change, and see the impact of her instructional practices. Sergiovanni (1982) sums it up best in the question he poses in Chapter 8, "How can we provide a context for supervision that best supports teacher growth and development on the one hand and releases the energy and talents of teachers to the fullest on the other?"

(p. 108). This is a question that I still think about daily, even from the superintendent's desk. I have yet to find a way to open the window that balances the new Ohio Teacher Evaluation System, growth measures, and other state and union evaluation requirements, while releasing the energy and talents of teachers who are developing the art of teaching. To achieve balance, I will find ways to reduce the importance of those requirements that do not align with my fundamental beliefs about evaluation.

DISSONANCE IN THE FUNDAMENTAL PRINCIPLES OF LEADERSHIP

In the beginning of this chapter, I referred briefly to my experience in the creation of the Hardin County Design Team, a team of six superintendents and school districts focused on creating a directional system aligning our core beliefs about education to the values, virtues, and traditions of our communities. The design team idea originated from our counties' attempt to secure a Straight A Grant from the state of Ohio and professional development aligned with the work of Phil Schlechty. Each individual district in our consortium has been working to fundamentally transform their critical systems to align with those of a learning organization versus a bureaucracy (Schelchty, 2009). Even though the book was written in 1982, Gerald R. Firth and Keith P. Eiken's Chapter 11, "Impact of the Schools' Bureaucratic Structure on Supervision," made a strong personal connection with me because the cognitive dissonance the authors' described is the same conflict I struggle with on a daily basis while embracing this work. What should the focus of our county directional system be? When those ideals conflict with the organizational structures created for us by the federal, state, and potentially local governments, how do we balance the dissonance? How do we create systems within the provided framework allowing us to lead, supervise, and evaluate teachers to offer the highest quality education possible for every student?

I took the initiative to do more research about Thomas Sergiovanni after finishing the book because the principles and ideas that I learned from others did not closely align with the excerpts provided in the *Supervision of Teaching* (Sergiovanni, 1982). I know I am still learning better ways to open the window of leadership in a balanced way, but it was my understanding that Thomas Sergiovanni had a breakthrough in the way he thought about leadership in the late 1980s and early 1990s. In an article I found from 1992 titled "On Rethinking Leadership: A conversation with Tom Sergiovanni," he shares a story of how his mindset shifted from the focus of leadership not being about a vision but about "a set of conceptions that become an idea structure for their schools" (Brandt, 1992, p. 48). He continues to say that "the more successful we are at establishing substitutes for leadership the less important it becomes to worry about who are leaders and who aren't" (Brandt, 1992, p. 48).

The story Sergiovanni shared was one from the 1980s where he was presenting a leadership seminar in the Philippines. His entire lecture focused on the idea of leadership as a process based on situations and how to be effective as a leader. Over the course of several days, a person in the audience continued to question him on what the word effective meant. Essentially, the audience member wanted to know how Sergiovanni was defining the word effective? At first, he found the question annoying, but in the weeks that followed, it was that single question that caused him to rethink and open the window of leadership a different way (Brandt, 1992, p. 47). This was the turning point and the end of his cognitive dissonance about leadership. Sergiovanni's viewpoint was changing.

"The only thing that makes the leader special is that she or he is a better follower: better at articulating the purposes of the community; more passionate about goals, more willing to take time to pursue them" (Brandt, 1992, p. 47). Sergiovanni wanted to abandon the word "teacher" and replace it with the phrase principal teacher, "a kind of community with teachers" (Brandt, 1992, p. 48). He believes that principals are leaders of leaders, the people who "develop the instructional leadership in their teachers" (Brandt, 1992, p. 48). He also begins to share his idea of schools as communities in the interview, which is what we hope to do on a county-level in our districts.

One of the first steps we took to develop a sense of community and a learning organization, where teachers are designers of instruction and principals are leaders of leaders, was to learn from our past to drive our future. We reflected on the defining moments in our history and used those moments to help inform and understand the way we had opened the window to education in the past. We compiled all the information about the educational, historical, and societal events of the various decades, and debated different viewpoints about what was happening in our district and community during each time frame. Some decades were easier than others, but the defining moments were easily remembered by all. We used this information to determine our previous core values and beliefs about education. We utilized these components to drive our new directional system focus of inspiring all to inquire, dream, and excel.

This was not an easy process, and the tension we worked through as a team over the course of several months brought about a common understanding of the similarities and differences in the core beliefs of our staff. As we finalized the words of our vision, I became stuck on the last word, "excel." I believed the word should be "achieve." My belief was for all our students and staff to achieve whatever goal was put in front of them. The question was repeatedly raised by a department head, what are we working to achieve? When I was mentally ready to look through a different lens, he shared his perspective on what the word excel meant to him. Achieve, assumes that there is a specific goal with one outcome. We only want others to achieve the goal. He insisted that based on our work, we wanted higher expectations for all of our district. We did not simply want others to achieve our goals but excel past them.

Looking through his lens brought balance to my tension, and as a leader of leaders, a principal teacher, in Sergiovanni's terms, played a major role eliminating dissonance and creating harmony in the directional system and core beliefs of our district. The teacher had lessened the importance of my dissonance with the word "achieve" by adding more consonance to the word "excel." If we had used a hierarchical or bureaucratic practice, the teacher may not have had a safe space to share his perspective. Our vision was stronger as a result and resolution of the cognitive dissonance.

Around the same time of the interview, Sergiovanni's (1994) book *Building Community in Schools* was released. Schools should be bound together with a common purpose and commitment that connect people much like that of a community. He goes on to talk about the four developmental stages leaders go through when building community centered around value-added leadership. The first of these is *bartering*. In the bartering stage, the teacher and principal simply strike a bargain with both sides getting something they want. This is what I feel happens in negotiations between the board of education and teachers' unions. In the second stage, building, the principal creates a climate of support and opportunities for staff to thrive and grow as professionals. Our district leadership team designs organizational and operational infrastructures to ensure a positive school culture. The bonding stage is where intentional relationships are formed around common core beliefs and values. We accomplish this through our professional learning communities and teacher-based teams. The binding process is what makes the community strong where there is a common purpose and commitment. This would be the stage I achieved with my staff when we worked through the revisioning process of the directional system described earlier (Sergiovanni, 1994, pp. 192–193).

When I was hired as superintendent, my school community was in need of new facilities. They attempted to pass a bond issue for a decade with no success and were preparing to run a new campaign with a new leader. Through the extensive work done with both internal and external stakeholders, we were able to bond around the educational experience for our students. The tension was centered around financial dissonance. No one felt that the facilities were acceptable or that the students of our district did not deserve a better learning environment. However, there was a tremendous amount of dissonance when a high poverty community had to give more money in taxes that they usually don't have. I cannot express in words the experience of a school community bonding over educational opportunities for our students. People helped each other understand the financial dissonance and how the educational benefit of our students outweighed that dissonance. This is what we hope to achieve with our county design team. We are in the building stage moving towards bonding.

EMBRACING THE NEW WINDOW

Pulling from the chapters in the *Supervision of Teaching* (Sergiovanni, 1982), and from Thomas J. Sergiovanni's other works, I hope to combine what I have learned about the various viewpoints of supervision and leadership to open a new leadership window enhancing my current practice. I will use this work as a stepping stone for future studies to enhance my viewpoint of supervision and leadership within my district and within the Hardin County Design Team. As I grow in my profession as superintendent, I continue to improve my understanding of the importance of perspective. A leader must clearly see what is easily visible, but also what is not. I go back to my readings of Eisner and think about implicit, explicit, and null curriculum. Just because we cannot see something or because it is not intentionally taught does not mean it does not exist. All aspects of curriculum and instruction impact the context in which educational leaders work.

*   *   *

As you dive into the ocean, the color red is eliminated from your field of vision. You often don't even notice it has been lost because you are immersed by so many variations of blues and greens. Essentially, your vision is so saturated with the dissonance of blues and greens it overpowers your thought about the loss of the color red. It is not until you put a red filter on your mask or camera lens, that you realize the color red exists all around you. The color was just hidden.

My husband and I scuba dive off the island of Cozumel, Mexico. About 5 years ago we were wreck diving at 60 feet when I cut my hand. This was my first scuba accident and I was prepared for what I needed to do. What I was not told in my training was the color red is not visible in 60 feet of water. I was having a serious moment of cognitive dissonance as my brain could not process why my blood was green. Fortunately, the dive master knew why I was concerned and wrote on a sketch pad, "blood is green at 60 feet." I looked at him with confusion, and he gave me a red filter. When I held the lens in front of my mask, my blood was red. The most magical moment was not that my cognitive dissonance was resolved by the filter, but that the filter exposed an ocean full of not only reds, but also of oranges and yellows. The coral was beautiful. Without the filter, you could not see the colors, and would have missed the most beautiful perspective of the ocean.

I walk away from this book thinking about how curriculum and instruction may be the red in my ocean when it comes to supervision, leadership, and evaluation. I am distracted by so many other things that until I put a specific filter over my current lens, I simply forget the other colors exist. Once I look through the filter, I realize that red (curriculum) surrounds me and is embedded in every aspect of my surroundings. I am still allowing myself to absorb the red from this book and questioning how I think about curriculum, supervision, leadership, and evaluation. I will continue to find new windows and learn how to open them.

REFERENCES

Brandt, R. (1992). On rethinking leadership: A conversation with Tom Sergiovanni. *Educational Leadership, 49*(5), 46–49.

Festinger, L. (1962). Cognitive dissonance. *Scientific American, 207*(4), 93–106.

Schlechty, P. C. (2009). *Leading for learning: How to transform schools into learning organizations.* Jossey-Bass Publishers.

Sergiovanni, T. J. (1982). *Supervision of teaching.* Association for Supervision and Curriculum Development.

Sergiovanni, T. J. (1994). *Building community in schools* (1st ed.). Jossey-Bass Publishers.

CHAPTER 29

RISING TENSIONS

A Shift in Union Leadership

Kasey A. Perkins

Author/Book studied:

Weiner, L. (2012). *The future of our schools: Teacher unions and social justice.* Haymarket Books.

> *With more than 3 million members and vast political networks,*
> *the teacher unions are the most powerful force in American education.*
> *That won't change, but they'll have to make peace with reform.*
>
> —Toch, 2011

Lois Weiner's (2012) *The Future of Our Schools* dives into a behind the scenes look at teacher unions and their significance in creating a socially just education system. Weiner writes the book for teachers who are interested in the democratic way of challenging a school district. She wanted to help unions build a strong foundation among educators passionate about teaching, social justice, and creating a new social movement with advocates from various entities. Teacher unions need to work together to combat the neoliberal ideology that weakens the public education system and supports school of choice.

Weiner (2012) points out that teachers did not create the inequalities that are present in today's education system; however, they have done little to break down these barriers and promote positive change. She highlights the isolation of teacher unions and the political breakdown over time that has lessened the support from public and political entities. Weiner uses her own experience combined with research to help teacher leaders pave the way to a socially just union in their district. She encourages union leaders to set aside their confusion and step into the limelight to help transcend the isolation that has overcome unions. Her contributions to education are paramount, since many who have read her work have experienced a transformation in their involvement in the union.

My personal involvement with teachers' unions and my journey from an educator to an administrator was the driving force behind my interest in Weiner's (2012) book. Having spent a portion of my career as a teacher and a significant portion as an administrator, my contributions and assessments of unions have vastly changed over time. Although I was not an active participant in political contributions or negotiations during my time spent as a union member, I did see positive outcomes from those that represented me during my teaching tenure. As I ventured into administration, my experiences with the union started shifting in a different direction. As a principal, I began working with my union leadership with teacher discipline and step one grievances. These opportunities afforded me the chance to work in a collaborative nature with union leadership while learning to appreciate the role the union played in my building. When I transitioned to an assistant superintendent, my view of the union drastically changed. I was now on the side of the "unsupportive district" that was often seen in a negative light by union leadership.

The portrayal of the district administrators and the way situations were contorted to benefit one side began to really distort my view of unions. Two teacher negotiations later I had decided I was anti-union and did not see their place within a school system. The hope in selecting this book was to shift my mindset back to where it began and to see the positive way unions can work with a variety of stakeholders to create a socially just environment for staff.

This chapter will unfold the tensions that have arisen over time with unions inside the public education system and tell the story of unions and their drive for equity and social justice as seen through the lens of an educator with 20 years experience both as a teacher and administrator. The evolution of the teachers' union and its impact on their practice, pedagogy, and evaluation system will help provide the framework to years of interminable conflicts. Tensions over time between unions, policy makers, administrators, and politicians help pave the path to what is often perceived as a socially unjust education system.

As Weiner wrote a resource to help teachers increase their strength of unions, this chapter will share two sides to a story with my personal perspective on both. Weiner attempts to share her passion for the labor side of unions without considering the possibility of how unions can work in a collaborative nature with administration to move education in a positive direction.

DISORIENTATION OF UNION MEMBERS

Educational inequalities with unintentional consequences were created from the inception of teacher unions (Weiner, 2012). Educators and politicians truly cared about an equal education for poor children but caused more harm than good in the interim. Unions were often confused and disoriented with a poor approach to leadership and management of its members. They became a threat to the public and community as they isolated themselves and narrowed their allies and support system over time (Weiner, 2012).

Lois Weiner, a life-long teacher and union activist wrote *The Future of Our Schools: Teacher Unions and Social Justice* (Weiner, 2012) to help fellow educators who had a commitment to social justice and democracy within our schools. Weiner served as a union activist for three different unions during her teaching tenure. Her book empowered teachers to work together to create a democratic environment while serving and working with multiple constituents. A new union would need to be created working with parents, community activists, and other local unions. Her commitment to social justice and democracy was the driving force behind her writing (Weiner, 2012).

Classrooms, teachers, and unions are all impacted by the social, economic, and political lives that surround them. Weiner is passionate about the importance of regaining strength in teacher unions and helping to reshape them into democratic and progressive entities (Weiner, 2012). Over the course of time, union leadership was pressured to respond to issues that were popular among their members. This impeded union leadership from focusing on concerns of social justice that made all members feel their contributions were valued and they were part of a democratic organization (Weiner, 2012).

Weiner (2012) dives deep into how educators must understand the impact of what goes on outside of their classroom and the tools necessary to help take politically aware educators and turn them into active leaders within the union. One of the main goals of a teachers' union is to fight for tenure, due process, and academic freedom of teachers. If schools remain undemocratic, it is challenging to have a democratic society (Weiner, 2012). "More than 90% of the 2.6 million public educators belong to the American Federation of Teachers (AFT) or the National Education Association"

(NEA; Hawley & Jones, n.d., para. 1). A study argues that teachers in the NEA had a larger voice in professional matters before the NEA engaged in collective bargaining (Weiner, 2012). Weiner's goal was to help unions create a social movement that brings allies together on educational issues by examining the problem and coming to a consensus. In order to achieve a social movement, a current union must stretch its boundaries and define what is important to their members. Activism must be present using the union as a vehicle for social justice work (Weiner, 2012). Unions are losing political ground because they have surrendered the battle about the purposes of schooling. Weiner, through her writing, fought to empower unions to not surrender or concede defeat.

Weiner (2012) stated, "Our opponents may confuse idealism with naiveté, but unions should not" (p. 26). In a social movement union, bargaining starts with union leadership organizing ways to have members in each chapter discuss their vision of what they want. It can be detrimental to a union to enter into negotiations with demands that benefit the members without benefitting the students. Parents and community members look for essential items to benefit their personal needs for students. Demands on salary and benefits without considerations regarding class size and other conditions that impact students do not help improve the perceptions of negotiations among community members (Weiner, 2012). Members need to be empowered to stand up for their rights but at the same time recognize the rights of the students they represent every day.

Weiner shares how to build social movements among teacher unions. The need to eliminate hierarchical and paternalistic unions and move them in the direction of social movement unions is vital for continued success. A union needs democratization in order to serve the greater good. The goals of the union should not be restricted to members' immediate economic concerns. They need to be open to serving the needs of all members and in a fashion that puts students first (Weiner, 2012). Teachers are fearful of unions and attacks on teachers. Over time, union leadership put demands on teachers and governed with an iron fist instead of in a collaborative and democratic fashion.

Jon A. Stone conducted a study in 2000 where his findings found limited connections between collective bargaining and an improvement in student achievement (Hawley & Jones, n.d.). Unions can help increase student achievement with strong teacher induction programs, ongoing research based professional development, performance rewards, and peer reviews. Interest based bargaining, aligned with a socially just union, fosters discussions with an effort to find solutions between both sides (Hawley & Jones, n.d.).

Albert Shanker (as cited in Toch, 2001) notes that "unless we go beyond collective bargaining to teacher professionalism, we will fail," (p. 73). Shanker realized early on the need for non-adversarial unions where members instead received professional development training and colle-giality. Similar to Shanker, Nel Noddings shared the need to make unions more caring and nurturing towards all the people. By empowering ele-mentary teachers to be more actively involved, the union would include all sides of public education, not just that of the typical high school staff. Nod-dings recognized the typical male dominated high school union leader who was now forced to be more caring and empathetic towards the needs of the elementary teachers (Weiner, 2012).

My own personal experience has been working with male high school teachers serving as union president. Only recently, when the current union recognized a need for a more democratic and representative approach was an elementary teacher elected as a co-president. How many times have we seen union leadership positions held by male high school figures? When this happens during negotiations, the needs of the high school staff are met while the lower grade levels are often tossed aside or forgotten. The addition of an elementary leader meant equal rights and advocacy for all grade levels.

Peterson (2014) said, "If we don't transform teacher unions now, our schools, our profession, and our democracy-what's left of it-will likely be destroyed" (p. 5). Teacher unions across the nation are standing up against union attacks. It is considered an important force across the nation to de-fend not only unions but the public-school systems. By defending the very unions that support educators, an improvement in the communities, public school system, and democratic institutions is vital for a socially just system (Peterson, 2014). To transform national unions the lines of communication must be improved with a collaborative environment fostered among activ-ists (Weiner, 2012).

THE POLITICAL ARENA

The political sides of unions have changed drastically over time. Public edu-cation is one of the few sectors that are still heavily unionized. Until Lyn-don Johnson took office in the 1960s, the responsibility of public education fell solely on the state. Johnson advocated for the involvement of federal funding to help educational deficiencies that hurt disadvantaged students (Weiner, 2012). Jimmy Carter attempted to clean up the public education mess left behind by his predecessors. However, he didn't have the means to offer the financial backing needed to resolve the crisis facing school sys-tems. Bill Clinton, during his presidency, advocated for charter schools and school choice. Al Gore and John Kerry had teacher reform policies at the forefront of their presidential campaigns.

The Obama administration looked at teacher reform and union issues head on. "Race to the Top" was created to bring change to the teacher evaluation system—correlating student achievement to teacher compensation (Toch, 2011). Reformist democratic mayors from larger cities like New York created a group called Democrats for School Reform in an attempt to focus their efforts on that platform.

As politicians fought for school reform, unions continued to lose public support. Right wing political candidates expressed anger at teacher unions, placing the blame on the unions for all of the problems in public education. While infiltrating themselves into reform movements, Democratic candidates were taking a more active approach to teacher unions. Some democratic activists for the reform movement were questioning union goals (Givan, 2014).

Givan (2014) stated the following:

> The teachers unions are going to have to explain why when every tough decision is made to reform the school system they are at the lead in opposing it...if you are going to be at the front like in preventing reform, then I believe that the bad outweighs the good. (p. 68)

Topics like evaluation, tenure, and staffing have not garnered the necessary support needed by the public. Newer generations of college graduates appreciate union support but do not believe in protecting ineffective teachers or seniority (Toch, 2011). Teachers coming from fast-track programs are unfamiliar with unions, their purpose, and are often hesitant to take on a substantial role within the organization (Weiner, 2012).

Politics are extremely influential on educational policy. The responsibility of making educational policy is a shared responsibility of the federal, state, and local governance. Bureaucratic differences, political interests, and political authorities all have roles in muddying the waters of educational policy. As political authorities became more involved in policy making, less attention was given to teacher unions and their influence on state policies. Historically, unions have been classified as one of the most active interest groups in politics. The policies that govern schools are decided primarily by public participation which is advantageous to unions (Hartney & Flavin, 2011).

A study conducted found that over 75% of teacher unions endorsed school-board candidates in elections. These political advantages help elect policy makers who favor teacher unions and their empathy causes labor-management relationships to be understudied (Hartney & Flavin, 2011).

NEOLIBERALISM MOVEMENT

Weiner dives into the neoliberalism movement which she claims is turning public education into a free market. She discusses how the movement has worked to create an education system focused merely on teaching students' skills that pave the way towards a bleak future of low paying jobs (Weiner, 2012). Teachers with minimum competencies are allowed to work in schools with a lack of training in this movement. Neoliberalism pushes a survival of the fittest thinking. The presumption by neoliberals is that people have to work together to protect their common interests (Weiner, 2012).

Our current government leaders have spent millions of dollars supporting the school of choice movement with charter school vouchers. By taking away funds from public schools to support the privatization of education, the public schools suffer from the loss of funding. In the interim, charter schools continue to close and new ones open with little to no state or federal accountability. They are not held to the same standards as public educators nor crucified in the eye of the public when these standards are not met. Betsy DeVos, the current education secretary, is a huge advocate for the school of choice movement championed by the neoliberals since the 1970s.

Neoliberal projects work to push the goals of the 1% of their political allies while destroying teachers' autonomy and their ability to create a socially just environment for students. The devastation brought on by neoliberals has grown to a global epidemic in today's public education and cannot be fixed by one individual or a few union members (Weiner, 2012). Weiner (2012) argues, "We need to reject the will of both political parties who advocate a system of education that leaves children and democracy behind" (p. 173). It is imperative that both teacher union members and administrators work together to combat the issue of privatizing schools and to recognize the complexities of all the issues that the neoliberals in today's society are using to ruin public education.

HISTORICAL BACKING

In 1904, Margaret Haley addressed the NEA's convention with her speech, "Why Teachers Should Organize" (Hlavacik, 2012). Haley was the first individual to advocate for a national effort to create a democratic, unionized environment for classroom teachers. Haley shared democratic goals of progressivism to make unionism appealing to teachers and administrators. Her speech was the first to formally outline union rhetoric which would lead to a transformation of the public education system throughout the 20th century (Hlavacik, 2012).

Herb Kohl, a prominent reformer in the 1960s, wrote about education and the damaged relationship between teachers and critics. Kohl scolds educators for blaming working conditions and students for their lack of effort in the classroom. He argued for an accountability system for teachers that holds them not just accountable for student achievement but their attitudes. Kohl placed the blame solely on teachers, their deficiencies, and their unions for the destruction of students. By their unwillingness to change, students and educators are harmed in the process. Weiner argues that Kohl failed to understand the bureaucratic system that prevented students from learning, and it was the system itself that was flawed, not the constituents (Weiner, 2012).

The New York City Board of Education stated in their 1969–1972 contract that (La Noue & Pilo, 1970) the board of education and the union recognize that the major problem of our school system is the failure to educate all of our students and the massive academic underachievement which exists especially among disadvantaged students. The board and the union therefore agreed to join in an effort, in cooperation with universities, community schools' boards, and parent organizations, to seek solutions to this major problem and to develop objective criteria of professional accountability.

Educational accountability was being demanded by all levels of the government in the 1970s. Richard Zwieback, member of the National School Boards Association, called for new bargaining. He suggested a salary schedule that recognized performance and rewarded performance while eliminating mediocrity; by eliminating low accountability standards, an improvement in teacher performance would be evident. This was also the time when individuals were beginning to discuss tuition vouchers and the need for privatizing education due to the current state of governance of public schools (La Noue & Pilo, 1970).

Public education was under scrutiny as skeptics doubted accountability within the public school system. Unions during this era were gaining national attention as the NEA and AFT union groups grew stronger and teachers became the prime target under criticism. The NEA focused on standards, ethics, and curriculum while the AFT focused on the protection of wages and working conditions (Lathan, 2011). Early on, the AFT and NEA developed teachers unions on a business union philosophy (Weiner, 2012).

The 1960s and 1970s brought about strong unions with the adoption of planning periods. John Dewey argued "that we can't have a democratic society without schools that are themselves democratic" (as cited in Weiner, 2012, p. 69). "We need to make real Dewey's slogan, 'Democracy in education. Education for democracy'" (Weiner, 2012, 0. 69). Over time, union activity was viewed as aggressive moves towards salary increases, working conditions, and protecting the rights of educators. Union leaders along with political influences have recognized the tension among union members between fighting for rights beneficial for teachers vs. reforms beneficial for students (Hawley & Jones, n.d.).

"Bread and butter" unions, as they are referred to by many in years past, supported the traditional view of what a union should be, that is a union focused on protecting its members without seeing the broader vision of the best interest of the community, school, and students. Internal democracy and membership engagement were two areas that would need concentrated change to break the barrier created by "bread and butter" unions (Peterson, 2014).

Later critics throughout the 1980s would come to blame the 1960s for the demise of public education. Through relaxed curricula, a lack of standards and accountability, and a failed effort to equalize opportunities for students, the reforms of the 1960s were viewed as failures by many. The 1970s brought back the framework of reading and writing along with the fundamentals, the back-to-basics movement. Right wing critics used these perceptions of school failure to support their case that liberal reforms were ruining schools (Weiner, 2012).

By the mid-1990s, both the AFT and NEA worked to enhance their efforts to increase student achievement and better conditions inside the schools to support both teachers and students. Both the AFT and NEA needed to work to become more social unions instead of business oriented. Merit pay was the first battle between AFT and NEA. Albert Shanker supported merit pay which led to many controversial conversations during his tenure as head of the AFT.

Albert Shanker's legacy, his political domination of teacher unionism, and his influence and educational politics for half a century were influential (Weiner, 2012). He was the founding father of a teacher's union in the early 1960s holding his leadership position within the AFT for many years. He went on to be one of many great leaders in educational reform throughout the 1980s and 1990s. He was an advocate for tough liberalism and was the head of the United Federation of Teachers in New York City and the AFT (Kahlenberg, 2008).

Shanker helped organize teachers to realize that a union was a professional organization where teachers could have a voice and be treated as professionals. He was an advocate for strikes if the ends justify the means. He helped shape the AFT and eventually the NEA into powerful organizations that helped teachers stand up for their rights. Shanker pointed to politics as the solution to the union and public education devastation (Kahelenberg, 2008).

"Political action is reduced to political retaliation, revolving door of promises, and betrayals" (Weiner, 2012 p. 102). During Shanker's rise, political life in this county was marked by the birth of social movements, such as the civil rights movement, Hispanic activists, and women's movements, which all pointed their attention at the social inequalities in our schools. Opportunities for equal education and an end to legally sanctioned discrimination were supported by Shanker. "His conservative ideas about schooling made him a perfect partner for the political forces initiating the counteroffensive to the reforms of the 1960s and 1970s" (Weiner, 2012, p. 89).

A NEW HORIZON

In today's public school system, democratic notions are secondary to economic issues. The U.S. Secretary of Education Arne Duncan, created Race to the Top (RttT). The agenda for the program called for a new partnership in educational reform with districts and unions collaboratively working to help accelerate the process. As a participant in RttT, I worked with teachers, administrators, and union leaders to engage conversations around growth, 21st century learners, effective teaching strategies, and plans for implementation. The RttT initiative came after years of political sides, liberals and conservatives discussing poor schooling and its responsibility for the moral and industrial decline in the American public education system. The classroom needs to be the starting line in any attempt to restore U.S. political and economic power (Weiner, 2012). In order to implement a successful process, administration and school leadership need to work in a democratic fashion with their union constituents.

A key problem is both national unions have accepted the use of standardized test scores to evaluate and pay teachers (Weiner, 2012). Reforms of the last decade say schools should be operated like a business, with students and parents as customers and funding dependent on test scores.

Weiner argues that schools can do more for students with better working conditions, teachers who are well prepared with strong resources, and an elimination of achievement conditions that are out of teachers' control (Weiner, 2012). This is an accurate statement but not one that comes without a need for direction and a strong working relationship between union leadership and district administration. It has been my experience that union leadership often feels a need to defend teachers who do not have any place in the classroom, nor should they be protected by their union. To eliminate achievement conditions means a need for an accountability system to ensure teachers that are not doing their jobs are not allowed to continue.

A strong union should fight for the rights of the many but not protect those that are potentially harmful to students. This is something Weiner fails to touch on throughout her book. Recent documentaries, like *Waiting for "Superman"* (Guggenheim, 2010), have the media criticizing teacher unions and portraying their role in slowing democracy and school reform. Unions are portrayed as selfish for protecting their personalized interests and defending and accepting status quo (Lathan, 2011). These are the exact reasons for my argument against Weiner's claim to eliminate accountability standards for the betterment of schools. Schools cannot eliminate standardized testing and teacher evaluation systems for fear of the lack of accountability and low expectations that may come from implementing low standards and expectations for our teachers.

Recently, I finished my second negotiations sitting on the side of the administrative team in the district. I, unfortunately, began to see why teacher unions often receive a bad name in the eye of the public. Although not the fault of the membership as a whole, those elected to serve in the capacity of the negotiations team represent union members. Their perceived greediness and desire for terms only impacting themselves without thinking of the students in the district was a challenging pill to swallow. Weiner wants teachers to feel empowered to work with various constituents for democracy and social justice. Her suggestion includes involving union membership to help make decisions that are centered on students. Of course, a negotiating team should ask for fair wages and strong working conditions. But unions also need to be willing to recognize what will benefit their students and items they are willing to bring to the table that will support these claims.

Shanker advocated for major reforms that still influence political debates in today's public education system. He was willing to admit that not all teachers were good teachers and those that were not needed to leave the profession. He called for a rigorous entrance exam where teachers would only be admitted into the profession if they passed the exam. He defended tenure for teachers but understood that incompetent teachers were being protected by their union leadership. So, he called for a peer review plan for master teachers to evaluate new and experienced teachers, recommending those that needed to leave the profession. He supported merit pay under the guidelines of high performing and accomplished board-certified teachers. Teachers could also receive merit pay for raising test scores (Kahlenberg, 2008). Shanker's ideas were all valuable ideas that are still controversial today in the political and public lens of our education system.

He helped build a powerful union movement with the sophistication to defeat political attacks against the movement. He believed in improving public education and wanted to prove critics of the system wrong. He was referred to by one journalist, "a Dewey" in the education system. These ideas, although advantageous to making a stronger teaching system, are not reinforced today by current unions. Some districts have been able to implement merit pay and to have a supportive collaborative system where failing teachers are not allowed to remain in the profession. On the other side of the barrier are unions where teachers hold leadership positions to invest in their personal interests. This is often at the forefront of their decisions and negotiation tools. Due to their own poor performance in the classroom, they would not agree to a merit pay system they may view as penial.

CONCLUSION

As Shanker explained, "Teachers are acting only in our own self-interest, wanting better salaries and smaller classes so our lives can be made easier" (as cited in Weiner, 2012, p. 125). In order to be recognized as professionals, union members must act on the behalf of their clients. The renaissance of teacher unions globally needs to start at the local level to create a socially just union. These courageous activists will help reshape our unions as Weiner so passionately advocated. Teachers, parents, politicians, and communities at large should be carefully watching this form of heroism moving across our unions in public education. The future of public education greatly depends on their outcome and drive (Weiner, 2012).

Union leadership and members need to work together against the charter school movement and the political entities that are causing opposition. By standing up to the media, teacher unions face the greatest challenge of rebuilding their relationship with the economy at large. Teachers and students are victimized by the absence of democracy in our schools. This battle cannot be fought by individuals concerned with their own self-interest in the classroom and the need to fulfill their own interests to make things better for themselves. Cooperation with parents, teachers, and a variety of community groups is key to determining factors that are mutually exclusive to the betterment of a school.

There must be a mutual understanding that prevails even when opposition is present with decisions impacting students and teachers. Everyone's individual self-interests must mold together in order to form a democratic learning environment and not at the expense of another constituent. Unless faced with incarceration, most Americans have a greater involvement within the public school system than any other public institution (Weiner, 2012). Typically the connections between a neighborhood and the school community are beneficial to its progress depending on those willing to participate within the work. Our school systems need to be rebuilt into a democratic environment that fosters the rights of all students. This challenge must be equal to that of their counterparts where all sides must learn to work together.

Interest based bargaining must drive the negotiations team with members from both sides sitting at the table to discuss how to improve education for all parties. The days of the union being sequestered to one individual room while the administrative team hides in another (or at least that is how it is perceived) has to end. To close one door, another must open. This door must lead to a collaborative environment where all parties participate in a democratic process with the end goal being a socially just learning environment for all. When this happens, a groundbreaking revolution will have occurred, and the public education system will begin to see a shift in how it is run in terms of union interactions with students and administrators.

REFERENCES

Givan, R. (2014). Why teachers unions make such useful scapegoats. *New Labor Forum, 23*(1), 68–75.

Guggenheim, D. (2010). *Waiting for "Superman"* [Documentary film]. Walden Media; Participant Media.

Hartney, M., & Flavin, P. (2011). From the schoolhouse to the statehouse: Teacher union political activism and U.S. state education reform policy. *State Politics & Policy Quarterly, 11*(3), 251–268.

Hawley, W. D., & Jones, D. R. (n.d.). *Teacher unions: Influence on instruction and other educational practices.* State University. https://education.stateuniversity.com/pages/2485/Teacher-Unions-INFLUENCE-ON-INSTRUCTION-OTHER-EDUCATIONAL-PRACTICES.html

Hlavacik, M. (2012). The democratic origins of teachers' union rhetoric: Margaret Haley's speech at the 1904 NEA convention. *Rhetoric and Public Affairs, 15*(3), 499–524.

Kahlenberg, R. (2008). Albert Shanker and the future of teacher unions. *The Phi Delta Kappan, 89*(10), 712–720.

La Noue, G., & Pilo, M. (1970). Teacher unions and educational accountability. *Proceedings of the Academy of Political Science, 30*(2), 146–158. https://doi.org/10.2307/1173371

Lathan, J. (2011). Letter from the editorial board: An unhappy union? *The High School Journal, 94*(4), 135–137.

Peterson, B. (2014). A revitalized teacher union movement. *Rethinking Schools, 29*(2), 5–9.

Toch, T. (2010). Teacher unions are dead! Long live teacher unions! *The Phi Delta Kappan, 92*(4), 72–73.

Weiner, L. (2012). Social movement unionism: Teachers can lead the way. *Race, Poverty, & the Environment, 19*(2), 37–40.

CHAPTER 30

WHO DO YOU TRUST?

Rhonda R. Phillips

Author/Book studied:

Meier, D., & Wood, G. (Eds.). (2004). *Many children left behind: How the No Child Left Behind Act is damaging our children and our schools.* Beacon Press.

The No Child Left Behind (NCLB) Act in 2002 was a bipartisan reauthorization of the 1965 Elementary and Secondary Education Act (Meier & Wood, 2004). Proponents of NCLB Act thought they were doing the right thing for children and public schools. However, many concerns surfaced that included underfunding, restrictive teacher qualification, and effects on subgroups (Meier & Wood, 2004). The promise of the Act was to increase quality, equity, and community for public schools. However, it became apparent that the design focused on one-size-fits-all testing. The solution would be to give parents choices for those schools not meeting the expected standardized test results. The consequences of providing vouchers for choice of schools led to publicly funding a privatized educational system.

Curriculum Windows Redux, pages 359–369
Copyright © 2022 by Information Age Publishing
www.infoagepub.com
359

The one-size-fits-all standardized test judges the schools based only on test scores. The inequities found in household income, child poverty rates, and health-care coverage are not measured in standardized tests (Meier & Wood, 2004). A testing system designed for one-size-fits-all in a world that is not the same size leaves public educational systems trying to develop a system to beat the mathematical trap. The use of standardized testing to rank and punish schools for poor rates encourages districts to develop ways to manipulate the results. These practices include student retention in a grade level to allow them more time to prepare for the standardized tests, teaching to the test, focusing only on the subjects that are tested, removing options for classes not tested, and drilling for skills instead of teaching critical thinking. Reliance on the test eliminates trust in teachers and mandates a prescribed curriculum for all students and does not address individualized learning. The one-size-fits-all educational system led to students becoming more likely to drop out of school so they are not counted in the data analysis (Meier & Wood, 2004). The cycle leads to many children being left behind through grade retention and dropout rates.

Standardized test scores become punitive and do not serve available diagnostic purposes such as academic improvement. The punishment is not only given to students but also to teachers. Teachers are threatened with losing their jobs if standardized test scores are not acceptable. Utilizing test scores for formative assessments and in determining the individualized needs of students would be beneficial. But, when the test scores are posted on the front page of the local newspaper and then utilized to rank districts throughout the state, formative purposes are not served. Testing impacts the overall trust of the teacher. The teacher who devoted 4 years to further education to make an impact on the future youth of our country is instead being criticized on the front page of the paper. The passion the teachers use to meet the individualized students is lost when the assessment is designed for all students as generic. The NCLB Act (2002) does not allow for individualization and does not take into account the broad range of outside school influences. The extreme pressure of standardized testing makes teachers choose between doing what is best for students or what will get the higher standardized test score. The professional judgment of a teacher is not valued and the trust is missing.

TRUST

What happened to the trust in public education? The implementation of standardized tests being used as punishment has led to teachers not being able to be the professionals they strive to be. Teachers want the ability to teach the individual students with a variety of instruction practices and assessments that meet the students' needs, not just for results on standardized tests. A doctor does not use the same treatment plan for all patients. Treatment depends on the patient's needs. All teachers should be able to develop an instructional plan for student improvement. Trusting professional educators, and local schools would eliminate the need to disrupt many of the educational practices. Instead, trust and professional practice would provide opportunities to develop critical thinking skills and offer a variety of classes including those that are not tested, such as field trips and recess. The community, local school board, administrators, and teachers need to be trusted to do what is best for the students, enabling them to use both formative and summative assessments to diagnose and improve student learning. Educators need to be trusted to use the assessment that best meets the students' needs instead of one-size-fits-all testing and to develop school reports that encompass multiple data points versus only standardized test scores. This would reduce the retention and dropout rates that currently occur so that we can stop the mathematical game of removing students not "performing."

When it comes to public education, "Whom do you trust?" Is the trust with the legislators who developed the NCLB Act in 2002 or is the trust with the professional teachers in the classroom for a minimum of 1,000 hours per year with the students? Most teacher professionals have been trained through a university program and required to complete ongoing continuing education for license renewal. But they still are not being trusted. Why grant a teaching license if society doesn't trust teachers to instruct students? This would be similar to receiving a driver's license and being required to take the bus everywhere. The legislators who are trusted to write federal education laws do not have training in education practice from a 4 year institution, have not been mandated to complete ongoing, continuous education hours in order to maintain their license, because most, if not all, are not licensed educators. Also, the legislators are not spending a minimum of 1,000 hours with the students. However, these legislators are trusted with making the decisions on standardizing American public education. The first free public education system was proposed by Thomas Jefferson (Meier & Wood, 2004). The first state superintendent of education, Horace Mann, promised public schooling to be the balance wheel of society (Meier & Wood, 2004). However, the NCLB Act (2002) did not provide a balance wheel. It and its continuation under Every Student Succeeds Act (ESSA, 2015) is in conflict with what is needed for today's society. Public education has compromised what was originally designed to provide a free public education to everyone in order to establish an educated democratic society, how it is an often autocratic exercise by the government not by teachers. This voice is standardizing public education to meet the needs of some, not all. Students who are competent to the set standards are left to the status quo because they already met the required standards and those that will never meet the standards are left behind despite the title of the federal law of NCLB Act. The law was written with the assumption that every student is the same. Standardizing the curriculum that is the same for all students has left no room for individualized instruction. This is what the teachers have been educated to do and should be trusted to deliver it to students.

The summer between my junior and senior year of college, I worked at a General Motors factory. The job paid very well which was extremely helpful in paying for my last year of college. I was getting ready to start my student teaching in the fall and would complete my bachelor's degree and receive my teaching license in the spring. I was earning a teaching license so that I could be trusted to educate the students and develop curriculum, not realizing that in the future, legislators would be mandating the curriculum. During this summer my job was to move ABS brake parts from the line that anodized the part to the next step of the assembly line. Every brake that came down the assembly line was identical. There weren't accelerated brake parts, average brake parts, and struggling brake parts coming down the line. All of them were identical so the assembly line worked efficiently in providing the needed steps to move the brake to the next step in the assembly line. Through all three shifts in the factory the same process occurred. There weren't any variables in the product or situation outside of the factory that influenced the brakes coming down the line. The factory line operator's responsibility was to hit the button and keep the parts moving.

I use this factory example to challenge the NCLB Act (2002). The act provides set standards to all students in all schools. There is no allowance for meeting the needs of individual students. If this law was written for the General Motors assembly line where all brakes are the same, then it could work. The identical brakes could be held to the same standards, tested to determine quality, and then the manufacturer would publicly announce the results of these standardized tests. The results could be posted on who was the most efficient in keeping the factory line moving so the brakes could be moved to the next step. However, I was taught to identify individual student needs. Teachers were taught the importance of being trusted to educate all students. When educating all students, measuring them identically does not fix the problem, it increases the problem. The problem with the standardized assessment is explained mathematically

> there is a fundamental problem that it is impossible to attain 100 percent proficiency levels for students on norm referenced tests (when 50 percent of students by definition must score below the norm and some proportion must by definition score below any cut point selected), which are the tests that have been adopted by an increasing number of states due to the specific annual testing requirements of NCLB. (Meier & Wood, 2004, p. 9)

Not only is the expectation flawed but again those trusted to make the decision forgot an important part of education, and that is the students. The students are not identical. The laws were written without consulting those that should be trusted, the teachers. Teachers are trusted to spend over 1,000 hours with students each year after receiving extensive training in child development and educational theory along with ongoing professional development. Why would they not be trusted in making the decisions with all students so they can be successful?

CURRICULUM

The lack of trust in the professional judgment of teachers has had an impact on curriculum development. The curriculum is being driven by a standard curriculum for all. A standardized curriculum leads to the same standards for all. Pinar et al. (2008) explains in *Understanding Curriculum* that with the loss of the individual we gain curriculum standardization and social control (Pinar et al., 2008). The NCLB Act (2002) is an example of the curriculum developed for social control for all students. The loss of understanding of individual students is evident in the assessments designed for the NCLB Act. If students were created on an assembly line at a factory, then standardized curriculum and assessment would work. However, students are all individuals. This is where the importance of trusting the teachers to develop and implement individually designed curriculum to meet the student as an individual is important. The NCLB Act does not trust the professional teacher to make this call. It not only controls the standardized curriculum and assessment but also punishes the teachers on yearly evaluations that can lead to loss of employment as a teacher. Again, if all students were created in a factory and were identical, the NCLB Act required assessments would work. However, the last time I checked students were not created in a factory. In fact students vary by classroom, school building, school district, state, and nationally. The professional educator, while completing a bachelor's degree, is trained in identifying and creating curriculum to meet the needs of all students as individuals.

The belief behind a group achievement test is that all students taking the test encounter the same test items (Eisner, 2002). The results from these tests can be compared statistically because the test questions and format are the same. The problem is that the students taking the test are not identical and the individuality of each student cannot be measured. Giving students options does cause difficulty in practice but allows for personal creativity and interpretation. This is true to the experiences the students will have in "the real world." The students are not created in a factory as a product on an assembly line and neither are the experiences they will encounter in a job or in life while navigating in "the real world" of life.

The curriculum reform movement that occurred in the 1960s was initiated by the fact that the Soviets space shuttle was the first in space (Eisner, 2002). This historical event had a tremendous impact on curriculum. The panic and fear that the United States was falling behind the Soviets led to curriculum reform. The goal was to develop students to think like scientists. This started the shift away from trusting the professional instructor. The panic led to curriculum designed and implemented with a top–down approach. The panic led to less trust in the teacher and more trust in the government. The goal was to make change as fast as possible so that the Soviets did not continue to advance more quickly in science and military than the United States. This approach has continued with the lack of trust in professional educators with the development of the NCLB Act (2002).

The concept of creating a standardized curriculum contradicts the federal Individuals With Disabilities Education Act (IDEA, 1990). A requirement of the individualized education plan is needed for every student. The IDEA recognizes that students are different and have different needs and the NCLB Act (2002) requires the same assessment for all students. The IDEA requires the development of an individual education plan for each student that is created by a team of professional educators. The process does trust the professional judgment of educators to develop the individual education plan. This concept of trust should be continued for future models. The NCLB Act does not allow for trusting professional educators.

ASSESSMENTS

There are other approaches to developing assessments that are not standardized and can account for the individual student. One example is developing community partnerships to help guide instruction to meet not only the individual needs of the students but also the needs of the community.

How do you develop partnerships? Community partnerships are needed to build trust in educational systems to prevent a one-size-fits-all assessment. A requirement for career technical education programs is the establishment of an advisory committee that meets at least twice a year. The advisory committee members are comprised of community members, including business representatives, parents, past graduates, postsecondary partners, and instructors. These meetings build trust among all members and guide the educational process to meet the needs of all students.

Another form of assessment is the 1 year follow-up data required to be reported for all career technical students. To help answer the question of students' career readiness, career technical programs complete a 1 year follow-up report to document what students are doing 1 year after completing a career technical program. The 1 year follow-up report is completed in March after a student graduates. This survey asks if the student is enrolled in postsecondary education, military, and/or working. The data collected is then submitted into the Ohio Department of Education through a database system called EMIS. The survey doesn't only ask if a student is enrolled in postsecondary education. The data collected provides excellent information to assess if the career technical program is meeting the needs of all students. Districts are trusted to collect and report the data. One method of collecting the data that has been very successful is having the career technical teachers contact the students. The district trusts the teachers to complete this task. The percentage of students located and completing the survey in one district is 99.2%. The teachers have developed a rapport with the students while they are in school and the teachers want to know what the students are doing and the students want to speak with their teacher. This is an example where trusting the teacher as a professional is very valuable. The teacher is the one that has devoted professional and personal time to helping students and teachers want to find out how students are doing. The purpose of the 1 year follow-up report is to make sure students are not left behind.

The other question to ask when determining the assessment, what does it mean to be a high school graduate? In other words, what are we trying to measure when a student graduates from high school? Ohio currently has three pathways to graduate for the Class of 2019. These three pathways are 18 points in specified areas on end of course tests, college readiness score on the ACT or SAT, or industry credentials approved by the Ohio Department of Education that total 12 points along with a score of 13 on the ACT WorkKeys assessment. All three of these pathways include a standardized assessment. This would indicate that we want a high school graduate to be a good test taker. When reviewing job postings, very few, if any, ask for the skill of a good test taker.

Ohio Superintendent of Public Instruction, Paolo DeMaria, in 2018, created an advisory committee for high school graduation requirements. Twenty-three members served on the advisory committee. These representatives included administrators, counselors, parents, state school-board members, and legislators. The goal of the committee was to develop recommendations for the high school graduation corhort Class of 2021 (Ohio Department of Education, 2021). While developing these recommendations, the committee decided on attributes of a graduate, which included things like "engaged citizens" and "cultural awareness" (p. 4).

What are the attributes of a graduate? Developing an assessment to measure this without a written test is possible. One example of an assessment that measures attributes that employers are wanting in a graduate is the Ohio Means Jobs Workforce Readiness Seal. The criteria established to earn the Ohio Means Jobs Workforce Readiness Seal are those needed to be successful in the workplace. The 15 skills established as the criteria were developed from reports by the National Association of Colleges and Employers (Ohio Department of Education, 2018). In order for students to earn the Ohio Means Jobs Readiness Seal, they must demonstrate designated professional skills and have at least three mentors validate these skills have been validated.

Another option that is a possibility is the development of a senior portfolio. This portfolio would be developed by the student and include specific evidence of requirements determined by a rubric and then evaluated by teachers. This would require trusting the teachers which is something that has been missing in other assessments. However, teachers are the professionals that grade the work to determine if they are earning the credits earned each year and the established grade point average used to enroll in postsecondary institutions. Shouldn't teachers be trusted to grade a portfolio created during the senior year. One example of a similar concept is a *career passport*. These are often given at career technical centers since students earn a diploma from the sending district. In the career passport, a student includes a résumé, references, list of technical skills obtained, awards, and certificates. This is then presented in a professional portfolio that can be used for future job interviews. Other items can be included such as goals, samples of work, and letters of reference. A portfolio assessment could also include documentation of experiential learning that included demonstration of technical skills, critical thinking, and professionalism. Demonstration of these skills would verify a student's career and college readiness after high school.

These are several examples of assessments that ensure curriculum needs are met, but do not require a standardized test. It is important to have accountability. However, accountability can be accomplished in many different ways such as the use of business and community partnerships. Eisner (2002) states, "If there is only one correct way to do something, those who hold other values or envision other means are going to be left out" (p. 121). The NCLB Act (2002) requirements for assessments only account for one way to do things. It does not allow trust in the professionals to determine multiple ways to measure and determine understanding. Providing multiple options for assessment allow options so that one-size-fits-all assessment models don't leave children behind.

Students are individuals that have other ways of interpreting or demonstrating knowledge. If these students are not given the opportunity to demonstrate this knowledge, they are going to be left behind. One example would be teaching the skill of changing brakes on a car. If we only used a written assessment to determine if a student could change brakes correctly, would you want to depend on them to work on your car? Would you feel safe with an automotive technician telling you they passed the written test but they have never changed brakes on an actual car? Would you feel confident that when driving down the road you would be able to stop when necessary? Or would you rather have a student that has practiced and demonstrated the skill of changing brakes and been evaluated by an expert prior to changing your brakes? Which automotive technician would you choose? Likewise, what kind of writer would you choose, one who has written or one who has passed a test on writing?

Eisner explains the need to reshape assessment in education. The features of the new would include the following: authentic assessment or situated learning, learning how to learn, intellectual community, cooperation within a group, more than one acceptable solution, curricular relevance, sensitivity to configurations, and students select a form to display what has been learned (Eisner, 2002). The eight elements of assessment trust the teacher to choose and manage multiple assessments to meet the needs of the students and the content being taught. The assessment requirements for the NCLB Act (2002) do not include any of the eight features shared above and do not trust the teacher to determine if the assessment is best for the student. The jobs being created now and the future will need students that can create and develop solutions that are not identical to others. Some of the jobs in the future for students when they graduate have not been created. The main feature listed in the eight elements of assessment is learning how to learn. The impact of the NCLB Act is that students have been taught to learn for the test. This should not be blamed on the teachers. They were not trusted in the first place with the NCLB Act. Many students only want the one right answer and get frustrated if they have to think. These students have not learned how to learn but only to memorize an answer for a standardized test. Students start taking the standardized tests in elementary school and know that the tests only measure memorization. This concept of simply learning to give the right answer on the test will continue to cause problems for our graduates and those who do not complete school. The skill of knowing how to learn is important to lifelong learning. History has shown there are always changes and integration of new innovations. This has been the strength of our country. However, this may not be the case in the future if we continue to standardize the curriculum and assessment. It is important to never stop learning. Will this generation even know how to start learning? Perhaps out of school learning experiences are enough to fill the gap. But, why would we design schools to leave children behind?

The impact on testing is so much more than the test scores. Students already are dealing with issues regarding mental health. The high stakes test scores are increasing the anxiety of both the teacher and student where they feel they are being bullied into only focusing on test scores (Meier & Wood, 2004). The pressure of passing the test is adding to an already stressful environment. In addition, a standardized test only measures a small portion of what is considered vital for success in life. It ignores the assessment of teamwork, reliability, initiative, and judgment (Meier & Wood, 2004). A veteran administrator shared with me, "Do not ask how smart a student is, but ask how the student is smart?" The NCLB Act (2002) only asks how smart a student is at one set time and with one type of assessment. Students are not all identical and this form of assessment is not a true measure of a student's knowledge or a teacher's skills in the classroom.

CONCLUSION

The use of standardized testing for all students does not measure the inequalities outside of the classroom. The one-size-fits-all model utilized in the current standardized testing model leaves children behind because not all students are the same. Trusting the educational professionals will prevent leaving children behind. The educated teachers know and understand that students are not identical. These same teachers realize they are not working on an assembly line educating identical students.

A district struggling with poor assessment results that often lead to loss of revenue from decreasing enrollment is fighting a battle that continues without a chance to make changes to address the issues. The never-ending cycle often happens to impoverished districts. These districts have diverse populations and economic inequalities. Their demographics do not align with the standardized curriculum and assessment of the NCLB Act (2002). These are the students and teachers that are left behind. As these districts continue not meeting the same standards enforced on all districts without taking into account that all students are not the same, the task of turning a district around becomes unmanageable. If students are not successful on the standardized test, it impacts many individuals including teachers and administrators. This causes the loss of teachers and the struggle to find replacements. School choice options reduce funding for the districts that are struggling. The loss of funds in a district already struggling to meet the standardized test score requirements causes the remaining students to be left behind. This situation will eventually be the demise of public education. What happens to these students left behind?

REFERENCES

Eisner, E. W. (2002). *The educational imagination: On the design and evaluation of school programs.* Pearson Education, Inc.

Meier, D., & Wood, G. (Eds.). (2004). *Many children left behind: How the No Child Left Behind Act is damaging our children and our schools.* Beacon Press.

Ohio Department of Education (2018, January 3). *OhioMeansJobs-Readiness Seal: What it means to employers and institutions of higher education.* https://education .ohio.gov/getattachment/Topics/New-Skills-for-Youth/SuccessBound/ OhioMeansJobs-Readiness-Seal/OhioMeansJobs-Readiness-Seal-Employers -HigherEd.pdf.aspx?lang=en-US

Ohio Department of Education. (2021). *Graduation requirements and high school redesign taskforce report: Recommendations for high school redesign in Ohio.* https:// education.ohio.gov/getattachment/Topics/Ohio-s-Graduation-Requirements/ HS-Redesign-Taskforce-Report-March-2021.pdf.aspx?lang=en-US

Pinar, W. F., Reynolds, W. M., Slattery, P., & Taubman, P. M. (2008). *Understanding curriculum: An introduction to the study of historical and contemporary curriculum discourses.* Peter Lang.

CHAPTER 31

FINDING MARK GLASS

The Responsibility of White Educators

Thomie Timmons

Author/Book studied:

West, C. (1994). *Race matters*. Vintage Books.

Mark laid there getting beaten on his own front porch. Racial slurs and fists slamming into his body and soul. Race mattered to him and to those who beat him. But this did not happen in the rural south. This was in Columbus, Ohio, after school in 1973, while his new friend stood across the street in horror and watched. It did not matter that Mark was kind, had a caring family who wanted no less than the best for him. It did not matter that the three fifth grade attackers were 2 years older than him. It only mattered that he was the only Black student at Binn's Elementary School. It was the first time his new friend understood that, no matter what his mother said about Mark Glass being just like them, equal in the eyes of God, just as capable, just as intelligent, Mark was going to have a harder

---

Curriculum Windows Redux, pages 371–381
Copyright © 2022 by Information Age Publishing
www.infoagepub.com

life. Mark never returned to school. His family moved. His new friend never forgot. The clear, brutal unfairness of this event became a story his new friend would later tell his students and sons. It became a defining moment for Mark's friend to never again watch from across the street. It became a lifetime search of finding Mark Glass.

Finding Mark Glass begins with understanding. The distinguished scholar Cornel West PhD gives a critical account of the state of Black America in the 1990s and how the history of racism has shaped the exclusion of an important culture in society. It is more than a commentary about racism, it is a testimony about why, as the book is titled, *Race Matters*. From the beginning of the book Cornel West (1994) tackles sensitive, and at times, taboo subjects that help create an understanding of the stark realities shaping the perceptions and politics of the time. Realities that continue to be relevant today and give poignant understanding to the significance of race.

West (1994) begins by identifying the White cultural ideals and Black stereotypes that unfavorably grind black culture in an often downward spiral of self-loathing which, he points out, are often influenced by market driven values and attitudes. He holds equal blame on Black leadership, as well as, liberal and conservative strategies that often do more to exacerbate rather than remedy the situation in which many Black Americans find themselves. This is not a neutral or unemotional dissection of these issues. It is a passionate commentary that calls for action from the heart while not separating this action from exceptional logic. Understanding these White cultural ideas and Black stereotypes is critical in the search for Mark Glass. How these two intersect, and how they breed confusion and misconceptions about people and problems that have real consequences, which often devolve into "us" versus "them."

In this vein, Dr. Cornel West (1994) takes exception to the Black conservative "blaming the victim perspective" (p. 85) which ignores the obstacles that are unique to Black participants in American society. He argues that the rise of Black conservatism highlights the inability of the liberals to manage a viable solution. Simultaneously, he points out that the new Black conservative ideas do not resonate with much of Black America. This argument parallels the critique of the affirmative action in which West identifies one of his two core issues of the fundamental crisis in Black America: Black poverty. Cornel West argues that, because Black poverty is a result of racial prejudice through markets and institutions, affirmative action is a necessary government intervention to redistribute wealth. He crafts this argument with the caveat that affirmative action is not "a major solution nor a sufficient means towards equality" (p. 95). Understanding the core drivers to Black poverty is critical in the search for Mark Glass. Although slavery laid the foundation for this poverty and should not be understated, the continued persistent racism that has followed, ranging from loan availability to concerns championed by the

Black Lives Matter movement, has clearly worked against any significant forward progress towards equity even in 2018.

Following up on the beginning of his book, Cornel West (1994) writes that the affirmation of humanity is the second core issue of the fundamental crisis in Black America. Black identity in the face of negative Black stereotypes and racism is hard fought, but essential to standing on equal ground. One of the forms of paralysis Dr. West describes as essential to understand, is the tendency not to have "any meaningful coalition with white progressives because of an undeniable white racist legacy of the modern Western world" (p. 98). Such a coalition is critical in the search for Mark Glass. Working together puts all members of the coalition in an intimate proximity that engenders empathy and understanding and builds upon shared values. This creates a potent alliance which builds upon the strengths of the diversity and variety of perspectives that reflect honest truth rather than supposition, suspicion, and misconceptions.

Black anti-semitism and Black sexuality are fearlessly critiqued by Dr. West as issues within Black America that create isolation and internal discord which need to be overcome by acceptance and compassion within Black culture. Cornel West (1994) further encourages a dialogue about the taboo, Black sexuality. Because of the many myths surrounding Black sexuality, he believes an open honest dialogue between races must be encouraged so that all races can be unafraid of recognizing each other's humanity. These hard and honest conversations typify the courageous honesty Dr. West is willing to imbue in his call to action. This courageous honesty is critical in the search for Mark Glass. Without courage to confront the truths that may expose the need to change, stagnation and ignorance is empowered.

It is this call to action which ends this book. It is an impassioned Black rage. West (1994) writes, "The young black generation are up against forces of death, destruction, and disease unprecedented in the everyday life of black urban people" (p. 149). West identifies Malcolm X as a great protagonist of Black rage. He artfully disagrees with Malcolm X's pessimism about White America's capacity for social justice and criticizes his inability to recognize structures in the Middle East that highlighted inequities in class, gender, and sexual orientation. However, in choosing Malcolm X's impassioned defiant candor as a model of confronting the new challenges created by racism in constructive ways, the scholar emphasizes why the future is so dependent on these actions. This urgency is critical in the search for Mark Glass. Quiet apathy must be replaced with impassioned empathy demonstrated through action and works that are defiant of surrender.

Overall, *Race Matters* by Cornel West (1994) emphasizes why the search for Mark Glass is important to education. Although Dr. West's book has no mention of curriculum, it has everything to do with the need to be mindful about curriculum. It has everything to do with the manner in which it becomes, what curriculum scholar Pinar et al. (1995) calls, "Curriculum as Racial Text." West's influence on Pinar's thinking is evident, as West (1990) is quoted in Pinar et al. (1995):

> Black cultural workers must constitute and sustain discursive formations and institutional networks that deconstruct earlier Black strategies for identity formation, demystify power relations that incorporate class, patriarchal, and homophobic biases, and construct more multivalent and multidimensional responses that articulate the complexity and diversity of Black practices in the modern and postmodern world. (p. 357)

Pinar et al. (1995) states that this is how "poststructuralist categories—such as deconstruction—can inform racial theory and produce political strategy" (p. 357). The value of the philosopher's ideas is also seen in the writings of the African American curriculum scholars contemporary to Pinar, such as the prolific curriculum scholar Gloria Ladson-Billings. This chapter of *Curriculum Windows* is a call to White educators to take action and participate in this search. Assumptions, such as, with the two term election of President Barack Obama racism was largely overcome, need to be replaced with a generous dose of skepticism. The White educator must resist the homogenous perspectives that come from a White domi-nant point of view and empathetically build relationships with communi-ties outside this comfort zone.

In *Race Matters*, West (1994) proposes a "prophetic framework" (p. 43) which "encourages a coalition strategy that solicits genuine solidarity with those deeply committed to anti-racist struggle" (p. 44). To be ready and able to take part in this coalition the White educator must not only be genu-ine but also willing to seek out personal prejudices, and institutional racial bias in the three curricula Elliot W. Eisner (2002) says all schools teach; the implicit, the explicit, and the null curriculum (p. 87). Prejudices and biases are as equally harmful as racial slurs and fist slamming into the African American body and soul. The need to find Mark Glass, cross the street, and end the madness requires a long and hard assessment of what is done and who does it. Ignorance is not an excuse White educators can afford, nor is inaction. Diligence is not enough. Commitment is not enough. Cornel West's words become as prophetically relevant today as they were in 1994, "We either hang together by combating the forces that degrade us or we hang separately" (p. 159). White educators must embrace the "us" and in doing so come to the understanding that enabling through inaction is a self-debilitating act. This passive acceptance of the status quo should not only be unacceptable, but also intolerable. The current polarizing politi-cal dialogue in 2018 lacks civility and more often than not has insidious racial undertones. This atmosphere has created a false binary that discour-ages empathy and encourages blame. In this atmosphere, and as educators begin to emphasize the whole child, it is imperative that the White educator join in championing curriculum that honors the whole child and does not devalue differences.

Being Mark Glass' friend has not been easy. There is much to overcome for the White educator but this is insignificant to the consequences of humanity. The nihilism West (1994) describes in the African American community can only be overcome "by love and care" (p. 29). Imagine the escalating power of partnering with fellow adventurers in this spiritual journey. This should not be done based on pity, the African American community is well able, by the example of Cornel West, to lay out significant solutions. However, as always, these tasks are bolstered by allies. For White educators this means shedding the role of bystander and participating in a framework of change guided by important questions:

> Does the curriculum celebrate and honor achievements of all races?
> Does the curriculum allow for a critical and honest reflection of race?
> Does the curriculum empower diversity rather than devalue the differences?
> Do the explicit and implicit curriculum get examined for bias that may harm rather than educate all students?
> Does the curriculum present an honest telling of the suffering brought about by racism both openly and institutionally?

With every question the street gets wider and more daunting. Potholes emerge. Finding Mark Glass becomes a more difficult task, especially from the safety of the other side of the road. Frightened children no longer, adults should make the journey the friend of Mark Glass could not make as a child. Walk across the street.

The steps in crossing the street are taken not by answering these questions but by asking these questions consistently and evaluating the issues that arise. As the issues are discovered, the work to solve them must be done hand-in-hand, knowing it will be challenged by a White supremacist ideology described as recently as 2008 by the authors of *Perpetuating Racial Inequities in Education: An Examination of Pre-Service Teachers' Interpretations of Racial Experiences* as they reviewed the literature:

> In *The Closing of the American Mind,* Allan Bloom (1988) charged that attempts to transform school curricula to incorporate non-Western thought and traditions undermined the fabric of American society. Non-Western students should simply assimilate culturally in order to succeed. Hernstein and Murray (1994) argued that the academic disparities between African and European American students was due to black intellectual inferiority. (Tripp & King-Jupiter, 2008, p. 34)

This article not only highlights the deplorable state of the ability of pre-service teachers to engage diversity, but it becomes an exemplar of how curriculum as a racial text can perpetuate ideologies that put students like Mark Glass at a systemic disadvantage. The White educator must develop the skills to overcome any ineptness to engage these issues, but often the greatest obstacle that needs to be addressed is the internal fear of discovering prejudices previously ignored. Only through intention can White educators overcome such ideologies by identifying internal prejudices and joining this noble cause, a cause that begins by addressing five questions.

Does the curriculum celebrate and honor achievements of all races? The mere fact that there is an African American month of acknowledgments in February should yell, "No!" In honest appraisal it is no more than a condescending pat on the head. An objective assessment of how this month is celebrated in a predominantly White school as compared to a school with significant diversity would serve as a poignant case study. Until this knowledge is embedded into the fabric of what is taught, it will never be seen as significant. In truth, these contributions are a critical part in the journey of becoming a citizen and reflect, in real numbers, the cultural and racial population of the United States. In 2017, 60% of the population identified themselves in the census as White (U.S. Census Bureau, n.d.). Yet, the persistence of a separation of educational content perpetuates the myth that all things White are more important. Worse yet, it perpetuates the idea that no significant achievements have been made by any other race. Until the answer to this question is a resolute "Yes!" educators continue to allow the disenfranchisement, not only of a particular race, but of the wonderful achievements of humanity. In contrast, the exposure to value and relevance of minority cultures, history, and achievements enriches the knowledge and perspectives of schools, particularly those lacking significant diversity. It is this exposure that creates the groundwork for empathy and understanding leading to a necessary foundation for fellowship.

Does the curriculum allow for a critical and honest reflection of race? If race matters, which West argues most convincingly it does, then the need for critical and honest reflection of how this shapes what is taught, how it is taught, and what is not taught must be ongoing. Attention must be maintained that includes all voices and engenders the willingness "to be disturbed" (Wheatley, 2002, p. 38); disturbed by facing personal assumptions and bias while listening to how these prejudices have intentionally and unintentionally impacted the value of others. White educators need to agree that to do anything else is to allow the insidious and destructive roots of White-Euro supremacy to grow stronger. Moreover, curriculum should encourage this racial dialogue among students to embed the skills and empathy to move forward in a diversified society. Students need to know how to celebrate these diversities and envision how this comes together to make a whole.

Alternatively, students need the skill to not only identify blatant racism, but also to identify the less obvious, institutionally driven racism. This includes the educational institution racism inherent in ACT scores, discipline rates, special education identification, to name a few. Students must be able to see how race impacts personal perceptions and actions. Then, with equal skill, challenge this racism with a greater understanding of the importance of action rather than passive acceptance of the status quo. None of this can be done in the absence of critical and honest reflections by all stakeholders, including White educators.

Does the curriculum empower diversity rather than devalue the differences? In recalling Eisner's (2002) discussion about null curriculum, what is not taught "has important effects on the kinds of options one is able to consider, the alternatives that one can examine, and the perspectives from which one can view a situation or problems" (p. 97). Diversity, achievements, and significant non-White contributions that shape our nation are ignored. Granted, it is all but impossible to remove bias, but this should not be an excuse to relent and make null significant content. When White educators advocate for the underrepresented, it does not demean the contributions of ancestors like an epic tragedy. It is important to examine the good, bad, and ugly. It is not valuable to romanticize and "whitewash" reality for the sake of false empowerment. Curriculum today is a long way from empowering diversity in race, gender, and sexuality, especially as those subjects intertwine in the fabric of American society. There is still a devaluation of diversity that needs attention. White educators must make a conscious effort to find the value missing from the curriculum beyond what is familiar. Reaching out to educational communities that do not reflect the homogeneity where the White educator practices to become part of this coalition may not seem urgent. Yet, without this change in mindset the White educator becomes a stumbling block. It is worth the effort. It is urgent.

Does the explicit and implicit curriculum get examined for bias that may harm rather than educate all students? Few practitioners, and less so White educators, examine curriculum for bias. The system makes it very uncomfortable to do so. The current system has teachers focused so intently on testing outcomes that the opportunity to be critical about curriculum is an opportunity not taken by most. The student has become an outcome and race a category exception for that outcome. Time and energy have been hyper focused on outcome results on market driven tests. "Tragically, concerns about unfairness have not altered the use, misuse, and abuse of tests for (mis)judging the abilities, capabilities, and potential of African Americans" (Ford & Helms, 2012, p. 188). The explicit curriculum needs to be challenged not only for the sake of African American students but for all students. The implicit curriculum which teaches the culture and values of the dominant group through inherent participation in the institution of school, however, often goes unnoticed. Racial disparities in advanced coursework, discipline rates and consequences, and validation of cultural identity, all create a harmful and repressive environment that goes too often without criticism. Educators cannot discount extraneous factors to the curriculum or school environment. However, in equal measure these factors should not be used as excuses. Educators must take action to impact that which is within their influence. The White educator must join in this good work of challenging bias and understanding the harm that can be incurred if this bias remains.

Does the curriculum present an honest telling of the suffering brought about by racism both openingly and institutionally? Curriculum must include honest discussion and uncomfortable awareness of how our society, government, and financial institutions have, and are, creating injustices. In examining the suffering there is much to learn. In 1998, Evelyn Hanssen (1998) wrote an article of her experience in an urban school called, "A White Teacher Reflects on Institutional Racism," which chronicles her experience and the obliviousness of other educators of this institutional problem. Institutional racism is not a new problem nor is it a problem easily seen without purposeful intent. Blatant overt racism is often attributed to a fringe, but recently has been exposed as more substantially part of contemporary life. Look no further than the war on drugs and the privatization of the prison system that has disproportionately impacted the Black community. Racism is not dead and that is where the dialogue begins. In examining the cause of the suffering there is much to learn. Honoring those who suffer motivates change. Confronting the absence of this honesty and presenting these injustices in any current educational community is daunting. Telling the story is different than letting the story be told. The White educator must be a co-participant engaging not only with empathy, but with understanding. Together in coalition, the plight of African Americans can be addressed. This coalition will "enrich the quality of life in America" (West, 1994, p. 44). The antithesis of this honesty is not only misrepresenting this suffering, but ignoring that this suffering exists. How can this be achieved? Organizations like Learn to Earn Dayton (2017) have created a great deal of discussion in Montgomery County, Ohio with easy to read charts and questions that focus attention on disparity in equity (Kurup, 2017). These questions are directed at closing the gap in school readiness, achievement, graduation, attendance, and college success. The result should not only bring awareness to the realities of being born into the Black race, but emphasize the importance of educators to advocate for changes in curriculum that make a difference.

Many White educators have joined this coalition. The e-article from Tolerance.org, "Why Talk About Whiteness? We Can't Talk About Racism Without It," by Emily Chiarello (2016) which references the Whiteness Project (Dow, 2016), is a good start to self-examination for White educators. With framing by the previously mentioned African American scholar, Gloria

Ladson-Billings, White educators can employ the three aspects of culturally relevant pedagogy she outlines on YouTube (Ladson-Billings, 2015). Identified as essential to success in teaching African American students, this pedagogy is a valuable tool for all educators and all students. This includes focusing on student learning that teaches beyond test scores, empowering cultural competence by encouraging students to embrace their own culture while acquiring fluency and facility in other cultures, and creating the critical consciousness of how the knowledge and skills students learn leads to additional knowledge. In the same video, Dr. Ladson-Billings (2015) says this is done "with laser-like focus" (1:12).

It is with similar laser-like focus that White educators must embrace and expand these five questions. For many White educators this means overcoming the perceptions imbedded into their experience from the curriculum that was in place when they were in school. There is a great deal to find and challenge. The task is not easy. However, education is a powerful tool and not meant to be easy. Understanding that, in education, curriculum as it is implemented in 2018 continues to share a substantial amount of the same bias and prejudices that were in place in 1973. Only through persistence and compassion does a learning community build strength in diversity. Cornel West (1994) states: "In these downbeat times, we need as much hope and courage as we do vision and analysis; we must accent the best of each other even as we point out the vicious effects of our racial divide" (p. 159). This is the "prophetic framework." This is the White educator's journey to find Mark Glass, to refuse the role of bystander, to walk across the street, navigate the potholes, refuse to stop no matter how wide the road seems to grow, and to reach out to stop the injustice. Allies will certainly be found in the crossing, but more powerfully, in this communion become a stronger "prophetic framework."

It is easy for a White educator to choose to look away, be a bystander, be silent in aberration of injustice until a gray numbness washes away the guilt of inaction. It is easy to be swaddled in the comfort of an illusion that race does not matter, walking head down, staring at the rhythmic lines in the sidewalk and daring not to look across the street despite being in the same neighborhood. Ignored are the cries of Mark Glass and the sounds of the insults and blows that fall upon him. White educators in this haze, wake up. Mark is in need. Join the journey to cross the street because despite this illusion, race matters. This more difficult path takes empathy, persistence, and unyielding faith that together in this common cause educators can create a curriculum for all students. A curriculum that empowers the greatness in all students while honestly reflecting the challenges and faults which would rather be ignored. A curriculum that gives students the skills to participate in the fullness of humanity.

It is not a random pseudonym chosen in the name for finding Mark Glass. The metaphor of a "window" is often used with great power in literature, often bringing perspective from the inside out or vice versa. Often used to frame a view, an opening, or passage. However, Mark Glass is the window pane. In this metaphor Mark is the glass and more than just a lens through which one side looks at another. A piece of glass is rarely noticed until it is rained on or becomes so dirty it changes the view. Typically the dirt and rain are seen in absence of the pane. The glass of the pane has many contrary characteristics such as strength and fragility. It can be smooth, or sharp if cracked or broken. In any case, the greatest care must be taken of the pane of glass in its construction, transportation, and installation. This metaphor is poignant to the idea that race matters and though intentional, does not attach enough humanity to the search White educators must join. In this, the White educators must see the glass in their windows but also understand that if this search only remains a metaphor without a personal connection, the glass breaks and the function of the window is destroyed.

It is in this search for Mark Glass that the scholar Cornel West is a valuable ally to the White educator. His critical insight in the book *Race Matters* (West, 1994) allows the White educator a view through his honest and insightful prose of the Black community that engenders empathetic understanding. Dr. West's words are an opportunity for a White educator to broaden understanding and challenge misconceptions. More importantly, it illustrates the urgent need for the White educator to actively participate with other like minded educators. White educators have significant responsibility. The National Center for Educational Statistics recent findings included two relevant findings. The first was that 84% of all public school teachers said they were able to influence curriculum. The second was that 80% of all public school teachers are White (Taie et al., 2017, p. 3). White educators have a significant proportion of influence in changing curriculum and a significant opportunity to join the friends of Mark Glass.

REFERENCES

Chiariello, E. (2016). Why talk about whiteness? *Learning for Justice.* https://www.tolerance.org/magazine/summer-2016/why-talk-about-whiteness

Dow, W. (2016). *Intersection of I* [Video Installation]. Tribecca Festival. https://tribecafilm.com/festival/archive/intersection-of-i-2016

Eisner, E. W. (2002). *The educational imagination: On the design and evaluation of school programs.* Prentice Hall.

Ford, D. Y., & Helms, J. E. (2012). Overview and introduction: Testing and assessing African Americans: "Unbiased" tests are still unfair. *The Journal of Negro Education, 81*(3), 186–189. https://doi.org/10.7709/jnegroeducation.81.3.0186

Hanssen, E. (1998). A White teacher reflects on institutional racism. *The Phi Delta Kappan, 79*(9), 694–698.

Ladson-Billings, G. (2015, October 23). Successful teachers of African American children [Video]. *YouTube.* https://www.youtube.com/watch?v=hmAZjNRmalI

Learn to Earn Dayton. (2017, January). *Know the gap, close the gap.* https://www.learntoearndayton.org/_files/ugd/a395ee_db99ced6f84d4c6a9504bd4458e43696.pdf

Pinar, W. F., Reynolds, W. M., Slattery, P., & Taubman, P. M. (1995). *Understanding curriculum.* Peter Lang.

Taie, S., Goldring, R., & Spiegelman, M. (2017). *Characteristics of public elementary and secondary school teachers in the United States: Results from the 2015-16 National Teacher and Principal Survey.* National Center for Education Statistics. https://nces.ed.gov/pubs2017/2017070.pdf

Tripp, L., & King-Jupiter, K. (2008). Perpetuating racial inequities in education: An examination of pre-service teachers' interpretations of racial experiences. *Journal of Thought, 43*(3/4), 33–45. https://doi.org/10.2307/jthought.43.3-4.33

U.S. Census Bureau. (n.d.). *QuickFacts: United States.* https://www.census.gov/quickfacts/fact/table/US/PST045217

West, C. (1994). *Race matters.* Beacon Press.

Wheatley, M. J. (2002). *Turning to one another: Simple conversations to restore hope to the future.* Berrett-Koshler Publishers, Inc.

CHAPTER 32

CURRICULUM AIMS

Is the Window Open or Closed?

Tammy Yockey

Author/Book studied:

Walker, D. F., & Soltis, J. F. (1997). *Curriculum and aims* (3rd ed.).
Teachers College Press.

*In fact, the curriculum and teaching are as inseparable from one another
as the skeleton is from the human body.*
—Walker & Soltis, 1997, p. 1

Have you ever fought for control of the thermostat in your home or car
and lost? What happens when you lose? If you are like me, if you are cool
you throw on a sweatshirt and call it a day, but if you are warm, you sneak
around the house and open a window or two. In the car, there is no sneak-
ing, you just roll down the window and let in the cool air. All of our actions are based on our perceived needs at the moment. We open and close

Curriculum Windows Redux, pages 383–395

our windows based on our needs and insulate ourselves when some of our needs are not being met. We repeat these actions multiple times in the course of a year, as seasons and our needs change. Throughout the history of education, political and economic forces have opened and closed the opportunity window to promote and support change in curriculum and its aims in education.

In 1997, Decker F. Walker and Jonas F. Soltis collaboratively authored a book entitled *Curriculum and Aims.* At the time of publication, Decker F. Walker was a professor of education at Stanford University and author of the *Fundamentals of Curriculum* (1989). Jonas F. Soltis was a William Heard Kilpatrick Professor Emeritus of Philosophy and Education at Teachers College, Columbia University, with a rich history in the philosophy of education (Walker & Soltis, 1997). In addition, Soltis served as "past president of both the John Dewey Society and the Philosophy of Education Society" (Teachers College Press, n.d.).

As a student in EDL 765: Seminar in Curriculum, Pedagogy, and Diversity and facing the thought of writing a chapter for a book that other people may read (Yikes!), I chose *Curriculum and Aims* (Walker & Soltis, 1997). *Curriculum and Aims* caught my attention when I read the title and table of contents. The title is not *Curriculum Aims* but *Curriculum and Aims,* indicating both are distinct and separate aspects of education. Planning and practice are often linked and become one concept rather than two distinct areas of focus. The subheadings in the first chapter alone are enough to process writing an entire book, let alone discuss in a brief review.

CHAPTER 1: THE TEACHER AND THE CURRICULUM

- Ambivalent Feelings About Curriculum Work
- Finding Time and Resources for Curriculum Work
- Who Has the Authority to Make Curriculum Decisions
- When Is a Curriculum Change a Change for the Better
- Preparing for Curriculum Work (Walker & Soltis, 1997)

I connected on both a personal and professional level with each item in Chapter 1. As an assistant principal in a district that is currently reviewing and refocusing efforts at identifying priority standards and resources that align with these standards, it has been a challenging task in a district where there are two middle schools serving Grades 6–8 and staff have varying viewpoints on each of the items listed in Chapter 1. Everyone involved in education sees curriculum through their lens and opens their window to let items in they agree with or need and closes their window if the perception is the need is not there or goes against their personal, professional belief. Teachers are working daily with different classes of students who have their own lens of the curriculum that is created by their teachers and outside interactions. State assessment vendors and creators have their own parameter for measuring the success of student achievement of state standards. Vendors all advertise they have a product that will help us meet our students' needs no matter how they are currently achieving. What happens when we disagree or there are forces outside of the school that are influencing who controls the thermostat? Do we constantly open and close our window to adjust for the temperature, or do we convince those in charge to reset the thermostat? We know curriculum and aims change, but are we introducing new and original curriculum and/or aims or are we recycling from previous generations?

TEACHER DIFFICULTIES WITH CURRICULUM

Walker and Soltis (1997) write that "curriculum and teaching are as inseparable from one another as the skeleton is from the human body" (p. 1). As professors of curriculum and curriculum theory, Walker and Soltis have identified three areas which present teachers with a challenge in regards to curriculum:

1. Teacher time and resources
2. Decision authority
3. Determining if change is for the better

As a practicing administrator these three challenges are present consistently in any and all curriculum work done in school. Finding time for teachers to be together as a group to discuss needs (both academic and resources) is a challenge. Teachers do not want to miss instructional time with students, so we begin to look at time outside of the school day or year, which presents a challenge for anyone who is unable to attend to have their voice heard and be a part of the process. Districts hire curriculum directors and solicit services from outside individuals to help find time, but the teachers who deliver the instruction may not have as much investment and/or be committed to the curriculum delivery if they were less involved in the process.

Challenge number two might be both one of the easiest and most difficult to answer. We know the legal answer is our local school boards have the ultimate authority in regards to our curriculum, but as well-educated individuals, we have a tendency to want to vote for change in any discussion. This guarantees our voice is heard, if not always the selected outcome. Clear guidelines need to be established at the beginning of a curriculum planning and developing process to ensure individuals know the goal of the process is to make an informed recommendation, but the authority for final decision-making lies outside of the teacher group.

"If I were only sure this would make a difference" is often heard as we work together to plan for curriculum delivery. We are often nervous that we do not know what will happen with change, so we stay put. Opportunities to open the window and let in new ideas and experiences can be lost as we insulate ourselves from change in anticipation of the strong winds we may face ahead.

TIMELINE

Have you ever heard the expression: "You will never know where you are going, unless you know where you have been?" Curriculum theorists of the past would most likely wish we kept this in mind as we make curricular decisions. Everything seems to come full circle and repeat itself. When political forces and perceived need are at their peaks, the window opens and new curriculum options are explored.

Three well-known philosophers who influenced education are discussed by Walker and Soltis (1997) in *Curriculum Aims.* As early as the fourth century, Plato outlined a framework in which the government and education institutions aimed to create a just state. By the 18th century, Jean-Jacques Rousseau theorized about education and freedom. Philosopher John Dewey was active in the 20th century when he wrote about the purpose of education being to promote individual growth and contribute to a progressive democratic society (p. 13).

Plato envisioned clear education aims for individuals in order to produce a just state. Educated individuals would be the individuals in power, those who demonstrated feats of strength and bravery would be charged to defend other citizens, and others whose talents "lie in the provision of goods and services should devote their lives to these needed tasks in society" (Walker & Soltis, 1997, p. 14). If you are my age, this might sound familiar. I remember sitting in my eighth grade homeroom and my high school counselor coming to speak with us about our choices in high school. We were given three paths to choose from that morning. He presented that the students who wanted to go on to professional careers would choose the college preparatory path, while those who were unsure would choose the general path, and those who wanted to go straight to work should choose the vocational path. I cringe when I remember the presentation. The paths were painted as life destinations as opposed to multiple options preparing students for continued growth. By age 14 we were expected to predict what we needed and wanted to do when we graduated from high school.

In 2018, all of these options still exist, but the focus has shifted from life pathways to allowing students to explore areas of interests to be better equipped to make decisions in the future. Many districts are formulating learner profiles or qualities of a graduate as opposed to predesignated life pathways. I think John Dewey would be proud and also argue more work can be done to promote individual growth. No longer are only a select number of students encouraged into college preparatory programs, but all students are encouraged to participate in college preparatory courses to keep the window to college open. During my high school years, vocational school was where students went who wanted to go straight to work after finishing high school. Few, if any, students who attended the vocational school went on to college. In the time since I have graduated high school, vocational schools have transformed into career centers, presenting students with both job ready skills, as well as maintaining the option for continued education while learning valuable skills that will be sought after by employers post high school.

Rousseau would shiver at the idea of pre-established pathways for children. Rousseau believed "natural lessons" (Walker & Soltis, 1997, p. 15) should be learned by children. Experience should be a child's teacher as opposed to learning from adults or books. Only after children had many experiences and gained an empathy and understanding for others were they reading for academic content knowledge which would make them an educated society member.

Plato and Rousseau would have a healthy debate when viewing curriculum practices of today. Plato argued for the needs of society as a whole, while Rousseau was focused on individual needs. If the conversation were to happen in the 1970s in the United States, Rousseau would have several supporters, while Plato would need to wait until the 1980s when the focus shifted to ensuring a consistent curriculum for all students to ensure our needs as a society were met.

John Dewey could be the moderator for the conversation and open the window for both points of view. Dewey believed democracy "was not just a form of government; it was a way of people's living and working together that provided for freedom of interaction among groups and for the widest possible sharing of experiences, interests, and values" (Walker & Soltis, 1997, p. 17).

While many philosophers and theorists have contributed to education between Plato and Dewey, many thoughts can be reduced to a progressive (think Dewey) versus a traditionalist point of view (think no change needed). As a nation, we have opened the window for progressive movements and methods when we feel (or outside forces influence) that we have gone too far in one direction and need to pull back. A standard curriculum began to take shape in the 1980s and has maintained strong momentum until recently. I would argue the desire for a consistent curriculum exists, but the desire for teachers, families, and students to have flexibility in demonstrating individual growth is beginning to change the tide.

WHAT IS A BASIC EDUCATION?

Is there an answer to this question that meets everyone's criteria of success? Most agree that all people should have the ability to read, write, and use basic mathematical practices. What about speaking a second language, developing an understanding and appreciation of the arts, developing social and emotional skills, or learning a trade skill that makes a person immediately employable? These and many more questions have been wrestled with over the course of time and intensely within the past century, as educators work to determine what is the content and aim of a general education.

"In 1893, the National Education Association appointed a committee, later called the Committee of Ten, to help standardize the high school curriculum" (Walker & Soltis, 1997, p. 28). The framework recommended by this committee, made up primarily by college instructors and private school headmasters, recommended four areas of focus for high school. The committee believed students should leave high school with a solid foundation in "classical, Latin-scientific, modern languages, and English" (Walker & Soltis, 1997, p. 28). The committee believed the goal of a high school education should be to prepare students for college.

In 1918, not long after the recommendation of the Committee of Ten, a group of progressive educators issued a report titled the *Cardinal Principles of Secondary Education* (Commission on the Reorganization of Secondary Education, 1918), which outlined not only what students need to be successful in college but what students should be able to do in life and for society. It is around this time schools began to divide into high school and junior high settings. High school became a more all encompassing setting where general studies, college preparatory, and vocational studies were offered.

In the 1940s, the faculty at Harvard went even further to recommend specific numbers of course offerings and requirements of high school graduates aimed at empowering students "to become productive citizens and fully honor their individual and talents and skills" (Walker & Soltis, 1997, p. 30). A window was opened to promote a blend of traditionalist and progressive curriculum material.

Currently, education practices revolve around many of the recommendations of these three reports. Many public school systems are divided into elementary, middle or junior high, and high school settings. High schools have gone even further to divide themselves into specialized learning systems. Most high schools now have career center options, college credit learning options, online courses, as well as flexible learning allowing students to learn at their own pace and focus on their specific interests and strengths. School districts have developed programming starting in elementary school to educate students identified as gifted, students with special learning needs, or English language learners. School districts no longer isolate achievement on academic assessments as an achievement of their student body. Districts and the students they serve are expected to do more than do well on an assessment. Service learning and extracurricular activities (academic, athletic, and the arts) are all recognized as important components of education. Current profiles of a learner and graduate include experiences and potential leadership skills in all of these areas.

HOW DO WE EDUCATE CONTRIBUTING LEARNERS?

No matter the aim or goal of education, a curriculum must be established to provide a guide to help teachers plan to meet these aims. Just as progressives and traditionalists may disagree on the primary purpose of a general education, the process of curriculum development can vary depending on whether the process is "subject-, learner-, or society centered" (Walker & Soltis, 1997, p. 53).

Our reality in current day education is that our students and our school systems must be focused on all three potential areas of curriculum development. Teachers who deliver the curriculum are required to be licensed to teach a content in a specific grade level, but must also be considered highly qualified for both the content and the grade level they are teaching. Depending on when teachers completed their licensing degree program, they can be licensed to teach a grade and content, but not deemed highly qualified using the state checklist or rubric.

Students should be at the focus of all curriculum decisions but are rarely involved in the process. No matter what standards and resources are selected, we must be able to meet the academic, functional, and emotional needs of our students. Throughout the 1990s and early 2000s, the focus of education has swung towards primarily subject- or content-driven decision-making in which the needs of the whole child have been neglected. Throughout 20 years in education, I have witnessed the number of students with anxiety, depression, and stress related concerns increase. Our students are coming to school in a mind frame that makes learning challenging. The focus of classroom practices led by the teacher and curriculum planning needs to keep this in mind. Students need an opportunity to develop their entire person and be taught how to face challenges, not just learn basic facts.

Unfortunately, the number of violent events towards self and society appears to be increasing. These events have opened the window for a great opportunity to develop and deliver a curriculum with a focus on social and emotional well-being, as well as social justice education. Our students are beginning to voice the need for change and their voice is being heard.

"Being prepared for society" is a phrase that can be left up to many interpretations. A progressive might argue the role of being prepared for society means being able to participate in the democratic processes of society, while others may argue prepared for society means financially contributing to the overall well-being of the society.

DEFINING PURPOSE, NOW WHAT?

In the early 1900s, school districts were viewed by many to be delivering an education that was wasteful from a fiscal standpoint. Schools were a lax environment. Schools seemed to be less efficient than factories and the military. Frederick Taylor was working with factories at the time to study worker movements and to determine the most efficient way to complete a task to increase production. Employee actions were broken down to the fewest steps needed in the quickest time to complete the task. Industrial windows are always open to maximizing human efficiency and production and his methods were quickly studied and adopted by industrial organizations. Public perception was if businesses could increase their efficiency, why would educational organizations not do the same? Could setting behavioral objectives in schools increase student productivity? Eisner (2002) stated "many of our most productive activities take the form of exploration or play" (p. 115). If learning is so scripted and prescribed that teachers and students do not get the opportunity to explore or play, then these options may be lost.

When I first started my career in an urban school district that was determined to be "low achieving" by the state, the district took steps to take away opportunities for play and exploration. Teachers were taken out of the curriculum decision-making equation and programs were purchased from vendors who advertised a guaranteed increase in student performance if their programs were followed to the letter. Teachers were asked to deliver a pre-made curriculum almost down to a daily script. Truly creative and caring teachers who wanted to meet the needs of students were forced to implement a one-size-fits-all approach. Teachers took students' temperature and measured how they were achieving, but were not given the freedom and choice to adjust the thermostat or open the window. Teachers were expected to deliver the next lesson in the prepackaged program. Teacher involvement in the selection of these resources was minimal. At the time, there were few of these standardized resources available, while today there are standardized options which promote the ability to differentiate based on student need. Results on state tests did not improve as drastically as districts had hoped and the importance of the teacher implementing a child specific (differentiated) learning plan window has reopened. While it is important to take the temperature to determine where students' skills are strong or weak, it is important to have the ability and knowledge to know when to adjust the thermostat, or instructional methods, to meet the needs of students.

Depending on which lens a group uses to determine the focus of education, the model and method for curriculum selection may vary greatly. One of the most influential frameworks used in curriculum design is known as the Tyler rationale. Established in 1949 by Ralph Tyler, Tyler

> organizes his rationale around four fundamental questions, which he claims must be answered in developing any curriculum:
>
> 1. What education purposes should the school seek to attain?
> 2. What educational experiences can be provided that are likely to attain these purposes?
> 3. How can these educational experiences be effectively organized?
> 4. How can we determine whether these purposes are being attained? (Walker & Soltis, 1997, p. 56)

Tyler would no doubt be a fan of clear and concise learning objectives. In current teacher evaluation systems, teachers are scored on the ability to communicate a clear learning target to students and establish criteria for mastery. This scoring has led to both positive and negative outcomes. Teachers are more aware of the student learning that needs to happen as a result of instruction, but sometimes the focus can become so narrowed that connecting the learning to other contents and future applications can become muddy. Learning is a continual process and not just "a collection of unrelated skills and knowledge" (Walker & Soltis, 1997, p. 57). As states have continued to develop standards for learning and testing to account for this learning, the focus has shifted from fact memorization to application of skills. Students are not performing as well on state assessments as they had previously. Is this because the content is truly that much more difficult, or have we not found the delivery method to ensure we are making repeat connections and applications in the content? Have we insulated ourselves against this change in format in hopes it will disappear as other state mandates have, or will we open the window to allow for this change of format and instructional delivery? Some schools and districts have already opened the window and established problem-based and authentic learning options for students, while making it a choice. How can something that is determined beneficial be a choice for teachers and students?

Paulo Freire, Brazilian educator and activist, who believed curriculum should "stimulate and sustain critical consciousness" (Walker & Soltis, 1997, p. 61), would most likely agree with current programs that promote problem-based education. He was a proponent of using daily world problems as sources for student learning. Teachers and students must work together to solve these problems. Freire determined an educational aim as consciousness raising. Freire's idea of thinking would be a socially focused curriculum.

WHO DECIDES?

The frameworks and focus for curriculum design, whether they be progressive, traditional, content, learner, or society focused, are all constantly working in either harmony or discord with educational reform. In 2018, Ohio school districts are evaluated on their progress towards meeting determined levels of achievement in math, science, social studies, language arts, educating students who are identified gifted or special education, student attendance rate, performance of racial groups, and college and career readiness of graduates (Ohio Department of Education, n.d.). Other states have similar evaluation measures or building and district report cards. All of these different measures are aimed at ensuring that all students are receiving what the state determines to be a basic curriculum and are being prepared to meet the demands of college or to enter a career upon graduation. These grades are published to community members with little explanation from the State, and districts are left to explain their results by offering differing or additional information about their students either in the frame of profiles of learners or qualities of a graduate, which portray their districts as favorable and as student-focused, rather than state-test-score-focused.

Current federal and state mandates have opened the window for an opportunity to examine curriculum practices at a local level and provide teachers and students the opportunities to grow; however, depending on the leadership and curriculum design process, the window can either be opened fully or slammed shut as schools insulate themselves from change and hope the reform momentum will pass just as many changes in education have done in the past.

As we continue to evolve as an education system, Eisner (2002) says it perfectly when he states, "Personality characteristics of the teacher are the electricity that brings the parts to life and determines the quality and ultimate effectiveness of teaching" (p. 328).

SHIFTING AIMS

Pinar et al. (2008) state that "the era of 'curriculum development' is past" (p. 5). I partially agree with this statement. As Walker and Soltis (1997) shared the three aims of curriculum theory as developing personal, social, and cultural curriculum, I think we are at a point in our nation when we will begin to focus on curriculum. We have merely treated curriculum, collectively, as a side notion in the past.

In my opinion, the window for academic content curriculum development is slowly shutting, while the window for social and emotional health curriculum development has been pushed wide open. States are adjusting the common core standards to *meet the needs* of their specific state and determining the best way to measure school and teacher success on the standards set forth within the curriculum. Open forums have been hosted to solicit feedback on the standards and set the direction of future planning around these standards and assessments. A greater number of families are now asking and expecting schools to develop an additional curriculum to meet the social, emotional, and cultural needs of their children. Long gone are the days when having a boilerplate character education program are enough to meet the needs of students.

As mentioned previously, the incidents of anxiety, depression, and other stress related challenges are increasing in schools. Schools will need to become proactive instead of reactive in terms of developing a curriculum and working with teachers who have had little professional training on how to implement a noncontent specific curriculum to their students. For teachers who struggle with anxiety and depression of their own, this will be a challenge. If I struggle with math, I might choose to become a math teacher, but perhaps a global language teacher. Educators have had the option to insulate themselves from areas of struggle and open the window and display personal strengths. This will not be a choice if implementing a curriculum becomes more encompassing around the social emotional needs of students.

I am personally reluctant to read or turn on the news on a daily basis. As a society, we are becoming polarized on issues of human difference, equity, and equality. Each of us comes with our own personal makeup, and we are in a position where some groups are exercising their voice indicating that individuality and difference is not okay, while others are embracing individuality and difference. Individuals in public power are all over the map when it comes to belief and treatment of individuals who are deemed different than themselves. As a nation we have had major movements where we have struggled over legal and political freedom of religion and equality of citizens, and now the window is open for a curriculum that educates teachers and students around ethical responsibility about the treatment of others. I believe this will be some of the most challenging discussions we have as an education organization. Is the aim of curriculum inclusive for all students personally, socially, and culturally or just those in a position of current or historical power?

HOW IS SUCCESS MEASURED?

Assuming a curriculum is developed to meet the aim of creating a more personal, social, and cultural education without losing the existing focus on content and college/career readiness, how will success of implementation be measured? Math, literacy, and so forth, can all be measured with assessments and there are right and wrong responses. The methods to solve the problem or question may be different, but the answer can be determined to be correct or incorrect. How does one measure the success of a curriculum which involves items such as social and emotional health, respect, and treatment of others? The pie in the sky answer is our children are living in an environment of less violence, hatred, negatively, and judgment, but how will progress be measured along the way towards this goal?

CONCLUSION

Deciding when to take the temperature of a group of students to determine their progress towards curriculum knowledge, when to adjust the thermostat, and when to open or close the window are all critical components when it comes to educating students and the adults who are charged with meeting all students' vast needs. Windows of curriculum opportunity are potentially opened based on perceived and actual needs, while political forces and potential fear of change try to close the window at the same time.

The best designed curriculum with the highest quality resources will not be effective at achieving any aim, without the opportunity for teachers to build relationships and care for their students in a manner in which students are willing to take risks and fail on the first attempt (or maybe second). Standardized assessments and reporting measures have created environments where opening the window to allow new ideas and techniques into the classroom is challenging. Fear of failure has created environments with few to no windows. For many districts, the aim of education has historically been doing well on standardized tests. Fortunately, many of these same districts are now opening the window and determining the criteria for a successful education to include more experiences and expectations in an education than doing well on an assessment.

Teachers are vital to the implementation of any curriculum, whether content, emotion, or socially oriented. Teachers need to have a voice at the table when curriculum outlines, resources, and implementation are discussed. Teachers need to lobby for when the window of curriculum opportunity needs to be open or shut. Political leaders and educators may have differing opinions on what society needs from our students. Both groups need to work together to ensure the curriculum planning process meets the needs of all students, not just a political agenda.

Teacher preparatory programs should have their windows wide open. Programs should prepare teachers to become advocates for high quality curriculum as well as prepare them to deliver high quality instruction. Teacher preparatory programs should work with students to make sure they have skills to develop relationships not only with students but other educators. Long gone are the days when going into your classroom and shutting the door are acceptable. Teachers must have the skills to open their window and communicate with those in their immediate environment as well as those beyond the horizon.

The window for curriculum and aims should be opened and closed repeatedly. The needs of our students and society are ever changing. Educators should take advantage of curriculum development opportunities and be a voice for our students who are not at the decision-making table. Educators should be knowledgeable of student needs and wants, and be willing to work collaboratively to make sure the curriculum matches the intended aim, our students are depending on it.

REFERENCES

Commission on the Reorganization of Secondary Education. (1918). *Cardinal principles of secondary education.* Department of the Interior, Bureau of Education. https://files.eric.ed.gov/fulltext/ED541063.pdf

Eisner, E. W. (2002). *The educational imagination: On the design and evaluation of school programs* (3rd ed.). Prentice Hall.

Ohio Department of Education. (n.d.). *Report card resources.* https://education.ohio.gov/Topics/Data/Report-Card-Resources

Pinar, W. F., Reynolds, W. M., Slattery, P., & Taubman, P. M. (2008). *Understanding curriculum.* Peter Lang.

Teachers College Press. (n.d.). *Jonas F. Soltis.* https://www.tcpress.com/jonas-f.-soltis

Walker, D. F. (1989). *Fundamentals of curriculum.* Harcourt College.

Walker, D. F., & Soltis, J. F. (1997). *Curriculum and aims* (3rd ed.). Teachers College Press.

CHAPTER 33

SHE WASN'T READY

Currere as a Practice for Critical Healing

Tiffany J. Williams

Author/Book studied:

hooks, b. (2000). *All about love: New visions.* Harper Collins
    Publishers.

July 14, 2018
Coffee . . . check.
Laptop . . . check.
Write something for Dr. Poetter . . .

I am PhinisheD! I submitted my dissertation to the graduate school for
format check. I have completed all of my edits. I have started packing my
apartment. I am leaving Oxford. Of course, I am coming back for graduation. My mother would have a fit if we did not. It is the finale. I have a PhD.
I am now Dr. Tiffany J. Williams.

Curriculum Windows Redux, pages 397–408
Copyright © 2022 by Information Age Publishing
www.infoagepub.com
All rights of reproduction in any form reserved.

For me, I guess this means little right now. When I talk about having a PhD, excuse me, earning a PhD, I feel nothing. Some say it just has not hit me yet. Others say I am in shock. The truth is, I feel the same as I did when I realized...

Let me start from the beginning.

LOOK THROUGH CURRICULUM WINDOWS

When I first arrived in Oxford to attend Miami University, I was traumatized. My trauma existed in more than one place so at the time I could not identify where said trauma was manifesting. I remember quitting the program, or at least I tried to quit. My advisor, Dr. Denise Taliaferro Baszile and my mentor Dr. Daniella Cook, were on a mission. I sent the two of them an email, which politely said, "Thank you so much. I quit. I am going home." At this point Dr. Cook called. "What's going on?" she said, to which I immediately started to cry. Trying to be professional, I composed my tears and said, "I can not do this." She continued to talk to me as Dr. Taliaferro Baszile was on her way to my apartment. I did not know this at the time but the two of them had already spoken and devised a plan to tag team the situation. One would talk me down and the other would come to my rescue.

Dr. Denise and I sat for the remainder of the day and created a plan: (a) what to do now, (b) what to do later, and (c) what to do in the process. I remember her saying, "The PhD is a journey." Needless to say, I did not leave but I was not sure why I stayed until now.

THE WINDOW: EDL762 AND EDL782

It was the spring semester. I was reading the syllabus for the class, Intro to Curriculum. Dr. Thomas Poetter, or Tom, is the instructor. He was talking emphatically about the course. He is waving, no, flailing his arms back and forth and walking around in a half circle while talking around the course. I was a bit startled. I wondered, "What the hell have I gotten myself into? I knew I should not have let Denise talk me into staying!"

I listened as Tom explained we would be writing a book together as a class. We would all pick a book from a particular decade to read and would write a chapter for which we would create a book. Our class read curriculum scholars from the 1970s. I chose *Multicultural Education: Issues and Perspectives* by James and Cherry Banks (1993). I was not thrilled about this idea. I was already struggling in the program, now he wanted me to write about it. As the weeks went by, we did practice exercises, which made me a bit more comfortable with the idea of writing. I loved to write. From my youth, I wrote short stories and poetry that expressed my thoughts, feelings, and lived experiences, but did not know this could be academic work. I was a writer, but had not realized that the kind of writing I loved to do had a name: *currere*.[1]

During this semester, I also was in class with Dr. Denise. She was teaching a course about race, curriculum, and education. This class gave me life! It was like she had written the syllabus to talk about all the things I wanted to discuss regarding how schooling and the curriculum did not fit those who lived outside White male bodies, ideologies, and ways of knowing. This is not to say, the class was not contentious. There were some who did not understand why we returned to race, sometimes gender and class, when talking about democracy, schooling, and curriculum. In the end, I learned scholarship that was inclusive and democratic to make space for those invisible, underrepresented, and ignored was not what some future academics wanted to explore. I did. I had two semesters of courses where most of the syllabi only included the work of White males. When I asked why there were no scholars of color and few women (mostly White), I was passively disregarded or did not get my questions answered. I felt invisible, silenced, and ignored. So, I wrote about it.

THE JOURNEY BEGINS: WHEN TIFFANY6 AND TIFFANY60[2] SHOWED UP

The semester before I was in Tom and Denise's classes, I already mentioned I was a wreck. I was leaving the program because I was overwhelmed and felt out of place. In the moments after Daniella and Denise's intervention, I decided to stay but I was still fragile. I felt broken on the inside and did not know how to put myself back together. I would sit and work, but my mind nor my heart, was in it. I wrote because I had to, not because I wanted to. In the midst of it all, I would pray asking for help. That is when they showed up.

I was sitting in my living room crying. I was silently praying for help to figure out my life. I was angry because I felt alone. I was afraid because I did not know what to do or what direction to go in. In this moment, Tiffany6 and Tiffany60 showed up. I wrote about these parts of myself, my past self and my future self, in my work from that moment forward. I talked about them from a *currerian* perspective. They helped me make sense of what and who I was, in relation to how I saw myself, and the world around me. In the end, I was the girl who saved herself.

EVERY WOMAN HAS A LITTLE GIRL INSIDE

In my work, I talk about the selves, Tiffany6 and Tiffany60, as a way forward for others to understand and make sense of their own lived experiences as a journey through *currere*. When I first learned of the process, I immediately gravitated to it because I felt it expressed how one could walk through critical curriculum moments without reliving trauma. For me, I had not begun to unpack my trauma as it related to schooling and the curriculum, but I knew they were linked. For the curriculum windows assignment, I started writing about one memory of school. This is when Tiffany6 began to tell her story.

I wrote a story called, *Through the Eyes of a Child: Windows to the Soul*, which later became *Critical Moment #1: Lion, Lambs, and Wild Horse: Teaching the Animals*, which I used in my dissertation work. I had written most of the story around my walk to school as a child. I talked about my school. I talked about my teacher. I talked about my relationship to schooling and education to what I saw happening in and outside the classroom. I talked about how I saw myself as a learner solely based upon my interactions with my teacher, the curriculum, and the schoolhouse.

I also talked about how destitute and impoverished my family was. I talked about how hungry I was and how that impacted my ability to learn. I talked about my mother's mental and emotional health and how this affected me in school. I talked about being invisible, silenced, and ignored and how this strained my relationship with schooling and education. I talked about how difficult it was to learn because I was invisible.

Katherine, my group partner, had the audacious task of reading my story. We were in class when I first shared it with her. She cried. Then Tom wanted us to share our work with other classmates. I was uncomfortable. I shared with Chloe and Danny. They both just looked at me. Chloe placed her hand on my shoulder. They did not know what to say to me. Neither of them had ever had such experiences in relation to schooling and education. As we talked, I tried not to shut down. I wanted for them to see my experience as one of many Black and Brown students they would possibly come across in their career as educators. I wanted them to see them, not pity them. I wanted them to hear their stories, not push them away because they were uncomfortable. I wanted them to know these stories live inside Black and Brown adults as a result of their little ones inside. I wrote this story in 2014, but it was not ready to be published until 2018.

STUDY OF THE SELF: SELF AS STORY

I say the story was not ready because Tiffany6 and I (my present self, Tiffany36) had not processed the trauma attached to the critical moment. I was working on being in a PhD program. I was writing and presenting at conferences. I was reading the work of Black and Brown scholars. I was gathering a language for what those thoughts and feelings were growing inside me. What I learned was I was not alone. I was in the midst of many scholars, particularly people of color and women, who had similar experiences with schooling, education, and the curriculum. Yet, I had not processed my own critical moment until then. Tiffany6 was still fragile because I had not opened myself to her, those experiences living inside me, as a part of the journey. In a way, I had silenced and erased her. It was through *currere* that I learned she was only hidden, yet visible to those around me.

The more I wrote, the angrier I became. I was angry because I felt wronged by the process of schooling and how it damaged and deformed me. I was angry because I was not recognizable to myself. I did not like who I had become. I was frail and broken yet powerful and outspoken. I was hurting inside but had become my own advocate. I spoke up when I felt I was being targeted by discrimination and microaggressions yet I continue in a process of self-hatred and self-defamation. I was still in pieces.

To story about the self is writing the self into existence. Traditionally people of color, Black women in particular, acted as orators who narrated themselves, their communities, and their histories. Black women used narrative as a way to tell a different story with regards to her body, her way of knowing and being. She spoke of the self in context as a way to disrupt and intervene on onto-epistemological, patriarchal, sexist, and racist critique.[3]

More recently, scholars have proposed the use of the self as a critical artifact for autobiographical inquiry in relation to identity, who we say we are in relation to how we see ourselves, its formation, and how it is influenced by external forces (social, political, cultural, economic, racial). In *Identity and Agency in Cultural Worlds*, for instance, Holland et al. (1998) discussed a theory they call self-in-practice. They suggested that "selves are socially constructed through the mediation of powerful discourses and their artifacts—tax forms, census categories, curriculum vitae, and the like" (p. 26). As readers of the socially constructed text, or the self in practice, we can reflect on ourselves in context as well as how we are conformed, deformed, and reformed. To this end, we either comply with the behavior in accordance or resist. Nevertheless, they stated, "the 'subject' of the self is always open to the power of the discourses and practices that describe it" (p. 27). They go on to suggest when looking at the self, there is a need for critical disruption in our way of thinking about the self as fixed as traditional Western thought would imply.

To live autobiographically, one must be a storyteller and her own protagonist. The story is lived while yet being written. She and her story coexist, much like Tiffany6 as she revealed her experiences. As I worked with *currere*, there were complicated conversations that came to the surface. I was in a dialectical dilemma because *currere* had brought me to a place, yet I could not enter. I was able to examine my lived experiences as *currere* made room for, but I could not process the moment in the prescribed linearity.

Additionally, although Pinar (1975) himself talks about poking holes in the theory, I still processed *currere* in a *White male* voice. This is where critical race feminist *currere*[4] became helpful.

CRITICAL RACE FEMINIST *CURRERE*: A KIND OF *CURRERE*

Critical race feminist *currere* intervenes on traditional notions of *currere* at the intersections of race, gender, and the curriculum. It makes room for curriculum to be explored as identity, difference, knowledge, and power. It gives permission for the self to be in process with the text, in critical examination and dialogue, as we seek a deeper understanding of the socially constructed self that is miseducated by the curriculum.

Although *currere* seeks to understand a deeper meaning to educational experience, the method foregrounds schooling as its central contextual space. I was also interested in how the external, non-schooling forces impacted educational experiences. Non-schooling experiences can refer to all the forces that interface with the schoolhouse yet exist outside of it. I wanted to know who I was in relation to schooling, but more important to my inquiries, I wanted to know how I became who I was in relation to all that is connected to schooling. That is the non-schooling. Delving into the onto-epistemological questions revolving around and centering the experiences of Black women and girls as the focal point of my work, critical race feminist *currere* can be used as a model for women of color (WOC) to make meaning of their schooling and non-schooling experiences. Additionally, it helps the researcher understand how race, gender, and the curriculum intersect, interact, or converge in academic, social, political, economic, and cultural lives.

POWER IN THE TELLING: ON THE JOURNEY TO CRITICAL HEALING

The interface between curriculum as story and story-ing the self-conjure up moments of contempt, trauma, adoration, or praise based upon how the curriculum was channeled in her, by her, and through her. Trauma that is attached to the stories of my past had become entangled with my present lived expressions. As I continue to process my lived experiences, the trauma I once experienced is lessened when I became aware of my power of authorship and the power of narration. I could not change what happened or how I felt, nor did I want to, but I had the power to tell how I felt and reacted in those critical educational moments. I also could reflect on what I know now or what I learned as a result of those experiences. I was no longer a victim to my story. I was the storyteller. I had power over the ending of the story. How I grew. How I lived now.

Brené Brown (2012), the author of *The Power of Vulnerability* suggests, in order to counteract shame, the trauma attached to it, and for healing to begin, you have to (a) return to the moment (recall it), (b) reconcile myself to it (speak to it/figure out what did I learn?), and (c) recover (begin again). Cynthia Dillard (2012) says it another way:

> But in order to heal, to put the pieces back together again, we must learn to remember the things that we've learned to forget, including engagement and dialogue and cross-cultural community that theorize our varying spiritualities, experiences, definitions, and meanings of Black womanhood. In this way, (re)membering becomes a radical and endarkened response to our individual and collective fragmentation at the spiritual and material levels, an endarkened response to the divisions created between mind, body, and spirit and an endarkened response to our ongoing experience and understanding of "*what difference differences makes.*" (Wright 2003, p. ix)

Through the process, I learned there could not be critical healing without anger, rage, trauma, love, and hope. Additionally, critical autobiographical work makes room for critical healing spaces. Critical healing occurs at the intersection of trauma and wellness, where the storyteller recognizes herself as author. She no longer sees herself in a traumatic state; therefore, she does not retell the story from a position of trauma. She sees herself whole, in the process of becoming whole. Critical healing provides for an in-depth analysis for understanding the complicated conversations that I lived, in my mind, and that are mapped onto my body. Trauma, pain, and rage can become all-consuming when it is not processed as a part of the critical healing process.

Baszile (2006) contends, "All work emerges from deep-seated autobiographical questions, whether those are made explicit or remain strategically or unconsciously implicit" (p. 90). Additionally, Baszile (2010) said

> All work is autobiographical. That is, we all bring our sorted histories, hopes, and desires to the project of curriculum theory, hooking onto familiar stories and creating new ones. And to the extent we are in dialogue, in conversation about these stories and the histories in which they are forever entangled, we produce, perform, and engage the "complicated conversations" that is curriculum theory. (p. 483)

Telling my own stories made me see myself differently, in ways I could not imagine. Just as the self is a part of the revolutionary process of hope, resistance, love, and joy, I learned I had to partake in my own pain, trauma, and anger to get to the other side. Healing was on the other side of trauma. Although at the time I did not realize my stories would help me heal, I know within me they were necessary to tell. It is in this evolution of the self that we undo, overthrow, and transform subjugation. We become subject and center in our own healing as an entry point toward collective healing. I heal so you can heal. I can show you how.

WHAT I KNOW NOW: LOVE AND HEALING LIVE TOGETHER

There is no critical healing without love. I speak of the kind of love that is beyond the physical or erotic. bell hooks talks about love as a critical point towards self-awareness and understanding that contributes to collective healing. In her book, *All About Love*, hooks (2000) discusses how love should be applied, not just as an intimate thing as it is generally discussed in Western Eurocentric thought, but as a mechanism of well-being and collective wholeness. She said, "A love ethic presupposes that everyone has the right to be free, to live fully and well. To bring a love ethic to every dimension of our lives, our society would need to embrace change" (p. 87). There had to be a commitment to critical self-love that exists within me for me to continue the process. While working on myself, I had begun to fall in love with myself. I loved my flaws. I laughed at my quirkiness. I loved how loud I talked, my Southern accent, and my maneuvering in and out of academes and hood speak in my work. I was gentle with myself when another story was being written. I gave myself time in the process ... to be ready.

I remember having a conversation with Dr. Poetter when I wrote the initial draft. I asked him if I needed to publish the paper in the book for a grade. He said, "No, you wrote the paper for the class; publishing is additional. I would like for you to publish it. You do not have to." I took this to mean, publish the paper. But I was not ready. Tiffany6 was not ready. She was a little girl hiding behind her mother, me, peaking while covering part of her face with my skirt tail. She was afraid to be seen. She was afraid to be consumed, like she had been previously in school. As she and I process through what schooling, education, and the curriculum did to us, she was no longer afraid. We knew what happened, why, and we were okay ... now. She knew I, Tiffany36, would speak up for us. She knew I would be able to articulate how necessary it is to recognize the need for representation in the curriculum. She knew I would challenge educators to examine their own relationship to schooling, education, and the curriculum as I did. She knew I would not let others speak on our behalf.

MEDITATION:[5] TIFFANY[6]: I SEE GOD IN YOU: BLACK GIRL LOVE STORY

8/31/17

I never really had a lot of friends. Growing up, most of my memories were of me playing alone, surrounded by what most folks would call "inanimate things." This is not to say, I was friendless, but I was more of a loner and completely content playing on my own. These "things" were my stuffed animals, dolls, and other "friends" that lived in my imagination. Many times, people or passerbys that caught a glimpse of my play, thought it looked as though I was talking to myself; arms flailing around, while marking my notebook and pointing my finger. For me, it was an active world, and I was the teacher. I could see them interacting with me as I interacted with them. We were connected although they were "inanimate."

I must say here that my interactions with inanimate things did not look the same as it would in popular cultural imagination such as Annabelle or Chucky. I was not mentally disturbed by any means. They did not tell me to do bad things nor were they demonic beings who wished to reincarnate so I should be afraid of them. Their lived experiences were generated from my own production of what they would or could be. They comforted me in the dark and we talked about future plans or what my life would look like. There was endless possibility embedded in those conversations although I was situated as a poor Black girl at the time. We talked about the reality I envisioned for myself although I had not reached the age of maturity to accomplish those things. I was fully aware that my companions were material yet motionless, breathless, and thoughtless but my words and belief in them gave them life. My "company" was in my consciousness and my consciousness was full of life!

As I got older, I was schooled by the curriculum of my household that big girls don't talk to themselves and that inanimate things were for kids. I learned that the two—the real world and the imagined—age of innocence and endless possibility and the age of consciousness and responsibility—could not exist in the same space. Additionally, my consciousness was not to be trusted because it was wayward by nature. Play and imagination were of no use to me in the material world because the imagination was for lazy dreamers and foolish people. I had to exist (lived) in the real world and invest in it because this reality was all I had to work with.

Within this frame of mind, I became a prisoner caught between what I knew and what I was being taught. I was embarrassed to interact with my friends from that point forward. I would be publicly shamed when I was caught talking to them. Over time, I stopped talking to them but every now and then they still talked to me. As I got older, I began to realize those voices were my own consciousness even though I had been taught to believe only crazy people talked to themselves (and responded back). It was insanity to interact with my own consciousness or take counsel in my own inner being because it was unseen therefore unknown.

Additionally, I was encouraged to pray to an external being that was invisible yet all seeing and all knowing; thus, crippling my own sense of connection with my highest self. Internal conflict is conflict with one's lower self! In order to rise up, I knew I had to return to my own consciousness.

In a religious world, this can be difficult to return to one's self because of certain dominant Christian principles. In particular, God as external savior and self as sinner in need of that savior was one principle I continued to struggle with. For me, salvation can be defined as an internal process of discipline to reach toward oneness within yourself or achieving higher spiritual levels of peace, happiness, or wholeness (i.e., Fruit of the Spirit). In contrast, Christian principles dictate that salvation was the journey away from damnation (i.e., hellfire and brimstone). To seek out the divine, one must lose themselves in the practice of self-deprivation. This, I was not interested in!

Parishioners as faithful or damned, according to principles of salvation, which live outside or external to one's own ability, being, or know-how to be self-determined, confined me. Spirit as savior is assigned to the external god principle not the self. In returning to what I knew as spirit, or as goddess in historical African tradition, the messages were conflicting with my way to salvation. Further, salvation as a concept of spiritual freedom in the hands of religion gets conflated into the external or material realm; thereby, disconnecting the self from its true path toward spiritual freedom.

As a child, I knew that some Christian principles and doctrines were wrong for me because it conflicted with my inner knowledge of self. This is not to say biblical truths are not relevant or hold universal truths. What is important for me is curriculums of religion; namely, self as sinner in need of salvation, did not resonate with my own understanding of the self as part of the collective divine. I understood my own oneness with God, or God consciousness (I am Goddess), as the same as oneness within myself. I was whole, complete, with no need for reconciliation to the divine; my reconciliation was with myself. Thus, my journey to salvation was the journey of (re)turning to myself.

The body as sinful and spirit as savior had been paramount to the Christian faith since its inception. As an adult, I had to come to understand salvation was connected to doing or acts of service and contrition. As a child, I understood I was spirit living in a body (material) and to achieve balance both spirit and body had to (must) coexist. Through religious means, the curriculum suggested my inferiority as female and that spirit was greater than body. Because of my body and nature as Eve, I could not possibly be one with spirit because my body was born sinful. God as external spirit, separate from human nature or being, was the way to salvation, not my own spiritual connection within.

In order to return to my own sense of divinity, I had to remember. I learned to forget my own nature, as divine, as wholly connected to the divine, and replace it with patriarchal and sexist ideology that suggests my inferiority was my own doing, never to be undone, never to be reconciled. I had to return to being whole as an act of resistance in love and hope as I stripped away negative, conformist understanding of what it meant to be a little Black girl. I had to return to my child-like understanding that god exists within me as an expression of love and wholeness, not as a solution to sin or disconnection.

The journey of returning to one's self begins when she acknowledges the Goddess within her. The practice of returning to one's self is through critical lessons and learning that works to cultivate the Goddess. The practice of returning to one's self is in the unlearning while revealing pain and trauma. The practice of returning to one's self is recognizing the shift inside from story character to storyteller. This can only happen when there is a shift in God consciousness from an outward expression to the curriculum from within. The greatest love story is the testament of self-love and care toward spiritual freedom. This love is demonstrated in process and (re)membering those things we have been taught to forget. It is in these moments whereby she exercises and exorcizes the psychological trauma that the curriculum may have caused. She begins to speak without sound. She sees with spiritual eyes. She knows beyond her present. She is Goddess. Only through practice do they live as one.

NOTES

1. For more on *currere*, see Pinar (1975). In this work, Pinar outlines *currere* as an educational process in which the individual, historically the student, writes about their educational experiences across the four temporal stages: regressive (focusing on past experiences), progressive (focusing on the future), analytical (focusing on the present), and the synthetical (integrating all the previous moments to take action towards liberation).
2. In my work, I discuss Tiffany6, Tiffany36, and Tiffany60 as critical selves as a way to examine critical educational moments using currere. I honor this tradition here. The shift to Arial Bold font signals a change in voice. It symbolizes the use of critical moments in past, present, or future throughout the paper.
3. bell hooks (1992) explained the process of self-liberation that leads to healing and self-awareness in *Black Looks*: To all of us who love Blackness, who dare to create in our daily lives, spaces of reconciliation and forgiveness where we let go of past hurt, fear, shame, and hold each other close. It is only in the act and practice of loving Blackness that we are able to reach out and embrace the world without destructive bitterness and ongoing collective rage (Dedication).
4. For more on critical race feminist *currere*, see Baszile (2015).

5. I refer to my self-reflective writing as meditations. These artifacts are journal entries. They do not necessarily reflect on academic work but sometimes have connections to academic work.

REFERENCES

Banks, J. A., & Banks, C. A. (1993). *Multicultural education: Issues and perspectives.* Allyn and Bacon.

Baszile, D. T. (2006). Rage in the interest of black self: Curriculum theorizing as dangerous knowledge. *Journal of Curriculum Theorizing, 22*(1), 89–98.

Baszile, D. T. (2010). In Ellisonian eyes: What is curriculum theory? In E. Malewski (Ed.), *Curriculum studies handbook: The next moment* (pp. 483–495). Routledge.

Baszile, D. T. (2015). Critical race feminist currere. In M. F. He, B. D. Shultz, & W. H. Schubert (Eds.), *The SAGE Guide to Curriculum in Education* (pp. 119–126). Sage Publications.

Brown, B. (2012). *The power of vulnerability: Teachings on authenticity, connection, and courage* (1st ed.). Sounds True.

Dillard, C. B. (2012). *Learning to (re)member the things we've learned to forget: Endarkened feminisms, spirituality, & the sacred nature of research and teaching.* Peter Lang.

Holland, D., Lachicotte, W., Jr., Skinner, D., & Cain, C. (1998). *Identity and agency in cultural worlds.* Harvard University Press.

hooks, b. (1992). *Black looks: Race and representation.* South End Press.

hooks, b. (2000b). *All about love: New visions.* Harper Collins Publishers.

Pinar, W. F. (1975, April). *The method of currere* [Paper presentation]. Annual meeting of the American Educational Research Association. Washington, DC.